Afghanistan

A CULTURAL AND POLITICAL HISTORY

Thomas Barfield

PRINCETON UNIVERSITY PRESS

PRINCETON & OXFORD

Copyright © 2010 by Princeton University Press
Published by Princeton University Press, 41 William Street, Princeton,
New Jersey 08540
In the United Kingdom: Princeton University Press, 6 Oxford Street,
Woodstock, Oxfordshire OX20 1TW
press.princeton.edu

All Rights Reserved

Ninth printing, and first paperback printing, 2012
Paperback ISBN 978-0-691-15441-1

The Library of Congress has cataloged the cloth edition of this book as follows

Barfield, Thomas J. (Thomas Jefferson), 1950–
Afghanistan : a cultural and political history / Thomas Barfield.
    p.   cm. — (Princeton studies in Muslim politics)
    Includes bibliographical references and index.
    ISBN 978-0-691-14568-6 (hardcover : alk. paper)
    1. Afghanistan—Politics and government.   2. Afghanistan—History.
3. Afghanistan—Social conditions.   4. Islam and politics—Afghanistan—
History.   I. Title.
DS357.5.B37 2010
958.1—dc22   2010002082

British Library Cataloging-in-Publication Data is available

This book has been composed in Adobe Garamond

Printed on acid-free paper. ∞

Printed in the United States of America

10

CONTENTS

ILLUSTRATIONS

PREFACE

I first entered Afghanistan traveling overland as a young student almost forty years ago. Like many travelers, I was awed by the country's scenery and fascinated by its people. Unlike most others I returned to learn more. That journey never ended but has often been detoured. It first encompassed years of ethnographic fieldwork among nomads in northern Afghanistan in the mid-1970s. I had a unique opportunity to experience life as it is actually lived in rural Afghanistan—something that seemed so easy to come by then and is so difficult now. It was a time of peace and security, when foreigners could travel the breadth of the country alone, armed only with a bit of common sense to ensure their safety. Political changes in Kabul rarely had any serious impact outside the capital. I was in Kabul the day that Zahir Shah (r. 1933–73) was overthrown in 1973. The biggest change was how quickly his pictures disappeared and how soon they were replaced by those of his cousin Daud.

This calm was deceptive, however, because others seeking power in Kabul, Communists and Islamists, sought to transform the country in radically different directions. The leftists had the first go in 1978 and provoked an insurgency, which the Soviet invasion in late 1979 was designed to quell. During the ten-year Soviet occupation I observed the country from the outside, informed by occasional trips to Pakistan to work with Afghan refugees. The Russian withdrawal in 1989 proved to be a false dawn of optimism. None of the great powers was willing to provide the necessary political and economic investment to forge an agreement between the Pakistan-based mujahideen (holy warriors) parties in Peshawar and the Soviet-backed regime in Kabul. The Russians wanted nothing more to do with the country, and the Americans lost all interest in it when the Soviet Union collapsed in 1991. This opened a ten-year civil war in which the Islamist leaders became dominate, and proved they could be every bit as ruthless and power hungry as the Communists they replaced. The nadir of this period produced the Taliban in the late 1990s.

From my safe perch in the United States I continued to follow the few reports that came out of Afghanistan, but was rarely asked about the country or its people. Critics of the university tenure system undoubtedly put me among those useless faculty who purveyed esoteric and irrelevant knowledge to the young without fear of termination. Wise policymakers had already determined that such remote places and people could be safely excluded from America's New World Order.

On September 11, 2001, Afghanistan suddenly became relevant. Now people wanted to know why we did not have more information on the country and its people. In 2002, I returned to northern Afghanistan after a twenty-five-year absence. The nomads I had lived with had survived and even prospered. (Regardless of ideology, everyone was still in the market for the mutton that the nomads produced.) But the country's infrastructure was destroyed and its security remained fragile. I began publishing more extensively, particularly on issues of customary law. In collaboration with other scholars, in 2003 I helped establish the American Institute for Afghanistan Studies. I was asked to give many scholarly presentations and occasionally advise policymakers. It proved difficult to explain Afghanistan and its politics to those who took an interest in it only after 2001. Not that it mattered much. Tired clichés passed as insights, and few policymakers thought of consulting any Afghans who could not speak English. There was, in any event, little appetite for real engagement in Afghanistan after 2002 because the Bush administration was preoccupied with Iraq.

During this period of neglect I began work on this book and its completion was made possible with the support of a Guggenheim Fellowship in 2007. Like the Afghans themselves, I take history seriously as the foundation for understanding the present. Because I am an anthropologist, I need to both give thanks and apologize to the historians whose work I use. They have provided me with the raw material to make my case but as a profession would be more conservative about drawing conclusions from it. They would certainly hesitate to comment on recent events. But with so much new attention on Afghanistan under the Obama administration, I have taken the risk of doing so.

There are far too many people who have helped me over the years to be able to thank individually. Nevertheless, I owe a particular debt to Awsif Nawsiri, my host and friend in Kunduz Province, for making my research in the 1970s possible and providing so many expert insights on what I was observing. A generation later I owed thanks to Neamat Nojumi, whose experience in the war against the Soviets in the 1980s and search for peace in its aftermath have helped me understand that period better. For understanding today's Afghanistan better I wish to thank Omar Sharifi, the Kabul director of the American Institute for Afghanistan Studies, who represents a new generation of Afghans keen to carve out a better future for their country. I received excellent advice on improving the book manuscript itself from Professor James Scott, Ambassador Ronald Neumann, and Dr. Whitney Azoy. I thank them for their close readings, suggestions, and corrections of errors. All remaining errors in fact or interpretation are, of course, my responsibility.

I dedicate this work to my father, whose continuing determination, intelligence, and energy make me proud of the old southern American tradition that gives us the same name.

Afghanistan

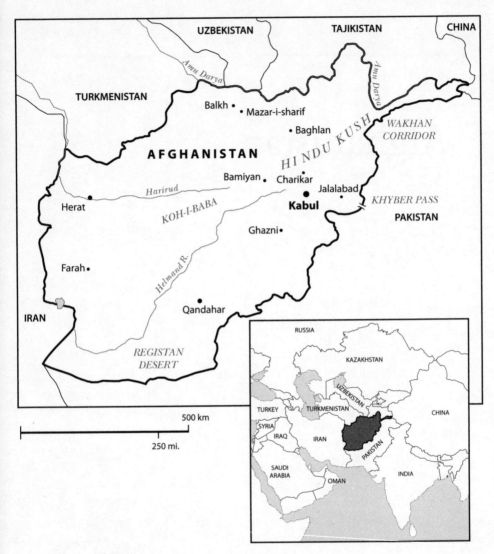

Map 1. Afghanistan

Introduction

Landlocked Afghanistan lies in the heart of Asia, and links three major cultural and geographic regions: the Indian subcontinent to the southeast, central Asia to the north, and the Iranian plateau in the west. Geography may not be destiny but it has set the course of Afghan history for millennia as the gateway for invaders spilling out of Iran or central Asia and into India: Cyrus the Great, Alexander the Great, Mahmud of Ghazni, Chinggis Khan, Tamerlane, and Babur, to mention some of the most illustrious examples. During this period, Afghanistan was part of many different empires ruled by outsiders and the center of a couple of its own. Its emergence in its modern guise began in the nineteenth century when the territory of Afghanistan was caught up in the great power rivalry between British India and czarist Russia, including two wars with the British. It remained peacefully neutral in the first and second world wars, although it experienced a brief civil war in 1929. But then in the mid-twentieth century Afghanistan was transformed into a cockpit for the cold war struggle between the United States and the Soviet Union that reached its climax with the Soviet invasion in 1979 and its withdrawal ten years later. In the subsequent civil war that erupted in the 1990s, Afghanistan became a failed state, ignored by the world. At the beginning of the twenty-first century it burst back on to the world scene when radical Muslim jihadists planned the 9/11 attack against the United States from there and provoked a U.S. invasion in retaliation. Since that time, a new Afghan government has struggled to bring stability to the country in the face of an Islamist insurgency.

All this focus on war and visiting conquerors overshadows the country's own inhabitants, except as the rough warriors who served as speed bumps on the highway of conquest or more recently earned a reputation for making the place ungovernable. As a result, Afghanistan itself remains just the vague backdrop in a long-running international drama where others hold the speaking parts. It often appears that the Afghans provide only an unchanging, turbaned chorus in this play—that is, except for their ever-newer weapons. This book takes a different tack. It views the Afghans themselves as the main players to understand the country and its political dynamics, examining the question of how rulers in Afghanistan obtained political legitimacy over the centuries and brought order to the land.

Discussing political order in the abstract often ignores culture and shies away from history, but the anthropological approach of this book gives prominence to both. This seems natural enough when discussing the differences, for example, between a multiethnic Switzerland and Yugoslavia, even though both are European and not so distant geographically. Yet for remote and culturally alien Afghanistan, such specificity seems a luxury that can be easily dispensed with. If the truth be told, the less the world knows about a place, the easier it is to generalize about it. Are not all ethnic and religious conflicts, Muslim societies, underdeveloped economies, terrorist movements, and failed states fundamentally alike in most ways, especially in poor countries? Unfortunately they are not, and assuming that they are imposes a uniformity that is dangerously deceptive. Afghanistan may well share similarities with other countries and societies, but these elements need to be documented rather than assumed.

THEMES

This book addresses four major questions that have particular relevance for understanding the country and its problems today.

International

- How did Afghanistan, which was overrun and ruled by a series of foreign dynasties for more than a thousand years, became renowned as the "graveyard of empires" in the nineteenth and twentieth centuries after forcing the withdrawal of both the British and Russians in a series of wars?

- Why did the U.S. invasion of 2001 that toppled the Taliban not immediately set off a similar national insurgency (as it did in Iraq), and despite that, still fail to bring stability to the country?
- Why have foreign attempts to change Afghanistan's politics, social structures, and government proved so ineffective?

Internal

- How did a ruling dynasty established in 1747 manage to hold power over such a fractious people until 1978, and why has the Afghan state since then experienced such difficulties in reestablishing a legitimate political order?
- Why did a country for which the term "Balkanized" appeared ideally suited show so few signs of disintegration as a national state in spite of its many divisions?
- How and why have splits in Afghan society since the 1920s over the structure of government and its policies led to so many periods of state collapse?

This book will argue that the most fruitful way to approach these questions is by examining the changing notions of power and political legitimacy in Afghanistan over a long period to understand how participation in national politics came to encompass an ever-wider circle of people. When the political structure was least open to competition, rulers found it easiest to maintain their legitimacy and authority because threats came from only a limited number of contenders. It was much harder to gain exclusive authority when the political system was more open and included more participants competing for power. Indeed, in the absence of an alternative political structure, such struggles for power threatened to disrupt society as a whole. In the worst cases it produced an unstable situation where no one could achieve enough power and legitimacy to restore political order without resort to continual armed conflict.

Afghanistan avoided this type of state collapse and political disorder for most of its history because the only people who competed for power were "professional rulers," hereditary elites who saw government as their business.

The right to rule was established by conquest and had two characteristics. The first was a lack of involvement (militarily or politically) by the subject population, which was often compared to a flock of sheep. The second characteristic was that competition for supreme power came only from within the dynastic elite or from outside invaders. Established rulers never feared replacement by subordinate groups within the polity because while such groups might act as their allies or enemies in political struggles, they did not conceive of themselves as potential rulers. Both of these characteristics were particularly evident in empires established by the Turko-Mongolian rulers who founded almost all the dynasties in the region from modern Turkey to northern India from the mid-tenth century to the beginning of the Western colonial era.

The emergence of a class of professional rulers was the product of a hierarchical political culture in which only men from certain elite descent groups were believed to have the right to rule or even compete for power. They did not have to rely on popular support because they employed mercenary armies (financed by tribute, or taxes on trade and agriculture) and feudal levies (provided by those to whom the ruler had granted landed estates). The only significant internal challengers to this exclusive political system were the tribal warriors organized into segmentary descent groups who inhabited marginal zones that states could not administer directly. They were egalitarian and rejected the legitimacy of any outside authority, but played a minor role in politics except when state power grew weak. In such a situation, tribal groups on the edge of the polity could topple a dynasty and seize the state for themselves. The structure of the system did not change, however, because the leaders of these tribal groups quickly monopolized power themselves and pushed their old followers back into the margins. For example, while Afghanistan's Durrani rulers (1747–1978) may have originated in an egalitarian Pashtun tribal system, they employed a classic hierarchical model of governance to maintain power exclusively within their own dynastic lines. They abandoned the democratic and federal political institutions commonly used among the Pashtun tribes at the local level, and replaced them with autocracy. Because of this, the relationship between the Pashtun tribes and their putative dynastic leaders was always a troubled one, in which cooperation (or conflict) depended on the issues involved.

This well-established tradition of exclusive elite authority began to erode in the nineteenth century as the increasing sway of Western colonial powers changed the political ecology of the region. Thus, from the founding of the Durrani dynasty in 1747 until 1838, Afghan rulers had only close relatives as rivals. Tribal groups stood aloof from such dynastic struggles, and only demanded that any victor continue to respect their traditional rights or pay them off. When the British invaded in 1839 and again in 1878, the pattern changed. The Afghans expelled the British each time, but only by employing rural militias in rebellions over which the dynastic elite had no control. This set up a contradictory dynamic in which the Afghan rulers encouraged armed resistance to expel foreign invaders, but then refused to share power when the war was over. It also valorized the defense of Islam and the Afghan nation as principles, yet at the cost of undermining the exclusivity of dynastic privilege. With each succeeding crisis and popular military mobilization, the restoration of state authority became harder and disputes over who had the right to rule the state became fiercer. During the nineteenth century such challenges to elite power remained largely inchoate because the cultural tradition of dynastic exclusivity remained so strong. After the First Anglo-Afghan War ended in 1842, the existing Muhammadzai dynasty continued to maintain its grip on power with no significant challenges by non-Muhammadzai rivals.

The situation changed in the wake of the Second Anglo-Afghan War after 1880. The new amir, Abdur Rahman, abolished the decentralized governmental system in which tribes and regions maintained a high degree of autonomy in exchange for submitting to the legal authority of the Kabul government. When faced with numerous revolts by his own relatives and regional groups, he waged war against his own people until he and his government had no rivals of any type. While effective, resentment of Abdur Rahman's heavy hand created a political backlash that over the longer term undermined his successors and led to a civil war in 1929 that forced the abdication of his grandson, King Amanullah (r. 1919–29). In the aftermath a Tajik usurper took power in Kabul for nine months until the royal elite rallied the Pashtun tribes against him and put a distant cousin, Nadir Shah, on the throne. Political participation appeared to widen with the establishment of a parliamentary system in 1964, but King Zahir Shah refused to cede any of his executive authority to it. He was ousted in a republican coup by his cousin, Daud in 1973. A Communist coup in 1978 ended Daud's life and his republic, terminating 230 years of dynastic rule. This change, however, ignited an uncontainable conflict in the wake of the Soviet invasion and occupation of Afghanistan (1979–89) that replicated on a grand scale the pattern of the Anglo-Afghan wars: the mobilization of groups throughout the country in resistance to (or support of) the new regime.

More than any other set of events, the Communist coup and Soviet invasion opened the question of political legitimacy in Afghanistan. The old dynastic tradition was in ruins, but there was nothing to replace it. This issue of who had the right to rule and on what basis was not resolved even after the Soviet Union withdrew in 1989 and its client regime collapsed in 1992. Lacking any overarching political unity among themselves, the various mujahideen resistance factions led the country into civil war and lay the groundwork for the rise of the Taliban. These conflicts eviscerated the formal state structure they were fighting to control and engulfed an ever-larger part of the Afghan population into political struggles from which they had been previously isolated. All the ethnic and regional groups in Afghanistan became politically and militarily empowered, reversing the process of centralization that had been imposed by Abdur Rahman.

Unfortunately the successful resistance strategy of making the country ungovernable for the Soviet occupier also ended up making Afghanistan ungovernable for the Afghans themselves. While the Afghans had recovered from many earlier periods of state collapse, the body politic was now afflicted with an autoimmune disorder in which the antibodies of resistance threatened to destroy any state structure, regardless of who controlled it or its ideology. Compounding this problem was a centuries-old structural weakness: the dependency of all Afghan governments on outside aid for financial stability. In the wake of the collapse of the Soviet Union, Afghanistan found itself without world-power patrons for the first time in 150 years and hence had no significant sources of outside revenue with which to fund a central government. In the face of indifference and a lack of aid by the major foreign powers and the international community in general, the country could no longer right itself as it had done so many times in the past.

The stalemated mujahideen civil war opened the door to interference in Afghan affairs by neighboring states, strengthened regional ethnic power brokers, and facilitated the exploitation of Afghanistan's weakness by foreign Islamist groups. At the forefront of these Islamist groups was the Afghan Taliban, which with the support of Pakistan and foreign jihadists, took power in Kabul in 1996. Although they justified their rule in Islamic terms, the Taliban were largely Pashtuns who saw all other ethnic groups as enemies. Even after they had conquered almost all the country, they never created a real government, and Afghanistan became a classic failed state. As an ally of Osama bin Laden's al Qaeda, the Taliban were the immediate target of U.S. retribution following the 9/11 attacks on New York and Washington, DC. The Taliban fell even more quickly than they rose: once it became clear that they would lose, every region of the country (including the Pashtun south) turned against them. Foreign troops were welcomed, against all expectations, because the Afghans saw them as a bulwark of protection against the very Afghan forces that had driven the country into ruin. More pragmatically it was equally clear that the Afghan government and economy could not be revived without massive infusions of foreign aid. If other wars had driven Afghans out of the country, the end of this one brought back about four million people, the largest repatriation of refugees ever seen (and one done largely by the Afghans themselves).

The question of creating political legitimacy was at the heart of reconstituting the Afghan government after its installation in 2002. A particularly delicate task would be installing a new political system without giving it the stigma of foreign imposition. Nothing undermined the legitimacy of any Afghan government faster than the charge that it was beholden to foreign masters. Despite the best of intentions, though, Afghan state building in the twenty-first century was fatally flawed because it attempted to restore a system designed for autocrats in a land where autocracy was no longer politically sustainable. The international community assumed that such a system would be considered legitimate if validated by elections. But Afghanistan had its own political traditions, in which elections played no part, and the virtues of majoritarian rule were not immediately obvious to the country's regional and ethnic minorities. Moreover, talk of democracy was difficult to reconcile with just how little power was delegated to any institution not part of the central government. The constitution of 2004 created a government barely distinguishable from the centralized monarchies and dictatorships that had characterized earlier regimes. Similarly, notwithstanding discussions about inclusivity and popular participation, neither were allowed at the local level. Provincial governors, police officials, and even schoolteachers would still be appointed exclusively by the central government in Kabul without consultation.

The rationale for this push toward centralization was the assertion that the country would break apart without firm control at the top. With the recent example of the former Yugoslavia firmly in mind, many international actors feared that the Afghans would inevitably seek to splinter the country along ethnic and regional lines if given the opportunity. Yet of all the country's many problems the push toward ethnic fragmentation had never been a powerful political force in Afghanistan because of a seeming paradox: ethnicity without nationalism and a pragmatic politics that was largely immune to ideology. While Afghanistan was divided into distinct regional and ethnic groups that could quite easily live without one another's company, there was no pressure to break the country into smaller parts. Afghans found the existence of a unitary state more advantageous than the alternatives, particularly because a larger state served as a barrier against undue meddling by its neighbors. Nor did Afghans have the political enthusiasm for such a project. Having suffered through both a radical socialist regime and a radical Islamist one, Afghans were not likely to be moved by anyone's new ethnic nationalist ideology.

The best means of attaining legitimacy in post-2001 Afghanistan would have been to recognize that the government's function was more important than its form: what it could do for the people who lived there. After a quarter century of war and social disruption, ordinary Afghans sought security, economic stability, and a chance to live normal lives. Ironically, this was what the traditional systems of elite dynastic rule historically provided over the centuries: security of life and property in exchange for obedience. Political participation of a modern democratic type was of course a nobler goal, and given the de facto autonomy of Afghanistan's regional and ethnic groups, more rather than less of it might be required to bring stability to the country today. But as the current difficulties suggest, practitioners of older and less attractive traditions of power understood that the first role of government was to offer security for its people from enemies without and against disorder from within. Before rejecting the past wholesale, it would be best to understand how Afghans achieved the feat so often.

STRUCTURE

The themes outlined above take place within a cultural and historic context, and this book presents them in this fashion. Chapter 1 provides a basic outline of Afghanistan's land and peoples. Specialists may wish to skip the descriptive parts because they are already familiar with them, but those for whom Afghanistan is largely a blank need to acquire a basic grasp of the country to make the more detailed material presented later comprehensible. Readers who fear they cannot possibly keep track of so many different groups should remember that they do so with ease when following their favorite sports teams, so thinking of this section as the "Afghan League" roster will make the task easier. So will remembering that some teams are more significant than others (the Manchester Uniteds or New York Yankees of Afghan politics), and that they generate similar passions of loyalty and hatred that more neutral observers find difficult to comprehend.

As important as knowing who the people are is also understanding how they live. Afghanistan is invariably described by casual visitors as "biblical" or "medieval." Rather than chide such observers for their ethnocentricity or Orientalist biases, I might note that there is some validity to this common trope. Afghanistan is medieval in the sense that religion still plays a determinative role in culture and politics, much as it did in Europe before the Enlightenment set the West on the road to secularization. Afghanistan is also biblical in the sense that it retains a nonmechanized rural subsistence economy, mud-brick architecture, and caravans of nomads that would not have appeared out of place two millennia ago. But physical appearances can be deceiving: these same "timeless" people shot Soviet helicopters from the sky using U.S. Stinger missiles in the 1980s and are now as addicted to cell phones as anyone else on the planet.

People also live their lives in a physical world. Afghanistan's mountain ranges and river systems define a number of distinct regions that are much older than the nation-state called Afghanistan today. These regions are more than just some names on a map; they have determined settlement patterns and trade routes as well as created different local cultures through the millennia. Each is centered around one of the country's major cities (Herat, Qandahar, Mazar-i-sharif, and Kabul), which serve as regional hubs within Afghanistan and link it with the outside world. Beyond the local identities that separate them, these regions share a common history and political-cultural tradition as part of Turko-Persia. Geographically, Turko-Persia encompasses the highlands stretching west to east from Anatolia and the Zagros Mountains through the Iranian plateau to the ragged edges of the Indian Plains, and north to south from central Asia to the Indian Ocean. It shares a common city-based Persianate culture interwoven with the legacy of the formerly nomadic Turkish ruling dynasties that came to dominate the region from the eleventh through the nineteenth centuries.

The final section of chapter 1 applies ibn Khaldun's classic model of Middle Eastern political organization to Afghanistan. In that fourteenth-century work he posited two quite different types of societies: a "desert civilization" based on subsistence agriculture and pastoralism in marginal zones; and a "sedentary civilization" based on the surplus agricultural production of the irrigated river valleys or plains that supported the cities. The social organization of the former was based on kinship ties, was relatively egalitarian, and displayed strong bonds of social solidarity in the midst of a general poverty of material resources. The latter's population maintained hierarchical social classes, concentrations of great wealth, and residence-based identities with little social solidarity but strong economic interdependence. This distinction still typifies Afghanistan and continues to have a profound impact on the country's governance. Far from participating in a single political sphere, Afghanistan has always been two worlds, interacting but unintegrated. These contrasting patterns of subsistence, social organization, and regional political structures underlie long-standing ethnic and tribal divisions. They also constitute elements of material life and social organization that have persisted for centuries, even millennia, and set the framework for daily life as it is ordinarily lived.

Chapter 2 examines the premodern patterns of political authority and the groups that wielded it. During this period nation-states did not exist and regions found themselves as parts of various empires. This chapter focuses on how (and what kinds of) territory was conquered, how conquerors legitimated their rule, and the relationship of such states with peoples at their margins.

In Turko-Persia, rulers did not seek to impose their authority uniformly across the landscape. Instead they imposed direct rule only in urban areas and on productive agricultural lands that paid more than it cost to administer them. They employed strategies of indirect rule when dealing with the peoples who had poor subsistence economies. These did not repay the cost of administration, and their location in remote mountains, deserts, and steppes provided natural bulwarks against attack. But the relationship between the center and these hinterlands was of great significance because when state authority weakened, it was tribal groups from the hinterlands that most often toppled existing regimes. The tribal groups that most commonly succeeded at this task were the Turks of central Asian steppe origin. Their hierarchical tribal structure gave them an advantage over more egalitarian tribal groups, which had more difficulty unifying and supporting a single leader. The Turks were also heirs to a horse cavalry tradition that remained militarily decisive against people who fought on foot until gunpowder weapons entered the picture.

The long-term dominance of Turkish dynasties in the region has been underplayed in a modern Afghan history that gives primacy to the Pashtuns as the country's rulers. But in reality the Pashtuns were never rulers in Afghanistan before the mid-eighteenth century. Only at that time, after serving as military auxiliaries to the Safavid and Afsharid empires in Iran, did the Durrani Pashtuns come to power by adopting the governmental structure and military organization of their former overlords. Indeed Ahmad Shah Durrani, the founder of the Afghan Empire, inherited the lands he ruled only after his Iranian patron, Nadir Shah Afshar, was assassinated. He and his heirs imposed the Turkish tradition of royal succession that demanded the ruler be chosen from only within the royal lineage. During this period the Afghan Empire slowly lost its most valuable provinces and retreated into the boundaries similar to those of today's Afghanistan.

Chapter 3 examines the erosion of traditional elite authority and new models of modern state building in the nineteenth century. The Anglo-Afghan wars were the crucibles that transformed the Afghan state and society. The focus is less on the wars themselves than the consequences they had for Afghanistan. In terms of foreign relations, the rulers of Afghanistan found themselves in the paradoxical state of becoming ever more dependent on the subsidies from the British raj even as they pushed the Afghan people to become more antiforeign. Domestically successive rulers sought to make the central government more powerful, but did not succeed until Amir Abdur Rahman took the throne in 1880. Understanding what he did and at what cost remains significant for Afghanistan today. Every ruler in his wake has attempted to maintain his model of government even when it brought ruin on the country. They all subscribed to Abdur Rahman's belief that rulers should resist sharing power and that the Afghan population had no role in government. Although the "Iron Amir" has been dead for well over a century, his zombielike shadow still looms large over the country and its politics.

Chapter 4 analyzes the fate of Afghan rulers and their regimes in the twentieth century. Some were more successful than others, but one thing they had in common was unexpected ends to their reigns. Every Afghan leader during this period was either assassinated while in power or driven into exile. While these events may seem unduly complex on first encounter, they can be broken down into three distinctive periods: 1901–29, 1929–78, and 1978–2001.

- 1901–29: This period was characterized by demands for constitutional reform in Afghanistan and independence from British control. Both were achieved in the reign of Amanullah (1919–29), but the king's attempts to modernize Afghanistan led to a backlash and civil war that forced his abdication. A new Musahiban dynasty then took the throne under Nadir Shah after he rallied the eastern Pashtun tribes in opposition to the country's first Tajik amir.

- 1929–78: The Musahiban period was characterized by cautious economic and social reforms. Only after being on the throne for three decades did Zahir Shah agree to establish a limited parliamentary system in the constitution of 1964. But such political tinkering could not contain the pressures created by the military and economic modernization of the country, which was funded by the cold war competition between the United States and the Soviet Union. Zahir Shah was ousted in 1973 by his cousin Daud who reigned until his murder in 1978.

- 1978–2001: The last two decades of the twentieth century were bookmarked by the imposition of two extreme ideologies on Afghanistan. The first was a failed attempt to implement revolutionary social and economic policies by a Communist regime. It led to the Soviet invasion and occupation of the country in the 1980s. Russia's withdrawal in 1989 began a period of civil war that destroyed the formal state structure, and gave rise to the Taliban and their reactionary Islamist regime. Taliban policies for changing Afghan society were equally as radical as those of the Communists, but in the opposite direction.

Throughout this period there were a number of recurring conflicts. The most volatile was the issue of social change and its direction. Often described as a rural/urban or religious/secular divide, in reality the division was more complex since positions differed depending on the issue involved. What could not be denied, however, was that over the course of the twentieth century, a pattern developed in which factions with opposing ideologies replaced one another in an ever more violent manner—and displayed less willingness to compromise each time. As a result, the process of re-creating the state in the aftermath of conflict got progressively more difficult. The seemingly easy restoration of a central government after the civil war in 1929 can be contrasted with the absolute inability to restore internal stability during the 1990s. External factors that had changed included a lack of interest in Afghanistan by any major foreign power. This reduced the flow of aid to the county to a trickle and allowed neighboring states to interfere in Afghan affairs. There were also internal factors that made the restoration of political order more difficult. Regional and ethnic power brokers had emerged that stood in opposition to Kabul-based elite. Foreign Islamist groups had a greater role in Afghan politics and exploited Afghanistan's weakness for their own purposes. The state structure itself was also so weak that those who held the formal reins of power were not markedly stronger than their rivals who did not. But the most important wound was self-inflicted: having made Afghanistan ungovernable to induce a foreign occupier to withdraw, the Afghans found that they had inadvertently made it ungovernable by anyone else.

Chapter 5 looks at the first decade of the twenty-first century in Afghanistan. As the twentieth century ended, ever-larger numbers of Afghans had become caught up in political and military struggles from which they had been previously isolated. Whether as fighters, refugees, or just victims of war and disorder, few escaped the turmoil that roiled the country. Ethnic and regional groups in Afghanistan had become politically and militarily empowered, reversing the process of centralization that had been imposed by Amir Abdur Rahman. Yet when the international community set about creating the new Afghan constitution, it did not start afresh but attempted to restore the institutions of old. This brought to the surface long-simmering disputes about the relationship of the national government to local communities, the legitimacy of governments and rulers, and the relationship that Afghanistan should have with the outside world. Little attention was given to the consequences of promoting social policies concerning women, individual rights, and secular education in a country where these had long been contested. The initial success of the process stalled and started to break down by 2005. The Taliban, who had been driven from the country in 2001, returned to begin an insurgency in the south and east.

As I also explain in the conclusion, Afghanistan's problems during this new decade can best be understood by examining where they fit past patterns and where they break from them. The prospects for bringing stability to Afghanistan hinge on whether these problems can be rectified in a way that Afghans find acceptable.

APPROACH

Although this book is firmly grounded in the history of Afghanistan and its ruling elite, as an anthropologist, my original research experience was framed by ethnographic encounters with ordinary people. These people had little interest in anyone's ideology, in part because their own cultural and religious identities were so strongly fixed. If the book could be expanded beyond its already-considerable scope, it would be through the addition of a thicker description of how such peoples on the receiving end evaluated their leaders and their policies. But their role in national politics has always been restricted because they were more concerned with local issues. Should a government meet basic expectations and leave them alone, there was little concern with what rulers in Kabul chose to do. Should a government fail to meet basic expectations, then woe to the ruler who mistook people's traditional acquiescence of that leader's right to rule for political passivity in the face of policies that disrupted their lives. Emphasis on the tip of the iceberg should never blind one to the fact that it floats on a much larger mass, which although out of direct sight, sets the rhythm of its movement.

Combining an analysis of the contemporary Afghanistan and its longer-term history presents its own difficulties. The more distant past is always easier to condense than recent events, but comparing Afghanistan's last fifty years with earlier patterns provides an excellent opportunity to explore some of the underlying forces and structures that have shaped contemporary Afghan politics and distinguish it from previous centuries. Still, writing authoritatively of the twentieth century (let alone the twenty-first) as history does not come easily to one who has spent his life within it, and for good reason. As William Faulkner said of the American South, in Afghanistan (where centuries merge as fluidly as decades do in other countries) the past isn't even past there yet. The obstacles are also great: people are still alive who will object that they were there and saw it differently. On the other hand, such contemporary observers almost always failed to recognize the significance of events as they happened, and were prone to partisanship and wishful thinking. (Read any yellowing old newspaper if you want proof.) While the history of contemporary Afghanistan is complex, it is not opaque; rather, it is best understood by giving historical context its due because it still plays a crucial role in politics today. Future readers will have the luxury of more accurately determining whether I was insightful or woefully misleading.

The underlying structure of analysis seeks to test theoretical models against events and events against theoretical models to throw light on both. At the same time, the material is presented with a story line, so those readers who have little interest in the models may still find the book engaging. This approach violates a postmodern axiom that authors should avoid imposing a "master narrative" on events, particularly recent ones, since no one view or interpretation should be privileged over any other. Alas, this author is as addicted to narrative (master or otherwise) as any opium smoker is to their pipe. It is useless to chide him for privileging his own interpretations in his own book. It will not stop or even embarrass him. Other writers fired up to prove him wrong can be counted on to do that, and the more wrong he is, the better their books will be. While no interpretation can ever truly stand as the last word, each book should present its own. This is mine.

CHAPTER ONE

People and Places

Political scientists often give primacy to individuals, political parties, and ideologies in their studies. Those that employ models of "rational choice" assume that individuals always try to maximize their interests or minimize their pain when it comes to making decisions. When people are presented with the same alternatives, they will respond in the same way whether you are in Kansas or Qandahar. Anthropologists are less keen on this approach and its assumptions, not because they believe people to be less rational, but because they are familiar with societies in which group interest regularly trumps individual interest. That is, individuals support decisions made by their group even when such support has negative consequences for themselves. Anthropologists also believe that cost-benefit calculations are shaped by cultural predispositions about what is considered important. In an aristocratic society where honor is the highest ideal, the willingness to die to preserve it strikes observers as noble; in a commercial society where money takes precedence, such behavior is considered lunacy.

Afghanistan, particularly rural Afghanistan, provides an excellent example of a place where tribal and ethnic groups take primacy over the individual. As a result, any student of Afghan politics must become intimately familiar with such groups and their relationships with one another. This chapter outlines them and describes how they work because they have all played key roles in Afghanistan history. They remain vital in understanding current events there. Furthermore, this chapter introduces what Afghans themselves take for granted: their geography, religion, subsistence economy, and architecture, along with the persistent aspects of social organization in which they ground their lives. Whether one traveled to the land of the Hindu Kush when the region was Zoroastrian and Buddhist or after it became thoroughly Islamic, many of these factors would strike an observer as similar over time. Even as new peoples and languages entered the region, the continuities remained more profound than the discontinuities. They constitute, as noted in the introduction, what the French historian, Fernand Braudel, classically defined as elements of the *longue durée*: aspects of material life and social organization that have persisted for centuries, even millennia, and set the framework for daily life as it is ordinarily lived.[1] This is the context out of which politics and government emerges in Afghanistan. Though more subject to change, political institutions remain deeply rooted in Afghan cultural values and social organization, which outsiders ignore at their peril.

THE SOCIAL CONTEXT OF TRIBES AND ETHNIC GROUPS

The outstanding social feature of life in Afghanistan is its local tribal or ethnic divisions. People's primary loyalty is, respectively, to their own kin, village, tribe, or ethnic group, generally glossed as *qawm*. Afghanistan's population is divided into a myriad of these groups at the local level. But the term qawm is flexible and expandable, so its reference is contextual depending on who is asking. It therefore applies not only to these smallest units but by extension to the country's major ethnic groups as well. The most important of these by population are the Pashtuns, Tajiks, Hazaras, Uzbeks, Turkmen, and Aimaqs, although a number of smaller ethnic groups have regionally important roles (most notably the Nuristanis and Baluch). While a simplified map of these ethnic groups at the national level is useful and orients an outsider to gross patterns, it is also misleading. First, ethnic group definitions are based on multiple criteria that are often locally idiosyncratic. Criteria considered critical in one region may be deemed irrelevant in another. Moreover, two groups in a local context may declare themselves distinct (and even hostile), but also accept as unproblematic a common ethnic label at the regional or national level. Ethnic groups, in this respect, are more descriptive than operational. Thus, the larger the ethnic category being mapped, the less meaning that category will have. It is a mistake to see Afghan ethnic groups as fixed "nationalities" that have some overriding commonality and history that demands political unity. Finally, even when mapped at a fine scale, ethnic boundaries are always problematic on the ground. They frequently overlap in areas with

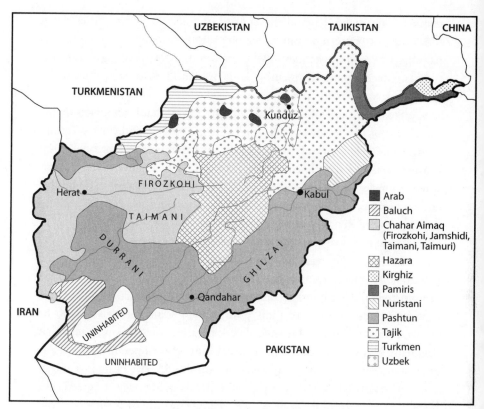

Map 2. Distribution of ethnic groups

mixed populations, and hide the crosscutting patterns of intermarriage, bilingualism, and unity through common geography. People of a shared locality (*manteqa*) may display more solidarity with their immediate neighbors of different ethnicities than they do with coethnics from other parts of the country.

Whether large or small, the varied ethnic groups residing in Afghanistan are all products of history. Since the end of the Bronze Age, if not before, new peoples have arrived (mostly from the north and west), bringing with them new languages and cultural practices. These new groups partially displaced, but more often amalgamated with, older populations in the major river valleys and urban centers. At the same time, Afghanistan's rugged terrain provided refuge for older groups to maintain their distinct ways of life beyond the control of rulers in distant cities. Even today the lofty eastern mountain region of Afghanistan remains a linguist's paradise where narrow valleys shelter communities speaking a dozen distinct languages, many representing language families that were once widespread but are now otherwise extinct.

Unlike other parts of the world, no group in Afghanistan makes mythical claims of having always been on the same plot of land since creation. Instead one listens gravely to stories of how the ancestors of one group conquered the land and bequeathed it to their descendants. Or how pressure from below pushed people into the mountains, where they could live as they pleased. Or how nomads seeking new pasture and farmers seeking new land were invited (or forcibly deported) by one ruler or another to settle where they live now. Such recounted stories are deeply rooted in the past, but remain such vital memories that they might as well have occurred yesterday. An illiterate man in northern Afghanistan gave me a detailed (and historically accurate) account of the Mongol destruction there while excoriating the memory of that "pure infidel" Chinggis Khan (who he claimed was an Uzbek). He then described a great irrigation system that originally had six major canals, of which only three operated today. "Afghanistan was a much better place then; you should have visited us at that time," he declared, as if I had just missed this golden age. I agreed, but knew that he was speaking of an age well beyond my own time horizon, since the Mongols had attacked in 1222. But by Afghan standards that was still recent enough to provoke strong emotion; an Uzbek listening to this story vehemently denied that his group had any relationship to the pagan Mongols. Across the border, a Pashtun example of taking the long view was famously expressed by the activist politician Abdul Wali Khan in the 1970s when questioned about his loyalty to Pakistan. He scornfully declared, "I have been a Pakistani for thirty years, a Muslim for fourteen hundred years, and a Pashtun for five thousand years."[2]

But what do I mean by the term ethnic identity, and how are ethnic groups in Afghanistan to be distinguished? Following the work of Fredrik Barth, they are most commonly defined as social groups that meet four criteria: they are biologically replicating, share fundamental cultural values, constitute a field of communication and interaction, and are defined through self-definition and definition by others.[3] The last criterion is the most important because it sets the boundaries of an ethnic group, and it is at the boundaries where we discern the most critical variables that people actually employ to distinguish themselves from others living beside them. The specific cultural content they share or the signs that mark that identity may change, but the group remains distinct as long its members assert (or are forced to accept) an identity that outsiders recognize and respond to. It does not matter whether that group defines itself primarily by descent from a common ancestor, language, religion, cultural practice, place of birth, physical characteristic, or (most commonly) combination of these. Nor does it matter whether their claim of distinction can be empirically validated. Whether rooted in documented history or invented whole cloth, its members (or the people around them) believe that it is true and unchangeable, and act accordingly. There is a practical rule of thumb for sorting out the large number of ethnic groups in Afghanistan: if people identify themselves as the "such and such," and their neighbors agree that they are the such and such, then they *are* the such and such.

This practical definition has not stopped scholars from crossing swords over just how fixed and unchanging ethnic identity really is.[4] Political scientists in particular tend to see ethnic groups as fixed and primordial, the product of a deep history that produces permanent groups with firm and unchanging boundaries. Conflict between ethnic groups is therefore especially difficult to resolve because the group identity is so inflexible. Anthropologists, on the other hand, are all too prone to argue that ethnicity is only circumstantial, and open to both choice and change, with individuals making strategic decisions on how to define themselves. For them, changing identity often appears to involve little more than picking the costume most appropriate to the situation at hand—a popular fiction that can be rewritten at will. Neither of these perspectives captures the essence of ethnicity in Afghanistan. People do assert that ethnicity is both fixed and historically rooted. All ethnic groups give themselves elaborate histories that stress their unchanging character. Specifically, they deny that an individual or group could change identity.

In practice, however, it is clear that flexibility and the strategic manipulation of identity has and does occur in Afghanistan. Within a tribal group it can be manipulated by changing a significant ancestor in an oral genealogy to reflect social distance. Groups in conflict prune ties to make their lineages appear more distant and hence less worthy of cooperation. This can also justify cooperation by incorporating a neighboring group and grafting their genealogy onto one's own at a higher level—a process that happened frequently enough among Pashtuns to create internal arguments as to which groups were the "true" Pashtuns. An individual or group could also convert to a different religious sect, where membership creates ethnic boundaries. The current distribution of sects in central Afghanistan must have been the product of such a process, even though current residents state that coversion from one sect to another never occurred.[5] So another rule of thumb is this: the success in manipulating personal, ethnic, or tribal identity in Afghanistan is inversely related to the degree of public suspicion induced by the change. Like the well-crafted patina on fake antiquities that convinces a buyer they are genuine, a successful social fabrication has the greatest legitimacy when its genuineness appears unquestionable or is at least difficult to challenge.

Ethnic groups in Afghanistan come in two flavors: tribal and nontribal. Tribes are a type of ethnic group that defines its membership through the unilineal descent from a common ancestor, real or assumed. In Afghanistan such descent is through the male line. The Pashtuns are the best example of this, with their ability to link scores of lineages comprising millions of people into a single genealogy backward through time to their founding ancestor. When the common ancestor is not known or is simply assumed to exist, the highest level of organization is a set of clans that assert a relationship with one another as a single group but cannot trace it. This system—characteristic of the Uzbeks, Turkmen, Hazaras, Kirghiz, and Aimaqs—is somewhat easier to manipulate, since it is easier to drop or add clans to the system. While the Turkmen and many Uzbeks maintain detailed lineages within their own clans, there is a tendency over time for these systems to lose their genealogical character, at which point it is only the clan name that is inherited. By contrast, nontribal ethnic groups make no claim of genealogical relationship among their members. The Persian-speaking Tajiks are the largest such nontribal group in Afghanistan. Mostly Sunni by sect, they do not assert a common descent but do maintain a common identity, distinguishing themselves primarily by residence. And, although the Hazaras have a tribal organization internally, externally they are defined not by this descent but rather by their common Shia religious faith, Persian language, and reputed Mongol ancestry.

Afghans often assert that ethnic groups are so distinct that they can be identified by their physical appearance alone, which is sometimes true when an individual fits an ethnic stereotype. Still, because of long-standing intermarriage, there is such a wide diversity within any single ethnic group, particularly large ones, that exceptions are as common as the rule. In practice, the belief that ethnic identity can be recognized visually stems as much from cues that men themselves provide through their style of dress (robes and headgear particularly). Women in rural areas often have even more ethnically distinct styles of dress and jewelry, but most never appear before strangers or are anonymously veiled when in public.

Ethnic Groups in Afghanistan

There are dozens of major and minor ethnic groups in Afghanistan, few of which have been well studied.[6] Two caveats must be tied to any estimates of their numbers. The first is that statistics in Afghanistan are validated more through repetition than by any data. The second is that partisans of different ethnic groups, even scholarly ones, turn chauvinistic when estimating their own group's numbers.

No one has ever really agreed on Afghanistan's population. From the 1970s to 1990s, sixteen million was the most frequently cited figure.* Today it is thirty million. This may or may not be an accurate figure. As a common Pashto saying has it, "God knows; I don't." It would be a useful piece of information to have, but promised surveys always seem to have a way of ending before their results become known. This is because population figures by region, let alone by ethnic group, are politically sensitive.

---

*The choice of this figure is instructive. In the early 1970s the Afghan government had claimed a population of twenty million—a figure that the United Nations used to calculate per capita poverty and aid. When a census found that there were only twelve million people in the country, the United Nations threatened to reduce its aid drastically. A typically Afghan solution was found by splitting the difference: each side gave four million to come to a compromise figure of sixteen million—a number invariably cited for the next twenty years.

Census takers have generally been prohibited from asking about group membership.

In the absence of real data, Pashtun-dominated governments have always asserted that Pashtuns constitute an absolute majority in Afghanistan, although they probably comprise only its largest plurality. More recently, Hazaras have entered the numbers game to make themselves equal to the Tajiks. The Uzbeks have similarly inflated the number of Turkish speakers. And Tajiks are either a larger or smaller part of the total depending on whether they are subdivided by region or included as a single group. If one were to give equal weight to all of these partisan estimates and offer offense to none, it would be safe to say that the five largest ethnic groups in Afghanistan comprise approximately 185 percent of the country's total population with smaller groups accounting for another 15 percent. This is not a statistic I expect will be validated through repetition, so below I employ the most common ones that add up to 100 percent.

Large Groups

PASHTUNS

Pashtuns have been the dominant ethnic group in modern Afghanistan since the mid-eighteenth century and currently comprise about 40 percent of the country's total population. An even larger number of Pashtuns reside on the Pakistan side of the border concentrated in the Northwest Frontier Province (NWFP) and the northern parts of Baluchistan. Historically, "Afghan" was so synonymous with "Pashtun" that Afghanistan could be equally glossed not only as the "land of the Afghans" but the "land of the Pashtuns" as well. More recently, Afghan has acquired a more national character, especially because this is how the outside world labels its people regardless of ethnic origin. Yet the use of Afghan in this national context is still contested. Some non-Pashtuns argue for the use of "Afghani" (formerly used only to denote the country's unit of currency) or "Afghanistani" as a national label on the grounds that Afghan still implies Pashtun identity inside the country.

Pashtun-descent groups are composed of lineages (Pashto -*zai*, "sons of") that trace their origin to Qais, the putative common ancestor of all

Pashtuns.[7] These lineages unite into larger clans (Pashto -*khel*), which in turn are grouped in four maximal-descent groups:

- The Durrani (known earlier as the Abdali) are the descendants from Qais's first son. In Afghanistan, they are located in the south and southwest. Their major tribal components are divided between the Zirak (Popalzai, Alikozai, Barakzai, and Achakzai,) and the Panjpao (Nurzai, Alizai, and Isaqzai). The most prominent Pashtun tribes in Peshawar, such as the Yusefzai, Shinwari, and Mohmand, also claim descent through this line.
- The Ghilzais (also called Khalji or Ghalji) are descendants of Qais' second son, but through his daughter. Located throughout the east they are Afghanistan's largest Pashtun group, and include tribes such as the Hotaki, Tokhi, Kharoti, Nasiri, Taraki, Sulaiman khel, and Ahmadzai, among others.
- The Gurghusht are descendants of Qais's third son. They include tribes such as the Kakar and Musa Khel (bordering the Baluch) and the Safi (in the Kunar region).
- The Karlanri (often labeled Pathans by the British) are asserted to be descendants of an adopted child of uncertain origin. They straddle the Afghan Pakistan border, but the bulk of their population lies in the NWFP. Their tribal components include the Wardak, Orakzai, Afridi, Wazir, Jaji, Tani, Khattak, Zadran, Mangal, Mahsud, and Khugiani.

In addition to descent, the Pashtuns ideally define themselves by their adherence to a code of conduct, the Pashtunwali, and their ability to speak Pashto. Many Pashtuns by descent who have lived for generations in Persian-speaking towns, though, no longer speak Pashto or conduct themselves according to tribal honor codes. These lapses call their Pashtun identity into question in the eyes of hill tribesmen, but since they also constituted the country's ruling elite, this opinion has never been shared by Afghan governments or the country's other ethnic groups. Most rural Pashtuns are subsistence farmers, but a minority of them are nomads. These seasonally migrating pastoralists (*kuchi* or *maldar*) do not constitute exclusive descent groups. Among the Durrani, the bulk of them are Nurzai, while the Kharoti and Nasiri have the largest nomadic components among the Ghilzais.

There are also large migrant Pashtun communities in the north—a product of the Afghan government policies of ethnic transfer begun in the 1880s.

TAJIKS

The Tajiks, usually defined as nontribal Persian-speaking Sunni Muslims, constitute about 30 percent of Afghanistan's population. Of all the ethnic groups in Afghanistan, the Tajiks have the least internal coherence. They traditionally made up the majority of urban residents in Kabul, Herat, and Mazar, but the bulk of their population is spread out over the mountains of the northeast. If asked about their identity, most so-called Tajiks will respond only by giving you their regional affiliation (Badakhshi, Panjshiri, Shomali, Salangi, etc.) or city residence (Kabuli or Herati). Rural Tajiks practice subsistence farming, but those in urban areas have historically been the bedrock of the merchant community, bureaucrats, and educated clergy. Their literacy in Persian, long the regional language of government administration, high culture, and foreign relations, gave them a powerful role no matter who was ruling the country.[8]

HAZARAS

The Hazaras make up about 15 percent of Afghanistan's population. Their homeland lies in the central range of the Hindu Kush, a region known as Hazarajat. They are Shia Muslims who engage in alpine subsistence agriculture and livestock breeding. Although their language is a dialect of Persian, the Hazaras are said to descend from the Mongol armies that conquered Iran and often display strong Mongoloid features. They maintained independent control of Hazarajat until the end of the nineteenth century, when Amir Abdur Rahman conquered the region. At that time the Hazaras were victimized and even sold as slaves in Kabul. But this population transfer, reinforced by the later settlement of migrant workers seeking casual employment in the capital, increased their numbers to such an extent that they made up a third of Kabul's population in the 1970s. As historic victims of prejudice on religious and racial grounds, the Hazaras found social mobility difficult. They ranked at the bottom of Afghanistan's ethnic hierarchy, and were systematically excluded from almost all government positions and educational opportunities by the Pashtun-dominated governments. They were particular targets of persecution by the Taliban, but most recently achieved parity with other groups under the constitution of 2004, which specifically recognized the legitimacy of Shia legal practices.[9]

UZBEKS AND TURKMEN

The Uzbeks and Turkmen make up about 10 percent of the country's population. They are Sunni Turkish-speaking groups that descend from nomadic tribal confederations that arrived in a series of waves from central Asia. They became politically dominant in the region from about AD 950. The Uzbeks arrived in northern Afghanistan during the sixteenth century as nomadic conquerors, but most later settled in the irrigated valleys or loess steppes, where they became sedentary farmers. The Uzbeks in Afghanistan are an extension of the Uzbek population across the border in Uzbekistan.[10] A large number fled from there to Afghanistan following the Russian revolution and later during the Stalinist period.[11] The related Turkmen tribes are found in the northwest on the borders with Turkmenistan and Iran. They remained much more nomadic than the Uzbeks, and often raided northern Iran and northern Afghanistan for slaves and other loot until the late nineteenth century, when the Russian conquest of Khiva and Merv ended their autonomy.[12] A number of Turkmen groups moved to Afghan territory after this, particularly following the establishment of the Soviet Union. They are closely related to the larger Turkmen populations in Turkmenistan and Iran. The Turkmen play an important economic role because they produce Afghanistan's famed carpets and karakul sheepskins, both of which are major export earners. Until recently, Turkish speakers were an invisible minority in Afghanistan. They had few representatives in government, and their languages were not taught in schools. During the Soviet war period and the civil war, they regained considerable autonomy and once again became a political force in the north.

AIMAQS

The Aimaqs are tribally organized Sunni Muslims who speak Persian but are sometimes said to be of Turkish descent.[13] They are the smallest of the regionally important groups, probably about half the size of the neighboring

Uzbeks and Turkmen. Historically, they occupied the mountainous territory east of Herat and west of Hazarajat, the ancient territory of Ghor. They also occupied some of the steppes and desert lands north and east of Herat. Often known as "Chahar Aimaq" (Four Tribes), their major divisions include the Jamshidi, Firozkohi, Taimani, and Taimuri. The Aimaqs suffered greatly during the wars launched by the Kabul government in the late nineteenth century, and many were dispersed to parts of northern Afghanistan. They probably number about a half-million people, although estimates vary widely. There is even some dispute as to whether they should be considered a set of small groups rather than one larger ethnic group. The term *aimaq* itself is a generic Turkish idiom for tribe. In rural areas they are seminomadic, with more emphasis on pastoralism than their neighbors.

Smaller Groups

The remaining ethnic groups of Afghanistan are quite diverse, but represent only 3 percent or less of the country's population. Individually, their populations range from one to two hundred thousand. Some of these groups, however, have had historical significance beyond their numbers. Afghan rulers frequently followed an old political strategy of appointing members of small ethnic minorities to high positions in the government and military. It was believed that they would be more loyal because they had no political base of their own within the larger population and were therefore less likely to betray their masters.

NURISTANIS AND PASHAI

The Nuristanis live in the mountains northeast of Kabul, where they inhabit isolated valleys.[14] Until the late nineteenth century they were independent, maintaining their own polytheistic religion and a distinctive culture based on goats and cattle as well as terraced agriculture. Forcibly converted to Islam after the conquest in 1895, the descendants of those who were moved to Kabul later became a critical part of the government and military in spite of their small numbers. Their languages are unrelated to any others in Afghanistan, and the population shows a high rate of blond-ism (a characteristic associated in legend with the conquest of Alexander the Great). Nuristani is an example of an imposed ethnonym, since inter-nally the Nuristanis are divided into a number of distinct tribes that oc-cupy separate valleys and speak different languages. The Pashais are cultur-ally similar to their immediate neighbors in Nuristan, but maintain their own identity and adopted Islam earlier.[15]

QIZILBASH

The Qizilbash originally made up the Shiite Turkish military units that helped to found the Afghan state during the turmoil of the mid-eighteenth century. They played a vital political role as defenders of the Afghan state against tribal revolts in the late eighteenth and early nineteenth centuries. Today they are a Persian-speaking urban population, key in government and trade. As Shias, they were distinct from the Sunni population, but they did not suffer from the severe discrimination inflicted on the Hazaras because of their long incorporation into the Kabul elite.

BALUCH

The Baluch are located south of the Pashtuns in the desert. They are extensions of much larger populations found in Iran and Pakistan. The Baluch have their own language, Baluchi, which (like Pashto) is related to Persian. On their ethnic border with Pashtun areas many Baluch speak Pashto, and the distinction between Baluch and Pashtun rests primarily on political allegiance to Baluch khans rather than language or descent. They are mostly pastoral nomads in Afghanistan. In the past they often made ends meet by raiding villages; today the Baluch are still renowned as smug-glers linking Iran and India.

ARABS

The Arabs of Afghanistan claim descent from the Arabian armies that conquered central Asia in the eighth century, but none of these groups still speak Arabic as a native language. They are now Persian speakers, and in the north they are bilingual in Uzbeki as well. They have a tradition of pastoralism, yet one that is well integrated into market production. These Arabs are frequently confused with *sayyids* (descendants of the Prophet), but they claim no such descent for themselves, and *sayyids* (representatives of which can be found among a variety of ethnic groups) reject any kinship with them. The Arabs have been relatively invisible in Afghanistan's ethnic politics. In part this is because culturally and linguistically, they have assimilated into the regional culture.[16]

PAMIRIS

Russian ethnographers have misleadingly referred to all the Ismaili groups inhabiting the headwaters of the Oxus River (Darya Panj) on both sides of the border as the "mountain Tajiks" or "Pamir Tajiks"—a tradition still followed in neighboring Tajikistan. As non-Sunnis speaking their own languages, however, they are not considered Tajiks in Afghanistan and often have antagonistic relations with their Persian-speaking Sunni neighbors in Badakhshan. They tend to identify themselves by valley, each of which has its own language, such as Wakhi, Shugni, or Roshani. There is a striking cultural difference between those Pamiris living in Tajikistan—who received infrastructure development and high levels of education under Soviet rule—and those on the Afghan side—who are largely illiterate and engage in subsistence agriculture.[17]

And Yes, Even Smaller Groups

JUGIS AND JATS

In Afghanistan, there are a variety of endogamous itinerant communities, which engage in specialized crafts (such as sieve and knife making or haircutting), or are peddlers and providers of exotic services (monkey and snake trainers or prostitution). Attributed with foreign (generally Indian) origins, their communities are typically labeled Jugis and Jats, a gloss similar to the use of "gypsy" in Europe. They reject such labels and use more specific terms (Shaykh Mohammad and Ghorbat), but all share a common marginal social status in Afghan society.[18]

KIRGHIZ

The Kirghiz are the smallest of the Turkic groups in Afghanistan. Numbering less than a thousand people today, they are pastoral nomads inhabiting the Wakhan corridor, and are related to larger Kirghiz populations residing in the Pamir range of Tajikistan, Kirghizstan, and Chinese Xinjiang. Their strategic location on "the roof of the world" has given them a political significance well beyond their numbers in this remote territory.[19]

NON-MUSLIMS

Afghanistan has only a tiny non-Muslim population, consisting of perhaps ten to twenty thousand Sikhs and Hindus long resident in Kabul and a few other cities. They were particularly important historically in Afghanistan's international trade and still play a large role in the currency market. Until the mid-twentieth century Afghanistan had small but old Jewish communities in Kabul, Herat, and the cities of the north. Most Afghan Jews emigrated to Israel in the 1950s, and the older members who stayed behind died off, so the community has now disappeared.

WAYS OF LIVING

One of the earliest sociological definitions of "culture" described it as the "complex whole which includes knowledge, belief, art, morals, law, custom, and any other capabilities and habits acquired by man as a member of society."[20] This holistic aspect has inspired anthropologists to stress the interconnections among these elements and not simply run a checklist on each society they encounter. Here I will sketch what the French anthropologist Pierre Bourdieu has called a "habitus," the ingrained patterns of apprehending the world and interacting with it.[21] In the realm of the power of ideas, the two most significant are conceptions of group identity (explored above) and the cultural framework of Islam. But people also exist in a material world that encompasses how they live their lives on a daily basis and the built environments they inhabit. This material habitus is as unremarkable to Afghans as it is distinct to outsiders. Indeed, it is so taken for granted that it is invisible, even when of critical importance. This is not surprising. Anyone who has experienced living in another culture soon realizes that the things that most struck them as unique and remarkable on first encounter quite quickly recede into the commonplace, everyday, and unremarkable with the passing of time. The human psyche seems to be hardwired into fixating on the exceptional while passing over the conventional.* Accounts of outsiders (like Alexis de Tocqueville's *Democracy in America*, or Mountstuart Elphinstone's *Kingdom of Caubul*) retain their value centuries after they were written precisely because they cogently analyzed what their interlocutors took as boringly self-evident.

Rural Economy

Afghanistan is a land of small villages, which traditionally accounted for about 80 percent of the population, spread out over a territory the size of France (or Texas, if you prefer). The practice of subsistence farming and pastoralism has always given these villages considerable autonomy. Although agricultural practices and crops vary from region to region, the national economy is based on rural production with no modern industries. Cities, although always politically dominant historically, constituted no greater percentage of the country's population than did the country's nomads (about one million each before 1978). The population throughout the first three-quarters of the twentieth century was about twelve million—a figure first estimated by the British in 1912 and reconfirmed in an unpublished Afghan census in 1974. This lack of growth is simple to explain. Afghanistan had a demographic profile typical of a premodern society in which a high birthrate was matched by a high death rate. In part because of higher growth rates among refugee populations that have returned to Afghanistan, the country's current estimated population of twenty-five to thirty million is now significantly larger, although neighboring Pakistan

---

*The bane of historians are those local accounts that excitingly proclaim "the famine was so severe that a *seer* of wheat cost fifty *kaldars!*" but never report the ordinary price of wheat. These accounts simply assume that everyone already knows this, along with how much a *seer* weighs and a *kaldar* is worth.

and Iran showed much higher rates of growth over the same period. As part of a war-induced urbanization that began with the Soviet invasion, cities and towns also now house a much greater percentage of the population. Before 1978 Kabul had about a population of a half million, and today is home to between three and four million.

Until only a couple centuries ago the vast majority of the world's people everywhere engaged in agriculture, mostly of a subsistence variety. In only the past century and a half, this formerly pervasive economic activity has been reduced to a specialty in industrial societies involving less than 2 percent of the population. But people still eat, and given growing rates of obesity worldwide, they eat much more and do much less physical work than when most everyone was a farmer. A corollary of this fact is that few readers of this book are likely to be familiar with the world of subsistence agricultural production that their immediate ancestors took for granted. Worse, wealthy residents of Europe and the United States are now prone to idealize it as "closer to nature"—and to boot, organic. So another set of caveats and fair warnings are noted below.

On the negative side: Subsistence agriculture in Afghanistan involves an almost-unimaginable daily life of toil, where one gets up at dawn because there is light and goes to sleep soon after dark because there is not. Such a physically demanding life makes people appear a lot older than they really are—that is, if they even survive long enough to look old. Rural Afghanistan has some of the highest infant and maternal mortality rates in the world. The seasonality of work is based on men plowing, sowing, harvesting, threshing, and then milling grain. The bulk of this will be set aside for a family's use, not sold on the market. Women spend most of their time doing basic tasks, such as getting water, making wood fires and meals from scratch, taking care of children, and engaging in household management, sometimes also combined with craft production. This work is done through human and animal labor because machines are rare, and electricity or piped water are rarer. There is the communal labor of cleaning irrigation channels and repairing any damage wrought by floods. There are heated disputes about the distribution of water when shortages occur, and the sometimes deadlier arguments over property boundaries. After all, just by plowing one extra furrow into your neighbor's land each year and moving the boundary marker a little, you can make a lot of their land your own in a decade. People kill neighbors over such issues. And farmers who do not have irrigation and rely on rain-fed fields are at the mercy of the weather. A good rain or snowfall produces a bumper crop; if there is no rain or snow, there may be a famine. Being a nomad isn't any easier either, even though they insist it is a better way of life than farming. A nomad will extol the virtues of sheep that reproduce geometrically while wheatfields remain fixed—a Malthusian road to pastoral wealth. But then after listing incidents of early blizzards, epidemics, droughts, thefts, and other disasters that can cut a flock in half overnight, the nomad will tell you the best strategy is to use sheep profits to buy irrigated land because "land never dies." When I once opined that perhaps the Afghan government should help its pastoralists through price supports as is done in other countries, a shepherd laughed and retorted sarcastically that "here, when the price of sheep gets too low, we eat them."

On the positive side: Subsistence agriculture provides its practitioners with a degree of autonomy unknown in a market economy. Prices for grain may fluctuate widely and often severely, but since farmers first set aside grain for their own consumption, such swings have less impact than in urban areas. From seed to wheat to flour to bread, every aspect of production remains at the household or village level. What they cannot produce themselves, farmers buy from local merchants and artisans, often by growing some cash crops, selling domestic animals, or engaging in craft production. But maximizing cash income is not their goal; they sell just enough to buy the items they need to consume. Similarly, after they satisfy their subsistence needs, they stop working. As the nineteenth-century Russian economist Alexander Chayanov documented among peasants there, given a choice between producing more or working less, subsistence farmers opt to work less (see the baseline of daily toil above).[22] It is a world of reciprocal obligations where hired domestic laborers are for all practical purposes incorporated into the extended household. Sharecroppers are generally neighbors of the landlords from whom they rent the land they farm. Such a robust structure can weather major economic and political disruptions that would collapse more complex systems. To those who wonder how the Afghans survived the recent decades of war and political disorder in better shape than other places in the world, look to this strategy of production to meet basic economic needs, and the tight network of family and social ties that draw people together as well as protect them.

Settlement Patterns

Settlement patterns in Afghanistan can be divided into three basic types: rural villages, nomadic encampments, and towns. There is a close link among them. Villages depend on towns to supply them with manufactured goods, and the wealth of the towns depends on the surplus that their hinterlands provide. Nowhere is this clearer than on "bazaar day," a once or twice weekly event during which the people of the countryside swarm into town to buy or sell, or just to experience the crowd. Sleepy towns that on other days of the week do not seem to justify the scores of shops lining their unpaved streets are on these days bustling with mercantile activity, with the caravansaries full of parked donkeys, and the teahouses overflowing with people eager for news and gossip. Nomads camped on uncultivated land away from towns and villages, by contrast, seem to live in a world of their own. But this is an illusion. In spite of their migrations and mobile tents, nomads travel by regular routes, and have close economic connections with towns in their winter areas and rural villages in their summer areas. In many parts of the country they also own land, so the distinction between nomad and villager is not a strict one.

The wide-ranging cultural diversity in Afghanistan can be seen in the amazing variety of building types found there. One study documented forty-four distinct types of nomadic, transhumant, and sedentary structures in rural areas.[23] This wide variety of tents, huts, yurts, flat and curved roofs, stone or mud walls, single buildings, and village complexes is large because it all evolved to meet a range of geographic conditions, climatic variations, and inherited cultural traditions. Each building type is specialized and refined in a way that maintains an equilibrium between the physical context and cultural needs. More remarkably to outsiders, buildings in rural areas are constructed by their inhabitants, not specialists, and they make use of the most common materials at hand. The adaptation of materials to the sites is such that they often appear to be an organic part of the landscape rather than intruders.

VILLAGES

Villages follow a number of settlement patterns depending on the availability of water and the need for defense. The key distinction in agriculture is whether the land is irrigated (*abi*) or unirrigated (*lalmi*). Except for the mountain and foothill regions that depend on unirrigated agriculture, most villages are sited in relation to an irrigation network of *jui* or channels. In large valleys, these may depend on a barrage or dam system that diverts river water in the main canals, from which it is then moved by gravity to smaller channels and finally to the fields. In mountainous areas, small streams may be diverted at high elevations for use by the villages below. In the western and southern parts of Afghanistan a system of underground conduits (*qanat* or *karez*) are also employed, but these require a large capital investment and need more maintenance than other systems. In all of these cases, the villages are located on the least fertile areas so that little agricultural land is lost. Village houses on the plains are usually surrounded by three- to four-meter-high mud walls. Indeed in those villages of the *qala* houses (see figure 1 and 2), walls are an integral part of the structure itself and are designed to serve as fortresses as well as houses.

Another house type found in the area from Herat to Tashqurghan employs domed roofs, while in most other parts of Afghanistan village houses use flat roofs. Typically square or rectangular in plan, they make use of sun-dried clay brick as their main building material. In the treeless high mountain areas, stone replaces mud, and in forested Nuristan the extensive use of wooden beams, frames, and columns creates a style of architecture unique to the region.

Village life is based on households working small plots of land, usually owned by an individual household. Tenant farming has always been far less prevalent in Afghanistan than in neighboring Iran or Pakistan. Wheat is the basic crop throughout the country. In irrigated lowland regions rice, cotton, melons, and citrus fruit are also grown. Most highland agriculture is unirrigated, with wheat the preferred crop at lower altitudes and barley the preferred one at higher elevations. Large tracts of land are plowed and sown in anticipation that a good snowfall or spring rains will produce a good crop. Highland villages tend to be smaller in population than those in the lowland areas. Mountain villages also irrigate groves of trees to pro-

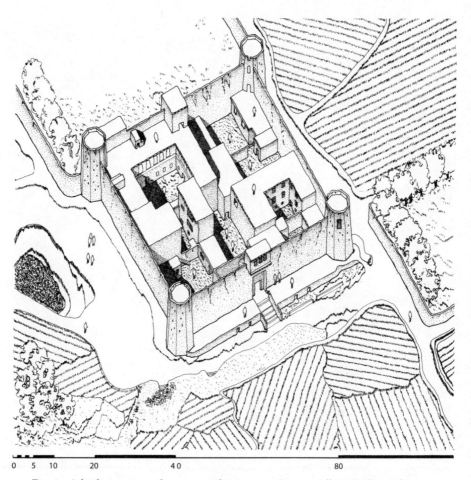

0   5   10   20   4 0   80

Fig. 1. A high-prestige qala, measured in meters. Source: Albert Szabo and
Thomas Barfield, *Afghanistan: An Atlas of Indigenous Domestic Architecture.*
Austin, 1991: University of Texas Press, p. 188.

duce crops such as mulberries, stone fruit, and nuts. Livestock, mostly
cows and goats, are an important component of the economy, but mountain villagers must limit their numbers to those that can be stall fed through
the winter. The livestock is moved to available pasture in the summer. To
facilitate this, people establish special summer villages (*ailoq*) or, particularly in central Afghanistan, make use of portable huts that provide seasonal dwellings.

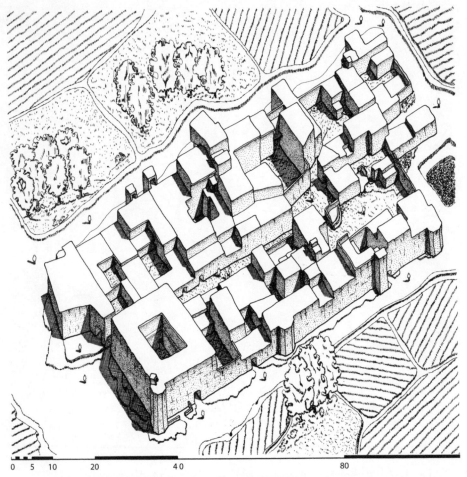

0   5   10   20   40   80

Fig. 2. A farm village qala, measured in meters. Source: Albert Szabo and Thomas Barfield, *An Atlas of Indigenous Domestic Architecture*. Austin, 1991: University of Texas Press, p. 164.

PASTORAL NOMADS

Raising livestock is the primary occupation of nomadic pastoralists in Afghanistan, who by some estimates number more than a million people.[24] These nomads take advantage of seasonally changing pastures, spending the winter in the lowlands and the summers in the mountains. They raise sheep and use camels to transport their baggage. The map of nomadic

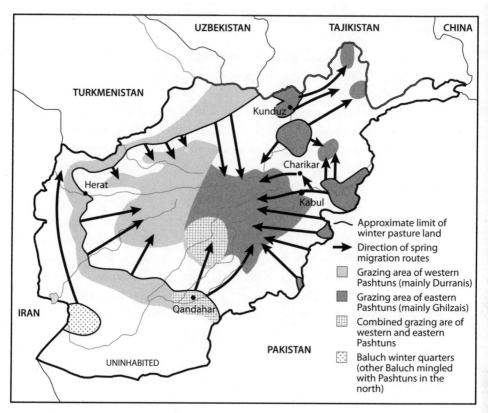

Map 3. Nomadic migration routes

migrations shows that nomads move toward the highlands of the Hindu Kush in the center of the country or the northeast toward the highland pastures of Badakhshan. Most of the nomads involved in these long-range migrations are Pashtuns, who use black goat-hair tents. Nomads from the Uzbek, Turkmen, or Kirghiz groups normally move their animals only short distances, often moving from winter pastures in the valleys to spring and summer pastures on the steppes and nearby foothills. They live in yurts. A few groups also engage in the caravan trade. All are dependent on the sale of animals, cheese, clarified butter, dried yogurt, wool, or skins to urban markets for cash, with which they then buy wheat. Wheat bread is the main food even of nomads in Afghanistan.

TOWNS

Towns act as centers of trade, where agricultural and pastoral products are exchanged for manufactured goods. Local artisans produce many of the items that are essential for village and nomadic life. Town populations are diverse, including members of many different ethnic groups. In the winter especially, young men from mountain villages will seek temporary work in the towns, returning home in time to help with the new agricultural season. Other migrants settle to form ethnic communities within an urban setting. Because of this, no matter how remote a village may seem, it often has links to regional urban centers. Towns are also centers of government administration, but links between officials there and more rural villagers have traditionally been brittle. While frequently more elaborate in towns, house forms employ the same type of construction techniques as do those in the villages. Like their village counterparts, urban houses are normally surrounded by high walls so that little detail of domestic architecture is visible from the street. In large cities multistoried buildings are common, based on multiples of the same construction type.

Religion

It perhaps goes without saying that Afghanistan is a Muslim country, mostly Sunni (85 percent) with a minority (15 percent) of Shias and Ismailis. While today it seems that every book on Afghanistan has "Islam" somewhere in the title or subtitle, earlier works did not. Some suggest this is evidence that past researchers underestimated the significance of Islam in the country, deceived by the values of the small secular elite in Kabul.[25] I would argue that a different dynamic was at work, and that it is relevant to this day. Afghanistan is an example of an older form of Islamic society in which religion is not an ideology but remains an all-encompassing way of life. If earlier investigators did not give Islam priority, it was because they took its overwhelming importance too much for granted and therefore in little need of explication. Today, by contrast, there is an intense focus on Islam, but one largely limited to its political guise—a perspective that flattens the distinctions between Afghanistan and other Muslim societies.

When religion is a way of life, it permeates all aspects of everyday social relations, and nothing is separate from it. This is the state of Islam in Afghanistan. Its influence is ever present in people's everyday conversations, business transactions, dispute resolutions, and moral judgments. There is no relationship, whether political, economic, or social, that is not validated by religion. Hard bargaining can be brought to a smooth end by a simple prayer that blesses and sanctifies the final agreement. Similarly, disputing parties that refuse to give any ground (because it might show weakness) can be moved to compromise when a mediator asks for it "in the name of God." Who can refuse a request like that?

In such a society it is impossible to separate religion from politics because the two are so closely intertwined. It is therefore hard for most Afghans to even conceive of the separation of religion and government because in their minds the two are so intrinsically linked. It would be like asking a fish to separate itself from the water it swims in.* Indeed, because Islam is so much a part of everyday life, the declaration of an "Islamic Republic of Afghanistan" in the constitution of 2004 provoked neither discussion nor concern. This was because the Afghan view of an Islamic government is descriptive, not prescriptive. It is a government composed of good Muslims, not one empowered to impose a particular religious or political agenda.[26]

In Afghanistan, this intrinsic Islamic identity is also fused with a strong cultural identity. Issues of identity politics and cultural practice that spark debate in other Islamic countries, which originated in their experiences of a colonial past, mass education, urbanization, rapid economic changes, and mass mobilization through explicitly political parties, have had little resonance in Afghanistan. Afghanistan was never a colony. It has low levels of literacy and an economy that is still overwhelmingly agrarian. Kinship and ethnic ties have always trumped political relations based on ideologies. Afghanistan is a place where the concept of Islamic politics is little debated, but only because its people assume there can be any be no other type.

---

*Such a pervasive role for religion was also characteristic of Christianity in medieval Europe, where questions of salvation took precedence over more material concerns. Since the rise of the modern West was characterized by the retreat of religion as the dominant influence in society, it now takes a leap of imagination to appreciate a society in which religion still plays that culturally dominating role.

Few peoples in the world, particularly the Islamic world, have maintained such a strong and unproblematic sense of themselves, their culture, and their superiority as the Afghans. In abstract terms all foreigners, especially non-Muslims, are viewed as inferior to Afghans. Although the great powers might have been militarily, technologically, and economically stronger, because they were nonbelievers, or infidels, their values and way of life were naturally suspect. Afghanistan's Muslim neighbors, however, fared only slightly better in (Sunni) Afghan eyes. The Uzbeks must have been asleep to allow the Russians to occupy central Asia for more than a century; Pakistan is a suspect land of recent Muslim converts from Hinduism (Pashtuns and Baluch excepted) that never should have become a nation; and Iran is a nest of Shiite heretics who speak Persian with a ludicrous accent. Convinced they are natural-born Muslims, Afghans cede precedence to no one in matters of religion. They refused to take doctrinal advice from foreign Salafis, who claimed they had a superior vision of Islam, coming as they did from the Islam's Arabian heartland. Instead, even under the Taliban, Afghans continued to bedeck graves commemorating martyrs with poles and flags, tied cloth swatches to sacred trees, made pilgrimages to the shrines of saints reputed to cure illnesses or help women conceive, and placed magical charms on their children and valuable domestic animals to ward off the evil eye. Afghans responded to any criticism of these practices by arguing that since there are no purer or stronger believers in Islam than themselves, their customs must be consistent with Islam. Otherwise they would not practice them. Islamic Sufi orders (Nakhshbanidya and Chisti particularly) are also well established in the country and give a mystic turn to what sometimes appears to be an austere faith.

GEOGRAPHY

Afghanistan's physical geography has had a profound impact on the country's history and culture. The complex set of mountains that lie at the heart of the country is one of the most obvious features. They are worth discussing in some detail because they set the limits on agriculture by altitude and determine the water available for irrigation through the river systems that flow from them. Specific river systems and their watersheds have also sus-

Map 4. Afghanistan's regions

tained Afghanistan's distinct regions: Herat in the west, Qandahar in the south, Mazar-i-sharif (Balkh) in the north, and the Kabul-Peshawar axis in the east. These regions (and Afghanistan itself) are part of the larger cultural-historical unit of Turko-Persia that encompasses the entire Iranian plateau.

Mountains and Rivers

When the Indian tectonic plate slammed into Asia millions of years ago, it raised up an arc of mountain ranges that are among the highest in the world. Afghanistan lies within the most eastern sector of this arc. The main ranges include the Paropamisus, which extends eastward from Herat and merges into the mighty Hindu Kush rising north of Kabul. The Hindu Kush in turn merges with the edge of the Pamir and Karakoram ranges in the far northeast. Because these mountains are still growing, the area experiences frequent and sometimes-severe earthquakes. Although Afghanistan's mountain regions are only sparsely populated, they are the country's key geographic feature because their height and location determine wind and precipitation patterns, temperature, vegetation, and the flow of snow-fed rivers. The central mountains bisect Afghanistan and catch the precipitation from the Indian subcontinent to the southeast as the monsoon winds exhaust themselves. This makes eastern Afghanistan the wettest part of the country and the only place where natural forests are found. The drier winds from inland Eurasia are blocked by the north wall of the Hindu Kush and Pamir chains. Precipitation falls mostly as snow at the higher elevations. The deserts of the southwest receive little precipitation and constitute a major dry belt swept by seasonal winds that blow for months on end. The most important mountain resource is its snowpack.

Rapid altitude changes give the land great ecological diversity over surprisingly short linear distances because the warm and cold areas of Afghanistan are determined largely by altitude. You can escape the freezing winter snows and winds of Kabul by taking only a three-hour drive east through the Silk Gorge to Jalalabad, where oranges are being harvested. You can escape the humid summer heat in marshy Kunduz, where temperatures often exceed forty degrees Celsius, by moving to the mountains of Badakhshan. But while the lowland regions are also warmer, in a mountainous country like Afghanistan, lowland is a truly relative term and defined by the local context. The grape-growing area of Parwan north of Kabul and the grain belt in Logar River valley to Kabul's south are relatively high in comparison to Qandahar or Herat, but both are low in relation to Hazarajat or Badakhshan. Traders take advantage of these differences by moving both highland and lowland products to city bazaars, giving these markets a diversity that is unrivaled in neighboring countries. In the mountains, alpine farmers typically exploit elevation differences by spending three seasons in a lower-altitude main village situated within a protected valley surrounded by their well-tended orchards and fields. In the summer as the snow melts, they move to a high-altitude village or camp with huts on the mountain slopes that tower above them to graze their cows and goats. Similarly, migrating pastoral nomads use the same principle over much longer distances. They pack their tents on camels, and migrate with their sheep and goats to mountain pastures that lie between three and four thousand meters in elevation in order to escape the summer heat and burned pastures of the plains. They return during August to avoid the onset of snows, which fall early in the highlands, and seek shelter in the warmer lowlands for the winter. Before the creation of Pakistan, Afghan nomads would migrate as far as the plains of India to spend the winter.

The mountainous central massif at the center of Afghanistan is rugged and discourages easy travel. Even today, the lack of drivable roads makes these areas difficult to access. Villages are cut off from the rest of the country for large parts of the year when winter snows block the passes or just make travel dangerous. Such regions appear, and often are, out of touch with the rest of Afghanistan, let alone the rest of the world. Who, other than the people who live there, would even think of venturing into such a high, trackless maze? Yet for millennia people have moved in and out of these mountains regularly. These regions provide migrant laborers, mostly young men, who leave their resource-poor villages for seasonal work in the lowland valleys or cities. Some venture even further to neighboring countries and beyond for work. Distant mountain villages therefore often have ties to the wider world through local families that have settled elsewhere but maintain strong ties to their natal villages, or more directly by sending remittances though complex trade networks to support their families with resources from abroad. Alessandro Monsutti has shown that the remote Hazarajat survived a drought in the late 1990s that would have otherwise created widespread famine through hundreds of millions of dollars in foreign remittances, which pulled up the economy.[27]

What has been more historically significant, however, is that while the mountain peoples live in a world dominated by problems of basic subsistence, many of the routes through the mountains have been conduits of international trade that have consistently brought outsiders and high levels of culture through these regions. Like a high-voltage electricity line, these routes run through such regions not because they have an intrinsic value in themselves but because they link regions with resources that do. As a consequence, they serve as economic and cultural interfaces between different worlds. This influence rubs off economically, culturally, and politically.

The highlands separate the country's distinctive regions north and south of the Paropamisus and Hindu Kush. The former had strong ties to the trans–Oxus River valleys and steppes to the north in central Asia, and the latter to India and Iran. Movement between these areas exploited a series of passes that pierced the Hindu Kush, the two most important of which historically were the Shibar Pass through Bamiyan and the Khawak Pass through the Panjshir Valley north of Kabul. (They were superseded by a drivable road built through the Salang Pass in 1964.) The old northeastern caravan route through Wakhan in the Pamirs, called the roof of the world in Persian, led into the western deserts of Turkistan with direct connections to China. A lower set of passes led from Afghanistan to India, including the famous Khyber Pass from Kabul and Jalalabad to Peshawar and the Bolan Pass from Qandahar to Quetta. These passes were well-known historically, and were well-traveled international byways of commerce. They were already old when the Silk Route caravans were young, bringing exotic goods, people, and beliefs into some of the region's remotest areas. The royal blue lapis lazuli found in five-thousand-year-old Sumerian tombs and inlaid into the three-thousand-year-old gold mummy case of the ancient Egyptian King Tutankhamen comes only from a single high mountain mine in Badakhshan. And along these routes centuries later Buddhism moved from India to China using Afghanistan as a key transmitter. Nothing reinforces this evidence of these international connections more than the long-abandoned remains of the massive Buddhist monastic complex in the Bamiyan Valley dating from the third to sixth centuries. Here, in a remote mountain valley at the center of the north-south routes crossing the Hindu Kush, stood the world's tallest carved Buddhas until the Taliban destroyed them. Later the beautifully tiled minaret of Jam, the tallest in the Islamic world, would be erected to the west by the Ghorid kings in the tenth century along the now little-used highland mountain track that linked their kingdom to Kabul and Herat.

Afghanistan's river systems all begin in the mountains, and their degree of flow depends entirely on the amount of snowpack there and how fast it melts. These rivers make irrigated agriculture possible throughout most of the country as they drain from the central mountains north to Balkh, south to Qandahar, east to Kabul, and west to Herat. But do not mistake the long blue lines on the map as evidence of easy access to the country or a way to ship bulk cargo. In fact, do not mistake most of them for year-round rivers. At least half of Afghanistan's rivers that burst their banks at flood stages barely trickle at other times of the year. Worse for trade and communication, all of Afghanistan's rivers (with the exception of the Kabul River) lie within the interior drainage basin of central Eurasia. This means that none of them reach the ocean. Instead of being a link to the outside world, following Afghanistan's rivers will eventually lead you nowhere. Most of the northern rivers fail even to reach the Amu drainage but are instead wrung dry for irrigation by a string of cities from Tashqurghan to Balkh to Maimana on the northern plain. Those that do reach the Amu from the northeast continue on, but only into the isolated and ever-shrinking Aral Sea. The great Helmand River and its tributaries end up in the desert marshes of Seistan on the Iranian border, squeezed between the Registan ("Land of Sand") on one side and the Dasht-i-Margo ("Waterless Plain of Death") on the other. And the Kabul River, which does connect with the Indus River just east of Peshawar in Pakistan, descends through so many deep gorges at such a rapid rate that its tributaries are suitable only for white-water rafting—a sport currently unknown to the Afghans. Rivers in Afghanistan therefore do not connect the country to the outside world or facilitate trade. Should you wish to cross the rivers by boat rather than ford them, at best you will find a few hand-pulled ferry boats (if you are lucky) or rafts lashed to inflated goatskins (if you are not). For this reason, rulers who built bridges were thought of kindly.

Regions That Persist over Time

Afghanistan has not always existed within its present historical boundaries, or for that matter existed at all as a single entity. Its international borders are arbitrary and divide communities that continue to see themselves as one. They also include people and places that at other times and under different political orders had only limited connections to today's Afghani-stan. Of course, the same could be said more cuttingly of Afghanistan's northern neighbors in central Asia, whose boundaries and ethnic character were bequeathed by Joseph Stalin. And an even greater historic wrong, in the eyes of the Afghans, was the imposition in 1893 of the Durand Line, which split the region's Pashtun population between British India and Afghanistan. For this reason no Afghan government (royalist, republican, socialist, Islamist, or democratic) has ever accepted the border between it and the NWFP of Pakistan as truly legitimate. Thus it distorts reality to use the modern nation-state as a fixed unit of historical analysis, particularly when its boundaries are projected into the past. Afghanistan, the land of the Hindu Kush, does have an ancient history, but its current form is only one of its many incarnations.

What has continually existed are Afghanistan's main regional components. These, like toy Lego blocks, have been fitted together in many different ways over the course of time, but each block has always remained recognizable as such. Sometimes they were provinces within world empires, like that of the ancient Persians in the fifth century BC who united everything from Egypt and the Mediterranean coast to the India's Punjab. Sometimes they were themselves the centers of regional empires, like those established by the Kushans (in the second century) or Ghaznavids (during the tenth to eleventh centuries). Sometimes, as in the sixteenth and seventeenth centuries, they were the contested and bloody frontiers of rival regional empires: the Uzbeks in central Asia, the Safavids in Iran, and the Mughals in India. And for many periods they were either independent kingdoms, ungoverned by any central power at all, or autonomous principalities that paid tribute and homage to a political center but remained locally autonomous in all other ways, including the right to raise revenue and troops.

Today's Afghanistan has four of these basic regional building blocks. They can be most easily identified by their ancient urban centers: Herat in the west, Qandahar in the south, Balkh (Mazar-i-sharif) in the north, and Kabul in the east. Peshawar and the NWFP constitute a fifth region, Afghanistan's phantom limb that was bequeathed to Pakistan when the British departed. Each of these regions dominates well-irrigated plains or river valleys that produce great agricultural surpluses, and have supported urban life for millennia. All had their own fluctuating frontiers in terms of how much of their adjacent mountain, steppe, and desert hinterland they controlled. But each survives and reemerges as a distinct region no matter the changes in political organization, arrivals of new populations or religions, or attempts to impose larger and more uniform identities on them.

HERAT AND THE WEST

Herat is a city with ancient roots located in the lowlands of western Afghanistan along the Iranian border. It is 920 meters in elevation and lies in an arid zone that experiences hot currents of air in the summer, a season known as the "Wind of 120 days." Herat was the capital of Areia in the Persian Empire and has remained one of the region's key urban centers since that time. Both the name of the city and region are derived from the main river that supports irrigated agriculture, the Harirud, as it leaves the mountains and enters the Herat-Farah lowlands. Villages are also irrigated by the use of the *karez* (also known as *qanat*), a system of constructed underground water conduits that tap the water table of the foothills and bring it down to the lowlands. A *karez* system requires continual maintenance, yet makes it possible to farm beyond the range of the river valleys and reduces the amount of water lost to evaporation.

Culturally and politically, Herat has long been tied into the Iranian world as one of the major cities of Khorasan. It owed its importance both to its agricultural productivity and its advantageous location for international trade. It was a junction city that linked the Iranian plateau to China via the central Asian silk routes. Herat was also a key city in Indian trade. Goods moved along the relatively flat route that ran south of the Hindu Kush to Qandahar and from there to India. In medieval times Herat was reputed to be home to a million people before the Mongols destroyed the city and depopulated the region in 1222. The region's productive potential was so high, however, that Herat eventually overcame even this disaster and in the fifteenth century served as an imperial capital of the Timurid Empire. During this period Herat was a center of art and literature, particularly renowned for its production of Persian miniature paintings and poetry. By the eighteenth century Herat had declined in status, but remained a crucial provincial city in the Iranian Safavid state on the frontier with the Uzbek khanates to its north.

Herat's population has always been predominantly Persian speaking, and composed of a mixture of Sunni and Shia elements. Herat claimed regional sovereignty over the various Sunni Aimaq tribes that lived in the mountains to the east in Ghor and on the steppes to the north in Badghis. On its southern flank, it also had a substantial Abdali (Durrani) Pashtun population, which by the eighteenth century had become politically dominant. For this reason, Herat was one of the core principalities of the Durrani Empire and the Afghan state. Its governor was always a powerful member of the royal dynasty. Kabul's control of its western region was often tenuous, though, and the Persians besieged Herat many times in the nineteenth century in hopes of reclaiming the city. Only the active intervention by the British raj (which viewed Herat as the main western gateway to India) prevented the Iranian Qajar dynasty from attaining this goal and preserved Afghan rule in the west.

QANDAHAR AND THE SOUTH

Qandahar is southern Afghanistan's dominant city and has been its regional political center for more than five centuries. It lies in Afghanistan's southern desert, but has thrived as a rich agricultural zone because it tapped the waters of the Helmand River and its tributaries, particularly the Argandab River. The ancient Persians called the region Arachosia after the name of that river. In ancient and medieval times Seistan, at the end of the Helmand's drainage, rivaled Qandahar in importance, but then declined to insignificance when its irrigation system failed. Like Herat, Qandahar expanded the range of irrigated land by using both river water and *karez* systems. In addition to its bumper harvest of wheat, the region was well-known for its fruit crops, especially its grapes and pomegranates. It grew cotton as a cash crop and more recently has been the center of opium production. At an altitude of a thousand meters, it has warm winters and hot summers. For such a large region the south's population is relatively small because so much of the surrounding area is a desert that can be used only by nomads on a seasonal basis. It had the lowest population density of the country's main regions in the 1950s: seven people per square kilometer versus twenty-two per square kilometer in the north, thirty-six in the east, and ten in the west.[28]

In early periods Qandahar was a constant bone of contention between empires based in Iran and those based in India. Its political affiliation shifted between them regularly. It was a key trade center, serving as the junction for goods in transit from India that had earlier passed through Kabul on their way west, and more directly as a direct link to Sind via the Bolan Pass and Quetta. Qandahar is the center of the Durrani (Abdali) Pashtun tribal confederation population, which extends from there to Herat. It borders the rival Ghilzai Pashtun tribal confederation, which had in an earlier era dominated Qandahar until it was displaced north toward Ghazni and Gardez. Qandahar's Pashtun identity became politically significant after Ahmad Shah Durrani established a Durrani Pashtun dynasty there in 1747—a dynasty that ruled Afghanistan until 1978. Although the capital was moved to Kabul at his death, Qandahar remained the most important of its principalities. It is the only one of the country's four largest cities where Pashtuns constituted the majority of the urban population and Pashto is the dominant language.

BALKH AND THE NORTH

Balkh, the "mother of cities" as the Arabs called it, is one of the oldest urban centers in the world. The capital of ancient Bactria, it was reputed to be the home of Zoroaster and the richest of all the provinces in the Persian Empire. Sitting on the northern plains at an altitude of 380 meters between the Hindu Kush and the Amu River, Balkh's climate is semiarid with cool winters and hot summers. The many rivers that flow out of the mountains and onto the loess steppes provide abundant water for irrigation. In some areas water is plentiful enough to sustain the crops of rice, cotton, and melons (*kharbuza*). In addition, the loess foothills support extensive unirrigated agriculture (*lalmi*), which produces great harvests of wheat and barley when the rains fall. The surrounding steppes also support vast herds of sheep, and the region is still renowned for its fine breed of horses, which were exported south to India in earlier times.

Balkh was the dominant city on the northern plains for millennia, although the outlying districts of Maimana on the west and Kunduz (Qataghan) on the east were often administratively autonomous. Today Balkh is just an impressive set of ruins, having been displaced by nearby Mazar-i-sharif in the nineteenth century as the region's major city. But Mazar still plays the same dominant role in the north as did Balkh, and as the site of Afghanistan's major Islamic shrine, attracts a large number of pilgrims.

Balkh's location north of the Hindu Kush put it outside the normal south Asian political sphere. It took a high degree of military and political power to control the northern plains from capitals based south of the Hindu Kush, so when that power weakened for any reason the north was the first region to be lost. By contrast, it was far easier to dominate the region from nearby Bukhara and Samarqand in central Asia—a connection that was later reinforced by the shared Turkish ethnicity among rulers there. Over the course of the past thousand years so many waves of Turkish-speaking nomads arrived in the region that it became known as Turkistan. Yet these immigrants (who became the Uzbeks and Turkmen of today) did not so much displace the older Persian population as merge with it. Persian remained the language of the cities and the valley populations, reinforced by Tajik and Hazara migrants from the mountains.

KABUL AND THE EAST

Eastern Afghanistan, with Kabul at its center, is the heart of the Afghan state. The eastern region encompasses the drainage basin for the Kabul River and its tributaries as well as the area around Gardez and Ghazni to the south. From ancient times, the area has been the strategic link to the passes through the Hindu Kush to its north and the passes to India to its east. It was the region's location rather than its intrinsic wealth that made it a center of political power. Because of its higher altitude (Kabul at eighteen hundred meters, Ghazni at twenty-two hundred meters, and Gardez at twenty-three hundred meters), the east has cool summers and cold winters. One unusual aspect of the east has been the close connection and incorporation of the cities in the highlands with counterparts in the semitropical lowlands. This pattern is similar to that seen in the Andes of South America, where as part of a "vertical archipelago," a single state exploited a variety of different ecological zones created by rapid altitude changes.[29] The upland districts that are over fifteen hundred meters in elevation have cold winters, and agriculture there supports wheat, barley, grapes, and trees yielding fruits and nuts. The lower valleys like Laghman and Jalalabad that are under a thousand meters are warm throughout the year, and produce wet rice and citrus crops. The variation in climate is most visible during the winter, when oranges grown in Jalalabad flood the snowy streets of Kabul.

This vertical archipelago strategy is also seen in the characteristic use of dual capitals on a seasonal basis. The Afghan state first rotated its administrative capital between Kabul and Peshawar. When Peshawar was lost to the Sikhs in the early nineteenth century, Jalalabad (at 620 meters) became the winter capital. In this Afghans were following a well-established precedent. The ancient Kushans, for example, had major cities in both the highlands (Kapisa) and lowlands (Taxila), and the Mughal governor of the region moved annually to Kabul in the summer from Peshawar.

Eastern Afghanistan has historically had both the highest regional population densities in the country—four times that found in the south and twice that found in the northern plains—and the largest percentage of its country's population—30 percent.[30] Kabul also has closer connections with the higher mountain villages bordering the agricultural valleys than does Qandahar, Herat, or Balkh, since they lie so much closer. In modern times Kabul has been Afghanistan's leading city, with two and a half to three times the population of any other city in the county. Kabul and the east are also the most ethnically diverse parts of the country because they sit on an ethnic fracture zone. The plains north of Kabul and the city itself are home territory to the Tajiks; the lands south and east are home to the Ghilzai Pashtuns. Hazaras inhabit many sections of the city in substantial numbers, since their mountain homeland lies directly to the west. Kabul also has minority populations such as the Qizilbash and Nuristanis. With its current population approaching four million, it remains the most important urban center in the country.

PESHAWAR AND THE NWFP

Peshawar is Janus-faced. Sitting at the eastern end of the Khyber Pass and west of the Indus River, travelers coming down from Kabul feel they have now truly entered south Asia. By contrast, travelers arriving in the opposite direction from Lahore or Delhi believe they have entered the first frontier city of central Asia. Closely connected to Kabul as its historic winter capital for many centuries, the city fell from Afghan control when it was lost to the Sikhs in 1834. It became part of the British raj when it defeated the Sikhs. Residents of Peshawar are mostly Pashtun, but those living in the city or on its surrounding fertile plains have always been subject to regional governments. The more famous Pashtun tribes living in the mountain valleys above the Peshawar have never been answerable to these governments. They cross the frontier between Afghanistan and Pakistan without papers, openly carry guns, and refuse to recognize the Durand Line as a border. Many Afghans still believe that the region should have rightfully reverted to them when the British left, as Hong Kong reverted to China. This view, though perhaps not well grounded legally, has remained a long-standing irritant in terms of Afghanistan's relations with Pakistan. This predisposition was bolstered after many millions of Afghans sought refuge there during the Soviet occupation and subsequent civil war. Although the city is never likely to return to Afghan control, the status of the tribes in the NWFP that were never incorporated under British direct rule and previously owed some allegiance to the amirs in Kabul remains an issue fraught with difficulty. The territory may have been severed from Afghanistan long ago, but Afghans still sense the pain of its absence. In light of my earlier caution not to project today's national boundaries into the past, a land that has more Pashtuns than Afghanistan itself, and that has played such a large (and continuing) role in Afghan politics, deserves some recognition.

Turko-Persia: Fixing Afghanistan's Place in the World

Afghanistan always seems to find itself included only as the tail end of any area studies map. Is it the southernmost part of central Asia, the westernmost part of south Asia, or the easternmost edge of the Middle East? Whatever the choice, it will be regretfully noted that the inclusion of Afghanistan is problematic. In fact, Afghanistan is an integral and central part of Turko-Persia both culturally and geographically.[31] Geographically, Turko-Persia is that large area of highland Asia stretching east from Anatolia and the Zagros Mountains through the Iranian plateau to the Indian Plains. Its northern limits are the Caucasus in the west and the Eurasian steppe at the Syr Darya River in the east; its southern border runs through arid Baluchistan to the sea. It was the heartland of the ancient Persian Empire, and that foundation still shapes the region. While it is overwhelmingly Muslim today, its cultural ethos and continuities are far older. Indeed, the easiest way to draw this region's cultural boundaries is to include only those peoples who recognize and celebrate the pre-Islamic Nauruz holiday, which marks the beginning of the Persian New Year at the spring equinox, and exclude those (like the Arabs) who have never heard of this holiday. So strong is this Nauruz tradition that neither the Islamic revolution in Iran nor the Taliban regime in Afghanistan was ever able to enforce a ban on its celebration.

Linguistically Turko-Persia, as its name implies, is dominated by Persian and Turkish speakers, who are often intermixed and bilingual. It is a region in which culture, history, ways of living, languages, and political interactions have a strong commonality. This has been particularly noted by many travelers who have moved out of south Asia or the Arab world and found themselves in a new cultural landscape where the similarities are stronger than the differences. Coming up from India, Olaf Caroe declared:

> Again and again, when moving in what may be called the Iranian world, I have been struck by the conviction that the influence of Persia over all these lands is a much deeper, older thing than anything which springs from Islam. . . . There is indeed a sense in which all the uplands in Asia from the Tigris to the Indus is one country. The spirit of Persia has breathed over it, bringing an awareness of one background, one culture, one way of expression, a unity of spirit felt as far away as Peshawar and Quetta. He who has caught that breath has won to the heart of a mystery, and he will not forget.[32]

One aspect that Caroe perhaps neglects is the profound impact made by the large-scale immigration of Turkish peoples into the region over the past thousand years and their establishment of powerful dynasties there. So close was the fusion that a proverb even arose declaring that "a hat without a head is like a Turk without a Tajik."[33] At the height of their political and military power in the sixteenth century, empires based on this tradition dominated the Muslim world: Ottomans in Turkey, the Safavids in Iran, the Uzbeks in central Asia, and the Mughals in India. Boundaries imposed by Western powers later severed Turko-Persia into a Russian-dominated central Asia, a British-dominated south Asia, and (after the dismemberment of the Ottoman Empire) a mindless grab bag labeled the Middle East. The last was really just a gloss for the Arab world—a prejudice that relegated the Turks and Persians to the margins of the margins. This has begun to change with new political and economic relations between the ex-Soviet central Asian states, Iran, and Afghanistan, as well as subnational regions such as the NWFP, Baluchistan, and Kurdistan. Turko-Persia is back, and Afghanistan is a part of it.

Ibn Khaldun and Afghanistan

Regions and ethnic groups aside, there is a more profound binary division that is strongly marked in Afghanistan: the dichotomy between what the medieval Arab social historian ibn Khaldun labeled "desert civilization" and "sedentary civilization" in his *Muqaddimah*, or introduction, to a universal history that he began writing in 1375.[34] Desert civilizations were those human communities based on subsistence agriculture or pastoralism that organized themselves along kinship lines under conditions of low population density. They were located in geographically marginal areas, which proved difficult for outsiders to dominate effectively or that did not repay the cost of doing so. The specific examples he cited included desert nomads (camel-raising Bedouins), steppe nomads (Turks), and mountain villagers (Kurds and Berbers). Sedentary civilizations were those human communities based on surplus agricultural production that sustained dense populations and created complex economies. They were located in broad river valleys and irrigated plains, which allowed for the emergence of nucleated villages and cities. Such communities were organized on the basis of residency, but were divided by class and occupational structures with a considerable division of labor. They were centers of learning and high culture as well as markets for regional trade and international commerce. In filling a blank map, the communities at the margins overspread the greatest geographic space, but the people concentrated in the limited areas of irrigated agriculture or in urban centers equaled or exceeded them in numbers. More significantly, the sedentary areas controlled the region's productive capital and produced the bulk of its wealth.

The two systems were not sealed off from each other. On the contrary, they had intense interactions and close connections, particularly because of population movements. Ibn Khaldun contended that desert civilizations must have predated sedentary ones because they were less complex socially and simpler economically—a supposition confirmed by modern archaeology. Once cities arose, however, there was a constant population flow from the marginal subsistence areas in the mountains, deserts, and steppes toward the cities and irrigated valleys. By contrast, city residents showed no desire to take up the harder and more austere life of the desert nomad or mountain villager. The push factor in this equation was demographic: the healthier periphery produced more people than its limited subsistence base could support. The pull factor was cultural and economic: city life has always been more appealing than that found in mountain villages or nomad camps. Cities and productive agricultural lands provided opportunities to indulge in normally unavailable luxuries for the rich and powerful, while the poor were attracted by the constant demand for new workers. In fact, this population flow was essential to the survival of premodern cities because their death rates exceeded their birthrates. Urban centers could not maintain a stable population (let alone grow) without a constant influx of migrants. Over time, this could lead to what amounted to a wholesale population replacement. The disappearance of the Sumerian as a living language in ancient Mesopotamia was a product of the constant influx of Akkadian speakers from the countryside. But the reverse also was true because of the cultural power of city life was so strong. Immigrants drawn from many disparate groups of people adopted the lingua franca of the cities that they moved to and lost their own native tongues over the course of a few generations.

Desert Civilization

ECONOMIC STRUCTURE

In a subsistence economy nearly everyone produces the same things, so there are no great differences in standards of living or much internal trade. In desert civilization, therefore, the chief might eat and drink more than an ordinary person, but it is the same food and drink. Wealth is measured in terms of property (land and livestock particularly) rather than money. This was underscored for me by a nomad trader who showed me the goods that he had brought into the mountains to trade with Tajik villagers. I commented that his could not be much of a business because these villagers had no money. He rebuked me, saying, "Just because people have no money does not mean they are poor. Here they have livestock." He explained that villagers had goats with so little local value that they were eager to barter them for his imported goods. As an example, the trader showed me a box containing a half-dozen unbreakable tea glasses he had purchased for one hundred afghanis in a city bazaar that he would barter for a goat valued in the village at five hundred afghanis. I apologized and told the trader that this was indeed a good return, but he only laughed and remarked that I had missed the real profit in his trade. When his own flocks returned to the lowlands, each Tajik goat would then be worth fifteen hundred afghanis in the local bazaar, meaning that his initial hundred afghani investment would yield a fourteen hundred afghani profit per animal.

In the absence of a money economy, people support themselves at a basic level. When surplus comes their way they invest in relationships. Hospitality, communal feasts, gift giving, and other forms of redistribution raise the status of the givers, and it is this social esteem or fame that is more cherished than money. Leaders gain and retain power through their ability to give to the group in some fashion. Bedouin poetry in particular praises the sheikh who is so lavish with his hospitality that he keeps nothing for himself. But such a subsistence economic base provides little basis for class differentiation, economic specialization, or capital accumulation. If societies rooted in subsistence economies often seem timeless and unchanging, it is because their replication remains trapped within such narrow limits.

SOCIAL AND POLITICAL STRUCTURES

Desert civilizations had specific social attributes. The most important of these was their strong group solidarity based on kinship and descent. This generated 'asabiya, or group feeling, which bound all members of a social group together when facing the outside world. In such a system, the group interest trumps individual interest to such an extent that loyalty to the group supersedes everything else. Positive acts by any member of the group redounded to the group's benefit; any shame likewise tarnished the reputation of the group as a whole. More significantly, attacks or slights against an individual were met with a collective response. Take crime as an example. One did not seek justice through government institutions (which often did not exist) but by mobilizing the kin group to seek retribution or compensation. If one man murdered another, the murdered man's kin were collectively obligated to seek blood revenge. Similarly the murderer's kin were collectively responsible for his act (and might even be targets in revenge killings), even though they had no direct role in it. If compensation were agreed on to end the threat of revenge, the whole group was liable for its payment. Not only did overt acts such as assault, murder, or theft demand a collective response, so did threats to a group's honor and reputation. In Afghanistan, it is the Pashtuns who are the best example of this system through the Pashtunwali, a code of principles thoroughly rooted in the primacy of maintaining honor and reputation. The military advantage of this solidarity was particularly evident in times of conflict. When such groups entered into battle, they were renowned as fierce fighters because individuals would rather die than shame themselves in front of their kin by running away. Life would not be worth living afterward if they did. Of course, the group itself could decide to run away (and usually did) if the odds turned against them, but they retreated together. That was only good tactics, and there was no honor to be lost in deciding to fight another day when victory was more certain.

This strong group solidarity was undermined by a number of structural political weaknesses, however. The first was that these descent or locality groups were necessarily of small size. Second, because such groups had a strong cultural predisposition toward equality, it was difficult for a leader to consolidate power. In such a system every man and every group could at least imagine the possibility of becoming dominant, and resented being placed in a subordinate position. Anyone in a leadership position was therefore plagued by jealous rivals who would be happy to replace him or at least throw obstacles in his way if they could not. This pattern was so ubiquitous among close relatives in Afghanistan that it acquired a specific term in Pashto: *tarburwali* (the rivalry of agnatic cousins). Third, even if a man succeeded in surmounting this rivalry, the position of leader itself was structurally weak. It lacked the right of command and so depended on the ability to persuade others to follow. It was thus tough being a chief of a people whom you had to cajole into action and where criticism by rivals was constant. For this reason, ibn Khaldun noted, religious leaders were often more successful than tribal ones in uniting large groups. Coming from outside the system and calling on God's authority, they could better circumvent tribal rivalries.[35]

Sedentary Civilization

ECONOMY

Sedentary civilization has luxury as its defining characteristic. This luxury is the product of a complex division of labor where money trumps kinship. In cities, everything one needs or wants is obtained with money, and so kinship ties atrophy. Five hundred years later and half a world away from ibn Khaldun's medieval Islamic cities, Adam Smith made the same point more broadly, observing

> that without the assistance and co-operation of many thousands, the very meanest person in a civilized country could not be provided, even according to what we very falsely imagine, the easy and simple manner in which he is commonly accommodated. Compared, indeed, with the more extravagant luxury of the great, his accommodation must no doubt appear extremely simple and easy; and yet it may be true, perhaps, that the accommodation of an European prince does not always so much exceed that of an industrious and frugal peasant, as the accommodation of the latter exceeds that of many an African king, the absolute master of the lives and liberties of ten thousand naked savages.[36]

Cities also supported a wide range of locally produced and imported foods, goods, and services that ranged from the utilitarian to the extravagant. Many of these products were vital to the survival of even distant rural communities. These communities' need for goods that they could not produce for themselves forced subsistence mountain villagers and nomads into dependency relations with urban markets. As ibn Khaldun explained, "While (the Bedouins) need the cities for their necessities of life, the urban population needs (the Bedouins) [only] for conveniences and luxuries. . . . They must be active on the behalf of their interests and obey them whenever (the cities) ask and demand obedience from them."[37]

I experienced an example of this at firsthand with the salt trade in the mountainous province of Badakhshan in the 1970s. Although I had thought the summer nomad encampments were self-sufficient, in fact they continually sent donkey and horse caravans to the distant provincial capital of Faizabad to buy salt because it was a necessary dietary supplement for their grazing sheep. Since the local mountain villagers had cows and goats, they also made the same buying trip for salt as did the nomads, but purchased cloth, metal tools, sugar, and tea as well. Villagers were therefore keen to sell surplus wheat to the visiting nomads for the cash they would need for these purchases. It was clear that geographic isolation did not imply economic isolation.

The division of labor and surplus production also supported centers of learning and artistic production. While one might find Sufi mystics in remote regions, centers of orthodox Islamic education were always urban based. These centers were financed through government patronage, but also by private donations of money, irrigated land, and urban property to pious foundations, the revenue from which supported shrines and schools along with the members of the clergy that ran them.[38] These institutions served as bastions of power for orthodox religious sects. Heterodox sects, by contrast, tended to thrive in the marginal areas beyond the control of status quo institutions. It is no accident that the core Shia and Ismaili populations in Sunni-dominated Afghanistan are found in its most remote mountain regions, or that older pagan groups survived here until a century ago. Indeed, one scholar has suggested that this is a reoccurring pattern: whatever tradition the center holds as orthodox, the mountainous margins will set themselves off against it.[39] When Bamiyan was Buddhist, monks in the valley undoubtedly complained about the unholy heresies being expounded in the highlands around them.

SOCIAL AND POLITICAL STRUCTURES

Two defining social characteristics of sedentary civilization are identification by residence (not kinship) and hierarchical divisions based on class. It is a world of strangers who are economically dependent on one another in all aspects of daily life, but have no reason to interact socially. People may boast of having a particularly prestigious bloodline, yet such descent groups cannot survive intact in a world where the individual interests supersede group interests. More important, social rank had less to do with ancestors than the control of wealth. Signs of class inequality are ever present in dress, food, and housing. In fact, in this setting we are no longer dealing with undifferentiated commonalities ranked on a scale of more versus less. Here we experience differences in kind so large that no single generality can encompass them. We stop talking about food and explore the realm of cuisine in which members of different classes have different diets. Similarly, social status can be distinguished immediately by dress, some types of which may be legally mandated or prohibited to make their distinctions binding. Women in sedentary civilization are much more commonly veiled and secluded than their sisters in the countryside because they do no work outside the household.

The political strengths of sedentary civilization lay in its centralization, higher degree of wealth, and larger size. Political leaders had "royal authority," as Ibn Khaldun put it: the ability to issue commands with the expectation that they would be obeyed.[40] Unlike desert chieftains, rulers here were not consensus builders or redistributors of wealth but rather acquisitive autocrats. They secured their power by accumulating wealth for themselves and the state on a grand scale, through various forms of taxation, control of trade or markets, and the large-scale ownership of productive land. Such wealth was necessary because it undergirded centralized authority. It paid for a government bureaucracy composed of appointed subordinates who carried out the ruler's commands with a police force behind them. Punishment awaited those who refused to pay taxes or had the temerity to ignore a decree. Perhaps most crucially, the revenue paid for an army that protected the state from invasion from without and against rebellion from within. Such military forces in the medieval Islamic world consisted of paid mercenaries or slave soldiers. While ibn Khaldun takes this as a given, it is a significant departure from Western history. Although mercenary forces were never absent, the ancient Greek polis (city-state), Alexander the Great, or the Roman Republic and early Roman Empire all recruited soldiers from their own people, and frequently made military service an obligation of citizenship (or a way to obtain it). Even in feudal Europe, the nobility justified its dominance of society based on their obligation to provide military service as mounted knights, and they were expected to fight in battle themselves. In the Islamic world, such mass participation in warfare was characteristic only of desert civilization. Warfare by states was in the hands of military professionals, who were the often unruly but paid servants of the state, not the ordinary inhabitants of any class.

This very complexity, hierarchy, and wealth created political weaknesses as well as strengths. Urban and peasant populations were not as tough as the people from the margins, physically or mentally. A structure of centralized political authority where officials could easily abuse their authority and accumulate personal wealth tended to spawn corruption. This weakened the state by siphoning off its revenue and alienating the population. But perhaps most significantly these populations were uninvolved with government. As its passive inhabitants it mattered little to them who the ruler was, and hence concepts of patriotism, citizenship, or indeed any sense of political obligation to the state was almost entirely absent. This usually proved a fatal weakness because the wealth of cities served as magnets for attacks by poor but militarily powerful desert civilization peoples, particularly the camel-riding Bedouins and the horse-riding Turkish nomads. Ibn Khaldun remarked that most of the ruling dynasties in the medieval Islamic world had their origins within such groups, which formerly lived at the margins of powerful regional states and empires. Taking advantage of periodic military weakness and economic decline within sedentary states, they made themselves masters of societies far more complex than those in which they were born. In the process, peoples from the margins regularly established themselves as the ruling elite in those regions that they conquered and then settled.

Beyond Ethnicity and Region

The division of marginal areas in Afghanistan into mountain, steppe, and desert zones creates a pattern similar to that seen in north Africa or the Arab Near East, but the order of their importance is different. In this region, it was the Turko-Mongolian horse-riding nomads from the north who played the dominant political role historically—one that they did not lose until the rise of the Pashtuns in the mid-eighteenth century. Mountain peoples also played a larger role than elsewhere in the Islamic world. These include the Aimaqs in the Paropamisus, the Hazaras in the center of the country, the Tajiks in the northeastern mountains, the Pashtuns in the mountainous regions straddling the border between Pakistan and Afghanistan, and the small yet culturally distinctive linguistic groups in Nuristan and the Pamirs. By contrast, Afghanistan's indigenous nomads played an insignificant role, and unlike Arab Bedouins, they did not form exclusive tribal or ethnic groups. In particular, the Pashtun nomads in the south and east shared common descent groups with other Pashtuns who were sedentary, as did the much smaller number of Baluch in the deserts of the south.

Even now at the beginning of the twenty-first century, ibn Khaldun's model can be applied directly and fruitfully to Afghanistan. Although not untouched by the economic and social changes that have fundamentally transformed or even eliminated desert civilization communities in other parts of the Near East, north Africa, or central Asia, Afghanistan remains a place that ibn Khaldun would easily recognize. Its rural economy remains largely subsistence based, and its road and communication infrastructure only minimally developed. Once leaving the few main highways, especially in the mountainous areas, you quickly encounter a world in which people move only on horseback, on foot, or by riding donkeys. They measure travel time in days, not hours. Wherever your destination, these people will cheerfully tell you that the place is *dur nist* ("not far") so as not to disappoint you, even though it will still take all day or more to get there. These are people whose goal in agriculture is to feed themselves and their families, not to produce crops for the market. Although hospitable, they draw the boundaries of community tightly and distrust strangers. Differences in wealth, rank, and status are minimal when compared to those on the plains or in the cities. Most important, these communities are still beyond the direct control of a weak Afghan central government in Kabul. What power that state had gained in the century prior to the Communist coup of 1978 was then lost in the quarter century of war that followed.

Ibn Khaldun would also be familiar with the cultural tensions between the people of the plains and cities and those who inhabited the country's mountains, deserts, and steppes. To city people, those in the hinterlands are more barbarian than civilized. Who (except perhaps an anthropologist like myself) would live with such people voluntarily? As a foreigner, I was often more comfortable dealing with nomads and villagers than some of my urban Afghan acquaintances. I at least respected their culture, which most city people (particularly educated ones) either held in contempt or feared. In return, people in the hinterlands viewed city dwellers as weak willed and corrupt. And people in the countryside had little good to say about the political elite in the capital, regardless of their ethnic origin. Yet one of the most interesting things about this divide, unlike so many others in Afghanistan, was that it could be crossed by individuals. People migrating to the cities who may have been steeped in rural values found these traditions impossible to maintain in an urban setting. Or perhaps it would be safer to say that their children found it impossible to do so.

In light of this, the traditional stress on ethnicity and region as the most significant divisions in Afghanistan needs some nuance. Important though they are, these values assume a commonality that is deceptive and even false. Members of different ethnic groups living together in cities or irrigated valleys often have more in common with each other than they do with coethnics who reside in completely different economic and social worlds. The urbanized Pashtun in Qandahar or a Tajik in Kabul experiences a political, occupational, and cultural milieu far removed from their fellow Pashtuns or Tajiks inhabiting remote mountainous Uruzghan or Badakhshan. In cities, money is more important than kinship, the circles of acquaintanceship are larger, and the levels of education are higher. On first sight, the harsh restrictions that the Taliban imposed on daily life in Kabul (no music, no games or kite flying, and required beards and prayers) appear rooted solely in their severe vision of Islam. But beneath the surface lay an older and deeper conflict that ibn Khaldun would have understood. The Taliban's hatred of the residents of Kabul, and the Kabul people's contempt and fear of the Taliban, had less to do with Islam than it did with the long-standing clash of values between luxury-loving urbanites and the puritanical rural villagers who had come to wield power over them. As ibn Khaldun also observed, though, if these mountain puritans saw themselves as closer to being good in a moral sense than were city people, it was only because their rural life offered far fewer opportunities for corruption. And having power and wealth in an urban setting could always be counted on to change that equation over time.

CHAPTER TWO

Conquering and Ruling Premodern Afghanistan

During its premodern history, the territory of today's Afghanistan was conquered and ruled by foreign invaders. Indeed it had a positively magnetic attraction for conquerors, not because they coveted the wealth of Afghanistan, but rather because control of Afghan territory gave them access to more prosperous places like India or central Asia, or because it gave them control of regional trade routes. Located on a fracture zone linking Iran in the west, central Asia in the north, and south Asia in the east, it was the route of choice for armies moving across the Hindu Kush (or south of it) toward the plains of India. For the same reason, empires based in India saw the domination of this region as their first line of defense. While the popular press often repeats the claim that no conqueror, including such figures as Alexander the Great or Chinggis Khan, ever succeeded in subduing the country, this is untrue. Most of these figures did subjugate the lands that now comprise Afghanistan and then occupied the territory they had won. The main problem they faced after establishing their power was attacks by rival states, not rebellions by the inhabitants.

As a result, for most of the past two and a half millennia the lands of the Hindu Kush were component parts of larger empires, and constituted a frontier zone of conflict between neighboring states. These had their centers in Iran (Achaemenid, Parthian, Sassanian, Seljukid, Il khanate, Safavid, and Afsharid), India (Mauryan and Mughal), or central Asia (Mongol, Timurid, and Uzbek). When Afghanistan itself was the center of an empire (Kushan, Ghaznavid, Ghorid, and Durrani), it served primarily as a base of operations for states that drew most of their revenue from India or Khorasan. What might strike contemporary Afghans as surprising was that only the Durrani Empire was ruled by Pashtuns. From the mid-tenth century to the mid-eighteenth century, every dynasty that ruled in this region

was either of Turko-Mongolian origin or had a military that was dominated by Turko-Mongolian peoples. The Pashtuns would only create Afghanistan as we know it today (and become its exclusive governing elite)
after 1747. Yet the structure of that state represented less of a break with
the past than might be expected since it drew more strongly from the
structures of its Turko-Mongolian predecessors than Pashtun tribal tradition. To explain this phenomenon, we need to look at three aspects of war
and government in premodern Turko-Persia. The first considers what territory was being conquered and ruled. The second examines how conquerors legitimated their rule. The third explores the relationship of states with
peoples at the margins.

STATES AND EMPIRES: A TALE OF TWO CHEESES

The modern view of a state is monolithic, with empires exemplifying its
largest and most highly dominant form. It is a processed American cheese
model in which each slice is expected to be uniform in texture and the
same as any other (although the size and thickness may vary). Internally,
deviations from this ideal represent quality control problems that the state
needs to address. Externally, lines on a map indicate precise boundaries.
One immediately leaves the jurisdiction of one state and enters the jurisdiction of another simply by crossing that line. These boundaries even divide unpopulated wastelands, and go offshore to define the ownership of
seabed and ocean resources. It does not matter that such lines may be artificial and split communities that have more in common with each other
than they do with the states that claim them. People in such states are treated
as monolithic too: one law to rule them all. But perhaps most important,
state control is deemed to be theoretically universal and absolute within its
boundaries, whether one is in the capital or at its farthest margins.

It is this American cheese model that is implicitly projected onto the
past. We look for boundaries, and then fill them all with a single color to
define a historic state or empire. This model applies fairly well to such classic
empires as Rome, China, and Egypt, where the goal was to create a uniform administration and even a common elite culture within the imperial

sphere. People radically different from themselves were only found at the margins. Such a model does not apply well to those parts of the world such as Turko-Persia where empires were cobbled together with large stretches of sparsely populated territory separating the main centers of agriculture and urban life. Rulers here sought direct control of these centers and the lines of communication among them while largely ignoring the rest. They employed a Swiss cheese model of the polity that did not assume uniformity across the landscape or their control of it. With Swiss cheese, you not only expect to find holes in every slice but also understand that each slice has holes of a different shape and size. These holes do not constitute defects (as they would in American cheese) but are instead the products of the very process that created the cheese in the first place. In other words, when dealing with unevenly distributed resources and populations, it is better to judge the value of your cheese by weight rather than volume, since you know that each slice will have lots of holes.

As a consequence, the ruling strategy for states and empires in Turko-Persia was to control the best bits themselves, and leave at arm's length territories deemed unprofitable to rule or of little strategic value. This was a far looser policy than those found in empires where populations and resources were more evenly distributed. Historical maps that stress the extent of their undifferentiated territory thus give a misleading impression because rulers there defined their conquests as the cheesy parts they ruled directly. Elsewhere the ploy was to assert nominal sovereignty over people in marginal areas within the boundaries of the state without bothering them much. They need not be ruled directly or subject to the same style of government as were the peoples of the irrigated plains and valleys. If such potentially troublesome peoples living in deserts, steppes, and mountains did cause problems, rulers employed policies that included both carrots (alliances or subsidies) and sticks (punitive campaigns or trade embargoes) to keep them in line.

These troublesome peoples came in two varieties: the elusive and the fixed. The first included nomads who used mobility as their main defense. They would move themselves, their tents, and their livestock away from any invading army, retreating endlessly until their pursuers exhausted themselves and had to return home. They knew their lands could not be occupied by such invaders because they were empty of resources and people. Herodotus attributed the defeat of the great Persian army by the Scythians in the sixth century BC to this "runaway" tactic.[1] Those peoples who inhabited mountainous valleys were by contrast as fixed in place as any plains peasant farmer, but harder to crack than the black walnuts that grew around their villages. It was always difficult to move invading troops into mountainous terrain, and even harder to fight effectively there. Enemies were subject to ambush, and the greatest military powers could find themselves stymied. The difficulties that Alexander the Great faced in fighting the mountain tribes in the Kunar Valley in the fourth century BC were not that much different from those faced by the Americans there in the twentieth-first century, except that the former dropped boulders and the latter shot rockets from their mountain perches. It was easier to come to an accommodation with such people than continually fight them, and most state powers chose that policy.

This inability to assert full state control in mountain areas and the large stretches of steppe or desert that divided neighboring states or empires should remind us of another reality. States were more likely to establish flexible frontiers with such regions than precise borders. Unlike their borders with abutting states, there was never a single line in these areas that determined absolute inclusion or exclusion. Rather, zones of control ran from direct at the core, through indirect at the margins, to the purely theoretical or symbolic in the outlands. In Afghanistan, such ungoverned spaces were often labeled *yagistan*, which could be translated either as "rebel lands" or just "lawless places."[2] Where to call an end to sovereignty was frequently a vexing question. Usually the answer was practical. Land empires stopped when they reached an ecological barrier (deserts, steppes, mountains, or jungles) that they could not effectively penetrate or make use of. But it was also a political question, such as when a military advance was halted to create a more defensible frontier or where the cost of administration outweighed the benefit of occupation. Thus, even the Great Wall of China or Hadrian's Wall in Britain was not a boundary in the modern sense but rather a self-imposed limit designed to prevent the empire's unraveling through overextension, just as a hem is used as a finish for the raw edge of a garment.

Returning to Afghanistan, the lesson from these comparisons is that premodern conquerors took control of the cheese in a land where the holes occupied a large percentage of the slice. Just how concentrated these areas are can be seen by looking at a map of the most significant agriculture regions (see map 5). The compact darker spots indicate the key agricultural districts (mostly irrigated) that a conqueror would be seeking and these constitute less than 5 percent of the country's total land area.[3] If you control these, you control the major sources of wealth and the population. The problem for states centering on the territory of today's Afghanistan, however, was that its territory had more margins than cores. Regionally productive areas divided by deserts and mountain ranges were hard to integrate into a single state structure and by default maintained considerable autonomy. More often they were divided among rival imperial polities that looked at all of Afghanistan as a frontier zone.

One thing that all premodern state rulers agreed on in this part of the world was that the direct administration of the marginal territory was not always necessary or even desirable. The resistance of the Pashtun tribes against the Babur's Mughal dynasty successors in the sixteenth and seventeenth centuries, for example, generally flared up when rulers sought to impose direct control in such areas. But since it was access to the passes through their territories that was really important, it was cheaper to buy them off or negotiate a political accommodation with them. The Pashtuns could therefore rightfully boast that their mountain fastnesses had never been conquered, but that was because successive empires chose to bypass them or else imposed only symbolic elements of sovereignty. To extend their claim of autonomy to all of today's Afghanistan involved more than a little exaggeration. Even among the Pashtuns, those who inhabited the irrigated plains around Qandahar, Peshawar, or Herat experienced foreign rule on a regular basis because their territories constituted the productive hearts of their regions that no ruler would willingly ignore.

Yet one might ask, since the productive regions of Afghanistan have not changed significantly in the past five hundred years (and may even be somewhat reduced), why the same strategy did not work for the British in the nineteenth century or the Russians in the twentieth century. A partial answer lies in a second question: how conquerors came to legitimate their rule. The use of force may be militarily decisive, but the government that a conqueror imposes only sticks when it comes to be accepted as permanent and legitimate. In this realm premodern Turko-Persian conquerors

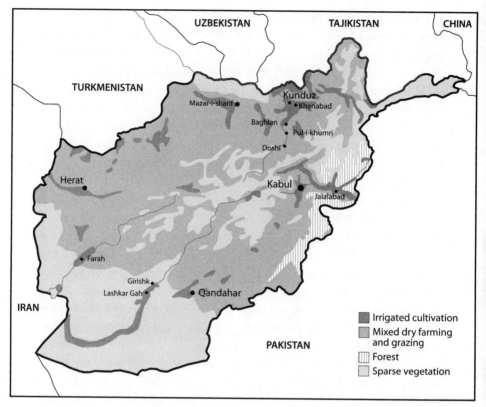

Map 5. Land use in Afghanistan

were fortunate. They worked within a political system where the number of contestants for power was limited and they were only rarely challenged by the people they ruled.

Premodern Patterns of Establishing Legitimacy in Central Asia and Beyond

States have historically used wars of conquest as the primary means to incorporate contested territory into their polities. For premodern states, wars of conquest were largely competitions among rival elites to control a subject population because the state as an institution was viewed as the property of the ruling elite that ran it. For this reason, territories could also be transferred from one polity to another through inheritance, gift, marriage alliances, and peace agreements. Conquerors were not at war with the people of the territory but rather with their rulers (although they still might end up killing a lot of ordinary folks in the process and destroying their property). Since control was the issue, it was common to allow defeated rulers to retain local power after they had acknowledged their submission to a new overlord and agreed to pay tribute, so that wars did not so much wipe the board clean as redistribute the existing pieces. And for most of history despised "foreign" rule was not only legitimate, it was the norm. There are few societies in Eurasia today that did not have a long experience of being ruled by people different from themselves. Because it was relatively easy to turn raw physical coercion into legitimate authority, all foreign rulers and their successors needed to achieve was the restoration of public order, and perhaps put down a rebellion or two. They could then count on religious institutions, economic power brokers, and other states to recognize them as legitimate rulers so as to minimize the disruption that would ensue by resisting such claims. The greatest asset for achieving long-term acceptance, however, was sheer inertia: as generations passed, the "force and usurpation" that David Hume claimed was the source of all royal executive power became routinized and traditional.[4] For example, Afghanistan's half century of peace from 1929 to 1978 under the Musahiban dynasty owed far more to this tradition of acquiescence than to its ability to project coercive power.

This may be a difficult mind-set for a contemporary reader to grasp, because since the Napoleonic period in Europe, warfare has involved the mass military and political mobilization of people in defense (or expansion) of their motherlands, fatherlands, promised lands, ancestral lands, homelands, holy lands, native lands, and other now-sacralized territories. Nor did this sacralization remain just a Western cultural fixation. The anti-colonial movements of the twentieth century in Asia and Africa all asserted the right of resident peoples (or at least their elite) to rule themselves, and declared foreign rule and occupation fundamentally illegitimate. We do, though, have a present-day analogy that captures both the feel and dynamic of this earlier age: corporate mergers and acquisitions. As factory workers and paper pushers continue their normal production of widgets and patterns of work, rival teams of mercenary bankers and corporate law-yers wielding proxy votes engage in furious battle to gain majority control of the target corporation's stock. On victory, the winning side purges the losing executive board members and appoints its own. The new CEO dis-misses most of the high-ranking staff (though often compensating them with golden parachutes to ease their pain), keeps on those they think can provide key local knowledge, and then installs their own loyalists who have no previous ties to this company. The new owners and managers may even be from different countries. Nothing changes on the factory floor during this process, and workers are not expected to take part in the struggle. They are not required to ratify its outcome even though they have more to lose or gain from the new owners' policies than other players. It is beyond their control whether the company will be squeezed like a lemon for its asset value, improved and run more profitably, or turned over again through a new takeover or merger. Rulers in Turko-Persia also viewed their subjects as economic assets rather than political actors, and there was no necessary connection between the rulers and the lands they ruled.

Acts of violence and physical coercion that first gained possession of a territory were transformed into legitimate authority by drawing on politi-cal theories supported by Islamic jurisprudence.[5] These put few barriers between de facto conquest and swift de jure recognition. One of the first actions that any new Muslim ruler took was to have the *khutba*, the Friday Islamic sermon at the main mosque, read in his name. Because Sunni Islam lacked a clerical hierarchy, the decision of what ruler's name to use was in the hands of the local prayer leaders—those in the least good position to reject such a demand. Announcing the ruler's name in the khutba signified both recognition of his sovereignty and gave public proof of his control. The other step to asserting legitimate sovereignty was to mint coins in the name and title of the new ruler. Such changes did not always stem from conquest. A regional ruler who decided to declare his independence or compete for supreme power would begin that bid by having the khutba read in his own name in his own territory and (if he had enough time) minting new coins.

Underlying this normally rapid acceptance of a new regime's legitimacy, whatever its limitations, was the fear of *fitna* (disorder, sedition, or civil war) and the consequences it could bring.[6] In the Islamic legal tradition, rebellion against an established Muslim ruler by his subjects was illegitimate because it created fitna. Students of Western political science will note that this line of reasoning closely parallels that of Thomas Hobbes's *Leviathan*, in which he justified the need for absolute rulers.[7] Himself a refugee from the disorder wrought by the English Civil War in the seventeenth century, Hobbes argued that any government was superior to lawlessness. As a consequence, subjects had a positive duty to obey their rulers, who in turn were obliged to protect their subjects' lives from the predation of other people within the state and invaders from without. Subjects should therefore accept as legitimate any ruler who was capable of protecting them, even if that ruler was defective or abusive in other ways. Rulers were not accountable to their subjects, but subjects had no obligation to remain loyal to leaders who could not fulfill their roles as protectors. In Hobbes's view, civil war or rebellion was the worst of all political conditions. Given the choice between that and accepting a conquest imposed by foreign invasion, he freely recommended the latter. Civil war could destroy society itself. Conquest (even foreign conquest) only threatened to change a society's leaders.

Although removed in time, place, and culture from the English Civil War that inspired Hobbes's observations, the rulers of Turko-Persian states viewed their political world in much the same way. For example, in 1006 the city of Balkh in northern Afghanistan was attacked by the Qarakhanids, a dynasty ruling a confederation of nomad tribes that had recently come out of the central Asian steppes to conquer today's Uzbekistan. The inhabitants of Balkh put up stiff resistance against the invaders, but in the end the city fell. Balkh was pillaged, and the main bazaar (owned by the sultan) was burned to the ground. Mahmud of Ghazni, the displaced sultan, quickly dispatched a large army and drove the invaders out. He then berated the people of Balkh for attempting to defend their city:

> What do subjects have to do with war? It is natural that your town was destroyed and that they burnt property belonging to me, which had brought in such revenues. You should be required to pay an indemnity for the losses, but we pardoned you; only see to it that it does not happen again: if any king (at a given moment) proves himself the stronger, and requires taxes of you and protects you, you must pay taxes and thereby save yourselves.[8]

Turko-Persian rulers thus looked on war and conquest as an unsentimental business that had little or nothing to do with the inhabitants of the territory. The ultimate targets of this expropriation were viewed as passive, and such people could only muddy the waters by entering the political or military realm. This vision of politics completely ruled out such notions such as patriotism, resistance, or consent. It would not be going too far to say that in the region's hierarchical political culture rulers and subjects might just as well have been different species. Sultan Sanjar, a powerful twelfth-century ruler of Seljuk Iran, explained that ordinary people were a breed apart: "They do not know the language of kings, and any idea either of agreeing with their rulers or of revolting against them is beyond them; all their efforts are devoted to one aim, to acquire the means of existence and maintain wife and children; obviously they are not to be blamed for this, and for enjoying constant peace."[9]

Only certain men from ruling descent groups were believed to have the right to compete for power. Hence, the constant theme in central Asian politics of a losing prince from one state appearing with a small band of followers in another, raising troops and setting out to establish his own empire. If politics was your hereditary business, then the question was how to find a new niche if you lost your old one. The most classic example of this was Babur, the Timurid prince who lost his original kingdom in Samarqand in 1501. Moving south to Badakhshan, he raised an army and conquered Kabul in 1504. After some unsuccessful attempts to defeat the growing power of the Uzbeks in his old home in trans-Oxiana, Babur turned his attention south. He captured Qandahar after a long siege in 1522 to protect his flank and then took Delhi by storm in 1526 to found the Mughal dynasty in India that would endure until 1857. Neither he nor the people he ruled seemed concerned that he had few previous connections with Kabul or the groups living south of the Hindu Kush.[10] In his business, victory in war was the main ingredient for political success, although making the right alliances was also helpful in gaining support. You need not convince the new population of your rights but instead merely dispossess the existing elite or make them your clients. War was thus an effective way to gain and retain power because victory provided legitimacy. While conquered cities often rebelled after a conquest, this was less a challenge to the legitimacy of its government than a test of its staying power. Populations were rarely punished for such acts beyond the execution of the ringleaders and the confiscation of their property.*

Success in war demanded an army, the bulk of which consisted of cavalry. Until around 1500 the compound bow was the main weapon, but after that time gunpowder weapons became more and more important. Such armies were expensive to maintain because they consisted primarily of costly mercenaries or even more costly slave soldiers (*mameluq*). Professional soldiers received their pay directly from the ruler or were given state-owned territories (*iqta* or *jagir*) to support them. Slave soldiers were attached to the household of the ruler with such titles as *ghulamshah* or *ghulambacha*. They were best known in the West through the janissaries, elite Ottoman troops, but similar institutions were common elsewhere in the Islamic world.[11] Because slave soldiers had no kinship ties of their own, rulers consistently promoted them to powerful positions with the belief that they would be more loyal to the throne than to their relatives. This was not always the case. Subuktigin, the founder of the Ghaznavid dynasty in the late tenth century, began his career as a slave soldier before taking control himself. Similarly, a mameluq dynasty governed Egypt for more than 250 years after its founding in 1250.[12] Additional military personnel were raised by bringing in tribal auxiliaries who volunteered to fight in a particular campaign either for pay or the opportunity to pillage. Campaigns directed against northern India attracted the participation of many otherwise-autonomous Pashtun tribes for whom the country's wealth was legendary.

It was the army that constituted the real body politic, because in a world where the danger of armed conflict was ever present, its lack of support doomed a ruler to defeat. Such troops were usually a fickle bunch. In William Shakespeare's *Henry the Fifth*, the English king is portrayed as successfully rousing his outnumbered and beleaguered troops against the French at Agincourt by appealing to their patriotism, but such an approach would not help a Turko-Persian shah, sultan, or amir. His soldiers worked on the "show me the money" principle. The survival of more than one kingdom hung on the question of whether its ruler could capture or raise enough treasure to keep his troops loyal and active. This problem was

---

*Except for the Mongol Empire's Chinggis Khan, who, not respecting the quasi-ritual nature of such challenges, had the populations of rebellious cities exterminated so that there would be no cities to rebel against him in the future.

so well-known that it became ingrained in popular culture. The famous thirteenth-century Persian poet Sa'di devoted a whole section of his stories and verse to the rulers and their courts, including their capricious armies:

> One of the ancient kings neglected the government of his realm and kept the army in distress. Accordingly the whole of it ran away when a powerful enemy appeared.

> If he refrains from giving treasure to the troops
> They refrain from putting their hands to the sword.
> What bravery will they display in battle array
> When their hands are empty and affairs deplorable?

> A sultan who grudges money to his troops, they cannot bravely risk their lives for him.

> Give gold to the soldier that he may serve thee.
> If thou witholdest gold, he will serve elsewhere.

> When a warrior is full, he will be brave in fight but if his belly be empty, he will be brave in flight.[13]

Caveat emptor, imperator!

Failures of Incorporation at the Margins of Empire

If there was an alternative model to this autocratic system, it was to be found among the tribal warriors who inhabited the marginal zones of the steppes, mountains, and deserts of the region. They had long experience with state societies, and a capacity to resist or cooperate with them. In ibn Khaldun's terms, these communities were examples of desert civilization: poor, tough, mean, and fractious people, but with strong community solidarity. If these people had simply remained at the margins, they would have not have presented a pressing problem. For example, the Roman Empire had unruly Germanic tribes on its frontier, but these were no threat to the imperial government until the empire itself weakened and then collapsed. Similarly, Chinese dynasties looked at steppe nomads north of the Great Wall as a foreign policy problem, not a domestic one. What made the difference in Turko-Persia (as well as the Arab world) was that the unruly people at the margins politically often lay within the claimed territory of the state and sometimes uncomfortably close to its centers of power. There was also a long tradition of peoples at the margins taking power as the region's ruling dynasties. At times of weakness at the center, leaders drawn from tribal peoples would seize the reins of government and restore political stability to the states they conquered, thereby becoming the rulers of people more sophisticated than themselves.

Because tribal peoples share a common organizational structure based on descent and kinship, it might seem that variations among them would have little practical significance. But this is not the case. Tribes in the Near East and Turko-Persia in fact drew on two different cultural traditions, which produced dissimilar political organizations. These differences had profound consequences for the region's history in general and Afghanistan's in particular. The first, an egalitarian type classically associated with the Bedouins of Arabia, was characteristic of the Pashtuns in Afghanistan and the NWFP. Organized through segmentary descent groups that were egalitarian in social structure and prone to reject the legitimacy of any hereditary leadership, it had an open political structure that was fluid. The maximum size of such groups as operational political units rarely exceeded ten thousand people. The second, a hierarchical type, was most closely associated with the nomadic horse-breeding steppe tribes (Turks and Mongols) that had originally entered Turko-Persia from the Eurasian steppes. It was organized through ranked sets of lineages, clans, and tribes, in which leadership was hereditary and limited to specific descent groups. This tradition produced tribal confederations an order of magnitude larger than egalitarian ones, ranging from one hundred thousand to as many as a million people under the rule of a single leader.[14]

EGALITARIAN LINEAGE SYSTEMS

The political dynamics of egalitarian lineage systems are "segmentary," which means that cooperation or hostility between particular groups is determined by the scope of the problem at hand. This dynamic gave rise to the ethnographic cliché, "Me against my brothers; my brothers and me against our cousins; my brothers, cousins, and me against the world."

When faced with a common threat, people set aside the numerous petty disputes that ordinarily divided them, but they immediately resumed their old rivalries and disputes once the common enemy was gone. To outsiders they might seem highly united, but internally they were hamstrung by divisions.

Leaders of egalitarian lineages did not have the power to command and served as a "first among equals." They were effective only when they mustered a consensus to support the actions they proposed. This was no easy job in a world where followers were loath to admit they were taking commands from anyone. For example, the Pashtun tribal assembly, or *jirga*, put so much stress on the nominal equality of its participants that men sat in a circle to avoid even symbolic hierarchy. This forced effective leaders to build alliances and greatly limited their authority to negotiate independently. Akbar Ahmed observed that attempts by the British raj to co-opt Pashtun tribal leaders in the NWFP through bribery provoked local outrage primarily because such payments created a distinction between leaders and followers: "The prejudice against ranks and titles and the hierarchy they imply is strong in tribal society and is summed up by the choice the Mahsud *mahshar* [headman], speaking on behalf of the clan elders, gave the British, 'Blow us all up with cannons or make all eighteen thousand of us Nawabs.'"[15]

The egalitarian nature of these societies made them particularly resistant to accepting the authority of paramount leaders who came from rival kin groups. The larger the group, therefore, the harder it was to maintain unity. For this reason, as ibn Khaldun first noted, a leader who stood outside the tribal system, generally in the guise of a religious prophet, had the best prospect of gaining the cooperation of enough quarreling tribes to create a supratribal organization that could overcome its inherent divisions.

Bedouins can acquire royal authority only by making use of religious coloring, such as prophethood or sainthood, or some great religious event in general. The reason is because of their savagery, the Bedouins are the least willing of all nations to subordinate themselves to each other, as they are rude, proud, ambitious and eager to be leaders. Their individual aspirations rarely coincide. But when there is religion (among them) through prophethood or sainthood, then they have some restraining influence upon themselves. The qualities of haughtiness and jealousy leave them. It is easy then to unite (as a social organization). . . . This is illustrated by the Arab dynasty of Islam. Religion cemented their leadership with religious law and its ordinances, which, explicitly and implicitly, are concerned with what is good for civilization.[16]

This helps explain why the egalitarian Arab tribes achieved the height of their political power during the early days of Islam, when they reached Afghanistan after overcoming the Sassanian Empire. From there they then expanded north as far as the land of the steppe nomads and to the borders of India in the east. But the brilliance of the early Islamic conquests should not blind us to their exceptional nature. After this time, the Bedouin tribes of Arabia never again established hegemony over the region. They could not match the military power of the horse-riding steppe tribes, whose hierarchical tribal organization was more easily adapted to ruling large states while maintaining political cohesion.

HIERARCHICAL LINEAGES

The leaders of the Eurasian horse-raising nomadic tribes had a different concept of political organization. They drew on a hierarchical cultural tradition originating in Mongolia, where pastoral tribes had created a series of outsized steppe nomadic states beginning in 200 BC under the Xiongnu Empire. This empire was not only large but also forced China to recognize it as an equal and sent it subsidies to avoid war. It was also remarkably stable under a single royal dynasty that retained power for 500 years—the first 250 years of which it ruled the entire steppe. Its medieval successors, the Turks and Mongols, maintained an even stronger pattern of centralized rule that allowed them to create bigger and more powerful empires.[17] In a series of mass migrations over many centuries, nomads from this tradition expanded westward into Turko-Persia. In some cases their conquests were centrally directed by states based in Mongolia, with the Mongol Empire founded by Chinggis Khan being the most famous example. But more commonly it was the losers of battles in the east who would migrate west to preserve their autonomy. Their military skills in horse archery and their greater political cohesion allowed them to regroup, and they eventually became the new rulers of the sedentary civilizations throughout Turko-Persia and beyond.

Turko-Mongolian tribal systems proved strong because their people, unlike the more egalitarian Bedouins and Pashtuns, accepted the legitimacy of hierarchical differences. Indeed, hierarchy was embedded into the very DNA of their social organization, with ranking distinctions between elder and younger brothers, senior and junior generations, noble and common clans, and ultimately the ruling dynasty and everyone else.[18] The acceptance of hierarchy as a normal feature of tribal life made it much easier for their leaders to create supratribal confederations by variously incorporating individuals, local lineages, clans, and whole tribes as the building blocks of a political/military organization that could present a united front to the outside world. These imperial confederacies combined people from a variety of tribes whose political unity was often all they had in common. The authority of a ruling dynasty, once established, became strictly hereditary and was rarely challenged from below. Their khans met ibn Khaldun's criteria for having true royal authority: they possessed the right to command obedience (by using force if necessary), collect taxes, administer justice, and handle all external political relations.[19] It was only a small step for a ruler of a complex confederation of tribes to see himself as the ruler of a more complex sedentary state.

Dueling Dynastic Dynamics

Egalitarian and hierarchical tribes displayed different characteristics of dynastic development after they conquered state societies and became rulers. The divergences lay both in the tribal traditions each represented and the resources available in the lands they ruled. Ruling dynasties originating from egalitarian tribes were short-lived and replaced regularly—a pattern so common in Arab north Africa and the Near East that ibn Khaldun posited a four-generation dynastic cycle model to explain it. By contrast, ruling dynasties produced by hierarchical tribes could be quite long-lived, and were almost impossible to remove internally even after their rulers became weak and incompetent. The hierarchical type, however, needed a much larger economic base to maintain itself, and was therefore character-istic of large states and empires. The egalitarian type required fewer re-sources and was most commonly found in places where the revenue base was too marginal to support a more hierarchical political structure. It also emerged during periods of state collapse, when regions that had been com-ponents of empires took the opportunity to become independent. Afghan-istan had both types of tribes and experienced polities based on each of these systems, so it is worth exploring each in more detail.

GLORY AND COLLAPSE: IBN KHALDUN'S FOUR-GENERATION MODEL

The rise and fall of dynasties in egalitarian lineage systems had a regular cycle of replacement, which completed itself in four generations as de-scribed below.[20] Weak dynasties in sedentary states, ibn Khaldun argued, were inherently vulnerable to attack and replacement by tribesmen who possessed military ability and superior 'asabiya, or as mentioned earlier, group feeling. 'Asabiya was the product of the close kinship ties or patron-client relationships that developed most strongly among tribal peoples. In times of warfare, such bonds better ensured mutual aid and cooperation than did the weaker political or economic self-interests motivating the mercenary armies employed by states. And the mercenaries of sedentary states were the least motivated when the dynasties that employed them lacked money to pay them. It was at this time that people from the mar-gins, who had earlier been dominated by dynasties based in urban centers, had an opportunity to displace dynasties. As noted previously, they need not overcome the large resident population but rather only defeat and re-place the dynasty that ruled over them.

The tribal leader who established a dynastic line by conquest found himself in a new political environment with fresh opportunities. Ibn Khal-dun called such a founder the builder of glory, a leader who through his personal struggles had achieved a success that he could rightly claim was the product of his own ability. He experienced the difficulties inherent in establishing his political dominance, and after obtaining power, retained those qualities that had allowed him to succeed in the first place. Having lived most of his life under rough conditions, he remained tough-minded and parsimonious, determined to maintain a simple life even when surrounded by luxuries. Stereotypically such a man would spurn the palace bedroom in favor of a tent pitched in a courtyard. He would dismiss his predecessor's large staff of cooks, barbers, valets, perfumers, eunuchs, poets, and musicians to end unnecessary and wasteful expenses. His cheapness meant that the treasury's tax receipts remained in surplus because such a ruler accumulated money but disliked spending it. He was often willing to share power with his immediate relatives, or at least seek their counsel on important decisions, because he still respected the bonds of kinship. On a larger scale, he would play the role of the generous chief by giving feasts, minor gifts, and sometimes stipends to the people who had helped him come to power.

The second-generation ruler differed from the first because he inherited leadership and did not have to struggle to create it. If the son of the founder seemed to lack the raw vitality and originality of his father, this was the product of his socialization and not necessarily an absence of innate talent. Groomed to rule, the son learned how to govern by observing his father rather than through direct experience. And growing up in the palace surrounded by wealth and luxuries he took for granted, he probably chafed at his father's cheapness as well as lack of manners and culture, and grew bored listening to endless tales of how many miles of desert the old man had walked through in his youth. On taking power, second-generation rulers were characterized by the luxury of their royal courts and the establishment of institutionalized royal authority. This required the elimination, frequently by murder, of the old tribal elite that had previously expected to share power. The founder's brothers and their heirs were particularly targets. After such a purge, the ruler appointed court officials from the ranks of men who had no independent power of their own and abolished the stipends paid to old tribal allies in favor of a greater reliance on the dynasty's mercenary military force. This generation also devoted its increasing tax revenues to large public works projects, but the budget remained in balance.

Third-generation leaders began a period of seeming greatness that disguised an institutional decline. Content with simple imitation and reliance on tradition, they lacked independent judgment. They habitually implemented policies even when they were ineffective or destructive. For all the pomp of their municipal projects and patronage of the arts, these rulers were cowardly, and dependent on sycophantic and corrupt advisers. Officials at all levels siphoned off the state's revenue for themselves. The treasury started to run large deficits as expenses mounted but revenues declined. As a result, the fourth-generation successors were doomed to a bad end. Inheriting both a bankrupt treasury and a mismanaged government, they had none of the skills needed to reverse the decline. Instead, assuming the right to rule was theirs by birth, they demanded the automatic respect of their subjects, but their arrogance and misrule destroyed what little remained of their political base. When disaffection in outlying areas turned to revolt, the dynasty was without revenues to pay its troops, which promptly abandoned it. Now damned and defenseless, it was only a matter of time before some fresh "founder of glory" swept in from the margins to begin the cycle anew.

The idea that dynasties start off with strong and competent rulers, and end with weak and incompetent ones, was hardly unique to ibn Khaldun. Chinese Confucian historiography in particular had a long tradition of assigning responsibility for dynastic collapse to the immorality of a "bad last emperor," whether he was the son of the founder or a tenth-generation descendant. But ibn Khaldun's model was sociological, based on the many historic cases from the Arab world that he was familiar with and his examination of their financial records archived at the courts where he served as a bureaucrat. He also put these observations in their cultural and social context. Ibn Khaldun observed that the acceptance of any noble class or caste status that permanently separated leaders from followers was impossible within an egalitarian social structure characteristic of Bedouin Arabs. Unlike in hierarchical social structures, where leadership and authority was vested in specific elite social groups, among the egalitarian Arabs no lineage was believed to have an innate claim on leadership. This meant that no tribal dynasty could assert a permanent right to rule on the basis of inheritance, divine right, or some other innate superiority. In egalitarian lineages anyone could envision his own rise to the top, and the political field was always open to rivals. Most important, there was no cultural or ideological barrier to the acceptance of talented new rulers as dynastic founders, regardless of their background. They need not hide their ambition behind some puppet ruler whose ancestry was more prestigious nor try to invent a better ancestry for themselves. Success wiped the slate clean and was its own validation, but such success could never be made permanent.

Hierarchy and Empire Building: A Turko-Mongolian Hegemony

Imagine for a moment a history of Rome in which the emperors were not only always German but where the empire's Latin speakers considered this to be the normal way of politics and helped facilitate the stabilization of their rule. Substitute Turk (or their Mongol cousins) for German and Persian for Latin, and you have the situation that developed in medieval Turko-Persia. Beginning with the Ghaznavids in eastern Afghanistan at the end of the tenth century, every major empire from the borders of northern India to trans-Oxiana, Iran, and Anatolia was founded by the Turks or Mongols. Once established these dynasties could be remarkably long-lived. The Ottoman Turkish sultans, for example, maintained an 800-year unbroken lineage lasting until the twentieth century, while India's Mughal dynasty survived for more than 300 years, until abolished by the British in the nineteenth century. Afghanistan would be continually ruled by such Turkish and Mongol groups for 750 years, until the rise of the Pashtuns in the mid-eighteenth century. Why was this pattern so different than the cycle of short-lived dynasties documented by ibn Khaldun, and what was the political legacy of this "ancient supremacy" for successor states?[21]

The answer comes in four parts. The first is military. The Turks and Mongols were nomads (or descendants of nomads), originally from the Eurasian steppe, whose horse cavalry gave them military superiority over the sedentary people they conquered. The second is organizational. The Turks and Mongols maintained states that were much larger in size, more centralized in organization, and economically more stable than those established egalitarian tribes. The third is cultural. Turkish and Mongol rulers were quick to incorporate aspects of the more sophisticated cultures they encountered to strengthen their governments. The fourth is dynastic cohesion. Only the descendants of the charismatic founder could inherit the throne, and the unrivaled prestige of the dynasty made replacing them politically difficult.

The nomads of the Eurasian steppe may have been less sophisticated than the sedentary peoples they encountered when they first migrated into Turko-Persia, but they were equal or superior to them in the arts of war. Employing the deadly compound bow, the nomads were masters of a mounted archery that could devastate an opposing army even while retreating with the so-called Parthian shot. They had an unlimited number of horses at their disposal because they raised them. Each man was trained from childhood to be a warrior—a skill so valued by their enemies that Turks taken from the steppe constituted the bulk of the early Islamic world's slave soldiers. These nomads had no need of standing armies (and bearing the costs of maintaining them) because their warriors were only assembled when needed to fight. This permitted steppe societies to mobilize a far higher percentage of their population for war than sedentary people with less disruption to their economy. Far from being a drain on state finances, steppe nomads saw war as a potentially profitable business. Each warrior brought his own weapons, horses, and supplies with him. In return he got a share of the loot.

This pure steppe tradition of warfare was initially focused on raiding rather than conquest and was often highly destructive. The first Mongol invasions of the thirteenth century devastated whole regions. But as invading tribes became permanent residents of Turko-Persia, their way of life and political objectives changed. In particular, their leaders began to conquer and tax regions rather than just raid them. This sometimes required educating fellow tribesmen on the elementary principles of government. For example, when the Seljuqs first entered Khorasan and conquered Nishapur in 1038, their leader, Toghril, had difficulty in restraining his brothers from looting the city. He had to point out to them that as the conquerors and new rulers of the land, they were in fact now destroying their own property.[22] Because settled agricultural lands bordered seasonal grasslands and mountain pastures, nomads could rule such areas without having to sedentarize all of their people. Instead many remained nomads but developed a style of pastoralism that was more integrated with sedentary agriculture. Pastoral products were exchanged for grain with local villagers, so the nomads' diet became dependent on grain. This was also true for their horses. With a ready supply of surplus barley, they began to breed much larger and stronger horses that could no longer survive on pasture alone. This, in turn, permitted the use of heavier armor and chain mail, which made their cavalry more formidable—a practice that previous steppe nomadic conquerors such as the Parthians had pioneered as early as the first century BC.

The hierarchical tribal structure found among the Turks and Mongols facilitated the creation and maintenance of large tribal confederations even before they conquered sedentary regions. Along the Mongolian frontier with China, these highly centralized imperial confederacies employed tribal social organization at the local level, but imperial rule in military affairs and foreign relations. These imperial confederacies used their power to extort resources from Chinese governments and then redistributed them to their members.[23] If egalitarian tribal groups were bound together by ʿasabiya, hierarchical Turko-Mongolian polities were bound together by their ability to distribute benefits. Steppe nomad leaders moving west brought this form of organization and its aggressive military strategies with them, but in Turko-Persia they became rulers rather than raiders. What did not change was their seemingly endless pursuit of wealth to redistribute as political capital. This struck their sedentary advisers as peculiar since they believed in taxing subject populations and hoarding the money in order to finance the state structure and army. Saʿdi actually made such a debate the focus of one of his tales, in which a ruler of tribal origin suggested that he might gain everlasting fame if he gave the entire treasury away as gifts to his subjects. His experienced Persian vizier argued that the ruler needed to look at revenues differently now that he ruled a settled state:

If you disburse a treasure to the masses
Each family gets but a grain of rice.
Why not take from each just a barley seed of silver
So that you can everyday accumulate a treasure?[24]

Turkish and Mongol rulers learned this lesson, and soon diverted their increased revenues to new mercenary armies and state officials, allowing them to sideline their old tribal followers. But they still proved relentless in their determination to increase the size of their states, because the fixed costs of the army and bureaucracy demanded a large and regular flow of revenues. Rulers therefore saw continued outward expansion as the best way to secure dynastic stability internally—a process that often continued through a series of rulers. For instance, the Ottoman Empire underwent expansion for five hundred years, until it finally spanned the Balkans, southeastern Europe, Anatolia, Syria, Mesopotamia, Arabia, Egypt, and north Africa at its height. The Mughals controlled more of India than any previous dynasty, but it took many generations to reach that size. And not content with the huge chunk of Turko-Persia that he already controlled after a lifetime of warfare, an aging Tamerlane was planning an improbable campaign against distant China when he died in 1400. Of course, since they all had Chinggis Khan's record-breaking world empire as a benchmark, the bar of success was set high. The end result, however, was that their outsized ambitions bequeathed their successors so much territory, wealth, and military power that their dynasties continued for centuries, surviving military defeats and periods of decline that would have collapsed less robust polities.

Conquest and military power was one thing, providing effective administration was another. The Chinese had a saying that while an empire could be won on horseback, it could not be ruled from there. Turko-Mongolian rulers seemed to understand this intuitively. They never let pride in their military successes blind them to their inexperience as administrators. Rulers solved this problem by creating states with dual organizations. Administration was placed in the hands of "men of the pen," literate Persian speakers familiar with government, while military commands were allocated to "men of the sword," tribal Turks or slave soldiers. This interaction between a Turko-Mongolian military elite and an older Persian tradition of civil administration, culture, and religion produced a synthesis that was the political foundation of Turko-Persian states for centuries to come.[25] It was also the source of innovations in religion and the arts. In religion the Turks, in earlier times pagans who had converted to Islam, eclipsed the Arabs as the prime defenders of the faith against non-Muslims and were the patrons of the Sufi orders that brought a new vitality to Islam. In art and architecture, the most brilliant productions of the Islamic world came under the patronage of the Timurids in central Asia, the Ottomans in Turkey, the Safavids in Iran, and the Mughals in India. Persian miniatures of this period were never surpassed.

A final aspect of dynastic stability was its limitation on who could hold high office. In an egalitarian system, the failure of the ruler placed the government itself at risk. In a hierarchical system, no rival outside the imperial line could compete for the position. Such limitations did not prevent succession struggles but did strictly limit who could compete for power in them. In most dynasties the death of the ruler immediately set in train a process of "bloody tanistry," a succession rule among Turko-Mongolian peoples in which the most talented male member of the royal dynasty inherited the throne.[26] Any disputes over who the most talented heir might be were decided by warfare and murder. This made violence the final arbiter of rightful succession among rival uncles, brothers, or cousins. When such internal succession struggles ended quickly, they tended to produce strong rulers without doing too much damage to the state structure. But over time the tradition of dynastic succession within a single lineage was so powerful that even promoting a series of idiots to the throne was seen as preferable to seeking a ruler from the outside. This was reinforced by the long-standing Persian (and Byzantine) imperial tradition that invested the ruling shah or sultan with absolute power. Rising leaders who came from outside this charmed circle found it safer to replace one royal heir with another (even if the appointment was symbolic) rather than risk abolishing the dynasty itself. The descendants of Chinggis Khan were classic examples of such a charismatic line. Only they could be the paramount sovereigns of Mongol successor states, but over the centuries their appointments to high office became purely ceremonial. Still, so strong was this tradition that even as famous a ruler as Tamerlane, a Barlas Turk, felt it necessary to employ such "tame Chinggisids" as the official rulers of his state during his own lifetime, even after he had built an empire that stretched from Samarqand to Damascus.[27]

The real secret to the centuries of continuity in such a hierarchical system was the need to work within it. In egalitarian systems, the pace of change was rapid and there was every incentive to replace failing rulers with outsiders when they faltered; in hierarchical systems, change was ponderously slow and there was every incentive to sustain a moribund dynastic line because the powers behind the throne lacked the prestige to rule overtly.

The strengths and weaknesses of the two systems can be seen in the rise of the Pashtuns, and particularly in the long-running rivalry between the western Durrani Pashtuns and the eastern Ghilzai Pashtuns. The more egalitarian Ghilzai Pashtuns would topple the Safavids, Persia's longest-lived dynasty, but then prove incapable of building an empire of their own. A generation later their more hierarchical cousins, the Durrani Pashtuns, would be more successful by adopting many of the structural characteristics of the Turkish Afsharid Empire, in which they had served as soldiers. They established an Afghan empire and created a powerful dynastic charisma that would keep the Durranis on the throne for 230 years. Yet this hierarchical transplant into the Pashtun body politic always remained a bit alien. Such was the egalitarian bias in the Pashtun system that struggles for supremacy by various lineages within the Durrani line had all the characteristics of egalitarian infighting. Rival lineages seized and lost power almost precisely according to ibn Khaldun's schedule of dynastic rise, decline, and replacement. Nor did the Ghilzai Pashtuns ever truly subscribe to the belief that the Durranis were superior to themselves—simply that they were more clever and manipulative. But it was not until 1978 that Ghilzais in the guise of Communists were finally able to abolish the royal line and rule themselves, only to split into murderous factions that would have collapsed the government had the Soviets not invaded and killed their leaders in the hopes of stabilizing the political situation. I am getting ahead of myself, though.

THE RISE OF THE PASHTUNS

Pashtun Prehistory

Although the Pashtuns trace their roots to the earliest inhabitants of Afghanistan, it is difficult to document their existence, let alone their political history and subunits, until about 1500. While some historians see evidence of Pashtun tribes in Afghanistan as far back as the Achaemenids twenty-five hundred years ago, this conclusion is based only on geographic toponyms and tribal names that appear similar to historic Pashtun groups. Even the history of the Turkish Ghaznavids, whose eleventh-century capital lay in the heart of what would become Ghilzai territory, does not delineate them clearly. Perhaps this lack of documentation should not be surprising, since for so much of its history Afghanistan's territory was the eastern frontier of various Persian-based empires and then Turko-Mongolian ones. In these empires, people at the margins rarely attracted the attention of the center. But perhaps this is fortunate, since more details would call into question some foundational elements of Pashtun cultural identity: first, that they have always constituted a single group based on common descent; and second, that their allegiance to Islam was earlier than other groups in the region and that they never resisted the adoption of the new faith.

Caroe contends that while Pashtuns undoubtedly have an ancient history, we must see their creation as a tribal group as a process that took some time to develop and incorporated a number of diverse peoples. In regard to common descent, he maintains that striking anomalies in the basic genealogies themselves hint at this more complex origin. In a society where all descent is patrilineal, only the senior line (Abdali in the west and Yusefzai in the east) and the Gurgusht claim an unbroken patrilineal descent from the founder. By contrast, the Ghilzai genealogies trace their line to a Pashtun ancestress who married a Ghorid prince after having a child with him out of wedlock (the founding male ancestor of the Ghilzais). The Karlanri tribes, which constitute the most important groups in today's NWFP, have no genealogical link at all (male or female) to the sons of Qais, the Pashtun's apical ancestor. They are the descendants of an adopted child of uncertain origins raised by Pashtuns. Genealogies are not histories, but Caroe makes a persuasive argument that they reflect a tradition by which the Pashtuns expanded not only through conquest but by intermarriage and assimilation as well. The Ghilzais appear to have intermarried and absorbed many of the different groups, particularly the Turks, who passed through eastern Afghanistan. The bulk of the Karlanri, by contrast, appear to be the indigenous inhabitants of the mountains of the NWFP who mixed little with outsiders, but who became Pashtuns (or more precisely Pakhtuns) by adopting their language and culture, and then discarding their older identities.[28]

If matters of genealogy have left a number of loose ends, the Pashtuns are emphatic that their Muslim identity cannot be challenged. It is a core belief among all Pashtuns that their founding ancestor, Qais, adopted Islam in the lifetime of the Prophet in Arabia and that Pashtuns became the strongest defenders of the faith from that time forward. But a look at the early Arab conquests shows that only parts of Afghanistan fell under their control: the northern region from Herat to Balkh and on into central Asia, and south through Siestan and Qandahar toward Sind. The mountainous areas of the Hindu Kush eastward to Kabul and Peshawar remained holdouts against Islam for many centuries. Kabul in particular was a Hindu kingdom at war with the Ghaznavids well into the eleventh century, and Ghaznavid sources have undifferentiated Afghans listed both as ghazis, fighters for the faith, and enemies fighting against them.[29] The idea that it may have taken four or five centuries for the conversion to Islam to be completed in what constitutes the core territory of the Pashtuns (and that some of their ancestors may have vigorously resisted the process) would doubtless be viewed as a deadly insult today, even if it were historically correct.

But exactly what occurred at the local level in Afghanistan from the fall of the Ghaznavid Empire at the end of the twelfth century through the foundation of the Mughal dynasty at the start of the sixteenth is lost in the shadow play of greater powers. These shadows include a period of unprecedented destruction and population movements induced by the Mongol invasions of Chinggis Khan and his grandson Hulegu in the thirteenth century. It was followed by the rise and decline of the Timurids in central Asia in the fifteenth century—a period of which our knowledge of the north and west is good (Herat served as a Timurid capital), but that of the south and east is much poorer. And certainly by 1500 when details do become specific, all Pashtuns are Muslim and keen to spread the faith to the plains of Hindu India. So that is where our story resumes.

Pashtuns on the Frontiers of Persia and India

Around 1500, three great empires with Turkish roots arose almost simultaneously and divided today's Afghanistan equally between them: the Safavids in Iran, the Mughals in India, and the Uzbeks in trans-Oxiana. The Uzbeks held the cities on the plains north of the Hindu Kush (Maimana, Balkh, and Kunduz). Kabul, eastern Afghanistan, and down through the Khyber Pass to Peshawar was held by India's Mughal dynasty, whose founder, Babur, had Kabul as his capital. The Iranian Safavid dynasty held Herat and the lower Helmand region of Seistan. Both the Mughals and Safavids periodically ruled Qandahar, which passed permanently into Safavid control during the mid-seventeenth century. At that time, the Ghilzai Pashtuns were the dominant group in eastern Afghanistan in a region stretching from Ghazni to Qandahar, and the Abdali (Durrani) Pashtuns dominated the west from Helmand to Herat. The Pashtuns appearance in all these plains areas, or at least their rise to prominence there, appears to have coincided with the emergence of these empires as well.

Babur's expansion into northern India displaced a dynasty of Afghan origin, the Lodis (1451–1526). Although in a collateral line with the Ghilzais, the dynasty's chroniclers left no details about their homeland or just what tribes might have followed them eastward. But their expansion into India showed three classic features that ibn Khaldun attributed to egalitarian tribes. First, the Lodis came to power as opportunists in a period of political turmoil and state collapse, when northern India was easy prey to a leader who could raise an army on the frontier. Second, they abandoned their marginal mountain homelands to resettle as conquerors in rich agricultural lands on the plains and, having left, never sought to control that frontier. Third, they suffered from the same cycle of dynastic decline that seemed structurally inherent in states ruled by egalitarian tribes. Lacking hereditary dynastic charisma, they could not recover from the decisive defeat that Babur inflicted on them in 1526. A revanchist dynasty of Suri Afghans (1540–55) would attempt to hold the lands beyond the Indus against the Mughals, but Humayan, Babur's successor, would win this territory back, leaving only a rump Afghan state ruling over Bengal until 1576.[30] During this same period we hear nothing specific about the Abdali Pashtuns in the west, who came under Safavid control.

The political activity of Pashtun groups that engaged in contests for power on the plains of India stood in stark contrast to those that remained in the Pashtun heartland. During the early sixteenth century those Pashtuns living on the irrigated plains near Peshawar, Kabul, Qandahar, and Herat all became subjects of either the Indian Mughals or Persian Safavids. Because local populations took such foreign rulership as part of the inevitable ebb and flow of the region's political dynamics, they did not resist it. Instead, for the next two hundred years, they concerned themselves with establishing good connections to their respective centers. This was relatively straightforward except in Qandahar, which was hotly contested by both the Mughals and Safavids. This placed both the Abdali and Ghilzai Pashtuns living in the region in a strategically advantageous position because they could play the two sides off against each other. Their options were still limited to which empire would rule the territory, however. In the end, it was the Iranians who ousted the Mughals and took control of today's southern Afghanistan. Even though the Safavids were Shiites, the Pashtuns in Qandahar found their rule more accommodating than that previously delivered by the Sunni Mughals and so saw no reason to reject their government. Like the alien origin of ruling dynasties, sectarian differences did not affect the political legitimacy of a government.

The relationships that various Pashtun groups established with their respective imperial centers did have a profound impact on their internal political development by introducing them to new models of administration and military organization. As frontier feudatories who linked their tribes to the Safavids, the leaders of the ruling Abdali and Ghilzai Pashtun clans had an advantage over other Pashtuns: an access to sources of revenue, and the political backing needed to rise above the petty disputes among rival tribes and lineages that had previously preoccupied them. This was because any leader who could extract resources from the imperial center and obtain a government appointment had an advantage over rivals who depended only on their kinsmen. But not just any type of appointment: their success depended on becoming the governor of a city that dominated its region. Before they became governors of cities such as Qandahar and Herat, Ghilzai and Abdali chieftains had little political influence beyond their own people. After gaining such appointments they became players in regional politics, in which control of a major provincial city was a necessary base. As centers of cultural sophistication, economic productivity, and political power, such cities were essential in bids for power (or to keep what one had). Experience in these urban environments also gave Pashtun tribal leaders a needed lesson in the basics of dual political organization that their Turkish overlords had long taken for granted. That is, the leader of a strong tribal military force needed Persian administrators to organize the military's finances and manage its bureaucracy, without which no state could survive for long.

Resistance against imperial rule among the Pashtuns, by contrast, was confined to the mountain glens of today's NWFP, an area in the Mughal sphere of influence, where tribes adamantly rejected all attempts at direct control. These tribes maintained their traditional forms of subsistence agriculture, and no clan or tribe had access to resources that could permanently place it above any other. Similarly, without a connection to the state system, no leader within the tribe could amass enough influence to make his leadership paramount. None of the powerful tribes there had an urban base they could call their own. But while opposition to direct Mughal administration was intense and mostly successful in the mountainous areas, the lure of Mughal wealth and the possibilities for personal advancement always remained strong. Just as common as the practice of war and conflict with Delhi was a Pashtun tradition of seeking out Mughal subsidies in exchange for peace, volunteering for paid military service, and establishing political alliances that provided advantages in local disputes. The Mughals therefore found paying subsidies for the right to use the Khyber Pass cheaper (and ultimately more efficient) than fighting in the mountains. Even the most famous Pashtun warrior poet, Khushal Khan Khattak (1613–90), who railed against the attempts of the Mughal emperor Aurangzeb to impose his authority in the autonomous tribal areas, came from a family that had served the Mughals loyally as allies for generations. He only split when Delhi made friendly overtures to his hereditary enemies, the Yusefzais in Swat, and abolished the road and ferry tolls that had been his family's traditional source of income.[31]

It was not until the beginning of the eighteenth century—when both the Safavids and Mughals had entered periods of rapid military decline— that the Pashtuns started to play an independent political role. This role would lead directly to the destruction of the Safavid dynasty itself and initiate a period of regional disorder that opened Mughal India to attack from all sides. At this time the Ghilzai Pashtuns were the dominant force in the Safavid-controlled territories of eastern Afghanistan, having earlier displaced the Abdalis in Qandahar during the reign of Shah Abbas the Great (1587–1629). But they also retained strong economic ties to Mughal India. Ghilzai nomads would move their flocks from their summer pastures in the Hindu Kush down to the Indian plains for the winter. Such a pastoral cycle was easy to combine with the caravan trade, which made Ghilzai chiefs rich. At the beginning of the eighteenth century the Ghilzai were estimated to number fifty thousand families. They remained loyal to the Safavids until an army of Georgians sent by the shah to repel a Baluch invasion in 1704 alienated the population and provoked a rebellion, which was quickly suppressed. Mir Wais, the wealthy Hotak chief who had previously governed Qandahar, was deported to the royal Safavid court in Isfahan as punishment and to keep him from causing further trouble. This tactic backfired because Mir Wais used the opportunity to buy friends as well as influence the shah. He also discovered how weak and dysfunctional the Safavid government had become. On his return to Qandahar in 1709, he instigated a greater and more successful rebellion. He beat back a Safavid punitive expedition, and expelled them and their Abdali Pashtun allies in 1711. The latter then also revolted against the Safavids and made Herat independent in 1717. It was notable that unlike the tribes of the Khyber that rebelled against the very idea of Mughal state control, revolts by the Ghilzais and Abdalis against Safavid rule were not designed to end state authority in their regions. Instead, these revolts were waged to increase the autonomy and influence that existing leaders had within a regional state structure.

The failure of the Safavids to control their Afghan frontier opened them to attack by the Ghilzais, both because their military capacity had been proved hollow and because the Abdalis were too consumed by deadly factional disputes to stand in their way. Led by Mir Wais's son, Mahmud, a Ghilzai force with no heavy weapons and probably numbering only about fifteen thousand seized the Safavid capital of Isfahan in 1722. They deposed the shah and then killed most of the ruling family. Once having seized power, though, the Ghilzais proved incapable of consolidating their rule. Mahmud was mentally unbalanced, and within a year his excesses provoked a coup led by his cousin Ashraf (whose own father had been murdered earlier by Mahmud). Although they were able to fend off an Ottoman invasion, Ghilzai authority in Iran quickly waned. As frontier feudatories, they lacked the administrative experience necessary to govern such a complex state and were Sunni rulers in a Shiite land. They were also fractured by tarburwali-style internal divisions. Their relatives in Qandahar were among the first to reject their authority.[32]

In reaction to the fall of the Safavids, Iran experienced a period of tribal resurgence in which Turkish groups from Khorasan came to the fore, most notably Nadir Shah Afshar (r. 1736–47). Nadir mobilized a wide variety of tribal forces (including the neighboring Abdali Pashtuns, whom he had first defeated) to create a powerful but ephemeral empire. For the first time in many centuries an Iranian power projected itself into India itself, when Nadir defeated the Mughals and then sacked Delhi in 1739. To hold his troops together, he rewarded them lavishly with loot from campaigns and payments derived from heavy taxes on all the territories under his rule. His state collapsed with his murder, but the eastern half was claimed by one of his lieutenants, Ahmad Khan, an Abdali Pashtun, who was proclaimed shah of the Durrani Empire in 1747.[33]

The Rise of the Durrani Empire

If not for Nadir Shah Afshar's untimely death, the Pashtuns might once again have found themselves a subordinate part in that long series of Turko-Mongolian empires that had so effectively dominated the region for the preceding eight hundred years. His assassination instead created a political vacuum in which to take power themselves. Not only was Iran in turmoil but Mughal India as well. The Mughals never recovered their power after Nadir's invasion, and their influence over their frontier west of the Indus River evaporated. They also faced challenges from the Marathas in the Deccan region, the Sikhs in the Punjab region, and the expansion of the British out of Bengal. To the north the Uzbeks were also in decline. Now divided into a number of petty khanates, the amir of Bukhara had only nominal control over the Uzbek lands south of the Oxus. This situation provided the Abdali Pashtuns a unique opportunity to build an independent Afghan-ruled state temporarily free from interference from Iran, India, or central Asia.

It was no accident that they, and not the unruly Pashtuns in the tribal hinterlands of the Mughal frontier, created the first Pashtun-ruled empire. Experienced servants of various empires, they had the ambition and tools to run one themselves. Because the establishment of the Durrani Empire is the usual starting point for the modern history of Afghanistan, however, there is a tendency to gloss over the large debt that the Afghans owed to the Afsharid and Safavid empires in creating it. The Durrani Empire, large as it was to be, would be glued together from the various pieces that Nadir Shah had previously conquered and governed with a Safavid model of administration. The Afghans were able to consolidate control over such distant provinces as Khorasan, Turkistan, Punjab, and Sind only because Nadir had first conquered them. He had even paved their way in Afghanistan itself by driving the Ghilzais out of Qandahar and seizing Kabul from the Mughals in 1738, the year before he sacked Delhi. This legacy becomes apparent when we look at how Ahmad Khan came to be the Durrani Empire's founder.

Ahmad Khan served as a leader in Nadir Shah's personal bodyguard and had led a contingent of four thousand Abdali horse cavalry. On Nadir's assassination in Iran in 1747, Ahmad immediately retreated east toward Qandahar with much of the old regime's portable treasure (including the famous Koh-i-nur diamond). The Abdali military commanders chose him en route as their leader in a tribal jirga. As the story goes, he did not seek this position but rather had it thrust on him during a deadlock among Abdali clan chieftains over who should lead them. A famous holy man intervened to end the dispute by declaring that Ahmad was the most deserving candidate and proclaiming him *Padshah, Durr-i-Durran* (Pearl of Pearls). Ahmad Khan thereafter became known as Ahmad Shah, and his Abdali clansmen thereafter styled themselves Durrani.[34]

The emphasis put on the importance of the jirga election in most Afghan histories implies that it was the Pashtuns alone who raised Ahmad to power, and that he was a product of the existing tribal structure. Neither supposition is accurate. His true power was based on his previous position as a potent Afshar official who had taken command of the old regime's troops in the area. In a world where money was an army's mother's milk, he had the largest amount of it at his disposal—a sum that was greatly augmented when he seized a large treasure caravan en route to Iran from India. He was also strongly supported by the non-Afghan Qizilbash, a Turkish Shiite group that had significant military strength in the army and no tribal connections with the local population. It is unlikely that the man who had run off with the bulk of Nadir's available treasure and had cavalry contingents under his personal command was really such a bashful presence in a council of his own people. Because Ahmad already had this broad base of support beyond the Pashtuns, the Durranis knew that it was only by rallying around him that they could hope to permanently displace their Ghilzai rivals in Qandahar, recover Herat, and expand beyond the Pashtun heartland.

On taking power, Ahmad Shah moved in two directions from his new capital in Qandahar. In the west he reestablished Durrani authority in Herat in 1750, and over the next two years displaced his Afshar rivals in Khorasan by taking Mashad and Nishapur. At the same time his agents seized control of today's northern Afghanistan from the Uzbek amir of Bukhara. Later in his reign, during 1768–70, he would have to again battle the Bukharan amir to reclaim this territory and signed a treaty recognizing the Amu Darya as Afghanistan's northern border. But he focused most of his attention on India in the east. Beginning in 1748, Ahmad mounted eight expeditions against India over the next twenty years. In spite of beating the Mughals and taking Delhi, Ahmad kept that dynasty in power and even defended it later from a powerful invasion from the south by the Marathas. The necessity of preserving the Mughals was a fine example of the power of dynastic charisma. No matter how great a hero he was in Afghan eyes, Ahmad could not see himself as a replacement for such an old and prestigious lineage, and chose to cloak himself in its aura rather than risk the consequences of abolishing it. Such a move would have opened the question of who had the right to rule and upset the complex web of nominal vassalage that tied the north Indian states together. Acting as the dynasty's protector was more politically opportune, and was the policy later followed by the British when they expanded into northern India.

When Ahmad Shah died in 1772, his Durrani Empire encompassed all of today's Afghanistan, Baluchistan, Iranian Khorasan, and the former Mughal territories of Sind, Punjab, and Kashmir. It would begin to unravel under the reign of his successor, Timur (1772–93), and shrink even more in the early nineteenth century. In this process the Punjab would fall to the Sikhs, the Iranians would reclaim Khorasan and threaten Herat, and northern Afghanistan would regain its autonomy. To understand why we must examine the structure of the Durrani state and its vulnerabilities, many of which persisted in successor Afghan states.

STATE STRUCTURE

Ahmad Shah's Durrani Empire was a coat worn inside out. Traditionally an empire's core territories consisted of its most populous economically productive cities and the agricultural land that surrounded them. Its frontiers were territories where the population and the revenue stream thinned out. By contrast, the Durrani Empire's Pashtun core (Qandahar, Kabul, and Peshawar) was much poorer and more sparsely populated than its richer margins (Sind, Punjab, Kashmir, Khorasan, and Turkistan). For conquerors who got their start in Afghanistan, the historic solution to this problem was to move on. To adapt the old Chinese saying, you could conquer an Indian empire from Afghanistan, but you could not rule it from there. Babur may have loved Kabul, yet his Mughal successors made Delhi their imperial capital and never looked back. The Lodis had done the same thing a century earlier. Ahmad Shah refused to consider this strategy. Instead of ruling north India, he found it preferable to conduct a policy of continual raiding whenever he needed funds (much as the Ghaznavids had done). This may have been prudent: the rising power of the Sikhs in Punjab and the Marathas in Deccan (let alone the British in Bengal) would have made it difficult to secure his power there using Afghan troops alone. For example, even at the height of their influence the Afghans proved unable to retain consistent control over Lahore, their main bridgehead in Punjab. They finally lost that city to the Sikhs in 1767, years before Ahmad died. But the situation was not much better in the empire's other regions, such as Baluchistan, Khorasan, and Turkistan, where they were forced to utilize unreliable local ruling elites to govern under Durrani supervision. Thus the paradox: the Durrani Empire's greatest sources of revenue were derived from the territories it never directly controlled. And that revenue would only continue to flow as long as the Durranis remained militarily dominant.

The necessity to remain militarily dominant required the Durrani Empire to mobilize and maintain a large military machine to overawe its neighbors and cow wavering vassals. Beginning with an army of 16,000 at Ahmad Shah's ascension to power, the army soon expanded to 40,000 (mostly made up of Durranis, Ghilzais, and some Qizilbash) in its first campaigns. At its height the army would consist of about 120,000 men. Of these forces, one-third consisted of regular troops (mostly cavalry but also artillery) while the remaining two-thirds were made up of irregular troops (of those, three-quarters were cavalry and one-fourth were infantry). The regular army was paid in cash or granted military fiefs in the core territories of India as compensation. The irregular forces were recruited either by imposing levies on specific districts or through tribal chieftains, who were responsible for finding and equipping their own troops. Such irregular troops served for the duration of a campaign and then returned home. As compensation, they received tax remission for a year (and presumably got war loot). Their chiefs, who commanded the irregular forces and dealt with the government, received landed jagirs or cash payments to compensate them. Detachments of tribal cavalry were also recruited on a more regular basis to protect the frontiers, collect tax revenue, guard government stores, and serve as police. They were paid in cash and in-kind by the treasury, and their chiefs received jagirs.[35]

Like most previous conquerors in the region, Ahmad Shah saw his army, regardless of ethnic origin, as the true body politic. This was reflected in his renowned generosity to his troops. When a treasurer complained that his unpaid soldiers had helped themselves to royal funds during a campaign against Nishapur in 1751, Ahmad rebuked him and declared,

> Don't you know, you fool, that I am also one of them, that it is by their unanimity, and with the help of their swords, that I have been raised to this high position? I should certainly look upon my soldiers as partners in this wealth. If they make a demand upon my wealth, which, in reality is the result of their efforts, and I share it not with them, I stand condemned before man and God.[36]

Sustaining this military structure depended on the receipt of regular revenue, amounting to about thirty million rupees annually at the empire's height. Much of this was unavailable to the ruler because it was collected by those who held jagirs or was subtracted to finance local administration (and reward local client rulers). The bulk of the remainder funded the army. Because the Durrani Empire survived on the fruits of military extortion, a policy that Admad knew well from his years with Nadir Shah Afshar, he was almost constantly on campaign. Grand raids against India in particular brought in lots of revenue and were popular with his irregular troops because they yielded loot and could be fought in the name of Islam against Hindus and Sikhs. But the army's structure also restricted Ahmad's power. His irregular troops were rarely willing to spend more than a year away from home. As they constituted the bulk of his army, Ahmad was often forced to end his campaigns prematurely and could not always consolidate his great military successes. Neither could he rest peacefully for long because otherwise his vassals would refuse to pay their tribute obligations and his troops would become discontented. The Durranis therefore needed to return to the same battlefields again and again when funds grew short. This proved most effective early on when dealing with the weak Mughals, but the growing power of the Sikhs in Punjab made such incursions ever harder. Difficulties in India also inspired revolts in Khorasan and put pressure on their western holdings as well.

From a military perspective the empire was highly centralized, with all power vested in its creator, Ahmad Shah. But provincial governors handled local administration and were practically independent of Qandahar in most nonmilitary matters. Such positions gave them so much autonomy that they were virtual mini-kingdoms. Recognizing this, Ahmad appointed his own sons to key regions such as Herat and Lahore. Beyond these core areas, though, he was forced to depend on his defeated enemies to govern their own territories as vassals, like the grandson of Nadir Shah Afshar in Khorasan and the Baluch chief Nasir Khan in Baluchistan. Because these governors maintained their own local base of support and had their own troops, they could rebel at the first sign of Durrani weakness. In addition, the strategy of maintaining stability by appointing sons to important governorships was effective as long as the ruler lived, but had negative consequences after he died. Princes then used their provinces as bases to fight for their own succession to the throne.

After Ahmad Shah's reign, succession battles among the ruler's sons (or between uncles and nephews) would characterize and debilitate the Afghan state for more than a century. The Turko-Mongolian tradition that restricted the inheritance of legitimate political authority to a few exclusive descent groups protected the dynasty from usurpation by outsiders. Yet as generations passed, the number of rivals from within this charmed circle grew dangerously large, since the Turko-Mongolian political tradition had no means of permanently excluding collateral heirs. No way, that is, except through death or disablement, given that the principle of bloody tanistry recognized the legitimacy of any royal contender who successfully defeated his rivals. Such bitter fights became particularly acute among the Durrani elite in the nineteenth century and periodically left the Afghan state close to collapse. Rulers found that gaining the throne was only the first step to power as they often spent decades reconquering the territories over which they were technically sovereign. Worse, this slow work would need to begin again when their own deaths sparked a new cycle of bloody tanistry among a new set of heirs.

PASHTUN TRIBAL RELATIONS

The political role of the Pashtun tribes in the Durrani Empire was problematic. Ahmad Shah and his successors needed their cooperation, but wanted to restrict their independence. One of their great successes was the reduction of the Ghilzais to a permanently subordinate status. While they were involved in a number of failed rebellions, they remained excluded from elite politics. That a tribe as large as the Ghilzai, which had formerly held Qandahar and toppled the Safavids, could be dealt with so easily demands some explanation. Elphinstone, the first British envoy to visit the Durrani court in the early nineteenth century, attributed the Ghilzai's vulnerability to their more egalitarian and decentralized internal organization. They were easy to unite for profitable military campaigns in foreign countries or in defense of their local interests, but otherwise ungovernable:

The internal government of the Ghiljies is entirely different from that of the Dooraunees. The chiefs of the former have now lost all the authority which they possessed under their own royal government. There is reason to doubt whether that authority ever was so extensive, as that introduced among the Dooraunees on the Persian model. It is more probable that the power of even the King of the Ghiljies, was small in his own country, and that the tulmultuary consent of the people to support his measures abroad, was dictated more by a sense of the interest and glory of the tribe than by any deference to the King's commands. Some appearances however warrant a supposition that his power was sufficient to check murders and other great disorders. Whatever the power of the King may have had formerly, it is now at an end, and that the aristocracy has fallen with it; and although it has left sentiments of respect in the minds of the people, yet that respect is so entirely unmixed with fear, that it has no effect whatever in controlling their actions. No Khaun of a tribe, or Mullik of a village, ever interferes as a magistrate to settle a dispute, or at least a serious one; they keep their own families and immediate dependants in order, but leave the rest of the people to accommodate their differences as they can.[37]

But there was another powerful external factor as well. After their expulsion from Qandahar, the Ghilzais no longer had a major urban center to use as a base. This may have been neither here nor there to an ordinary Ghilzai, but history has shown that no Pashtun group can rise to state power without first dominating a regional center. Sandwiched between Kabul and Qandahar, the formerly ruling Hotak Ghilzai had no room to build a power base of their own there. While they might get some revenue-taxing trade caravans through Ghazni when the government was weak, or assist in rebellions, they were too far from the real centers of power. This was also true of the Ghilzais in Laghman to the east. Though they might periodically dominate Jalalabad, this secondary center, too, was sandwiched between the greater urban centers of Kabul and Peshawar.

Ahmad Shah's dealings with his own Durrani tribe were more complex. The Durranis supplied him with the bulk of the irregular troops he needed, but he was also keen to keep them in check. Elphinstone explained that Ahmad and his Sadozai successors did this in a number of ways. First, there was the policy of governing the tribes lightly while levying heavy taxes on the nontribal parts of the empire, so as "to get men from the western and money from the eastern; with the provinces also, the practice of the government has been to exact little from those in the west, and use them for defence alone; but to avail itself of the resources of the eastern provinces, and of the means they afforded for the extension of territory."[38] Second was the strategy of divide and rule, in which it was "the King's policy to keep the Dooraunees in subjection to himself, while he exalts them over other Afghauns. For this purpose, he protects the Taujiks, and all others whose power he can use to depress the nobles, without endangering the ascendancy of his tribe."[39] Third was the fact that the royal largess granted to the Durranis had strings attached that bound them more closely to the state than other tribes, because "the lands of the Dooraunees were actually given to them on the condition of military service, and the principal foundation of their right to possession is a grant of the King."[40] Finally, as Elphinstone described it, a ruler never granted any tribal leaders political autonomy except out of necessity:

The government of the tribe of Dooraunees centres in the King, though even there, he is generally obliged to attend to the wishes of the heads of the clans. He also interferes in the interior management of the tribes on the plains, and near great towns; but he contents himself with levying his supplies of men and money from the rest, without any further interference in their affairs, than is occasionally required to preserve public tranquility."[41]

It is true that by bringing the Durranis to power, Ahmad Shah is rightly seen as the founder of an independent Afghanistan that was no longer just a contested border region of Iran or India. But there remained a natural friction between the pretensions of the autocratic ruler who had founded an empire and a people whose politically egalitarian ethos rendered such claims to preeminence suspect. Ahmad smoothed over this problem by appointing a *majlis* (council) composed of Pashtun clan elders to advise him. Though this gave the appearance of a partnership, such clan leaders appear to have had little influence on policy. The real conflict between royal pretensions and tribal republicanism, however, would not emerge until the reigns of Ahmad's successors, who never treated the tribes as partners.

The Decline of the Durrani Empire

When Ahmad Shah died in 1772, his son and heir designate, Timur Shah, succeeded to the throne after suppressing a revolt within his own clan in favor of his brother and executing its ringleaders. Timur then moved the capital from Qandahar to Kabul (outside the Pashtun tribal territory) in an attempt to reduce the influence of the Pashtun tribes permanently. He also surrounded himself with Qizilbash cavalry as his personal bodyguard and counterweight to the Pashtun tribes. These Qizilbash troops put down a number of rebellions by the Pashtun tribes. If there was any doubt about whether the empire was a tribal patrimony or a dynastic monopoly, Timur ended it. In this he followed the typical pattern described by ibn Khaldun for the sons of tribal leaders who saw their father's kinsmen as rivals rather than allies. Elphinstone (as usual) provided a good deal of context in this matter, observing that "there is some distinction of interests between the

King and the nation, and still greater difference of opinion regarding his legal powers; the King, the Courtiers, and the Moollahs, maintaining that he has all the authority possessed by Asiatic despots; and the people of the tribes considering him a monarch with very limited prerogatives. This produces a good deal of diversity in the actual exercise of royal authority."[42]

Elphinstone also noted that Timur had sidelined the tribal elite who still held appointments granted by his father by instituting new offices or altering the duties of old ones so that he could appoint his own officials to the most powerful positions. He made sure that such officials were men of low standing who owed their power only to his appointment. Unlike his father (or his successors), he did not appoint his sons to important governorships but rather only "men of little weight and influence; by which Timour hoped to secure himself from rebellions and obtained for the present prompt obedience to his orders, and complete control of all revenue."[43] He retained important Durrani chiefs at court, where they had no access to their own troops and fell completely under his control, guarded by his well-paid Qizilbash allies. Timur's finances were in good order, and he maintained such strict control over expenditures that he was not forced to raise revenues by means of military campaigns, as was the custom of his father. He went to war only to put down rebellions.

Such a conservative policy over a twenty-year reign would likely have proved a great success if Timur had been the ruler only of a secure small state and not a large fragile empire. But Ahmad Shah had left Timur with conquered territories that had yet to be incorporated administratively. I noted earlier that aggressive multigenerational expansion had been characteristic of long-lived Turko-Mongolian empires in the region. Babur's Mughal Empire was only secured after many campaigns by his son Humayun (r. 1530–56) and grandson Akbar (r. 1556–1605). Similarly, the Safavid Empire became stable under the aggressive policies of Shah Tahmasp (r. 1524–76), the son of its founder, Shah Isma'il. Elphinstone was of the opinion that the Durrani Empire, too, could have taken a similar course under more aggressive leadership. If Ahmad Shah's "plans had been pursued, there is no doubt that a government sufficiently strong to have secured its own stability, would have soon and easily been introduced through the whole great empire." Instead, because his son Timur focused on maintaining internal order. As a result, the remote provinces gradually withdrew themselves from the control of the court; the government lost its reputation and influence abroad; and the states that had been obliged to preserve their own territories by submission to Ahmed Shauh, now began to meditate schemes for aggrandizing themselves at the expense of the Dooraunees. The decay was not severely felt in Timour Shah's time; but the commencement was even then observable, and it advanced in rapid strides under the reigns of his successors.[44]

Even if the Durrani state had been stronger, its stability would have been sorely tested by the period of bloody tanistry that followed Timur Shah's death in 1793. Timur had failed even to name an heir, and the empire was soon fractured by a series of civil wars mounted by his many sons. Each contender waited for an opportunity to betray his rivals, and at least a half dozen proclaimed themselves king at one time or another. They fought and replaced each another at such a dizzying pace that it was hard to keep track of even the successful plots, coups, and murders that brought three rulers to power, let alone the more numerous ones that failed and left their perpetrators blinded, exiled, or dead. Zaman Shah (r. 1793–1800) came to the fore initially. He attempted to restore Durrani hegemony in India but failed, both because of the rising power of the Sikhs and because his brother Shah Mahmud, the governor of Herat, aided a Persian revolt in Khorasan that diverted Afghan forces to the west. In 1800, Mahmud deposed Zaman and blinded him, only to fall victim himself to another brother, Shah Shuja (r. 1803–9, 1839–42). Lucky enough to be imprisoned rather than blinded or killed, Mahmud returned to the throne again (r. 1809–18) and Shuja was forced into exile in India, where he never ceased plotting a return to power.[45]

The successive civil wars mounted by the Sadozai Popalzai princes (all descendants of Ahmad Shah) against one another created an opening for the powerful Barakzai Muhammadzai lineage. The Barakzais were a rival Durrani clan whose political prominence rose as allies of various Sadozai factions seeking power against their rivals. They had served as viziers to the Sadozai shahs, and thus came to know how the government worked and the weakness of their masters. But because the Popalzais had an exclusive claim to legitimacy, the Barakzais initially contented themselves with being the powers behind the throne. This was a dangerous business, because even a weak shah could order the exile or execution of his viziers, so it was only a matter of time before the Barakzais acted to displace their rivals more permanently. Yet so strong was the concept of Sadozai exclusivity that it would take more than forty years, and a disastrous Sadozai alliance with the British, to complete this process.

The Barakzai Muhammadzai lineage traced its political rise to Payinda Khan. Born in 1758, he succeeded his brother as chief of the Barakzai clan in 1775, and was granted the title of Sarfraz Khan by Timur Shah. Given charge of the Ghilzais, Payinda Khan defeated a rebellion against Timur and was instrumental in placing Shah Zaman on the throne upon Timur's death in 1793. Zaman returned the favor by stripping him of office in 1799 and executing him soon thereafter in hopes of reducing the influence of this upstart lineage. His actions had the opposite effect, because Fitih Khan, the eldest of Payinda Khan's twenty-one sons, took immediate revenge by blinding Zaman and placing Shah Mahmud on the throne in 1800. Although Mahmud lost power to Shah Shuja a few years later, the Barkakzais remained loyal and helped him regain power in 1809. But this did not quell the Sadozais's suspicion of the Barakzais because they remained the power behind the throne. In 1818, Mahmud attempted to curb Barakzai influence by imprisoning Fatih Khan before having him blinded and then cut into pieces. Fatih's brothers responded by seizing the throne in the name of a series of puppet Sadozai shahs they promoted as their pawns.[46]

Unfortunately, this merely set the stage for further warfare among the Barakzais themselves. This ended only with the rise of Dost Mohammad, another one of Payinda Khan's sons, who declared himself amir in 1826. But his kingdom was just a pale reflection of the once-magnificent Durrani Empire. Now shorn of its richest Indian and Persian possessions, it had become the Kingdom of Kabul, with rival clans holding Qandahar and Herat as independent fiefdoms.

Despite the political turmoil that engulfed Afghanistan in the early nineteenth century, Ahmad Shah had bequeathed the Durrani Pashtuns a ruling charisma that would last for the next two centuries. While the failure of his direct Sadozai descendants to maintain their exclusive dynastic privilege reflected an even faster pace of decline than ibn Khaldun had described among dynasties of egalitarian tribes, the political competition to replace them remained restricted to the Durrani elite—a hierarchical notion of rule otherwise foreign to Pashtun thinking. This was the true "Pearl of Pearls" that maintained the Durrani as rulers of Afghanistan—an inheritance ultimately more valuable than the soon-to-be-lost Koh-i-nur diamond or even lovely Kashmir. As men seized power, lost power, and plotted to regain power, the patterns of authority differed little from that practiced centuries earlier: rivals for leadership were all members of a large dynastic house who were more concerned about coups from within than by displacement from without. Legitimacy meant seizing power and displacing relatives, not competing with other groups. And as much as the subordinate tribes and ethnic groups may have resented Durrani power, even potentially powerful groups such as the Ghilzai Pashtuns never effectively challenged their right to rule even when they revolted against them. Yet this traditional world and its conventions were about to be challenged by the growing influence of European colonial powers that would present Afghanistan and its rulers with entirely new sets of problems as well as opportunities.

CHAPTER THREE

Anglo-Afghan Wars and State Building in Afghanistan

At the beginning of the nineteenth century, Afghan concepts of political legitimacy were still firmly rooted in the past. Competition for state power was restricted to a small Durrani elite, and their replacement meant little to the ordinary people on the ground. The government structure was decentralized and fragmented, dependent largely on the feudal levies of troops and plagued by a shortage of resources. Much would change by the end of the century, however. Afghanistan became a nascent national state. A regular army replaced tribal levies and mercenaries. A centralized government with a national bureaucracy displaced formerly autonomous regional leaders and their feudal clients. The role of the Afghan people also changed. They became more involved in struggles to defend the nation against foreign invaders and yet found themselves more oppressed by their own governments in the aftermath. The crucible bringing about these changes was the two wars that the Afghans fought with the British (1839–42 and 1878–80), or more accurately the consequences of these wars.

But one thing that this crucible strengthened rather than destroyed was the domination of Afghanistan's existing political elite. Dost Muhammad initially lost his throne during the First Anglo-Afghan War, but then returned to rule the country again for another twenty years. By the end of his reign, Afghanistan was unified not only under a single government but also under one in which his family was paramount. Dost Muhammad's descendants continued to rule Afghanistan despite a new period of civil war and another British invasion. It was this Second Anglo-Afghan War that brought Afghanistan's so called Iron Amir, Abdur Rahman (r. 1880–

1901), to the throne. He so successfully centralized power that the national government in Kabul appeared all-powerful. For better and for worse, this model of administration would be the standard by which his successors judged themselves during the next three-quarters of the twentieth century. How so many changes could come about and yet leave the old ruling dynasty in place is the question I will explore here.

AMIR DOST MUHAMMAD AND THE KINGDOM OF KABUL

Dost Muhammad faced severe internal challenges when he declared himself amir in Kabul. The Sadozais disputed his right to the throne. His kingdom was much reduced in size and divided into regions that were all but independent, and his financial base was precarious. Externally, three new players arrived on the international scene and threatened Afghan territories. The Sikhs under Ranjit Singh (r. 1801–39) had shorn Afghanistan of its last Indian provinces, built a powerful state in Punjab, and looked prepared to advance further west. The Russians had arrived on Afghanistan's western borders and were supporting Persian campaigns to retake Herat. The British had sent envoys to Afghanistan and appeared to have possible designs of their own on the country.

The shakiness of the Barakzai claims to the throne was apparent in Dost Muhammad's choice of the title of amir rather than shah. The dynastic aura of Ahmad Shah Durrani was still so strong that only his direct descendants were believed to have the right to take the title of shah. From the time of the expulsion of Shuja in 1818, the Barakzais had respected this tradition by appointing figurehead Sadozai descendants to sit on the throne—a pattern common in Turko-Mongolian regimes. Dost Muhammad broke with that tradition in 1826 by ruling directly in his own name with the title of amir after being coronated as *padshah* in a ceremony designed to resemble Ahmad Shah's own elevation to rulership in 1747.[1] Despite this sleight of hand, many Afghans still considered the Barakzai Muhammadzai usurpers. Shah Shuja, the Sadozai who had received the first British embassy to Afghanistan, was still at large and continued to seek the restoration of his line from exile in India. Indeed, the legitimacy of the

Sadozai shahs remained so strong that, as we will see, the British asserted that they were only helping Shuja reclaim his rightful authority when they invaded in 1839. Of course, a more practical reason for assuming a title less grandiose than shah was that the kingdom of Kabul was only a pale reflection of the original Durrani Empire. Nor were its remaining territories under Dost Muhammad's secure control. Peshawar had been lost to the Sikhs in 1834. Herat was ruled by a Sadozai prince independent of Kabul. The Uzbek amirs of Turkistan maintained de facto independence. The Durrani heartland in the south was ruled by a set of Dost Muhammad's half brothers, the Qandahar sardars, who were themselves periodic rivals for the throne.

At the beginning of his reign, Dost Muhammad's financial base was quite small: around a half-million rupees, derived from Kabul and the plains to the north. By the 1830s, when he dominated most of eastern Afghanistan, his annual revenue had increased to about 2.5 million rupees.[2] By comparison with the Durrani Empire, however, even this figure was still low: less than 10 percent of the 30 million rupees in revenue that the Sadozai shahs had commanded forty years earlier. In part this was because the eastern provinces that had supplied the bulk of the Durrani Empire's revenue had been lost, and Dost Muhammad could collect no revenue from the provinces that he did not as yet control (Qandahar and Herat). But an even bigger obstacle was the structure of the revenue system itself—one largely unchanged from the time it was created by Ahmad Shah. It had liberally distributed land grants, jagirs, in return for military services, and these consumed between 50 and 60 percent of the state's nominal revenue, even before calculating the amounts needed for administration or payments for regular troops.[3] Neither the rates of taxation on the Durrani elite nor the grants themselves could be altered without a much stronger military and political power than Dost Muhammad possessed.

More significantly, because the Durrani Empire had found it so much easier to extract revenue from its Indian provinces, it had never bothered to raise much money from more marginal areas within Afghanistan. Politically this was a good choice since it reduced local opposition to the government in areas where it had historically recruited irregular troops.

But Dost Muhammad did not have this luxury. Like a poor student searching every pocket, drawer, and sofa seat for whatever loose coins might turn up, Dost Muhammad focused his revenue-raising attention on areas that his predecessors had ignored. Since his government was confined largely to the Kabul River basin, he greatly increased the rate of tax collection on communities there as soon as he came to control them. Groups that had been lightly taxed by the Sadozai shahs (the Tajik Kohistanis north of Kabul; the Ghilzai tribes of Laghman, Jalalabad, and Ghazni; and the Hazaras in Bamiyan and Hazarajat) all found themselves targets of new government demands. The methods of tax collections were harsh. These often included the use of troops whose actions in the name of the amir differed little from those of a pillaging foreign army of occupation. Josiah Harlan, a military officer of American origin in Dost Muhammad's employ, described from firsthand experience the usual means of collecting such taxes in more remote regions:

> A body of one thousand cavalry is annually sent to collect the revenue. This corps is dispersed over the district in small divisions, each one with orders to collect, and is quartered upon the husbandman, who is obliged to subsist the soldiers so long as the revenue is unpaid! . . . The accumulated mass is dispatched to Caubul, which is the nearest mart of general commerce; a portion is sold for necessary cash expenses, another part is traded off by means of reciprocal necessities and much of the grain is retained for family use. The slaves are sold by government contract, but the government levies . . . a percentage on the amount of sale.[4]

Not surprisingly, such methods provoked opposition and even periodic rebellions by unhappy subjects, particularly in those regions that had not been previously subject to severe taxation. Such a policy of "internal imperialism," however, was to be expected in a state that had inherited the expenses of an imperial structure yet retained only the resources of a small kingdom to finance them. Having few other sources of income, Dost Muhammad's policies were therefore heavily extractive.

The projection of state power into formerly autonomous regions to raise revenues came at a high political cost. Such tactics were thus employed more out of desperation than choice. This problematic trade-off of

raising revenue by risking rebellion forced regimes to make careful calculations. Depending on the period chosen, Afghan regimes seemed hell-bent
on either forcibly extracting as much revenue as they could from the
countryside or avoiding rural areas completely as a revenue base. The decision about which policy to employ rested on a simple equation: the degree
of revenue sought by any Afghan government from its countryside was
inversely related to the availability of other sources of income elsewhere. As
we will see, this encouraged Afghan rulers to seek foreign revenue sources
as a way to avoid political conflict with their own people.

For the first ten years of his reign, Dost Muhammad spent most of his
time consolidating his limited power and extending it beyond Kabul. Initially he had to contend with troubles caused by the old Sadozai ruler Shah
Shuja as well as rivalries within his own immediate family. He had external
enemies too, most notably the Sikhs. He organized a jihad against them
after they seized Peshawar both in hopes of recovering the city as well as to
buttress his own legitimacy as a Muslim ruler. While he won a battle against
them in 1836, he failed to restore Afghan control of the region. In further
hopes of doing so, he sought a diplomatic alliance with the British as a
counterweight to the Sikhs. He did not receive the alliance but did get
British aid in defending the city of Herat from the Persians (1837–38),
which brought the Russians in contact with Afghanistan. But the British
position on Afghanistan had by that time moved away from helpful neutrality to a more aggressive policy that sought the domination of Afghanistan as a client state to create a large defensive buffer between its Indian
holdings and the expanding power of Russia.

Dost Muhammad was willing to come to terms with the British, and
their key agent in Kabul, Alexander Burnes, believed that he would be a
more reliable ally than the aging and unpopular Shuja.[5] But Lord Auckland, governor-general of India, thought otherwise and struck a deal to
return Shuja to the throne with the help of a British invasion in alliance
with the Sikhs. In 1839, the "Army of the Indus," consisting of around
twenty-one thousand troops and accompanied by thirty-eight thousand
camp followers, crossed the Indus River and had reached Quetta by March
in preparation for its attack on Qandahar. Of those who later remained to
occupy Afghanistan, few would come back alive.

The First Anglo-Afghan War and Its Consequences

The Defeat and Surrender of Dost Muhammad Khan

Just how weak Dost Muhammad's position was became apparent when the British took his half brother's realm of Qandahar in April without opposition and then marched north. After taking Ghazni in a severe fight in July, the British were on the outskirts of Kabul a few weeks later. Unable to rouse a resistance against the British following the capture of Ghazni, even after invoking the religious necessity for all Muslims to come together in a jihad against an infidel invader, Dost Muhammad abandoned Kabul in early August. The British then occupied the city and reinstalled Shuja as the shah in the fortified palace complex of Bala Hissar. Dost Muhammad fled north seeking assistance from the amir of Bukhara, who instead made him a virtual prisoner. On his return to Afghanistan in August 1840, he raised Uzbek troops in the north, but these deserted him after a defeat by the British in Bamiyan. Dost Muhammad then moved to Kohistan, where the local Tajiks were already in rebellion against the British. In early November he led them to a victory in a battle north of Kabul. A day after this success, Dost Muhammad rode into Kabul and surrendered to the British, who promptly exiled him to India with all honors.

Interpreting Dost Muhammad's surrender has long presented difficulties for Afghan historians. How could the past (and future) amir, founder of the dynasty that would rule Afghanistan into the next century, desert his people and country at such a crucial time, particularly when his star now appeared to be in ascendancy? And after doing so, why did his reputation remain so untarnished that he was not only able to return and rule the country but also retain his place as one of Afghanistan's most respected leaders, even today? Part of the problem lies in an anachronistic view of loyalty, leadership, and nationhood in a time of change. The British invasion of Afghanistan was rooted in the belief that political legitimacy was the domain of an exclusive elite and the replacement of one Durrani leader in Kabul by another would not provoke a rebellion. Indeed, it was striking just how quickly the vast majority of the Durrani elite and their allies such as the Qizilbash (to whom Dost Muhammad was related through his mother) fell in line to support Shuja's restoration. The argument that he, as a Sadozai descendant of Ahmad Shah Durrani, had a better right to the throne than any Muhammadzai was powerful. (Dost Muhammad had even told the British that he would step down as amir in favor of Shuja if he could retain the role of vizier, the political relationship that formerly existed between the Sadozais and Muhammadzais earlier in the century.) That Shuja was returning to power on the point of British bayonets was no asset, and in fact would eventually prove his downfall, but he had a sound claim to the Afghan throne. Even if his claim were less sound, nonelite groups were expected to accept his fait accompli and get on with their lives.

The early collapse of elite resistance and their co-optation by the British was probably instrumental in bringing about Dost Muhammad's surrender. On his return from Bukhara, he found himself leading a weak resistance composed almost entirely of marginal ethnic groups with no personal loyalty to him. The Uzbeks had abandoned his cause after their first encounter with the British, and the Kohistanis were more anti-British than pro–Dost Muhammad. (Only a year earlier they had revolted against him to facilitate the return of Shuja.) Perhaps most important, Dost Muhammad could not conceive of popular rebellions as anything more than nuisances to a foe who was overwhelmingly superior in arms and had a seemingly endless supply of money. After all, he had only recently put down rebellions by these same groups employing only a fraction of the resources now available to the British. And the British had used their initial advantages with skill. The advance of their army into Afghanistan and the defeat of all forces that opposed them proved their military might. Their political agents moved swiftly to buy the support of prominent Durrani notables in the south and Ghilzai leaders in the east while subsidizing the clergy. Dost Muhammad might have been able to win a few more pieces in this bloody chess match, but he could see no way of avoiding eventual checkmate and so resigned the game.

The image of a chess game is more than metaphoric here. Rulers in Turko-Persia were professionals, and there was a political protocol open to losers—one that not only preserved their lives but also offered the possibility of a new game and their restoration to power. For example, at the lower level in the political hierarchy, leaders of tribal rebellions would often appear before the king with nooses around their necks or grass in their mouths (like cows) to express their abject submission. If their tribe was powerful, they would likely be fined and forgiven unless the ruler was truly vexed. (It was considered shortsighted to execute too many of today's rebels since they might be tomorrow's allies.) For the rulers of fallen states the possibilities were broader since they (unlike internal rebels) had a duty to fight, and a valiant reputation was respected by friend and foe alike. On defeat, they might flee to a neighboring state for refuge and wait for better times. Or particularly when confronted with an expanding empire, they might simply surrender to their victorious foe with the expectation of becoming his feudatory. Both the ruling clans of the Durranis and Ghilzais had come to power locally as feudatories of Safavids in this way. The Durrani Empire itself had reappointed local rulers as their governors in India and Khorasan after first defeating them. Before they were sacked by the Sikhs, the Muhammadzai sardars in Peshawar had accepted such a position under Ranjit Singh. Because modern historians overlook the cultural nuances of the political hierarchy in central Asia that the participants of the period took for granted, they see defeat and surrender as moral failings rather than the occupational hazards of being a professional ruler.

By riding into Kabul alone and voluntarily tendering his submission to William Macnaghten, Britain's political representative, Dost Muhammad was recognizing that a new empire had emerged, in which the British now reigned as the regional hegemonic power. In such a changing world Afghan rulers needed to adjust their policies to adapt. As professional rulers, they were accustomed to making hard choices and taking risks. Dost Muhammad rightly concluded that the British needed the cooperation of the old ruling elite to maintain control of places like Afghanistan that were difficult or impossible to rule directly. He also accepted the principle that

like the Mughal Emperors whom they had supplanted, the East India Company now held the right to appoint the ruler of his country. As a monarch in his own right, Dost Muhammad Khan also indicated to Macnaghten, the supreme representative of the British civil power in Afghanistan, that he was prepared to co-operate with the "new world order," rather than resist it. However in doing so, he made plain that he would do so as a ruler in his own right and not like the quisling, Shah

Shuja, who required the presence of a foreign, infidel army to keep him on the throne.[6]

The British, also familiar with this protocol, treated Dost Muhammad with great respect. They refused Shuja's demand that he be turned over to him for execution as a rebel, and sent Dost Muhammad to India with a tidy pension. Macnaghten even wrote a letter to Auckland explaining that the British owed him more deference than their client king, Shuja. "I trust the Dost will be treated with liberality. His case has been compared to Shah Shoojah; and I have seen it argued that he should not be treated more handsomely than His Majesty was; but surely the cases are not parallel. The Shah had no claim upon us. We had no hand in depriving him of his kingdom, whereas we ejected the Dost, who had never offended us, in support of our policy, of which he was the victim."[7]

And Dost Muhammad was not wrong in seeing the realm of rulership as the preserve of an elite and not ordinary people—a position held as strongly by the British in India as it was by the Durranis in Afghanistan. Like the professional ruler that he was, he took his refreshment and awaited the start of the next game—one he knew was bound to come, and come soon.

Restructuring the Afghan State

One of the first priorities of the British occupation was the reorganization of the Afghan state and its finances. Shah Shuja proved an obstacle in this process because he was a product of the old system and not inclined to change it except under pressure. The British therefore gradually took control of the government in order to make administrative and military reforms that would increase state power. These reforms and the unanticipated consequences of their own occupation soon made the British position in Afghanistan less rather than more secure.

The Durrani elite acquiesced to Shuja's return to the throne on the assumption that the traditional system of military payments would continue. Indeed, Shuja's legitimacy as a ruler depended as much on his ability to shower his followers with money as it did on his royal descent. The existing system was highly lucrative for both the officials who made such grants and for those who received them. Half the state's revenue was devoted to such payments, although the troops maintained in this fashion were of negligible military value and their numbers were inflated by adding fictional ones to the payroll. But this was not the point. Local chiefs used such funds and land grants to maintain powerful patronage networks, not to fight wars. In fact, their duties were largely limited to collecting the taxes needed to pay them. The British viewed the whole system as thoroughly corrupt and in need of reform. To increase the state's power, they planned to replace the old feudal cavalry with a professional infantry under the direct command of the central government.

This change would increase the power of the central government and reduce the autonomy of the chiefs—goals long sought by Afghan rulers too. Dost Muhammad himself had created an additional infantry force under foreign officers for this reason, but had not tampered with the organization of the costly irregular troops. At least some in the British command recognized the political trade-offs that had led to his hesitation in this matter. What the British condemned as the corrosion of corruption was unfortunately still the main glue that held the Afghan state in one piece. In 1840, Captain R. S. Trevor, the British officer given the command of these irregular forces, cautioned, "We must not look on the Irregular Cavalry merely as a military body. In that light 3 Regiments might annihilate it tomorrow, but as an instrument which enables H.M.'s principal subjects to appropriate a greater part of his revenues without making any return, and which has continued so long that its destruction would certainly be considered an invasion of private property."[8]

Two new corps, the Janbaz (one thousand men) and Hazirbash (eight hundred men), were created in June 1840 over the objections of Shuja, who saw the distribution of patronage passing from his hands to the British. The immediate savings were substantial: the payments to chiefs for irregular troops fell by more than one-quarter, from 1.3 million rupees in 1839 to 1 million rupees in 1841.[9] When the chiefs complained, Trevor was no longer sympathetic but instead bluntly expressed the view "that in the course of two years all the chiefs of the military class should be dismissed from his service, and that what support they may receive till that time they should consider as charity given to them."[10] Since it was the supply of feudal military units and the tax revenues granted to maintain them that sustained the Durrani elite, the threat to abolish the system undercut both their prosperity and political power. This was a deliberate act, for as Malcolm Yapp explained, "British policy was aimed ultimately at the destruction of these forces and constant efforts were made to abridge their privileges."[11]

Another blow to the system of redistributive allowances within the Afghan state was the sudden influx of vast sums of money into the economy. As part of the war effort, the British had flooded Afghanistan with silver rupees and letters of credit drawing on the Indian banking system to pay for their occupation, salaries for their soldiers, the administration of the country, and subsidies to influential Afghan leaders. (The total cost of the war to the British over three years was estimated at around eight million pounds, while Dost Muhammad's prewar income had amounted to less than the equivalent of two hundred thousand pounds annually, little of it in cash.) Influxes of cash money are always disruptive to any subsistence-based economy because they create new sets of winners and losers. In this case, it increased the power and influence of those engaged in trade, who provided needed commodities and services. It undermined the social and political standing of those whose influence was based on feudal obligations to the state, or who owned underproductive landed estates. Because the flow of British expenditures pouring into Afghanistan were so many orders of magnitude larger than those ever available to its Afghan rulers, their impact can be compared to plugging a table lamp into a high-voltage electric line.

The 4,500 troops and 11,500 camp followers who remained in Kabul put a huge burden on a poorly integrated Afghan domestic economy, and commodity prices rose sharply. Macnaghten complained that by June 1841, prices had risen by 500 percent. This may be an exaggeration or the result of a temporary supply problem, but even if prices had only doubled or tripled in two years, it would have justified Afghan complaints that the British had enriched the grain merchants, starved the poor, and made the chiefs destitute.[12] Inflation also hurt those classes of people, such as mullahs, who normally received fixed stipends for their services. In this context, the constant complaint that the British fostered immorality and prostitution among women in Kabul was also hardly surprising in a city now awash in cash and beyond the control of the "traditional authorities." The money economy penetrated the immediate countryside as well. The British reworked the tax system to make it more efficient, and in a single year increased tax receipts around Kabul from 225,000 to 900,000 rupees. This was done in part by selling tax farming rights to international fruit merchants, who encouraged the substitution of export cash crops like grapes for less profitable subsistence crops.[13]

The Defeat and Withdrawal of the British

Such rapid economic and political disruptions would likely have induced opposition under any circumstances, but the discontent was magnified by policy blunders and incompetence. With the restoration of Shah Shuja, the East India Company in Calcutta saw its costly invasion as a "mission accomplished" and soon put intense pressure on its officials in Kabul to reduce expenses. In response, these officials cut the annual stipends paid to the Ghilzai chiefs in the east from eighty to forty thousand rupees as part of a wide range of economies that included dropping stipends to the mullahs, whose support they had earlier paid for. The Ghilzai chiefs were outraged at this reduction, coming at a time when their original grants had already been eroded by inflation. They declared a jihad and revolted in September 1841, cutting communications with Jalalabad. Initially, this revolt was not designed to force the British out of the country but instead to restore their stipends. Troops from Kabul reopened the roads, but rather than conciliate the Ghilzai chiefs involved, Macnaghten threatened to replace them if they refused to accept the stipend cuts and deliver hostages for their good behavior as well.[14]

Meanwhile in Kabul disaffection was growing. The ulema complained that the British were interfering with their administration of justice in the name of fighting corruption. Such corruption unfortunately provided a great part of their income. The British were also seizing religious endowments (*waqf*) from local shrines and adding them to the state coffers. The Durrani elite at court, as noted earlier, were alienated by the rapid changes in government that reduced their income and influence. In such a volatile atmosphere, a riot by a small Kabul mob in November that resulted in the murder of Burnes quickly evolved into a large-scale attack on the British cantonment, which the Ghilzais and Kohistanis joined in. There was no unified leadership, and the chiefs involved acted as independent agents, many of whom sought British bribes as their price for going home. (The Ghilzais, for example, were demanding two hundred thousand rupees to depart.) Only with the arrival of Muhammad Akbar, Dost Muhammad's favorite son, did the fight against the British become well organized. Akbar put such pressure on the poorly positioned cantonment that the British sued for terms in December. By this time, however, events had transformed their bad situation into a desperate one. A series of negotiations between Akbar and Macnaghten designed to come to some accommodation ended only in Macnaghten's murder. In January 1842, the British agreed to withdraw their army and camp followers unconditionally from Kabul in return for Akbar's promise of safe passage. Those who were not taken prisoner were either massacred by the Ghilzais en route or froze to death in the mountain passes. Only one British survivor made it safely to Jalalabad.[15]

The well-known story of the destruction of the Kabul expeditionary force has overshadowed the internal changes that the British implemented—changes that would remain even after they had gone. Historians have instead argued over what caused this famous defeat.[16] According to most nationalist Afghan historians, reaction to the British occupation produced an inevitable and universal antiforeign, pro-Islamic, popular rebellion whose success was never in doubt. British accounts have tended to see the various uprisings as uncoordinated, prompted by religious fanaticism, and exacerbated by British policy blunders and incompetent leadership. From the standpoint of changing concepts of legitimacy, the two most significant aspects of the revolts against the British in winter 1841–42 were its new religious justifications and tribal participation.

Until 1840 religion had played a minor role in internal Afghan politics because fighting had always been Muslim on Muslim. Raising the banner of jihad had been a popular way to mobilize Afghans outward for invasions directed at the polytheists on the Indian plain or their Muslim rulers. But the British occupation of Afghanistan in support of Shuja raised the question of whether his regime had lost the authority normally inherent to a Muslim ruler. If Shuja's government was just a cloak for the rule of foreign infidels, then rebellion against it would be justified. The charge that the

government had betrayed Afghanistan's Muslims and deserved to be toppled was therefore a constant theme in the propaganda directed against the
British and Shuja. It had surprisingly little resonance when the British first
invaded. It gained traction as the occupation continued, particularly as the
British began to direct more of the government's workings themselves.
Putting Afghan opposition in a religious framework also made it more difficult for the British to mobilize previously willing allies among the Ghilzai
chiefs. These chiefs declared that it would be politically fatal to take a public stance against a popular jihad opposing foreign occupation when it was
so strongly supported by their followers. Of course, as ibn Khaldun had
observed, religion had always been the best way to unite tribes that were
otherwise too divided to unite on any other basis. It also ennobled more
self-interested political, economic, and personal motives. Shuja himself
complained that "these men are not influenced by considerations of religion, they give their lives for the wealth of this world and do not fear
death."[17] That may have been true, but leaping to a "defense of Islam" to
justify resisting a regime in Kabul or its policies would henceforth become
a sword that was rarely sheathed in Afghan politics, regardless of whether
foreigners were actually present on Afghan soil.

The rebellions against the British did not originate within Afghanistan's
Durrani elite. Although those who had experienced a loss of power may
have incited others to violence, they took on leadership roles only well
after the fighting had started. Instead, the first rebellions were mounted by
more marginal groups that had their own grievances. The most important
of these were the Pashtun Ghilzai tribes to the east and south of Kabul, and
the Tajik Kohistanis of the plains and mountains north of Kabul. Chiefs
and clergy from these regions who mobilized their own fighters were at the
center of the resistance, not the existing forces of the irregular cavalry that
were commanded by the Durranis. The trouble was also localized. The
Durranis in Qandahar did not rise at all until two months after Kabul had
fallen and then failed to take the city. Nor were there uprisings among the
Hazaras, the Uzbeks, or in distant Herat. But in spite of their crucial contributions to the success of the war, neither the Kohistanis nor the Ghilzais
took the opportunity to put themselves into power. They instead sought
out military and political leadership from the existing (and politically vacillating) Barakzai and Sadozai elite. For example, the Kohistanis initially

raised troops in the name of Shuja until he denounced them for using his name and forged seals to justify their rebellion. When it became clear that Shuja was sticking with the British, the Ghilzais and Kohistanis then rallied around Akbar when he took command of the forces besieging their cantonment in Kabul. Although it was he who took the lead in dealing with the British politically, Akbar's power then and in the months that followed depended more on his Ghilzai allies than his Barakzai kinsmen.[18]

The eighteen months after the British lost Kabul in January 1842 was a period of political complexity and rapid change, including the British reoccupation of Kabul in September 1842 and their departing the country for good before winter set in. It is therefore usually more convenient to take up the story when Dost Muhammad returned to Afghanistan from his Indian exile in June 1843 and began his second reign. But the period is worth examining briefly because it reveals just how tenacious the old patterns of political legitimacy and organization remained. In particular, it demonstrates that the return of the Barakzais was by no means a foregone conclusion, that defeating the British had done little to unite the Afghans internally, and that even the mobilization of a historically unprecedented range of people to fight the war had not dented the small Durrani elite's monopoly on power.

Shuja remained in Kabul after the British withdrawal in January 1842. In a political system where such concepts as patriotism or nationalism were as yet unknown, his previous actions may have been unpopular, but they did not trump his hereditary right to rule since a king cannot be a traitor to himself. Indeed, his political position actually improved over the next few months. Within the Bala Hissar fortress, a Hindustani and Arab garrison protected Shuja from attack. Still in possession of two million rupees that he had squirreled away during the previous two years, he could afford to maintain more troops than any of his rivals. Such resources were now critical in the renewed internal struggle for power between the Barakzais under Akbar and the Sadozais under Shuja, not to mention the large cast of more minor supporting characters still deciding which way (or on whom) to jump. Even as they both declared the necessity for Muslim unity to drive the remaining British forces back to India, they undercut each other politically at every turn.

Although now a hero of the jihad, Akbar's many problems included a lack of funds, competition with his elder cousin Zaman Khan over who should lead the Barakzais, and general opposition by many court factions to the restoration of Barakzai power. Shuja's main problem (besides the disappearance of his British protection) was his need to walk a dangerous tightrope. He had to prove that he was not "pro-infidel" while secretly keeping his ties to the British (who might return). Thus Shuja publicly proclaimed his support for the jihad and demanded the British withdraw from Jalalabad, but privately wrote to urge them to march on Kabul as soon as possible. His enemies suspected this double game and tested his fidelity by demanding that he participate personally in the war by leading reinforcements to Jalalabad. After receiving sworn promises from the Barakzais that they would be faithful to him, he emerged from the palace in early April and was promptly assassinated by a Barakzai. His son, Fath Jang, then declared himself shah. The struggle between the Barakzais and Sadozais now entered a new phase, which soon ended with Akbar's victory. Akbar captured Bala Hissar in June, garrisoned it with Ghilzai troops, and recognized Fath Jang (who was now his effective prisoner) as shah in a regime where he served as vizier and undisputed strongman. Akbar then fended off his cousin Zaman's bid for power by using his new government's resources to buy more allies and having a tribal council reaffirm that the exiled Dost Muhammad remained the true king.[19]

Installing a regime in which a strongman ruled in the name of a more prestigious though purely nominal head of state was a classic political ploy in Turko-Persian empires, where inherited hierarchy trumped mere talent. And seven centuries of experience within such empires had so deeply permeated Afghanistan's ruling elite's concepts of political legitimacy that they were uneasy about rewriting its rules. Afghan tribes might abandon their chiefs when they displeased them and refuse to recognize any inherited right to rule on principle, but the Durrani elite judged itself by the standards of a Persianate political system in which establishing the legitimacy of a new dynasty was much harder. Thus, the process of replacing the declining Sadozais with Barakzai rulers first begun in 1815 still lay uncompleted in 1842. In spite of all the opprobrium heaped on the Sadozais for their cooperation with the British and Akbar's own prestige as a leader of the jihad, the legacy of Ahmad Shah Durrani's dynastic charisma adhered so strongly to his direct descendants that removing them was politically dangerous. With so many factions still in play, the nominal recognition of a Sadozai shah as head of state had too many political advantages to dispense with. It allowed Akbar to avoid the charge of usurpation that had long plagued the Barakzais, isolate his cousin Zaman, and conciliate the Popalzais in Qandahar, and proved useful in negotiating with the British. It also neatly avoided the question of whether he was superseding his father as amir. Instead Akbar justified his own right to rule in terms of religion, putting himself above existing tribal and dynastic politics. He explained his actions this way in a letter to the Shinwari Pashtuns of the Khyber area after he took power in Kabul:

> As it was an object of paramount importance that in the contest with the race of misguided infidels the whole of the members of the true faith should be united together and the attainment and perfecting of this object appeared indispensable, therefore did the whole of the devoted followers of the true faith consent to choose me as their head, and to place themselves under my counsel. All the tribes and leaders of the Douranees, Ghilzyees, Kuzzilbashes and Ka[b]ulees and Kohistanees have submitted to me.[20]

This political restructuring might have had a more significant impact on Afghan history had the British withdrawn at this time, as the Afghans learned they had been ordered to do. But the situation changed dramatically when Calcutta reversed course and dispatched reinforcements to Jalalabad and Qandahar in August with instructions to retake Kabul. Akbar's troops were no match for these forces, and he had to flee, leaving the British to reoccupy the capital in September. They then lay waste to the city and the surrounding countryside. When Fath Jang, who had remained in the Bala Hissar palace, learned that the British had no intention of staying in Afghanistan or giving aid to any regime in Kabul (a new government in London having sworn off such adventures), he abdicated and left with them. A younger brother took his place, but this last of the Sadozai shahs fled to Peshawar before the year was out. The British then allowed Akbar's father, Dost Muhammad, to return to Kabul to rule again as amir.[21]

Dost Muhammad's Second Reign

Amir Dost Muhammad's second reign took place within a new political and economic environment. The Sadozais were now gone for good, and the structure of government was stronger. The amir was the main beneficiary of the domestic reforms that the British had put in place, particularly their creation of a more professional army and an improved tax structure. The Durrani tribal chiefs also had far less political influence at court—a goal that Dost Muhammad had long sought. The power of other groups also fractured once the British left. Following the expected pattern in segmentary political systems, once the enemy that united them was gone, the old internal disputes among the Ghilzais and Kohistanis came to the fore, allowing Dost Muhammad to follow a policy of divide and rule until his power became strong enough to subdue them directly. The proven superiority of a disciplined and well-trained army—a type of army that Dost Muhammad had long hoped to employ—finally gave the central government enough military power to exert its authority over the whole country. Externally, Dost Muhammad came to an understanding with the British not to interfere in Afghan affairs if he did not bother them. A disgruntled Akbar opposed this last policy and wanted to send Afghan troops once again to the plains of India. But he died, perhaps poisoned, in 1847, and none of Dost Muhammad's other sons had the same will to oppose their father.[22]

Whereas during the fourteen years of his first reign (1826–39) Dost Muhammad was barely able to control the region between Kabul and Ghazni, by the end of the twenty years of his second reign in 1863, he had retaken control of almost all of today's Afghanistan. During this process, he increased his annual revenue base from 2.5 to 7 million rupees. His first targets beyond Kabul were Jalalabad and Bamiyan. He then invaded northern Afghanistan. By 1849–50 most of the north fell under his control, although Badakhshan retained nominal independence until 1859, and Maimana remained in the orbit of Herat. Dost Muhammad subdued and taxed the powerful Ghilzai tribes around Ghazni in the early 1850s as he pushed Kabul's influence south. This put him in conflict with his half brothers, the Qandahar sardars, who had ruled the south (off and on) since 1820. The death of the last of these brothers allowed Dost Muhammad to dispossess their heirs and seize Qandahar in 1855. Herat, long under the nominal rule of a Sadozai prince, was finally annexed by Dost Muhammad in 1863, only a few months before his death.

Dost Muhammad was cautious in his external relations in a time of rapid change. Following the death of Ranjit Singh in 1839, the Sikhs' power declined. They lost two wars with the British (in 1845–46 and 1848–49), after which Punjab and other Sikh holdings became part of India. Since the British maintained the old Sikh frontiers, Afghanistan now had the British as its immediate neighbor in the east. British policy toward Afghanistan (and the Pashtun tribes of the NWFP) during this period was famously described as one of "masterly inactivity."[23] The same might be said of Dost Muhammad as well. While he was constantly on campaign internally, his attitude toward the British was wary but nonconfrontational. For example, when the Sikhs abandoned Peshawar, the Afghans reoccupied it in 1849, only to withdraw when the completeness of the British victory over the Sikhs became clear. Afghanistan's formal relations with British India resumed in 1855 with the Treaty of Peshawar. It promised peace and friendship as well as the respect of existing borders, along with a vague promise of mutual aid against common enemies. The recognition of existing borders meant that the amir was tacitly accepting Britain's occupation of Peshawar, formerly seen as an integral part of Afghanistan. Although not as a quid pro quo, Dost Muhammad did get British support for Kabul's claims on Herat and the west. That region was still ruled by strongmen in the name of the Sadozais. These individuals allied with the Persians, who occupied Herat in 1856. In response, the British first provided Dost Muhammad with four thousand muskets and five hundred thousand rupees to resist the Persian takeover. In 1857, they agreed to a second treaty that included another four thousand muskets and a hundred thousand rupees a month to last as long as the Persians remained a threat. The Persian threat soon vanished, though, after they lost a three-month war with the British, agreeing to withdraw and renounce their claims on Herat by treaty in 1857. Yet the amir's payments continued to arrive for an additional eighteen months after the war ended and eventually totaled 2.6 million rupees. Although not part of any formal agreement, the extra funds rewarded the amir for not assisting the Indian Mutiny of 1857, an earthquake that almost toppled the British raj.[24]

Dost Muhammad's failure to assist in what the Indians would later see as a war for independence was not popularly viewed by most Afghans. They saw the uprising by the raj's sepoy troops as an opportunity to follow up on their own victory, retake Peshawar, and perhaps expel the British from India entirely. Given the difficulties that the British faced, this result was not beyond the realm of possibility. The British representative then in Qandahar, Henry Bellew, certainly feared the consequences of an Afghan intervention because "a word from Dost Mohammad would have sent the tribes in a wave of fanatical irredentism to overrun and possess the rich valley of Peshawar and the Derajat."[25] But Dost Muhammad, ever the conservative realist, thought that outcome was unlikely. The British had just aided him in dealing with Herat, and far from expecting them to exit the stage, he believed they were not yet finished expanding their empire. He said so directly in response to a plea to intervene by the amir of Bukhara:

> How can I . . . believe the word of the King of Bokhara and break so good a union as one I have made with the British? If I had known the King of Bokhara to be true, I would have never joined with the British, and I well know that my own kingdom, and that of Bokhara, will one day be annexed to the British territories. I have therefore entered into an alliance . . . with the view to keeping my country as long as possible.[26]

Such an admission might appear surprising in the afterglow of the Afghan victory against the British a decade before. Dost Muhammad was, of course, also wrong about the threat to Bukhara, or at least about what country would do the annexing. It was Russia that went to war with Bukhara and added it to its empire in 1868. But Dost Muhammad was not wrong in foreseeing that the days of masterly inactivity would eventually end as British memories of their Afghan defeat faded and their fears of Russian expansion grew. Twenty years after Dost Muhammad's death, the British would indeed shift to a new and more aggressive "Forward Policy." This policy aimed to incorporate Afghanistan into the British Empire to create a "scientific frontier" that would preempt any danger to India from the north.[27] As to its inevitability, however, Dost Muhammad may have underestimated both the ability of the Afghans to resist and disrupt their plans and the growing British willingness to substitute rupees for bayonets to achieve their strategic ends when dealing with Afghanistan.

NEW FORCES IN AN OLD AFGHANISTAN

The interaction with the British had ended up strengthening the Durrani state and the elite who ran it, but at the same time it changed the nature of the relationship between the population and the central government. Part of this change can be explained in terms of the military technology available to both the central government and the rural population. It made rebellions far more dangerous than they had been in the past while also providing stronger tools for their suppression. The other change was more subtle, and took a longer time to develop or at least be recognized. This was the growing participation in politics by nonelite groups in the face of foreign intervention, which forced existing governments to make new calculations about what types of policies they should pursue.

The Changing Nature of Military Power in the Nineteenth Century

Through the beginning of the nineteenth century, the rulers of Afghanistan had measured their military strength in terms of controlling the horse cavalry. Expensive to maintain but overwhelmingly superior in battle, these forces made warfare the exclusive domain of elite groups. The categories of landed estates given to support these troops and their leaders consumed a major portion of a state's potential revenue. By contrast, the mobilization either of tribal mountaineers or rural peasants as infantry was militarily secondary. These auxiliaries could rarely turn the tide of war because they often had little or no experience in organized warfare, and fought on foot, armed only with shields, long knives, and spears. They were no match for the professional cavalry troops. While such groups frequently constituted the core of rebellions against the Mughal or Safavid rule, the best they could hope for was to keep these empires out of marginal regions, which were in any event unprofitable to occupy.

The First Anglo-Afghan War therefore marked a military watershed: nonstate forces that had previously played only a secondary role in the region's history had defeated the British. Whole sections of the Afghan population that had previously been excluded from politics had fought against the British in a national cause, even if they had not conceived of it as such. One reason they were able to do this was the changing technology and economics of warfare in south Asia, which made such a revolt far more dangerous than those in the past. Gunpowder weapons such as cannons and camel-mounted matchlock guns had been introduced into south Asia as early as the sixteenth century, but because they were expensive and needed professionals to operate them, they strengthened the hands of existing states. By the beginning of the nineteenth century, changes in the military strength of the people inhabiting marginal regions increased with the introduction of cheap muskets and later rifles. This allowed for wider (and more effective) participation in warfare by larger numbers of people.[28]

The mountaineers now came to war with their own gunpowder arms and could fight effectively at a distance, particularly in ambush. As Rudyard Kipling observed in an often-quoted line from "Arithmetic on the Frontier":

A scrimmage in a Border station—
A canter down a dark defile—
Two thousand pounds of education
Drops to a ten-rupee *jezail*.[29]

Such tactics, of course, were hallmarks of a classic guerrilla war strategy, in which the aim was to make it more costly for the invader to continue the occupation than to leave. The British had been driven from Afghanistan by the losses suffered at the hands of such irregulars, not because they lost pitched battles with regular armies. To prove this point (if only to themselves), the British returned to Kabul in fall 1842 to take revenge and easily defeated every Afghan force that resisted them.

Succeeding Afghan governments took a lesson from this. Their old feudal cavalry forces were not a match for a European-style army; but they also were no longer as effective countering rural rebellions against the state. It was not just weaponry that was involved, though. Cavalry troops continued to make up about half of the army, but they were now better organized, and combined with infantry and artillery. The real advantage of a well-trained and properly equipped army under professional officers was its consistency. Unlike the old feudal levies or tribal armies (*lashgar*), they did not depend on the cooperation of fickle chiefs, could regroup and fight again after a setback, and did not disperse seasonally. The creation of a European-style armed force therefore became a priority for all Afghan rulers in the nineteenth century. This military buildup was not designed to protect the country from invasion but rather to keep the rural population in line and the regions under Kabul's control. This marks an entirely new conception of warfare because in old Turko-Persia the fear was rebellion by subject princes, not subject populations. One simply ignored troublesome people in marginal areas. Yet in the wake of the expulsion of the British, Afghanistan's ruling elite could no longer dismiss the danger from these groups. The equations of power had altered, and this required a new and more complex strategy of government.

Postwar Reconsiderations and Recalculations

The political consequences of the First Anglo-Afghan War were profound, but the lessons that the British, the Durrani elite, and the Afghan people drew from it were quite different. As far as the British were concerned, the war proved that the Durrani elite were incapable of controlling their own people. Hence any future occupation of Afghanistan as a colony, even with the cooperation of its ruling class, would likely prove a questionable venture. At the very least, it would demand a military commitment far out of proportion from the value of the country. This strengthened those who favored a more indirect approach, in which British India would control Afghanistan's external affairs without actually occupying it through the support of compliant Durrani amirs. Since the Durrani amirs had always gotten along better with the British than their people did, establishing cordial relations with them by means of subsidies and military aid was certainly the easier objective to achieve. This policy proved remarkably fruitful, in part because it never demanded that the amirs act to help Britain overtly, only that they remain passive. As we have seen, the most notable example of this was Dost Muhammad's refusal to participate in the Indian Sepoy Rebellion of 1857, but it would not be the last.

The Durrani rulers drew a different set of lessons from the First Anglo-Afghan War. The first was that it was rebellions by its own population and not their own actions, government policies, or regular troops that had preserved Afghanistan's independence. This meant that unless they created a stronger state structure and a more centralized military, they too could fall victim to the same types of uprisings that had driven the British from the country. The second lesson was a corollary of the first: the Durrani dynasty needed to redefine its own political legitimacy in the eyes of its own people in a way that would command more popular support. To achieve the first objective, successive amirs solicited British aid to build a stronger state by arguing that only they could prevent a supposedly rebellious Afghan people from constituting a serious frontier problem for India and stand as a barrier to Russian expansion. The brilliance of this policy was that the amirs would receive payments to keep themselves in power while keeping the British out of the country. This helped in achieving their second objective of building internal political support by portraying themselves to the Afghan people as the necessary preservers of the nation's independence and Islamic religious identity against potential aggression by both the British raj and czarist Russia.

For the Afghan people, the First Anglo-Afghan War was a demonstration of a new political power. This was the first time that nonelite Afghan groups had taken a decisive role in national politics and proven their ability to remove a government. Because they were still culturally hobbled by traditional concepts of legitimacy, however, neither the Ghilzais nor the Kohistanis attempted to replace the old Durrani elite, or even force it into a power-sharing relationship. Instead, they continued to see themselves as mere allies of existing Sadozai or Muhammadzai Durrani factions, whose members they appointed as the leaders of their struggle. The clergy who framed their opposition to the British in terms of a religious jihad and not a national struggle reinforced this attitude. Therefore, almost all of the popular resistance was aimed specifically at the infidel British and only obliquely at their Afghan collaborators, including even Shah Shuja. Muhammadzai rulers would thus valorize the legitimacy of popular revolts against outsiders in religious and national terms, while simultaneously condemning as treasonous and illegitimate any revolts against their own governments.

All these lessons were put more clearly into play during the Second Anglo-Afghan War (1878–80) and its aftermath with the emergence of Amir Abdur Rahman and his project to build a centralized state.

THE SECOND ANGLO-AFGHAN WAR AND AMIR ABDUR RAHMAN

Civil War and State Building

Dost Muhammad's success at building up his military power was not accompanied by administrative centralization. His unification of Afghanistan merely incorporated the three most important regions that had previously been free of Kabul's control: Qandahar, Herat, and Turkistan. He was unable to rule them directly or change the structures of their administration. Indeed, his own style of administration was less sophisticated than his predecessors:

> Apart from the formalities like striking coins and the insertion of the Amir's name in the khutba, the administration of Dost Muhammad Khan's nascent state showed little resemblance with that of the bygone Sadozai Empire and was extremely rudimentary in nature. As if to obliterate all traces of Sadozai supremacy, Dost Muhammad Khan even did away with the physical remnants of that era, such as the office for records. During his reign, as during that of his successor, there were no government offices, and the state officials worked in their homes, carrying scraps of paper around in their pockets when reporting to the king.[30]

In other words, Dost Muhammad was not the ruler of a unified Afghan state but rather the last of its great patrimonial kings, who simply took regional administrative fragmentation for granted. His focus was on extracting revenue from his provinces (when he could), not ruling these regions from Kabul. His was a dynastic realm in which subjects had no role in government, despite the power they had demonstrated during the First

Anglo-Afghan War. Nor did the larger Durrani elite have much power for that matter; with few exceptions, Dost Muhammad's officials were all members of his immediate family.[31] This was most apparent in his appointment of his sons as governors of various cities and provinces, where he let them rule as they thought best. Although his sons were in constant competition with one another and complained when rivals got a territory better than their own, Dost Muhammad was at least confident of their loyalty to him. But since each province came with its own military and tax revenue, the governors acted more as little kings than as obedient servants of the amir. As political actors in their own right, they built patronage networks and political alliances in the regions they ruled, so that their success or failure at the national level now had immediate repercussions at the local level.

The use of sons as governors created stability during the lifetime of the amir, but guaranteed trouble on his demise for reasons that Afghans understood through bitter experience: sons might be loyal to their father yet not to each other. I have already noted the intense rivalry in Pashtun society among patrilineal cousins (tarburwali), but this paled in comparison to the rivalry among half brothers. In fact, since only one of them could succeed to the throne, even full brothers did not always support one another. This tendency was exacerbated by the sheer number of royal heirs. While Muslim law restricted a man to a maximum of four wives, Afghan rulers such as Timur Shah and Dost Muhammad never applied such a restriction to themselves. When Dost Muhammad died at age seventy-two, he had twenty-seven sons and twenty five daughters born to sixteen wives.[32] His children ranged in age from mere infants to mature men with sons of their own. Sons by different mothers (who varied widely in social rank and ethnic origin) saw their half brothers as deadly rivals, and the fragile ties that bound them broke with the death of their father.

The seeming unity of the Afghan state at the time of Dost Muhammad's death was more apparent than real. Even with the elimination of the Sadozais and the subordination of the Peshawar and Qandahar sardars, Muhammadzai cousin lineages, Dost Muhammad's immediate heirs were numerous enough to conduct a series of civil wars all by themselves. As at the death of Timur Shah, who also had an excess of wives and sons, bloody tanistry would once again rule the day and throw Afghanistan into another period of turmoil. One difference from earlier civil wars was that because Dost Muhammad's prestige was so high, he achieved a goal that had eluded earlier Muhammadzai rulers: an institutionalized dynastic charisma. The civil war following his death was not a political free-for-all. It was a limited war of succession restricted to his sons and grandsons, who avoided killing one another when possible.

The death of Dost Muhammad in 1863 opened a period of five years of unrest. Sher Ali initially took the throne. The third son of Dost Muhammad's favorite wife, he had come to be heir designate after the death of his more famous brothers, Muhammad Akbar (1847) and Ghulam Haidar (1858). His major rivals were his two half brothers, Muhammad Afzal and Muhammad Azam, whose mother was the amir's first wife, but who had a lower social ranking. As Dost Muhammad's eldest surviving son, Afzal thought the throne should be his and revolted with the aid of his brother Azam. The threat to Sher Ali was real because Afzal had been governor of Turkistan for a decade and built up a well-trained army of twenty-five thousand there. Sher Ali attacked Turkistan but decided to come to an accommodation with his half brother after an indecisive battle there in June 1864. As Sher Ali walked with Afzal through Mazar's holy shrine to conclude the peace, he learned of a plot against him by Abdur Rahman, Afzal's only son. Abdur Rahman had opposed the reconciliation because it deprived his father (and by extension himself) of his legitimate right to the throne. He planned to arrest the amir and shoot the heir apparent, Muhammad Ali Khan. Instead, Sher Ali arrested Afzal and transported him to Kabul, forcing Abdur Rahman to flee to Bukhara.

In 1865 Sher Ali faced a revolt in the south by his full brother, Muhammad Amin Khan, the governor of Qandahar. Sher Ali suppressed that rebellion, but the casualties included his rebel brother and, worse, his own heir, Muhammad Ali Khan. This threw the amir into a severe depression. He went into seclusion at the famous "Shrine of the Cloak" in Qandahar and refused all entreaties to resume his public life. Azam and Abdur Rahman used the opportunity to return to Afghanistan from exile, mobilize their allies, and attack Kabul. In May 1866 they freed Abdur Rahman's father, Afzal, and made him amir. This finally galvanized Sher Ali to raise an army to oppose them. But Sher Ali suffered a series of defeats with large casualties in 1866 and 1867, and so retreated to Herat, where his son

Yaqub Khan ruled as governor. Afzal died that year and was immediately replaced on the throne in Kabul by his full brother Azam, causing Abdur Rahman to return to Turkistan. It fell to Yaqub to reverse the family's fortunes by taking Qandahar from Azam's sons and then defeating the amir himself near Ghazni in 1868. Azam fled to Iran but died en route, and Abdur Rahman was soon forced to seek asylum in Samarqand as Sher Ali's forces moved north. The civil wars now over, Sher Ali would rule as amir for the next ten years.[33]

If Dost Muhammad was the last of the great patrimonial kings of Afghanistan, Sher Ali was the first of its state builders. He focused particularly on strengthening the army and making administrative reforms to support it.

Sher Ali's goal was to have a completely professional army. Dost Muhammad had built up some professional units, but now the new amir was determined to end the government's dependency on irregular troops led by the country's notables. When Sher Ali first visited India in 1869 he sought British aid to do this. Although the British agreed to make a few grants of arms to his government, they were otherwise disinclined to assist him directly or get involved in Afghanistan's internal politics. Yet they did permit Sher Ali to recruit retired noncommissioned officers from India who could train his soldiers and artisans who could provide these soldiers with weapons. By the end of his reign, he had fifty-six thousand troops divided into forty-two regiments of cavalry, seventy-three of infantry, and forty-eight of artillery batteries. It was still not quite a national army, since the units were identified by their region of recruitment and ethnic origin. Ghilzai and Wardak Pashtuns dominated the army, and also held high civil and military posts. By contrast, the Muhammadzais and the other Durrani aristocrats showed little interest in military service.[34] This was the beginning of a new pattern that would have significant consequences. In the past the Durrani had owed their preeminence to their military service; now they were becoming a more passive hereditary aristocracy.

Sher Ali sought administrative reforms to pay for his army. The army consumed a little more than 40 percent of the government's total revenue of thirteen million rupees. This burden was met by reforming the tax system so that it took in five million rupees more than his father had been able to raise. Sher Ali pushed to have some land taxes paid in cash rather than in-kind. He also imposed austerity measures on the court by decreasing royal allowances so that "every penny saved would go to strengthen the country's defense, which was that patriotic sovereign's one and only desire."[35] Despite increased military spending, the Afghan treasury continued to have a surplus in the years before he died. The organization of Sher Ali's government rested with a set of ministers, none of whom was a member of the royal dynasty. There was still little evidence of a bureaucratic structure, however, and the impact of Sher Ali's changes should not be exaggerated. New tax policies might have a direct impact on those districts from which it could actually be collected, but Hasan Kakar concluded that the average Afghan of the time remained only weakly within the orbit of Sher Ali's government and in many cases beyond its control entirely:

> Even after it had been reformed the government was still unable to rule directly over the entire country. It controlled only the cities, towns and their dependencies as well as those areas where contingents of troops were stationed. Tribal communities, especially those of the frontier regions, remained self-administered as before, and their affairs were settled by elders mainly through the *jirga*s in accord with the Shari'a and Pashtunwali (Pashtun code of behavior). In cases in which disputes between individuals and tribes were unsettled the conflicting parties often resorted to violence. Thus, in these communities anarchy and order coexisted, and the government intervened only when general order was disrupted.[36]

Nor did the reforms free Sher Ali from the typical political problems created by the competition among sons by multiple wives to succeed him. His eldest two sons, Yaqub and Ayyub Khan, used Herat as a base from which to project their own power. They threatened outright revolt or secession when their father appointed their much younger half brother as his new heir in 1873. Following a series of threats and reconciliations, Sher Ali gained the upper hand in this dispute. Yaqub found himself imprisoned in Kabul, while Ayyub sought exile in Persia.

In addition to buttressing his government's domestic power, Sher Ali was the first amir to judge Afghanistan by any international criteria. When he visited India in 1869, he came away with the strong impression that, in the words of his grandson, "all people are advancing in the arts of peace and civilization. It is only we Afghans who remain the ignorant asses we have always been."[37] Without making substantial changes he believed that the country would never command respect in the world and would not be treated in terms of equality by its powerful imperial neighbors, Russia and Britain. This was the earliest expression of two themes that would grow in influence among the rulers of Afghanistan in the twentieth century: a concern about how outsiders viewed their country, and the desire to change Afghanistan's economy and society to make them more progressive and modern. Previous rulers had been worried about what outside powers might *do* to Afghanistan, but they expressed no concern about what they might think of it. Similarly, previous rulers had made changes with an eye to strengthening their power, particularly in the army, but they never saw themselves as social engineers. Of course, accomplishing changes in either of these two areas would require the Afghan government to alter radically its relationship with its people as well. Whether such changes were necessary or desirable would become a recurring flash point in Afghan politics—and it remains unresolved even today.

Second Anglo-Afghan War

During Sher Ali's reign, the Russians expanded rapidly into central Asia. They reached the historic northern border of Afghanistan after annexing Samarqand and making the amir of Bukhara their client in 1868. Beginning in 1869, the British and Russians began engaging in discussions on their respective interests in central Asia. They finally came to an understanding in 1873 that the area south of the Oxus River (Amu Darya) would be considered Afghan territory. (This was the same boundary set earlier by Ahmad Shah Durrani and the amir of Bukhara in the mid-eighteenth century.) Russia also agreed that Afghanistan fell within the British sphere of influence. In this way Afghanistan became a buffer state between their two empires. While this agreement was made without Afghanistan's cooperation, it served the amir's interests by setting a limit on Russian expansion without forcing him to make new concessions to the British. But it did not entirely set his mind at rest. Saint Petersburg might have been satisfied with the agreed-on limits, but Russian expansion into central Asia was more often the product of aggressive local commanders than official policy. These commanders' definition of protecting Russia's frontiers included the right to expand them, with or without orders. General Constantine von Kaufman, the Russian governor general in Tashkent, was particularly aggressive in such matters. He made the Khivan khanate a protectorate in 1873 and occupied Kokand in 1876. The Russians then began attacks on the Turkmen tribes in Merv. Kaufman also sent letters to the amir in Kabul that implied that Russia's acceptance of Afghan sovereignty over its northern territories was conditional as well.[38]

The renewed Russian advances in central Asia coincided with a change in British foreign policy that was partly in response to them. Benjamin Disraeli had become Britain's prime minister in 1874 and he favored the Forward Policy. At a minimum, that policy demanded more direct control over Afghan affairs; at a maximum, it foresaw the dismemberment of Afghanistan into its component regions and their incorporation into British India. Evidence of this new policy became concrete in 1876, when the British occupied Quetta in Baluchistan, formerly an Afghan feudatory. At the same time, the British demanded that Sher Ali accept the appointment of an English political agent in Kabul. The new and aggressive British viceroy in India, Lord Edward Robert Lytton, saw this as a way to rule Afghanistan from within as a protectorate. Although Lytton was willing to make some concessions to the amir, such as protecting his dynastic rights against rivals, the loss of independence was too high a price, and Sher Ali refused to comply.

As tensions mounted, an uninvited Russian diplomatic delegation sent by Kaufman arrived in Kabul in July 1878. This infuriated the British, who immediately demanded equal treatment and insisted on the reception of their own delegation. When the Afghans refused, the British issued an ultimatum and then invaded Afghanistan in November. Kakar is of the opinion that Kaufman deliberately provoked the British in order to draw them into a costly Afghan conflict to facilitate Russia's own war with the Ottoman Turks, with whom Britain was allied. Of course, since Lytton was looking for a fight after Sher Ali rejected his demands, another excuse would have undoubtedly been found had not the Russians provided this one. If it was a ploy, Sher Ali was its main victim. Assuming he had a reliable ally, the amir evacuated his troops from Kabul to make a stand in northern Afghanistan, declaring, "I am leaving in order to unite with the Russians and acquire financial and military assistance so that I may return to avenge myself." [39] When he reached the north, however, Kaufman refused to provide him the promised aid. Sher Ali sought to appeal to the czar directly, but Kaufman foreclosed that option by refusing him entry to Russian territory. He instead recommended that the amir make his peace with the British. Frustrated and long debilitated by chronic illnesses, Sher Ali died in Mazar in February 1879.

The Second Anglo-Afghan War, like the first, began well for the British and ended badly. By January 1879, they had occupied Jalalabad with a force marching up the Khyber and Qandahar with a force from Quetta. Yaqub became amir on Sher Ali's death. He had only recently been released from prison to serve as regent in Kabul during his father's absence. With no Russian alliance in hand to stop further British inroads, Yaqub agreed to make peace on British terms. In May 1879 he signed the Treaty of Gandamak, which formally ceded various border territories to India (including the Khyber Pass), permitted a permanent British mission in Afghanistan, gave the British control of Afghanistan's foreign affairs, and made Afghanistan part of a free trade zone with India. It returned to the amir's sovereignty the areas under military occupation, and granted him and his heirs a subsidy of six hundred thousand rupees annually. [40]

With the hostilities now concluded, Sir Louis Cavagnari was dispatched to Kabul in July with a small escort to serve as the head of the British mission in Afghanistan. Housed in a less-than-secure part of the Bala Hissar palace complex, he proceeded to act like the proconsul that Lytton expected him to be. Ordinary Afghans welcomed neither Yaqub's treaty with Britain nor Cavagnari's presence in Kabul, but initially there was no overt opposition. As in the First Anglo-Afghan War, trouble began over a side issue that escalated out of control. In September, three regiments of unpaid Afghan soldiers from Herat took their grievances to the mission, seeing the British as the true rulers and paymasters of the country. Rioting broke out when they received no redress, and joined by a local mob, they overran the residence and murdered Cavagnari and his guards. The British responded quickly. General Frederick Roberts occupied Kabul in October. Yaqub was held prisoner, forced to abdicate, and eventually sent to India. Roberts sought to hang or shoot anyone involved in the uprising, and was none too particular about trials or evidence of guilt. The British also blew up the Bala Hissar palace complex, the historic seat of Afghan rulers.[41]

The British now ruled Afghanistan directly and gave every indication that this state of affairs would be permanent. Lytton concluded that if he could not rule Afghanistan through a compliant amir, he would dismember it first by establishing British India's line of defense at its scientific frontier on the northern slopes of the Hindu Kush, then severing Qandahar from Kabul, and perhaps giving Herat to the Persians. Since the empire was at the peak of its Victorian glory, the colonial hubris that underlay his confidence was perhaps inevitable. General Charles MacGregor, the chief of staff of the British military in Kabul, suggested that force was the only thing that the Afghans understood and recommended the following line of argumentation to bring them to their senses:

> You shall give in, you have killed Cavi, and his hundred men, but we are sending another representative with 10,000 men, and he shall stay there whether you like it or not. We wish one thing from you, and that is friendship, but whether we get this or not, we will have your obedience, you may chafe as much as you please, but we will be your masters, and you will find that the only escape from our heavy hand will be your entire submission.[42]

Instead of compliance, the imposition of direct foreign rule provoked regional revolts by the Ghilzai Pashtuns and Kohistani Tajiks, who together attacked Kabul in December. This tribal army was large—about fifty thousand men—but had no unified command. Having a better-organized and better-led army than in 1841, the British successfully held off the besiegers, who withdrew to Ghazni in the spring after looting the Qizilbash, Hazara, and Hindu sections of Kabul as well as those Muhammadzais they deemed pro-British. This Ghazni faction, or National Party, wanted the British out, and a return of one of Sher Ali's sons to the throne. At the same time, Amir Afzal's son, Abdur Rahman, had left Samarqand to raise an army of his own in the north in January 1880. Since his family had long supplied Kabul's governors in Turkistan, Abdur Rahman had established connections there. The continued resistance to their direct rule had convinced the British that they should seek a quick agreement with some Afghan ruler who would respect their interests after they left. Unsure of the reliability of Sher Ali's sons, they opened negotiations with Abdur Rahman, offering to make him amir of "Northern Afghanistan" (i.e., Kabul, eastern Afghanistan, and Turkistan). As Sir Lepel Griffin wrote the amir in June:

> With regard to limits of territory, I am directed to say that the whole province of Kandahar has been placed under a separate ruler, except Pishin and Sibi, which are retained in British possession. Consequently the Government is not able to enter into any negotiations with you on these points, nor in respect to arrangements with regard to the northwest frontier, which were concluded with the ex-Ameer Mahomed Yakoob Khan. With these reservations the British Government are willing that you should establish over Afghanistan (including Herat, the possession of which cannot be guaranteed to you, though Government are not disposed to hinder measures which you may take to obtain possession of it) as complete and extensive authority as has hitherto been exercised by any Ameer of your family.[43]

Abdur Rahman delayed accepting such an agreement since he would be sacrificing half of the country's existing territory. During this delay, Lytton was replaced as viceroy by Lord Ripon, who proposed returning the ex-amir Yaqub or his brother Ayyub to the throne. This possibility was foreclosed when Abdur Rahman, in concert with his cousin Ishaq Khan (Azam's son), arrived on the outskirts of Kabul in July 1880 and accepted the amirship on British terms.

Abdur Rahman's success came at the expense of the elite Durrani groups that favored Sher Ali's family. The new amir had bypassed them by appealing directly to the Ghilzais and Kohistanis, whose desire to see the British out of the country outweighed their existing loyalties to the heirs of Sher Ali. By getting first to Kabul and appealing to the people while striking a deal with the British, Abdur Rahman showed himself to be a more skilled politician than his rivals. Kakar notes, however, that his success came at a cost that both the amir and later historians of the dynasty would do their best to obscure, because "by accepting only 'Northern Afghanistan' he went along with the British scheme to divide Afghanistan. Furthermore, he surrendered the independence of the country for which his compatriots had fought."[44] That Abdur Rahman would in fact rule over an undivided

Afghanistan was a welcome but unexpected gift from his greatest rival, Sher Ali's son Ayyub, the ruler of Herat.

Even before coming to an agreement with Abdur Rahman, the British had recognized an independent *wali* (governor) of Qandahar in May 1880. Drawing on an obscure line of Sher Ali's cousins, the British proclaimed his rule to be hereditary, provided him with arms, had coins minted, and had the khutba read in his name. In return, they would control Qandahar's foreign relations and station political agents at court. But the stability of the new principality was challenged by Herat's governor, Ayyub, who had moved his army (forty-five hundred infantry, thirty-two hundred cavalry, and four thousand irregular ghazis) east. In July 1880, the army encountered a strong body of twenty-eight hundred British troops supported by two thousand followers at Maiwand. Although the British had superior arms, the Afghans were able to close on their formation by taking large casualties and they annihilated the enemy in fierce combat. If Ayyub had immediately followed up on his victory, he could have easily captured Qandahar. Instead he delayed ten days before besieging the city, giving the British enough time to regroup and fortify their position. Yet even without occupying Qandahar, had Ayyub chosen to march north on Kabul, the country would have risen with him.[45]

To get troops south to deal with Ayyub's siege of Qandahar, the British agreed to withdraw their army of ten thousand from Kabul if Abdur Rahman would convince the Ghilzai to allow it unhindered passage south. Abdur Rahman did this by presenting the British withdrawal from Kabul as an Afghan victory—an evacuation of the country that was not to be resisted. Perhaps surprisingly (given that a similar promise made by Akbar in the First Anglo-Afghan War had led to a massacre), Roberts covered the 324 miles to Qandahar in a record time of twenty-three days unhindered by attacks along the way. In September 1880, Roberts relieved the siege at Qandahar, and Ayyub retreated back to Herat. Afghanistan was now divided between the British in the south, Ayyub in the west, and Abdur Rahman in the east and north. The British had no intention of staying or maintaining an independent Qandahar, however, and were determined to completely evacuate the country before the summer heat set in. The amir opposed such a rapid withdrawal because Ayyub still remained at large, but he was given no choice since the government in London had ordered its Indian officials to withdraw. Qandahar was therefore turned over to Abdur Rahman's officials in April 1881. The war with the British was over, but the Afghan conflict that it spawned moved into high gear.

Abdur Rahman may have been named amir in Kabul, but his hold on power was precarious. The British had recognized his government, but would not move to sustain it in a civil war. Ayyub, as the victor at the Battle of Maiwand and Sher Ali's son, had both a stronger claim on the throne by descent and better nationalist credentials than Abdur Rahman. Ayyub also had more troops at his disposal. But Abdur Rahman had a number of assets to his credit. The new amir had spent much of his youth involved in military campaigns in northern Afghanistan and was therefore an experienced field commander who rarely hesitated to press home an attack if he sensed vulnerability. He was also a ruthless personality who might well have adopted Henry V's motto of carpe diem ("seize the day"). By contrast, Ayyub and his brothers had been powerful governors who had delegated military affairs to their Ghilzai officers. As was typical of conservative third-generation dynastic princes who had grown up with inherited power, they had a tendency to put off hard decisions and could rarely move themselves to take advantage of singular opportunities. In times of crisis they tended toward vacillation rather than resolution.

Ayyub reclaimed Qandahar in July 1881, well after the British evacuated the city. He had not done this earlier because Herat had revolted against his rule and it had taken some time to suppress this insurrection. (Heratis of many different ethnic groups had all agreed that this would be a good time to throw off Kabul's domination and become independent themselves.) His advisers urged him to take the offensive and march immediately on the amir in Kabul, but Ayyub preferred the defensive course, in part because his Durrani followers favored that as well. In Qandahar, he convinced important clerics to issue fatwas justifying the war on the grounds that the "*farangi* amir" was an infidel. In response, Abdur Rahman had his own clerics issue fatwas denouncing Ayyub as a rebel, but their cooperation was more grudging since the amir was forced to distribute gifts or money to them. Not content to let the situation become stalemated, Abdur Rahman consulted with Ghilzai and Kohistani leaders, and then marched south to Qandahar in August. Along the way, he distributed food and money lavishly to the Ghilzai tribes to win them over to his side.

While he had some success in this, there were also many Ghilzai in Ayyub's army as well, so this war of succession did not split entirely along tribal lines. As had happened during the First Anglo-Afghan War, the Ghilzais acted as allies of Durrani pretenders on both sides and did not see themselves as possible rulers.

When Abdur Rahman arrived at Qandahar, he commanded around fourteen thousand troops facing Ayyub's army of seventeen thousand. Such odds should have favored Ayyub, who had a prepared line of defense and a more secure line of retreat. But his army was disorganized and poorly led. Nor did Ayyub intend to put himself in harm's way by getting close to the action, taking up his view of the coming battle from the high ruined ramparts of the old city. By contrast, the amir led his troops in battle personally and routed Ayyub's army. Showing the temper that would characterize the next twenty years of his reign, Abdur Rahman then sought out one of the clerics who had issued a fatwa condemning his "blasphemous aid to infidels." Although the cleric had taken refuge in the sacred Shine of the Cloak, where violence was forbidden, the amir confronted him with a raised sword, and "with one stroke severed his head from his frail body and threw it out like a football."[46] Ayyub fled west, but Herat too revolted against him on learning of his defeat, and he had to seek asylum in Persia. In 1887, the British would offer him permanent asylum and a pension in India.

CREATING THE AFGHAN STATE

During the Second Anglo-Afghan War, the British recognized that their own occupation of Afghanistan in support of Yaqub's weak regime had destabilized the country. They therefore sought to find a new cooperative ruler who, in exchange for large subsidies and the right to rule an unoccupied Afghanistan, would agree to let Britain control the country's foreign affairs and respect British interests in India. Abdur Rahman was willing to meet these criteria, but he knew that securing his own power would be a longer-term project. His most immediate objective was to win the civil war with Ayyub. In achieving this goal, Abdur Rahman not only removed the most significant Durrani rival challenging his elevation to the throne but also gained control over the entire country (with the exception of Maimana, which would fall to him in 1884). What then distinguished Abdur Rahman from previous amirs was that after winning the by-now-customary war of succession, he began a series of new wars, which Louis Dupree labeled "internal imperialism," designed to destroy the old state structure in which the major urban centers and the tribal regions were autonomous.[47]

Abdur Rahman's goal was to rule Afghanistan directly and autocratically without relying on intermediaries.[48] His initial policy of consultation and largesse, which had characterized his civil war days, was now replaced by a policy that depended more on force than persuasion and grew harsher as his reign progressed. But imposing direct rule and taxes over a people who appreciated neither naturally raised opposition. During the course of his reign, the amir experienced over forty uprisings against his government. Had these been better coordinated or come all at once, Abdur Rahman would have undoubtedly been toppled. One of the amir's political strengths was that he aimed his attacks at specific targets and thereby kept conflict from spreading too widely against him at any one time. He also took on hostile tribes and regions in sequence, often rewarding victims of earlier repressions with opportunities to gain wealth and political influence by allying with him in later attacks on others. By the end of his reign, he had created a powerful police state in which even subversive talk that might offend the amir could land a person in jail or worse. The level of violence it took to bring Afghanistan to such a state has frequently been overlooked by historians and later political leaders, who instead lauded the amir's ability to bring order to such a fractured land.

Abdur Rahman's internal wars were designed to reduce the autonomous political authority and military power of three main groups: the eastern Pashtun tribes that had been the core of the anti-British resistance, his rival cousins who ruled Turkistan, and the non-Sunni ethnic groups in rugged parts of the country that had historically fallen outside Afghan state control. Over the course of the next fifteen years he would crush every autonomous group in Afghanistan one by one, aided by British subsidies that financed the creation of a powerful national army equipped with modern weapons that were purchased abroad or produced in his own factories.

Even more than Dost Muhammad, Abdur Rahman looked with suspicion on the tribal resistance that had led the British to withdraw. If the rebellious Tajiks or Ghilzais who attacked Kabul had leaders with more vision, or ambition, they could have seized power for themselves when the British left. Yet they appear to have been satisfied with the withdrawal of the British and once again left national politics to the Durranis. Abdur Rahman made sure they would not have the chance to change their minds. His campaigns began in the early 1880s, when he took control over a number of eastern Pashtun districts and tribes that had gained some autonomy during the war. He then fought a major war against the Ghilzais, who had revolted against his rule (1886–88).

The amir sparked this war by first arresting many influential Ghilzai leaders and then introducing a new tax scheme. As members of the National Party in Ghazni, the tribal leaders and clerics had come to wield great influence during the occupation, and many had supported the amir's rival cousin, Ayyub, in the civil war that followed. When in 1883 the amir had earlier arrested some of the most prominent and popular of these war leaders, including General Muhammad Jan Wardak, on trumped-up sedition charges, he was condemned by the most important Ghilzai cleric, Mullah Mushk-i-Alam: "Three thousand men who took defense during the British occupation and endured hardship in protecting the honor and the country of Islam are today in prison in Kabul. Therefore all people, including me, consider us in danger."[49]

The amir also changed the tax system applied to the Ghilzais. Formerly it was assessed as a fixed quota for each tribe and paid though the tribes' elders. The new tax was much higher (one-third of the agricultural produce from irrigated lands) and was collected from individual landowners. Adding insult to injury, the Ghilzais who had helped drive the British from Afghanistan were now expected to pay much higher taxes than the Durranis in the south. Although their role in the occupation was less than glorious and they had been fully supportive of Ayyub, the Durranis continued to benefit from the tax-free land grants they had inherited from the time of Ahmad Shah. The Ghilzais revolted against this treatment by the amir beginning in October 1886. Not wishing to be seen as pure rebels, they fought in the name of the exiled prince Ayyub. The amir appeared to have the upper hand when his best general, Ghulam Haidar, defeated the Ghilzais within weeks and dispatched two thousand heads to Kabul to build an exemplary "tower of skulls" to impress the populace. The amir's army also seized land from rebels and treated the inhabitants harshly. Such tactics only sharpened Ghilzai anger, though, and led to renewed attacks in spring 1887. The number of rebels exploded from twenty thousand in March to one hundred thousand in April. But they stood little chance against the amir's better-organized troops, which were armed and equipped with more modern weapons. More significantly the amir was able to constantly reinforce his army from Kabul, giving the Ghilzais no respite. By winter, the revolt waned after the loss of an estimated twenty-four thousand Ghilzais dead—far higher Afghan losses than ever experienced in their fighting with the British. The amir's postrevolt policy was designed to impoverish the Ghilzais on the theory that "when they have no money left with them, [they] will not raise disturbances."[50] And in fact, they never raised another large-scale revolt again.

Having extinguished his most dangerous tribal threat, the amir immediately turned his attention to his cousin Ishaq Khan, governor of Turkistan. As Azam's son, his cousin Ishaq would be the likely successor had Abdur Rahman died, because the amir's own sons were still children and he had no brothers. But a greater threat was their disagreement on how Afghanistan should be ruled. Ishaq was of the opinion that as in the past, Afghanistan was best ruled as a set of regions loyal to, yet autonomous from, Kabul. This view was shared earlier by Ayyub: he had proposed a political solution to the civil war in which each of the six remaining princes whose fathers had been an amir would get a province. Abdur Rahman wanted a true centralized state with himself as the only ruler. At the beginning of his reign he did not have the power to realize this goal. He was forced to recognize Ishaq's virtual autonomy in the north as governor of Turkistan because he commanded a strong provincial army and had his own revenue stream. It was a system that the amir was determined to limit, however. He first refused Ishaq's request to appoint his younger brothers to the newly opened governorships in Herat and Qandahar in 1881. Tension mounted again when the amir annexed Maimana in 1884 and then kept it out of his cousin's jurisdiction in Turkistan. Over the next few years the amir repeatedly requested Ishaq's presence at the court in Kabul, but Ishaq refused, fearing (rightly) that they were only ploys to remove him from office. In August 1888, Ishaq's passive resistance turned to rebellion when he permitted his subjects to declare him amir in open opposition to his cousin. This revolt was a far greater threat to the Abdur Rahman's authority than any other since his opponent filled the hereditary requirements to replace him. Not waiting for Ishaq to cross the Hindu Kush, the amir's army under Ghulam Haidar moved north. His outnumbered troops made contact with Ishaq at Ghazniak in September. The battle shifted back and forth, but ended suddenly when Ishaq took flight on hearing that his key regiments had been defeated. This news was false, yet Ishaq's loss of nerve at that critical moment led to the collapse of his army and its retreat from the field. Abdur Rahman now had direct control of the north, an area he knew well from his youth, and had driven the last of the possible royal pretenders out of the country.[51]

Abdur Rahman's final major campaigns were wars of conquest against non-Sunni areas that the Kabul government had never directly controlled: Hazarajat in central Afghanistan (1891–93) and Kafiristan in eastern Afghanistan (1895–96).[52] Previous Afghan governments had controlled only the edges of Hazarajat and ruled the rest indirectly. Abdur Rahman received the formal submission of the tribes there in 1890, although the terms to which they agreed remain open to dispute. It was the behavior of the officials and troops that the amir sent to the region that sparked rebellion in 1891. The war quickly took on a religious overtone when the amir had the Shia Hazaras declared infidels. This allowed both his army and the tribal levies that he raised to ignore the usual Islamic laws of war. In particular, the army could enslave those that they captured, and keep their land and property. This was especially important in recruiting Pashtun tribes, which agreed to participate in hopes of plunder. The amir mobilized a hundred thousand troops for this campaign—more than for any other. The army broke the power of the Hazaras, many of whom were enslaved, while a large number fled to Persia and Baluchistan, where they formed refugee communities. The amir's government reaped a large dividend from taxing this slave trade. Hazarajat itself was impoverished as neighboring Pashtun tribes expanded their territory into lands formerly controlled by the Hazaras. The war also opened vast new stretches of summer pasturelands to Pashtun nomads.

The campaign against the Kafirs, an ancient society that still maintained its pagan religion in mountainous eastern Afghanistan, was by contrast fought mostly for symbolic reasons. The amir had been portraying himself as a paragon of Islamic leadership, and the opportunity to engage in a war against true (and relatively powerless) infidels was too good to pass up. He also feared that if he did not assert his direct control there, the British or Russians might do so. A winter campaign in 1895 when the region was snowbound led to a quick victory. Unlike the incitement to violence in the Hazara campaign, the amir prohibited the enslavement of prisoners or the pillaging of property. The mass conversion of the region went quickly, and the region was renamed Nuristan, "Land of Light." The war had some surprising consequences. The amir recruited about ten thousand former Kafirs into the army, and this small ethnic group retained an important military role in Afghan governments for the next eighty years, much as the Qizilbash had done in the time of Ahmad Shah. The amir also built a pack animal road running through the Afghan territory that separated the Russian Pamir base at Khorog from British-controlled Chitral. He had the bright idea that if Russia was determined to invade India, then he would ease their way by building a road to make it easier—a road that would also direct the Russians away from any crucial Afghan territory.

These wars centralized political and economic power in Kabul, and made Abdur Rahman the undisputed ruler of Afghanistan. Previously major provinces such as Qandahar, Herat, and Turkistan had been autonomous because they had rich sources of revenue that could finance local armies. And because the relatives of the amir in Kabul usually administered them, they also became major sources of dynastic tension when the governors used them to create independent power bases, often by allying themselves with regional non-Muhammadzai political elites against the central government in Kabul. Abdur Rahman destroyed this autonomy by appointing governors that he could remove at will rather than immediate relatives. He also began a policy of subdividing provinces into smaller units so that they would never be large enough to serve as a base for revolt. This reduced the importance of the regional elites. For the next century, all national politics would be centered in Kabul, and the regional cities wilted in its shadow. The other notable aspect of these campaigns was how frequently they were directed at whole populations and not just their leaders. The destruction of life and property was severe, and at a level previously associated only with foreign invasion. This was magnified by the amir's regular policy of moving populations from their home regions to distant parts of the country to reduce their power. After the defeat of Ishaq, large numbers of defeated Ghilzais in the south were uprooted and exiled to northern Afghanistan. So many Shia Hazaras were deported to Kabul that they became a significant part of Kabul's population for the first time. Aimaqs in central Afghanistan and Nuristanis also found themselves in new places. It was becoming less and less possible to remain neutral in political struggles.

This inability to avoid state power extended into the economy as well. Direct taxation was imposed on tribes and regions that had previously been taxed only indirectly, if at all. In 1889, the amir had an annual income estimated at around fourteen million rupees. But by 1891 the figure had risen to fifty million rupees—four times higher than anything Sher Ali had ever raised. The bulk came from land taxes in an economy that remained subsistence based, and from populations that had not increased in number, so the sudden surge in government revenues came at the expense of ordinary Afghans, who were left destitute. Even members of the elite were targets. The amir found ready excuses for confiscating property and money from refugees, rebels, government officials, clerics, or indeed anyone whose wealth came to his attention.[53] He also increased his control over foreign trade. While previous Afghan governments had taxed trade running through their territories, they had not attempted to control the organization of the trade itself or its financial infrastructure. By contrast, as Shah Mahmoud Hanifi has shown, Abdur Rahman attempted to monopolize both in a way that eventually isolated and impoverished the Afghan people.[54] Such high levels of revenue collection inside Afghanistan were unprecedented, and went to fund the amir's professional army and nascent bureaucracy. But just how rudimentary the state administration remained could be seen in the fact that the amir was never able to determine his real income or expenses, only how much was taken in and how much was spent in any one year.

The increased tax burden was not offset by government investment in education, infrastructure, or communications, which were transforming neighboring Iran and India at the end of the nineteenth century. The amir refused foreign offers to construct railways and telegraph lines that would link Afghanistan and its economy to the outside world. He also forbade foreign investment in the country and made no attempt to develop Afghanistan's rich mineral deposits. The amir's arms factories that produced the bulk of the weapons for his army could not operate without importing iron from India, even though Afghanistan had much vaster ore deposits on its own territories. The amir feared that any economic or transport development would only make the country vulnerable to outside interference. He may have been correct about the danger, but such a strategy was like eschewing the acquisition of wealth because it might attract thieves. Abdur Rahman thus laid the foundation for the country's long-term economic stagnation and poverty, even though in terms of population density and available resources it had a stronger potential for growth than many of its neighbors.

The amir could ignore the country's structural economic problems because he received regular subsidies from the British. This began with an allowance of 1.2 million rupees annually in 1883, and it was raised by a third in 1893 to 1.8 million as part of the Durand Agreement. Altogether, with the addition of special grants and arms in 1880, 1881, and 1887, the amir collected 28.5 million rupees from the British during his reign.[55] This money alone was not enough to make Afghanistan a true rentier state (given the amir's high rate of internal taxation), but with the subsidy came access to the international arms market, which supplied the amir with all the guns and ammunition he needed to subdue his own people. It also paid for the machines and raw materials necessary to run his government-owned workshops, which were Afghanistan's only factories. But access to such arms and equipment came only with the cooperation of the British raj, since even if the amir had wanted to spend his own funds, all his international imports into Afghanistan by sea came through Indian ports.

The receipt of British subsidies returns us to a problem that Afghan rulers faced from the time of Dost Muhammad: how to justify their close relations with a non-Muslim power while maintaining their status as a defender of the faith and protector of Afghanistan's national integrity. The Durrani elite had always tied their fortunes to their alliance with the British. Yet this alliance was only effective to the extent that the British avoided a direct occupation of Afghanistan. The Second Anglo-Afghan War had convinced the British that the indirect approach was more fruitful in creating a barrier to Russian expansion. As a result, Afghanistan became a buffer state, and its northern and western borders were defined in international agreements, over which the Afghans had little influence. Although these borders were arbitrary, they were not artificial. They included the core areas of Herat, Turkistan, and Badakhshan, which had always constituted long-standing political and economic units. Although at the margins the Afghans may have lost some territory in some places, they gained it in others. These agreements, whatever their imperfections, protected Afghanistan from Russian expansion and Persian irredentism. In return, the amir not only received a large British subsidy but access to needed imports through India as well. The amir's dependence on this relationship became clear when the British imposed the Durand Line, which severed Afghan control over the territory that would become the NWFP. The amir vehemently opposed relinquishing his nominal sovereignty over the Pashtun tribes in the region. It took an economic embargo at the time that he was fighting the Hazaras in 1892 to force his compliance.[56] It was this economic embargo that exposed the amir's weakness: the British subsidies might now constitute a much smaller percentage of government revenue than they did early in his reign, but without the cooperation of the British he could import no arms and ammunition, or even the raw material with which to make them. Without having to mount a new Anglo-Afghan war, the British split what had been the Pashtun core of the Afghan state. This seems to validate in a more global context ibn Khaldun's belief that turbulent populations on their margins were easier to control economically than militarily.

The British got the obedience they demanded but left a sore that never healed. If changing the borders in the remote mountainous Pamirs or the deserts of Siestan had only minor consequences for a ruler in Kabul, this demarcation cut too close to the heart, even though it was not officially a border. Technically the Durand Line simply demarcated each country's zone of influence in the Pashtun tribal areas that neither directly administered at the time. But while the other borders were accepted without question, if only as a fait accompli, this frontier remained so problematic that no successor government in Afghanistan of whatever ideological persuasion was ever willing to recognize it as permanent.

Transforming the Afghan Polity

Abdur Rahman used force to centralize the state, but at the same time tried to give the government a broader political base. He did this in three ways. First, by the end of his reign he convinced the Pashtuns, at the expense of other ethnic groups, that they were part of the same governing elite that had oppressed them. Second, in spite of his own close alliance with the British, he made defense of Islam and jihad a feature of Afghan national identity when dealing with the outside world. Abdur Rahman made himself the arbiter of domestic religious and national ideology in a way that championed his primacy while hiding his compromises. Third, the modern Afghan state as currently constituted was his creation. The amir stressed the pure Islamic character of the Afghan state while creating a fundamentally secular government that dominated the religious establishment. He was the nationalist who declared the necessity of defending Afghanistan's borders to the death and never ceding Afghan land. Yet this was the same man who initially accepted the amirship of *northern* Afghanistan in 1880, knowing that it would mean the loss of Qandahar and Herat. Although he was politically vulnerable then, even at the height of his power in 1893 he was unwilling to risk war with the British to prevent the imposition of the Durand Line. He instead accepted the increased subsidy in compensation and moved on to finish the last of his internal wars.

Creating a Pashtun State

From 1881 until 1888, Abdur Rahman directed most of his campaigns against the Pashtuns, particularly the Ghilzais. Yet for the next ninety years, the Pashtuns as a whole would see themselves, and be seen by others, as the privileged ethnic group in the country. For if the Pashtuns were the prime victims of Abdur Rahman's early wars they were the beneficiaries of his later ones. For example, the amir's suppression of the Ghilzai revolt coincided with his recovery of Afghan Turkistan in 1888. This allowed him to punish large numbers of rebellious Pashtuns from the south by exiling

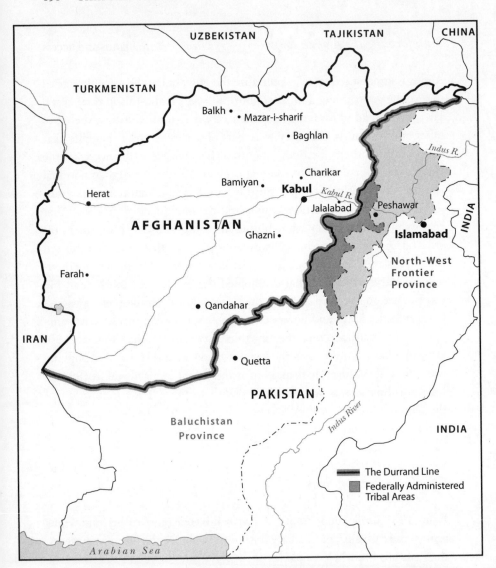

Map 6. Afghan state with modern boundary highlighting Durand line with Pakistan

them to Turkistan, a territory then inhabited primarily by Uzbeks and Tajiks. The deported Pashtuns were given rich agricultural lands and access to pastures for raising sheep in a territory that had been depopulated by wars among the former Uzbek amirs, slave raiding by the Turkmen nomads, and disease. Because these lands were generally much better than those they had lost, and because they were surrounded by other hostile ethnic groups, the former Pashtun rebels of the south became strong supporters of the government in the north.[57] Similarly, the war against the Hazaras employed large numbers of Pashtun tribesmen, who were given Hazara land and rights to sell captives in exchange for their participation. These Hazara conquests were particularly valuable to the Pashtun nomads, who were able to extend their summer range deep into the Hindu Kush, but also gave other neighboring sedentary Pashtun groups control over lands formerly owned by the Hazaras. The campaign in 1895–96 to conquer and convert the inhabitants of Kafiristan to Islam also benefited the Kunar Valley Pashtuns, who had long been in conflict with them. In the eyes of most non-Pashtuns, the Afghan government was now viewed as a Pashtun government and not just a Durrani dynasty. This created an ethnic status hierarchy that would typify Afghan society for the next century. In broad stokes it ranked Pashtuns at the top, followed by Persian-speaking Tajiks, who played a large role in the administration of government, and then Turks, who were largely ignored and rarely found outside their home region in the north. The Shia Hazaras fell at the bottom of this scale and bore the brunt of discrimination imposed by a Sunni majority.

Although the amir raised the status of Pashtuns as a group, he was not an ethnic nationalist. Unlike Sher Ali, who had attempted to make Pashto the national language, Abdur Rahman fell back on the use of Persian as the language of the government bureaucracy and court. Even among the Pashtuns, as Kakar notes, the main benefits went to a small Muhammadzai elite:

He likewise treated the Pashtuns differentially, raising the Mohammadzays to the top of the new polity. Even they he treated unequally, raising the descendants of his great-grandfather, Sardar Payanda Khan [Dost Muhammad's father], to a privileged position by providing them with regular allowances and making them partners of the state (sharik-e-dawlat). The Kabul Mohammadzays, who following the British intervention were in a twilight period, began to emerge as aristocrats among a people who were more or less egalitarian.[58]

Closing Ranks: Islam and Jihad

The amir referred to his country as the "God-granted State of Afghanistan" and proclaimed the religious necessity of defending its integrity against attacks by infidels.[59] Unlike eighteenth-century Afghan rulers, for whom jihad meant wars directed outward against Hindu India, the amir's vision of jihad was defensive, protecting Afghanistan from invasion by the Christian empires now to its north and south. In this manner he created a xenophobic atmosphere in which all non-Muslim foreigners and their foreign ways were suspect. He also stressed the importance of a unified leadership in such a defensive jihad. Since he had already declared himself the "light of the nation and religion," his Muslim subjects owed him double obedience to keep the infidels out. The amir developed these ideas in three treatises, which were widely distributed.[60] Although not a cleric himself, he had no hesitation about imposing his views forcefully. Fearing that any talk of harmony or brotherhood would undermine the spirit of jihad, he lashed out violently at any cleric who dared preach a softer line. For example, the amir once demanded that a mullah be put to death because he had preached that Muslims must regard Christians as brothers since they were a "people of the book." The first council of clerics refused and found him innocent of any charge of heresy. A second panel called to try the case again could only muster two clerics willing to uphold the death penalty, even after the amir made his wishes clear. One would have probably sufficed, since the amir immediately used this minority judgment to have the offending cleric stoned to death.[61]

The amir's focus on jihad served the purpose of directing aggression outward. For a man who fought all of his wars against his own people and who had killed many Afghan Muslims, but few if any infidel British, pressing his people to look outward for more evil enemies paid dividends. Only he could preserve the nation and thereby defend the faith. In the process, the amir linked elements of Islamic belief with Afghan tribal customs in ways that convinced his largely illiterate population that the two were identical. The tautology was that since all true Afghans were devout Muslims then all their customs must be Islamic as well, otherwise they could not be good Muslims (which they were by definition). Anyone proposing to change tradition could therefore be accused of attacking Islam itself. In other Muslim countries there was debate over responding to the Western colonial challenge by changing old traditions and reforming Islam, but not in Afghanistan. The amir's retrograde view of Islam combined with his policy of xenophobic isolation preserved Afghanistan's territorial integrity, yet closed the country off to new ideas, even those coming out of the Muslim world.

The Afghan National State

Afghanistan was formerly a country composed of distinct regions and tribes. Whether Qandahar was ruled by the Safavid Persia or Mughal India aroused little concern in Herat or Turkistan, which themselves might be part of a different polity. Indeed identifying with Afghanistan, "the land of the Afghans," was a bit of a stretch for an Uzbek in Balkh or a Tajik from Badakhshan. Being part of a larger polity was of interest to the kings and khans who ruled them, not ordinary people. One might appeal to the common defense of Islam, but a national identity did not bubble up from below. It was the amir's standardized taxes, laws, currency, conscription, and administrative structure that put all Afghans into a single system. An individual might not identify with other regions of the country but he now shared their problems.

This administration was fundamentally autocratic and secular. Abdur Rahman centralized the government and destroyed the power of the regional elites. Heretofore Afghanistan's rulers had never wielded exclusive power. The local-level power structures had remained resilient, and their leaders worked within a divided system of government. Afghan amirs also had to deal with rival lineages and even family members who developed independent power bases. The clergy was largely independent of government control. By eliminating the existing class of khans and community elders, Abdur Rahman removed the layers of protection that shielded local communities from the demands of a central government. The ability of these communities to organize was so debilitated that it was said that if the British invaded Afghanistan again, they would face no opposition.[62] The amir also put the clergy under his control by demanding that judges pass examinations that he devised. Those clerics who made judgments that displeased the amir found their positions and salaries terminated. Abdur Rahman also nationalized the country's Islamic endowments (*waqf*), which had long supported religious institutions independent of the government. Despite his many references to Islam, the amir viewed his government as a secular one in which his new state laws were deemed to take priority over both traditional religious law (sharia) and customary law. For better or worse, Afghanistan became a unitary state under Abdur Rahman's rule, and its inhabitants came to see it as such.

Abdur Rahman versus the Longue Durée

Abdur Rahman is justly credited with laying the foundation for a modern national state through his establishment of a highly centralized government in Kabul. Unlike his predecessors, Abdur Rahman clear-cut the political forest that had impeded his path to absolute authority by reducing what had been a complex political ecosystem into a much simpler one, in which no internal actors could challenge him or his government. Chancing on this altered scene of weeds and stumps that stretched to the horizon, all observers (internal and external) seemed to agree that the old political forest was no more and would never return. For better or worse, Afghanistan had passed a watershed in which the model of government created by Abdur Rahman became the new standard by which future regimes would be judged. Much as the establishment of the Durrani Empire by Ahmad Shah in 1747 is seen as the beginning of Afghan history, Amir Abdur Rahman's reign is seen as the beginning of Afghanistan as a nation-state. In particular, it appeared that he had permanently eliminated the autonomy and economic significance of the country's distinct regions and qawms that I earlier posited as being the core structural elements of Afghan history.

But to what extent was this really true? In the first chapter of this book, I examined Afghanistan in terms of the longue durée aspects of material life and social organization, which had persisted for centuries and even millennia. These included features of agricultural production, exchange relationships, ethnic groups, and cohesive geographic units. From this perspective, most of Abdur Rahman's achievements were ephemeral—political changes imposed from above at great cost that appeared transformative but were not. The amir had used his access to new military technology to outmatch his opponents, but he resolutely resisted the introduction of other new technologies (such as rail transport, steam engines, and telegraph lines) that were transforming the economic organization and social structure of his neighbors. As a result, the Afghan economy remained overwhelmingly subsistence based, and goods continued to move to markets as they always had—on the backs of donkeys, horses, and camels over unimproved caravan trails. Agricultural surpluses could not be profitable transported from one region of the country to another, let alone easily exported. The state industries that historians use as examples of the amir's innovations in fact simply equipped his military with modern arms and raised revenues for his government. They had no transformative impact on the Afghan economy because they were located almost exclusively in Kabul and required imported raw materials to function. Most significantly, while the amir had eliminated the old regional elites as political players and gained power over their territories by military force, he did not alter rural Afghan society. The social structure of qawms and the regional ties they represented still predominated at the village and provincial levels. They may have been subordinated to the Kabul government or displaced by warfare, but these social structures had not been eradicated or even greatly changed. Kabul therefore became the leading political and economic center of Afghanistan because it was the amir's capital and the exclusive seat of government. Yet it was a center only by default: Afghanistan's level of urbanization was higher in the fifteenth century under the Timurids, when Herat and Balkh were international centers of culture and commerce—something that late nineteenth-century Kabul (with a population of only fifty thousand) never came close to achieving.

Although the military and political successes gave Abdur Rahman supreme power over Afghanistan and its people, his centralized model of government went against the grain of Afghan tradition. Unlike Persia or the Ottoman Empire, where the authority of shahs and sultans was buttressed by a strong cultural tradition of autocracy, Afghan rulers were historically forced to work within a political system that was more federal and consultative. Though this older system of politics did appear to have been wiped out during Abdur Rahman's rule, it had not really disappeared but rather reappeared in new guises. For the next century and more, successive regimes that attempted to model their governments and style of rulership on that of Abdur Rahman's inevitably found themselves challenged by this tradition—in some cases, resulting in state collapse. Returning to the image of Abdur Rahman as a clear-cutting logger helps us understand why. His wars to create a centralized Afghan state destroyed what ecologists would call a "climax state," a self-perpetuating stable relationship among species in which the community is in equilibrium.[63] It remains constant over time until it is disrupted by some outside force. When a stable climax relationship among species is destroyed, it is replaced by a series of transitory communities, which then succeed one another in a predictable sequence until the old climax state is restored. Because the species composition of each successive stage is usually quite different from its successor and the whole cycle may be centuries long, the sequence of relationships (and whether they are transitory or stable) is not obvious to the casual observer at any one point in time. If this sounds too complicated, let me use a more commonplace example that Abdur Rahman would have appreciated: shaving someone's head does not make him permanently bald. Although they might look the same, a bald head is a hairless climax state, while a shaved head requires constant barbering to prevent the hair from returning.

The stable climax state in the "political ecology" of Afghanistan was characterized by a center (wherever it was) dominating distinct regions, which had their own political elites. Whether it was the Achemenids from Persepolis, Mughuls from Delhi, Safavids from Isfahan, or Afghan amirs in Kabul or Qandahar, the building blocks of the state were remarkably similar. Ruling dynasties either appointed powerful local elite to rule as their agents when their power was limited or sent an agent of their own to rule directly when they were strong. It was a fairly robust system, which buffered the regions from the consequences of political collapse at the center. In such cases these regions might be reshuffled into new polities, become independent, or perhaps become dominant political centers themselves. Abdur Rahman destroyed this historic political climax state when he stripped the regions of their autonomy and deprived them of economic resources. What he and his successors could not stop, however, was the tendency to revert back to that form, even if that took generations to become apparent. Abdur Rahman was a diligent barber, but the direction of change is clear if the perspective is a long-term rather than a short-term one. Of course, as human beings we tend to privilege the circumstances we experience in our own short life spans, so perhaps it is not surprising that current conditions are so readily projected into the future. In retrospect such assumptions often prove gravely mistaken. While Abdur Rahman may have viewed his centralized state as a permanent achievement, the next chapter will show how later governments that modeled themselves on his concepts of autocracy ended badly. The amazing thing is that to this day, governments in Kabul have emulated the Iron Amir despite the grief this has brought to the Afghan people. In some cases, it would appear that those who remember the past too uncritically are doomed to repeat it regularly.

CHAPTER FOUR

Afghanistan in the Twentieth Century:
State and Society in Conflict

Abdur Rahman's successors found it difficult to maintain the fearful degree of state supremacy that he had imposed on Afghanistan. Although every Afghan government aspired to achieve the same level of power and centralization attained by the Iron Amir, few succeeded. While twentieth-century technology provided them with better weapons, communications, and transport, none were able to similarly impose their will on the people of Afghanistan. Those Afghan leaders who would best succeed during the next century employed a "Wizard of Oz" strategy. They declared their governments all-powerful, but rarely risked testing that claim by implementing controversial policies. Conversely, the leaders who were most prone to failure and state collapse were those who assumed that they possessed the power to do as they pleased, and then provoked opposition that their regimes proved incapable of suppressing.

The periodic and often-rapid collapses of state power in Afghanistan during the twentieth century had their roots in the persistence of violence at the top of the system. Indeed, changes of power frequently appeared to be a throwback to the old, bloody tanistry system in which the right to rule demanded the elimination of all other rivals. Following Abdur Rahman's peaceful death in 1901, every succeeding Afghan head of state for the next one hundred years would either die violently at home or be driven into exile abroad. One might assume such a sanguinary record would have induced increasingly greater caution in the application of state power by every new ruler, but over time the opposite proved the case. State violence during the last quarter of the twentieth century dwarfed anything experienced during its first third but was no more successful. One reason for this was that after the fall of the monarchy in 1973, each succeeding regime had a weaker claim to political legitimacy than had its predecessor in the eyes of ordinary Afghans. Such regimes compensated for this defect by increasingly resorting to force to maintain their authority.

After 1980, armed conflicts and social disruptions became the norm. These reached unprecedented heights because each rival faction had an international patron willing to provide it with a seemingly endless supply of weapons and money. Afghanistan became a stage for a series of proxy wars in which Afghan blood would be shed in the name of ideologies that few Afghans shared. The outcome was a level of destruction far beyond what the Afghans could have accomplished themselves, and spawned conflicts that they lacked the capacity to control or resolve on their own. The Afghan people would have the unenviable distinction of experiencing oppression at the hands of both a radical socialist regime and a reactionary Islamist one. Neither had any respect for the wishes of the Afghan people, who would fall victim to their respective ideologies. The worst evil of civil war, Hobbes's cancer of the body politic that could destroy society itself, was let loose. As a consequence, the seemingly all-powerful centralized state that held Afghanistan in its thrall in 1901 would be reduced to a powerless shell by 2001.

A Short Walk through the Twentieth Century

The New Elite, New Goals, and Unexpected Outcomes

Even as its neighbors began to change, Afghanistan entered the twentieth century with its face firmly fixed on the past. Abdur Rahman had taxed the economy more heavily, but the country still remained subsistence based and its people culturally insular. In terms of transport, communications, industry, or education, little distinguished the Afghanistan of 1800 from that of 1900, beyond a few government-run factories in Kabul. Politically, however, Abdur Rahman had radically transformed the country. He centralized power so thoroughly that no city or region outside of Kabul had any significant influence on national policy. He destroyed or subordinated the regional elite in the north, west, and south who had previously challenged the national government's primacy in the nineteenth century to such an extent that one could be forgiven for thinking that they had been wiped from the map. The tribal structures of the Pashtun areas in the east remained intact, but the amir had so brutally repressed their rebellions that the Pashtuns withdrew from national politics entirely. The Islamic clerics and sufi *pirs* who had played such an independent political role at the end of the Second Anglo-Afghan War were reduced to being either arms of the state or apologists for it. The army was more professional and centralized than ever before, yet the amir never allowed a class of military leaders to develop that might challenge his power or influence his policies.

Paradoxically Abdur Rahman's high degree of centralization, imposed at a high cost, would prove detrimental to the stability of later Afghan governments. The amir had suppressed the dynastic rivalries, religious movements, and regional rebellions that plagued nineteenth-century rulers, but he left the Afghan state ill equipped to cope with the new social and economic challenges that would characterize the twentieth century. Afghan governments remained reactive rather than proactive, responding to problems when they became crises rather than averting them. This structural difficulty was compounded by an ever-widening cultural split between a rising elite in Kabul (a product of Abdur Rahman's state building) and the inhabitants of the countryside and provincial cities. The former increasingly espoused the cause of reform while the latter viewed change with suspicion. Although the urban elite were few in number, their influence was huge because they dominated government institutions. To them it seemed only natural that in the wake of Abdur Rahman's successful state building, the next goal should be Afghanistan's modernization. Compromise with opponents on this issue (except on a temporary basis) would be unnecessary since they could always be put down by the force of modern arms.

The new national political elite had a much narrower social, political, and regional base than those of nineteenth-century Afghanistan. Leaders then were politically autonomous and served as intermediaries in their people's dealings with the central government in Kabul. Such loyalties might be based on tribal ties, regional affiliations, religious networks, or descent from rival dynastic lines. Their followers were loyal to them first and Kabul second (if at all). Abdur Rahman's elite, by contrast, was created to serve him and his state, from which they derived their influence. They were drawn primarily from the ranks of tame Muhammadzai sardars, the descendants of Payinda Khan (the Muhammadzai founding ancestor), whose influence as a group had been declining for generations. But after the amir made them "partners of the state" (*sharik-i-dawlat*), which entitled them to receive regular government stipends and land on easy terms, they became the dominant class in Afghanistan. Not all Muhammadzais immediately qualified for this honor: the amir banished from the country all those whom he deemed too ambitious or influential, although they too returned after his death. Abdur Rahman's ruling class also included members of other groups that served the state, including urbanized Tajiks and ethnic minorities or provincials based in Kabul, many of whom began their ascent to power as lowly servants to the palace (*ghulambacha*). Unlike tribal Pashtuns, who were famously endogamous, the Muhammadzai elite periodically married their women to influential men outside their lineage, opening the way to social advancement and co-opting those who might have otherwise opposed the status quo in the absence of such ties.

Abdur Rahman's imprint would remain surprisingly strong over time, as Barnett Rubin discovered through a statistical analysis of who held prominent government positions eighty years later.

> The ethnic composition of the old regime [of the 1970s] was remarkably similar to that of the court circles originally recruited by Amir Abdur Rahman. The most salient characteristic of that elite was that it included more than ten times the concentration of Muhammadzais and Kabulis than the population as a whole. Other Pashtuns were also overrepresented, and the overrepresentation of Pashtuns and Muhammadzais was greater among the core power holders than it was in the elite as a whole. Tajiks (mostly Kabulis) were also quite predominant, but mainly in the legal, financial, and social ministries; Pashtuns held the core of power.[1]

The power base of this new elite stood in sharp contrast to the old feudal aristocracy, although it remained largely Pashtun in origin. The feudal aristocracy's economic power had rested on its landed estates in the provinces, and its political power was derived either from the troops that it could muster or its ability to mobilize its own people in support of (or opposition to) the national government. Abdur Rahman's elite drew its wealth and political influence either from state patronage that could be withdrawn at any time or their ability to influence state policy. Unlike previous Afghan elites, these people were not masters of a national government but rather its servants. It was a rentier aristocracy that would live in a hothouse world in which everyone knew everyone else (and where everyone not related by birth appeared to be connected by marriage). Members of the Muhammadzai clan in particular would come to display a paradoxical air of aristocratic hauteur undercut by a political servility that ill befit either Afghanistan's egalitarian ethos or its tribal emphasis on preserving personal autonomy.* More significantly for Afghanistan's future, they were city people in a land where the vast majority of the population still lived in rural villages. Their ties to, and understanding of, this "other Afghanistan" were weak. For the next eighty years, national politics would be restricted to the city of Kabul and the state-dependent elite that held the reins of power there.

Like a similar prerevolutionary aristocracy in France, a small but influential minority of their members were supporters of radical social and political change. They assumed that they would be the leaders of any progressive movement because they were the only educated people in the country. Yet the expansion of the government and economy in the 1960s began to produce a larger class of educated people, who lacked the same access to power and wealth, and the respect for the existing structures of power. Previously, the number of such people was so small that they could be incorporated into the older aristocracy directly or at least co-opted into its patronage network with government jobs. But by the 1970s, their numbers had become too large and their social origins too diverse for this tactic to be effective. The dominating role of Kabul in Afghan political life instead had the perverse effect of creating a mirror counter-elite that Rubin labeled "rentier revolutionaries."[2] While these groups spoke of radical socialist change that would transform Afghanistan, their means of achieving this goal were the same as their royal predecessors': to control the state's assets and use its power themselves.

---

* A non-Muhammadzai Pashtun explained this perceived alternation by quoting an old Afghan saying: "One man's master is another man's dog!"

Based almost exclusively in Kabul, this counter-elite had few ties to rural Afghanistan, even though many had provincial origins. They certainly had no political base there. Rather, they saw themselves as a socialist vanguard party that would use the state to reorganize the economy and Afghan society from the top down. Although more radical, they shared with the Muhammadzais a dependency on state institutions and state power to implement such changes. After taking control of the state structure in 1978, they assumed that they could use its power to impose their policies on the rest of the country at a rapid pace. Never was an assumption more unwarranted. The realities on the ground in Afghanistan would prove much more challenging and difficult, as this and all future governments would come to learn through hard experience. It would also raise questions long buried: What made a government legitimate, and who had the right to rule?

Three Different Afghan Eras

The history of twentieth century in Afghanistan in which these events played themselves out may seem unduly complex on first encounter, but it can be broken down into three main periods: 1901–29, 1929–78, and 1978–2001.

Amanullah's failed attempts to modernize Afghanistan after the conservative reign of his father, Amir Habibullah, frame the first period from 1901 to 1929. This era ended in a brief civil war, which drove Amanullah from power after a Tajik bandit named himself amir in Kabul and ruled for nine months, before being killed himself.

Under the rule of the Musahiban brothers and their sons, the second period from 1929 to 1978 gave Afghanistan its longest interval of peace and internal stability. This period began with the declaration of Nadir Khan as king in late 1929 by a national jirga composed primarily of Pashtun tribes that had opposed Amanullah. Although Nadir was assassinated in 1933, for the next fifty-five years his extended family would maintain an exclusive grip on power. During this time Afghanistan was politically stable, avoiding both international conflicts and any significant internal rebellion.

Under Nadir's brothers, who ruled in the name of his young son, King Zahir Shah, the Afghan state introduced few changes—and then only at a glacial pace. The tempo of reforms quickened with the arrival of a new generation, particularly under Daud Khan (Zahir Shah's cousin), who became prime minister in 1953 and ruled for the next ten years. Zahir Shah finally emerged in his own right after he dismissed Daud in 1963 and began to rule directly, thirty years after he first ascended the throne. He instituted a new constitution, which created a limited democratic government. During the 1960s, the economic and social development of Afghanistan accelerated at the fastest pace that the country had ever known as it opened itself more to the outside world, ending the severe isolation first imposed by Abdur Rahman. Both the monarchy and its experiment in democracy came to an abrupt end in 1973, when Daud ousted Zahir Shah in a coup. Since Daud was a member of the royal family, however, the Musahiban grip on power remained unchanged even though he declared himself president of a new Afghan republic.

Today, the period of Musahiban stability and peace has been showered with praise as a golden age. Like most such golden ages, it looks much better in hindsight than it did to the people of the time. In particular, a new generation of Afghans who had taken advantage of educational opportunities found themselves without much in the way of economic opportunity and excluded from political power. The bulk of these were modernists, for whom Amanullah was a model. But there was a minority of Islamists, also opposed to the government, who equally sought its downfall. Given the dynamics of Afghan history, it is not surprising that when Daud seized power in 1973, he devoted most of his attention to suppressing the Islamists. This proved a fatal error: a coup by his formerly socialist allies in 1978 resulted in his death and the end of Durrani (Sadozai and Barakzai) rule after 230 years. The Communists who replaced him were Ghilzai Pashtuns—sweet revenge perhaps for the many times that they had previously been excluded from power.

War and anarchy characterized the third and most complex period, from 1978 to 2001. In retrospect, Afghanistan's troubles over these twenty-three years can be divided into three unholy parts. The first phase began in 1978 with a bloody coup by members of the Marxist People's Democratic Party of Afghanistan (PDPA), who murdered Daud and declared a socialist regime. After only twenty months, internal dissent within the regime's own ranks and a growing insurrection against its radical policies brought the government to near collapse. In an attempt to stabilize the situation the Soviet Union invaded Afghanistan in December 1979. This initiated a ten-year occupation that pitted the Soviets and the PDPA against the Islamist-led mujahideen (holy warrior) factions that waged war against them. The mujahideen party leaders based themselves in Pakistan, but were funded by the United States and Saudi Arabia. The Soviet war would leave a million Afghans dead and create three million refugees before the Russians withdrew their troops in 1989. Against the odds, the PDPA regime under Najibullah (r. 1986–92) maintained its power in Kabul after the Russians left. Najibullah's stability, however, was fatally undermined when the Soviet Union collapsed. The PDPA dissolved itself in April 1992, and its internal factions joined with competing mujahideen parties, mostly on the basis of ethnicity or regional affiliation.

Since opposition to the PDPA was the only glue that bound rival mujahideen leaders together, the fall of the regime sparked an intense power struggle. This new phase was characterized by a bewildering and constantly shifting set of alliances and betrayals that produced a civil war no faction could win. While each faction dominated at least one region of the country, none was powerful enough to eliminate the others. Many parts of Kabul, which had remained undamaged during PDPA times, were destroyed in this fighting. Many Pashtun areas in the east and south fell into disorder. Chaos in the south led to the rise of the Taliban in 1994, a religious movement led by clerics from Qandahar that pledged to restore order in the name of Islam. Under the leadership of Mullah Omar the Taliban pursued policies every bit as radical as the PDPA, but in the opposite direction. With the support of Pakistan the Taliban expanded rapidly, opening the third and final third phase of this civil war. They seized Kabul in 1996 and by 1999 controlled all of Afghanistan, except the northeast. Despite their internal victories, the Taliban received little international recognition and took their friends where they could find them. They granted training bases to various international jihadists groups with whom they shared common values, such as Osama bin Ladin's al Qaeda. The cost of this cooperation proved fatal when al Qaeda operatives attacked New York and Washington, DC, on September 11, 2001. Before the year was out, the United States and its coalition allies expelled the Taliban from Afghanistan, and helped establish a new government in Kabul.

Issues That Never Died

Although these periods may appear quite different, the underlying problems that divided Afghanistan in the twentieth century remained the same throughout. The most volatile was the issue of social change and its direction. Neither those who sought to transform Afghanistan nor those who resisted change were ever able to displace their opponents permanently. Thus, whether the regime was conservative or reformist, radical or reactionary, each would be brought down by the defects of its own policies. Over the course of the twentieth century, regimes with opposed ideologies replaced one another in an ever more violent manner. Each began with the confident illusion that its new policies or crafty political compromises would break the old cycle for good, only to have its world collapse when it fatally underestimated the strength of the opposition. While activist regimes tended to fall apart more quickly than traditionalist ones, neither escaped this fate. Conservatives or reactionaries might temporarily suppress the unmet demands for faster, more profound changes and a better standard of living emanating out of Kabul, but not in the long run. Yet radicals or reformists making up for lost time by quickly imposing such changes countrywide never survived the wholesale rejection of their policies by a rural Afghan majority that still organized itself along qawm lines within a subsistence-based economy.

A dictum by Karl Marx was ignored by those seeking instant change, particularly Afghanistan's radical Marxists: a society is a product of its economic base. Reformers or revolutionaries could never hope to change Afghan society without first changing its economy—a daunting and unglamorous task, which would take generations and require its stronger integration into the wider world. But conservatives seeking to freeze Afghan society in place or return it to an idealized past could take little comfort in this fact. Centuries before Marx, and in a world where Islamic and tribal values remained unchallenged, ibn Khaldun had observed that the cash economy of the city undermined group solidarity and kinship ties by empowering the individual. Isolated as Afghanistan seemed, even the rural countryside could not escape the penetration of a growing money economy that brought ever more city values into the villages with each passing generation and every new road or school. The new economy gave people new ideas and new wants. Conservatives, let alone reactionaries, could never permanently maintain what they saw as traditional tribal or Islamic values in a world where economic opportunity and social mobility increasingly unhinged old status hierarchies. Going to war to defend such values only increased the rapidity of social change within the communities that fought them. Still, oblivious to these realities and regardless of its ideology, each regime that took power in Kabul and lasted long enough to hold a military parade assumed it was the natural master of the country and its inhabitants, and could dictate Afghanistan's future. Of course, beyond the edge of town where government influence historically ebbed and then vanished completely in villages where donkeys were more common than cars, these trumpets of state supremacy sounded faintly, if at all.

Abdur Rahman might have been the first to diagnose the continuing problem that led to his successors' demise—Amanullah in 1929, Daud in 1978, the Communists in 1992, and the Taliban in 2001. All had come to grief after employing state power to change Afghan society without the cooperation of its people. Abdur Rahman (and earlier Afghan amirs) was oppressive when it served his interests, but never conceived of the state as an instrument of social and economic change (or indeed of using it to provide any public services). Instead, he focused on gaining and maintaining political power. The unspoken quid pro quo in this arrangement was that government would not interfere in the lives of ordinary Afghans, except in the traditional areas of taxation and security. This was the policy followed by Abdur Rahman's son Habibullah in the first decade of the twentieth century and by the Musahiban monarchs (Nadir Shah and Zahir Shah) from 1929 to 1973. The irascible amir might also have observed that attaining his own limited goals had been difficult and bloody enough; transforming Afghanistan's economy, values, and attitudes was a task better left to God. Taking on this task in God's absence were a series of ever more radical Afghan governments that approached transforming their country with unbounded expectations and a missionary zeal that rejected compromise.

ACT I: AMANULLAH'S FAILED EXPERIMENT, 1901–29

The Legacies of Abdur Rahman

When Abdur Rahman died in 1901, his designated heir, Habibullah, succeeded him peacefully. For the first time in Afghan history there was no war of succession. Indeed, Abdur Rahman had left such a powerful impression of authority that even a century later, the Iron Amir still held a central place in the Afghan historical imagination. He was praised as a ruler whose reign, like that of Ahmad Shah Durrani or Dost Muhammad, writ Afghanistan anew and transformed. Unlike his illustrious predecessors, however, Abdur Rahman left a legacy of fear unmediated by affection. By his own estimate he killed more than a hundred thousand Afghans. His conception of the rights of rulers was superficially similar to those held by earlier Turko-Mongolian shahs and sultans: they all saw their subjects as having no role in government.[3] But there were two important differences. First Abdur Rahman reduced everyone, including his own sons, to the rank of subjects excluded from politics. He not only had no equals, he would brook no powerful subordinates, critics, or rivals of any type anywhere—not among his sons, in the harem, at court, in the provinces, among the tribes, or even within the clergy. He declared himself God's agent on earth and acted accordingly. But unlike the shahs and sultans of old, who wore their authority lightly because they took it for granted, Abdur Rahman felt the need to proclaim his rights and authority at every turn. For example, he demanded the production of a written contract between himself and the Afghan people that would bind his subjects to his will in perpetuity. These "Covenants of Unity," 194 in all, were collected from every stratum of society, starting with his Muhammadzai kinsmen and moving on to "Hindus, artisans, businessmen, nomads, soldiers, and civil and military officials." They were formally signed by local mullahs and tribal elders, and then sealed by *qazis* (religious judges) for delivery to the amir in 1896. In the fifth clause, the people agreed "not to deviate from [the amir's] will, to keep on obeying whether he is alive or dead, be on guard to dangers all the time, not to be ignorant of our responsibilities to ourselves, to our religion and honor and of other Muslims, and it is for his sons, neither for us nor for our descendants, to choose the inheritors."[4]

Although the amir had created an authoritarian state, the idea of popular sovereignty had still managed to permeate his court and even his own psyche. After all, he had used the Afghan people's war against British occupation to get the throne. But if he truly believed that subjects had nothing to do with government and particularly dynastic succession, then why demand their acquiescence to what was none of their business in the first place? The shahs and sultans of old would not have bothered because such a charade would have had no significance to them or their subjects. Similarly, why create an unprecedented number of spies, who infiltrated every sector of society, or severely punish anyone who passed on rumors of rebellions or talked of politics? (The amir once had a man's lips sewn shut as punishment for daring to discuss politics.)[5] The fact that the Iron Amir made all these efforts seeking public recognition of his authority laid bare a new fear: that national politics might not remain the unquestioned monopoly of an exclusive dynastic elite. Abdur Rahman's grandson, Amanullah, would learn this bitter lesson in less than thirty years, when the descendants of this covenant's signers would bring his government down.

Afghanistan Peeks Outward

Habibullah inherited the throne after his father's death in 1901 without a succession struggle, and Afghanistan maintained its internal stability. Secure in his own power and facing no rivals, the new amir recruited to his court many families that his father had left in exile. These included descendants of rival Muhammadzai lineages such as the Peshawar sardars from India (the Musahiban brothers) and Mamud Tarzi from Ottoman Syria. It also included representatives of influential Sufi movements such as the Mujaddadi family, the Naqshbandi Hazrats of the Shor Bazaar in Kabul, and Sayyid Hasan Gailani, whose brother was the head of the Qaderiyya Sufi order in Iraq. These exiles had an enormous impact on Afghan politics because they brought new ideas, both secular and religious, into a country that had long been cut off from the outside world. Indeed, the political divisions that would eventually tear Afghanistan apart later in the century all had their roots in ideologies that first came into Afghanistan at this time.

The exiles had direct experience with the outside world that their resident Afghan counterparts lacked. They were products of new movements in India and the Ottoman Empire that were now shaping politics throughout the Muslim world, but from which Afghanistan had been isolated. Particularly in the wake of Japan's victory over Russia in 1905, nationalists and modernists were pushing such causes as political reform, pan-Asian solidarity, anticolonial resistance, and national independence. They argued that Muslim societies needed to modernize by adopting or adapting cultural and economic innovations from the West to compete more effectively with it. Religious-based parties preached the cause of Muslim revival, unity through pan-Islamic solidarity, and resistance to non-Muslim domination by means of jihad. While these streams would diverge and later appear incompatible, at this time their proponents in Afghanistan had much in common because both were fervently anti-British and believed in a state based on Islamic principles.

The sources of their opposition differed, though. As Senzil Nawid observed, the ulema feared that the continued British domination of Afghan affairs would undermine the country's Islamic social and political order over the long-term, while the so-called Young Afghan movement saw British domination as more injurious to national pride and an obstacle to the country's progress. Also, while they supported pan-Islamic movements elsewhere, these Young Afghans felt that the Afghan religious establishment was too dominated by reactionary and obscurantist clerics. The structure of religious life and belief needed to be reformed or displaced before Afghan society could progress. The Islamic parties saw no such defect, arguing that if Muslim societies were weak, it was because they had been oppressed by the Western colonial powers, and needed to display stronger religious solidarity and stricter applications of the faith in order to become independent again.[6] The call for a religious revival had a stronger resonance in the broader Afghan population—especially the call to wage jihad against the British in India—but the nationalists and modernizers had a greater impact on a new generation at court, eager for change.

In a country where literacy was rare and power was concentrated in the hands of the amir, it was the court factions in Kabul that had the greatest influence on national policy. During Habibullah's reign there were two major factions, both pushing him to make changes. The first was a religious faction composed of ulema, Sufi leaders, and the more devout members of the royal family, the most significant of whom was the amir's younger brother Nasrullah. The second was a nationalist and modernist faction, drawn largely from the rising new generation influenced by Tarzi, who established Afghanistan's first newspaper in 1912. It included students in the new school that the amir had founded (Habibia College) and two of his own sons (Enyatullah and Amanullah), who would marry into the Tarzi family. Initially, Habibullah was content to let both camps flourish because while he was fairly devout himself, he was also keen to bring such innovations as electricity to Kabul.

Habibullah later retrenched after both these movements began to criticize him. He first lost the support of the ulema and religious faction after calling for a holy war against the British and then reversing his position to block it. The amir had made the threat to protest the Anglo-Russian convention in 1907 that delineated their respective spheres of influence without bothering to consult the Afghans. But by 1908–9, his call to jihad had proved so popular that the amir feared it was getting beyond his control. Under British pressure, he not only suppressed the jihad movement but also arrested and even executed some of its organizers. This infuriated his brother Nasrullah, who had clandestinely financed and armed many of these groups. The nationalists also attacked the amir for accepting limitations on Afghan sovereignty by giving in to British demands and not pushing for complete independence. Of more concern to the amir than this criticism was his discovery of a secret party of constitutionalists (*mashruta*), whose goal was to abolish the monarchy. Organized first among students in his own Habibia College, the party's allies included both nationalists, liberal ulema, and even (it was rumored) his own sons. In late 1909 the amir moved to arrest the plotters, many of whom were executed, alienating the larger number of more moderate Young Afghans, who continued to see themselves as the vanguard of change.[7]

This dispute was a dress rehearsal for a similar conflict that emerged over an even more unpopular policy: Habibullah's declaration of Afghan neutrality in the First World War. As far back as the Napoleonic period European wars had impacted Afghanistan, but for the last one hundred years it had been the rivalry between Britain and Russia in Asia that played the key role. Now a war had broken out that joined those two historic rivals as allies against Germany and the Ottoman Empire. The Ottoman sultan's call for the defense of the Muslim caliphate in the name of pan-Islamic unity was particularly powerful in India, where an anti-British movement arose in its name. In Afghanistan the call to arms had universal support among ordinary Afghans. The court factions were also pro-Turkish. The modernist nationalist faction saw the Young Turk movement there as a model for themselves, while the traditionalist clerical faction needed no new urging to renew its call for holy war on British in a pan-Islamic cause. The demand for war reached its highest pitch in fall 1915 with the arrival of a Turko-German delegation in Kabul armed with letters from the Turkish sultan and German kaiser seeking permission for Central Power troops to pass through the country to attack India. More realistically, they hoped to use Afghanistan as a base from which to inspire jihadist revolts against the British in the NWFP and perhaps beyond. Given the number of Indian troops that the British were deploying to other theaters, this would have had a large impact on the Allied war effort. Only the amir expressed strong reservations about going to war. He argued that a position of watchful neutrality served Afghan national interests better. To this end, he hedged his bets by drafting a secret treaty to join the German war effort on the arrival of a large military force in Afghanistan with a substantial supply of weapons for his army and gold for his government. The envoys left nine months later, and the amir maintained his policy of neutrality through the war's end.[8]

It is noteworthy that the British never sent a mission to Kabul to counter the Germans or threaten the Afghans, as they had always been quick to do when the Russians had made similar attempts to foment subversion there in the nineteenth century. But perhaps they did not feel the need. Both the regular eruption of fiercely anti-British prowar sentiments among the Afghan people and the conservative pragmatic response to damp them down by Afghan rulers had a long history. As we saw in the last chapter, the bedrock policy of all Muhammadzai monarchs dating back to Dost Muhammad's second reign in the 1840s was to excoriate the raj as an evil empire for popular Afghan consumption while remaining staunch allies of British India privately. In burnishing their antiforeign image at home, Af-

ghan rulers made it clear to the British that, without their continued cooperation, such a wildly militant people would constitute a serious frontier
problem for India. There was no greater master of this black art than
Habibullah's father, Abdur Rahman, who published books calling for
jihad, but only ones initiated and led by the amir himself. Amir Habibullah was more risk averse than his father and let others take the lead when
it came to stirring up trouble. Like many second-generation rulers who
had inherited power rather than fought for it, he had no desire to tempt
fate by initiating a war on behalf of the Turks or Germans whose outcome was
so uncertain. He of course expected compensation from the British equal to
his risk for taking such an unpopular position with his own people—in
particular, the fulfillment of Afghanistan's long-sought demands to be recognized as a sovereign nation with full independence.

When the British prevaricated on the issue of independence at the end
of the war it left the amir in a precarious situation. They did not seem to
realize that in the wake of the war and the collapse of the old order in Europe, the Middle East, and central Asia, the amir was bearing the brunt of
attacks by those unhappy with the outcome. The conservative religious
faction held him responsible for facilitating the defeat of the Ottoman
sultan that ended the last of Islam's great independent empires. As the experienced British diplomat Sir Percy Sykes remarked, "With the complete
defeat of Turkey by a Christian power and the occupation of the Holy
Places of Islam, fanaticism was aroused, together with the bitter feeling
that Afghanistan had failed Islam in its hour of need."[9] But even those who
had no interest in the caliphate found fault with the amir for failing to
extract independence from the British raj as the explicit price of his neutrality. And this nationalist modernist faction now had a new foreign ally
looking to undermine the amir: the Soviet Union. The emergence of a
radical socialist regime determined to spread its ideology from the ashes of
the old czarist empire was a wild card, yet it was surely not going to make
the world safer for monarchy. The legacy of Abdur Rahman's repressive
policies was still strong enough so that dissatisfaction with the amir never
resulted in significant popular revolts against him. It did not secure him
from enemies closer to home, including his closest relatives. One morning
in February 1919, during a hunting trip in Jalalabad, Habibullah was
found murdered in his tent, the victim of an unknown assassin. Just who

killed him, or arranged to have him killed, remains a subject of speculation to this day. "How far the unpopularity of his war policy may have been among the causes of his assassination it is difficult to say," read the conclusion of a note prepared by the Political Department of the Indian Office, which praised the "fidelity of the late ruler to the British connection."[10] Still, perhaps it was less his war policy than Britain's postwar failure to reward him adequately for it that led to his murder and laid the groundwork for the Third Anglo-Afghan War.

In the aftermath of Habibullah's death, his brother Nasrullah proclaimed himself amir following an agreement struck during Abdur Rahman's lifetime. Habibullah's two eldest sons, Enayatullah and Hayatullah, both immediately swore their allegiance to their uncle and helped him bury their father in Jalalabad. Such dynastic bargains were always fraught with tension, however, because as a ruler's sons reached manhood they were prone to reject such understandings. They knew that the longer any amir ruled, the more he would seek to exclude his brothers or nephews in favor of his own sons. In any event, Afghan dynastic disputes were never settled by debating the finer points of inheritance law or by a gentlemen's agreement; they ended only when a challenger proved himself supreme by blinding, jailing, exiling, or killing his rivals. It was Amanullah, Habibullah's third son, who rose to this challenge. Calling for revenge, he condemned his uncle as a traitor and his father's assassin. Unlike his brothers, Amanullah had the advantage of serving as vice regent in Kabul during his father's absence, from which he seized control of the army and national armory on learning of his father's death. He was also a leader in the nationalist modernist faction at court and quickly gained its support against Nasrullah, who was more popular with the ulema and the border tribes.

In the nineteenth century the next step would have been a series of bloody battles, but government resources were now so concentrated in Kabul that whoever controlled them had an overwhelming advantage. Once Amanullah secured the support of the military, his uncle decided his position was untenable and abdicated in favor of Amanullah (who had already disinherited his brothers for siding with their uncle). The British were of the opinion that Nasrullah could have raised the frontier tribes to fight for him with the support of the ulema, but princes who had raised the flag of revolt in earlier periods always had a firm regional base to fall back on and a good deal of time to prepare. Nasrullah lacked a regional base, and events moved against him so quickly that he was a self-declared amir for less than ten days. What was also different was the political nature of the struggle. The opposing factions now represented different ideologies rather than just different tribal or regional networks, although their respective leaders were of the same dynastic house. Looking at the growing wave of nationalist movements elsewhere, another British observer declared that Amanullah's swift victory was "an illustration of the broad fact already noticed that the impulse behind recent movements in the East is nationalist rather than religious in character, and that when the two forces come into conflict the advantage lies with the nationalist."[11] Some things did not change: Amanullah immediately imprisoned his uncle in Kabul, where he died a few years later.

Amanullah: Reforms and Response

Amanullah moved quickly to consolidate his gains. He named his father-in-law Mahmud Tarzi foreign minister—a provocation since Britain had forbidden Afghanistan from establishing any direct relations with foreign states. In April 1919 he proclaimed a war of independence, beginning what was also known as the Third Anglo-Afghan War.[12] He also issued a call for jihad to the border tribes against the British. These were brilliant moves domestically because they united the conservative religious faction with the nationalists in a common struggle. Even those clerics who had supported his uncle's bid for power now moved enthusiastically to endorse the young amir. The army attacked British positions in three places across the frontier, but with the exception of Nadir Khan's short occupation of Tank, they were unsuccessful and the Afghans asked for an armistice in May. Under continuing pressure from the jihadist revolts in the tribal areas and wearied by the Great War, the British were also keen to seek a solution despite their victories against regular Afghan forces, which included the first aerial bombing of the country. By August 1919, the Treaty of Rawalpindi that recognized Afghanistan as a sovereign state was ready for signing. Although a tremendous victory for the country, the agreement potentially weakened the ruling dynasty because the British stopped their subsidy payments to the amir and initially refused to allow him to import arms through India. Amanullah got some leverage back when he established diplomatic relations with the Soviet Union in 1920, forcing the British to make concessions of their own when he signed a new treaty with them in 1921. This reestablished Afghanistan's salience in that already long-running balance of power saga that Kipling had called the "The Great Game."[13]

Such victories raised the status of Afghanistan and its amir across the Muslim world. Amanullah became engaged in pan-Islamic causes such as the defense of the caliphate, support for Indian Muslims and their anti-British *khalifat* independence movement, an attempt to preserve the independence of Khiva and Bukhara, and support for the *basmachi* resistance movement against the Soviets in central Asia. The conservative Afghan ulema rewarded him with the title of Ghazi as victor of a holy war. This Islamic phase of his reign ended fairly quickly as world events undermined the pan-Islamists. The Russians incorporated Khiva and Bukhara into the Soviet Union in 1920, and then forced Amanullah to abandon his support of the basmachi. When the Turks under Mustafa Kemal abolished the caliphate in 1924, to the horror of the Afghans, the anti-British khalifat movement in India collapsed. Although Amanullah considered declaring Afghanistan the home of a new caliphate, the idea had little support in the wider Muslim world and was quickly abandoned.

Still, Amanullah's prestige among the more religious factions undoubtedly facilitated his main goal, which was to modernize Afghanistan from the top down. He issued a blizzard of state regulations (*nizamnama*) designed to do just that. The most important of these was the constitution of 1923, which laid out the structure of the government, and gave the amir supreme executive and legal authority, but also established the Council of Ministers to run the government and the State Council to advise it. After forty years of conservative rule under his father and grandfather, the sweep of Amanullah's reforms was so broad that even Nawid's short summary of the most basic ones leaves the reader breathless:

> These regulations laid the foundation for ambitious administrative, legal, financial and social reforms. Administrative functions were better organized and centralized. A new tax law was introduced, and the legal

system unified. Social reforms included the abolition of slavery; expansion of the educational system, including formal education for women and reformation of the mosque schools; the imposition of universal conscription; and attempts to curtail polygamy, child marriage, and Pashtun customs relating to the treatment of women. Family matters were defined by a written uniform code of law.[14]

THE KHOST REBELLION

Reaction to these changes was not long in coming in the form of the Khost Rebellion of 1924, which would soon force the amir to retreat on a number of fronts and illustrated the weakness of his government. The rebellion got its start among the eastern Pashtuns, who saw their traditional way of life under threat. Although public objections to the reforms would be grounded in religious terms (that they were in violation of orthodox Islamic practices), the real problem lay in Amanullah's attempt to extend central government power into provincial areas in a way that affected peoples' lives directly. This threat came from three directions: taxation, conscription, and perceived interference in family life.

Fighting the war of independence had exhausted the national treasury and ended the long-standing British subsidies. This would have created a problem for any Afghan government, but it was a particular problem for Amanullah, whose ambitious building plans now relied on revenue derived primarily from the country's rural economy. The most notable of these was the construction of a new modern suburb of Kabul, Darulaman, at an estimated cost of ten million rupees or one-third of the state's normal annual income. To increase revenue, Amanullah revised the tax system to make it more efficient, required that taxes be paid in cash, and raised the tax rates on irrigated land that had remained unchanged since the mid-nineteenth century. He instituted new taxes as well, including a poll tax in Kabul and a tax to support education supplemented with "voluntary contributions" extracted even from poor provinces. Since even this increased revenue flow did not cover the costs of his projects, Amanullah lowered military spending and cut the stipends previously paid to the Muhammadzai

elite and religious leaders.* Even if the Afghan government had been administered by model bureaucrats who were content to live simply on their
modest salaries, the increased taxes and their more efficient collection
would have been unpopular. But in Afghanistan, no tax revenue ever
reached the central treasury without first being skimmed by its collectors.
In the past, the village head had served as the middleman and he had some
self-interest into not mulcting his own people too severely. The new tax
administration was run by civil servants with unprecedented powers to
intimidate local people. Cash tax receipts were also easier for officials to
pocket than was agricultural produce. Corruption flourished, both discredit-
ing the government and reducing the amount of revenue it received.[15]

Conscription was the second issue that upset rural communities, particularly among the Pashtun border tribes. Some had previously been
exempt from conscription entirely for political reasons (Barakzais, Mangals, Zadrans, and Ahmadzais), but most others traditionally supplied one
able-bodied man for every eight eligible ones (*hasht-nafari*). The community chose who would go and was responsible for supporting his family
during his absence. Tribal leaders saw the power to choose conscripts and
negotiate with the state on behalf of their communities as one of their
most important roles. Under the Conscription and Identity Card Act of
1923 the system changed to cut out such intermediaries. Conscription
became compulsory and universal, although the wealthy could buy an ex-
emption. There were no provisions to support a conscript's family during
his absence. In fact, after Turkish military advisers had modified the system
of compensating conscripts to one they were more familiar with, soldiers
could barely feed themselves. The law also required that all men registering
for conscription get a government identity card (*tazkera*), which allowed
the government to keep track of an individual. The law further required
the presentation of such state identity cards to file a court case, register a
marriage, or even engage in business. In this way the government hoped to
use its identity card system to enforce its unpopular new family law by

---

* Despite the tax changes, the estimated government revenue of thirty million rupee a year
appears significantly less than the fifty million annually claimed by Abdur Rahman after
1891. But given the nature of government record keeping and the use of different base figures,
the comparisons from one reign to another are problematic. Astute readers may recall that the
abolition of in-kind tax payments was also attributed to Sher Ali sixty years earlier, so that the
claim of administrative reforms was not always matched by their implementation either.

keeping track of what individuals were doing. Unlike conscription, requiring the state registration of individuals and marriages was entirely new, and strongly resented as unwarranted state interference in community life.[16]

The reforms aimed at marriage customs and the treatment of women were the most controversial. Amanullah was keen to discourage plural marriages, restrict marriage payments, ban child engagements, and end the custom of settling blood feuds by an exchange of women. The Pashtuns in rural areas had always prided themselves on their adherence to Pashtunwali, their code of honor, which placed great emphasis on personal autonomy and resistance to state power. The state (or even the local community) had no right to interfere in family affairs. The marriage laws threatened to do just that by imposing state supervision on what Pashtuns (and other rural Afghans) felt was a private matter or already covered by sharia law principles used by local clergy. This threat was mostly theoretical, however. Unlike in the Soviet Union or Turkey where powerful state structures allowed secular modernists to reach right down to the local level and impose social change, the Afghan government had no such capacity. Villages experienced annual taxation and conscription directly, along with the corrupt officials sent to collect the men and money. But the new laws relating to marriage and the status of women were mostly the stuff of inflammatory rumors that few people personally encountered since they had been only recently promulgated. Still, even the imagined fear that the state would undermine fundamental social relations sanctioned by Islam and the Pashtunwali had a powerful impact. It stoked up the level of hostility to an already-unpopular government in tribal areas. Pashtuns famously proclaimed that they fought for only three things, *zar*, *zan*, and *zamin* (gold, women, and land). Within three years of coming to power, Amanullah had squarely pushed two of these hot buttons with his taxation (gold) and social laws (women). In a society concerned with preserving the appearance of honor and autonomy, men often felt compelled to act well before such threats became a reality. Because honor itself was judged in the theoretical realm, perception could be more important than reality.

The rebellion that began in Khost in March 1924 lasted nine months. Its leaders were local clergy who saw the new law codes as a threat to their authority and livelihood. Unlike the higher-level ulema based in cities who had cooperated with Amanullah (despite their misgivings), these local firebrands condemned all of his new laws as illegitimate and contrary to Islamic sharia. The use of such rhetoric was important because by the same Islamic principles there was no right to resist a Muslim ruler's demand for taxes or conscripts. Nevertheless, beginning with the Mangals, it was the tribes that had most resented conscription that formed the base of the rebellion. The rebellion soon spread to the other Pashtun tribes of eastern Afghanistan after government troops failed to repress it. Realizing that his regime needed a broader political base to confront the rebels, in July Amanullah summoned a thousand prominent delegates representing the tribes, the ulema, and landowners to participate in a *loya jirga* (national constitutional assembly) in Kabul. Amanullah had called such a body together in 1923 to rubber stamp his constitution and he now expected them to renew their support of his laws to counter rebel criticism. Instead, they turned on the amir and expressed their long-repressed misgivings about his laws. The ulema wanted to subject the new codes to their interpretation of orthodox Sunni Hanifi legal principles and receive assurances that the new state legal system would not displace the traditional system of qazi judges. Stung by rebel charges that they had abandoned their religious scruples, the clerics also demanded that Amanullah restore the legal distinctions between Muslims and non-Muslims as well as abandon his restrictions on polygamy. Humiliating as it was for the amir to back down on these issues, the urban ulema did give their blessing to the reforms that most rankled the rebels. They declared the amir was within his rights to raise taxes and change the mode of conscription as he pleased. To this end, they issued a fatwa labeling the rebel clergy and their tribal supporters traitors, subject to the most severe punishment.[17]

The rebels continued to grow in strength through the summer in part because they had added a dynastic component to their struggle after naming Abdul Karim, one of Amir Yaqub Khan's sons, as their new amir. Abdul Karim had crossed into Afghanistan from India and won the support of the Ghilzai tribes by proclaiming that he would govern justly with a council of forty ulema. The addition of the powerful Ghilzais put Amanullah's regime in great danger. Rebel armies defeated his troops and advanced within eight miles of Kabul itself, pillaging the prosperous villages they passed through. Unfortunately, as Abdul Karim himself later observed, "this victory rather proved to me to be the source of ruin in that almost all my soldiers left hurriedly for their homes with the loot." Amanullah had an opportunity to regroup and then turn the tables on the rebels by declaring that Abdul Karim's appearance in Afghanistan was a British plot designed to regain control of the country. (Actually, the British themselves were at a loss to know how Abdul Karim had gotten to Afghanistan and who was financing him there.) This anti-British propaganda enabled Amanullah to change the war's discourse away from the legitimacy of his laws to defending Afghanistan from a foreign threat. The government rallied neighboring tribes to its cause under the banner of jihad and helped crush the insurgents with great loss of life by the end of the year. Abdul Karim fled back to India, but sixty leading rebels were taken to Kabul and publicly executed, though at least one roundly condemned Amanullah to the crowd as an infidel before he was shot.[18]

The Khost Rebellion left the regime intact, but graphically illustrated its weakness. It had not proved fatal because historically Afghan rulers were displaced by popular rebellions only in the context of a foreign invation— and then only when they spread across regional and ethnic lines. Still, even though this rebellion was confined to the eastern Pashtuns, Amanullah's relative neglect of the military had led to disastrous setbacks in what should have been a minor conflict. It also drained his treasury of an estimated two years' income to pay for the fighting. The necessity of calling on the tribes for military assistance only heightened the perception that his government was weak. More important, it punctured the aura of military invincibility that the Afghan state had nurtured for more than two generations. Both Amanullah's father and grandfather had so concentrated government resources on the army that after 1890, no tribe or region ever meaningfully challenged Kabul's hegemony. This was no longer the case after the Khost Rebellion. To compensate for his military setbacks, Amanullah had reached out for an alliance with the conservative clergy, rolling back social reforms but maintaining administrative ones.

In most analyses of twentieth-century Afghan politics the conservative Islamic clerics, tribes, and rural population are portrayed as equally unified against urban-based reformers like Amanullah and the nationalists. But as the loya jirga of 1924 demonstrated, the orthodox clergy could be readily enlisted as supporters of state power if their own interests were protected. Had the period of compromise continued longer, it is possible that

Amanullah would have eventually recovered enough strength to sustain his reforms, albeit at a slower pace. Instead, inspired by a world trip that made Afghanistan seem even more backward to the amir, he would return to Kabul determined to light a fire under the country. He did, and was then consumed by it.

The Civil War of 1929

In the wake of the Khost Rebellion, the amir improved his own popularity by making inspection tours of Jalalabad (1925) and Qandahar (1926), and pushing his governors elsewhere to better maintain order. Even conscription now proceeded regularly in both the eastern and southern Pashtun regions. Only two years after making so many concessions to the conservatives in the loya jirga of 1924, Amanullah now rescinded many of them and even reopened the schools for girls to which the clergy had so objected.[19] Amanullah was also now confident enough in the stability of the country to undertake a world tour in the company of his wife, Queen Soraya. The trip lasted from November 1927 until June 1928, and included stops in India, Egypt, Britain, Italy, France, Germany, the Soviet Union, Turkey, and Iran. It was unprecedented. It was the first time any reigning Afghan amir had ever traveled beyond India, let alone visited non-Muslim Europe. Nor had any ruler ever left Afghanistan for such a long period or allowed his wife to play a public role. Many of Amanullah's advisers objected to the trip's high cost and worried that the amir's long absence would weaken the government. Amanullah's enemies accused him of endangering his Islamic faith by visiting wine-drinking infidel lands and allowing the queen to appear unveiled.

The trip proved a great success as public relations. It put Afghanistan on the diplomatic map, and garnered favorable press in Europe and the Middle East—credits that played well at home too.[20] But its greatest impact was on Amanullah himself because it inspired him to renew his program of radical reform. In August 1928, he convened another loya jirga of a thousand selected representatives that approved his new laws with little dissent. These laws included plans for economic development, education, the creation of the National Assembly, and more reforms of the legal system, including family law and women's issues. In October he styled himself a "revolutionary ruler" and pushed even harder on the social front, demanding that Afghans now wear Western-style suits and hats in the government precincts of Kabul, changing the traditional Friday weekly holiday to Thursday, requiring compulsory coeducation in elementary schools, prohibiting polygamy among government officials, and declaring that the court system would now be run by secular government-trained judges, who would replace the existing qazis.[21] Amanullah also pushed to end the seclusion of women and abolish the veil. The amir's goal was no less than a new Afghanistan that would break decisively with its past:

> I am compelled to say that the great secret of progress for our country lies in discarding old outworn ideas and customs, and as the proverb goes, march with the times. Rest assured that it rests with our generation to rebuild this country in the fullest sense. . . . We must show [other countries] that we are no longer an ignorant people and that we are determined to stand upon our own feet, without leaning on others.[22]

Such changes naturally alienated the clerical establishment, even those who had supported the amir in the past. But Amanullah had already decided to confront them directly, and break their power and influence. On his return to Afghanistan the amir cut his ties with the clerical establishment entirely, refusing to meet with even its most prominent representatives, ending their stipends, and forbidding membership in Sufi orders by government officials. Amanullah harshly condemned the existing religious structure, determined to "purge the practice of Islam in Afghanistan of its folk ways, traditional taboos, and superstitions, which he claimed were espoused by ignorant and self-interested clergy."[23]

While opposition from the clerics was to be expected, Amanullah had opponents in the modernist camp as well. Although they shared common goals, modernists such as Nadir Khan had long argued that changes should be made only in selected areas rather than through the comprehensive packages favored by the amir. He recommended concentrating on economic development, and going cautiously whenever addressing women's rights and family law, which were the focus of conservative opposition. Mahmud Tarzi, the amir's father-in-law, approved of the radical social changes, but like many observers worried that the pace of change was too fast for the country to absorb. Because Amanullah refused to take advice that he did not want to hear, both men had left Afghanistan for Europe by the mid-1920s. Less publicly, liberal Young Afghans complained that the amir's plans, while progressive, left his unrestrained autocratic government unaltered. In their minds, the inherited shackles of the past that the amir so roundly condemned included Afghanistan's monarchy as well as its clergy.

For the bulk of the population in Afghanistan, the problems with the amir's reform program were less theoretical than practical. Corruption had risen to new heights during Amanullah's trip abroad, further eroding his popular support. The loya jirga in 1928 had largely rubber stamped the amir's proposals even as it put new burdens on the people, including raising the period of military conscription service from two to three years. Taxes on practically everything in rural areas had doubled or tripled under Amanullah, so that land and animal taxes amounted to almost two-thirds of his government's revenue. The urban areas were also hard hit by taxes and high import duties on an ever-wider set of goods.[24] Summarizing these miseries, Roland Wild observed that

> the tax-gatherers were more pressing than they had ever been in the past. Hardly a month went by but they came with news of a new valuation. There were taxes on houses, and new demands on weddings and funerals and village ceremonies. There seemed to be more taxation officers than tax-payers. Gradually the peasant began to know the other side of "reform." . . . The peasant paid, and when he could not suffered the annexation of his land in the cruel winter."[25]

Few of the radical new policies announced by Amanullah in 1928 had time to be implemented. Within months he was faced with uprisings similar to the earlier Khost Rebellion, but because so much more of the population had turned against him, they had expanded well beyond the perennially discontented Pashtun border tribes. The Shinwari Pashtuns were the first to revolt in November after a clash with government troops. They then attacked Jalalabad, burning the amir's winter palace to the ground. Discontented clerics soon gave this tribal rebellion a religious turn by declaring the amir an infidel. Amanullah responded with the same tactics that he had employed in 1924: promising to cancel the most inflammatory reforms and seeking the cooperation of the ulema. But the revolt had already taken a fatal turn when it was joined by the Kohistanis north of Kabul, led by a bandit named Habibullah Kalakani. Supported by the clergy, Habibullah was soon at the gates of Kabul. New offers by the amir to suspend all his reforms were rejected. In January 1929, after government troops had begun defecting to the rebels, Amanullah abdicated in favor of his brother Enayatullah and decamped to Qandahar. Within a few days Habibullah's forces were in the city and Enayatullah also abdicated. Habibullah declared himself amir. He was not the only one: Ali Ahmad, the former governor of Kabul, was proclaimed amir by the Shinwaris, and within weeks Amanullah renounced his own abdication and mustered troops in Qandahar to fight against Habibullah.

Civil wars in Afghanistan fell into two categories. The first and most common were the wars of succession confined to the existing dynastic line. The time it took to settle such conflicts ran from a few weeks to a few years, but rarely disrupted the country as a whole. The second and more deadly type of civil war was directed against the government itself. In the nineteenth century, these had only occurred under the pressure of foreign invasion and occupation because driving the foreigners out also required bringing down the governments that they had installed. Such conflicts involved much larger numbers of people and a wider array of ethnic groups, and inflicted high levels of destruction on the regions where they were fought. More important they ended with the replacement of existing ruling lineages by new ones, albeit ones still confined to a narrow elite. The Sadozais had been permanently replaced by the Muhammadzais at the end of the First Anglo-Afghan War; Abdur Rahman had dethroned the sons of Sher Ali at the end of the Second Anglo-Afghan War. Amanullah had the dubious distinction of provoking a civil war against his own government by acting as if he were a foreign occupier himself.

The revolts that drove him from power closely resembled the wars against the British. First, Amanullah faced the same pincer movement against Kabul from Tajik rebels in Kohistan to the north and Pashtun tribes from the east—the groups that took the lead in the nineteenth-century wars against the British. Second, the war against him was portrayed as a jihad against a now-illegitimate amir and had strong clerical backing. Third, it was Kabul centered; Qandahar, Herat, or Mazar did not join in the civil war until after Amanullah left the country. But there were also some differences. Amanullah's abdication when faced with defeat was unprecedented. Nineteenth-century amirs, even defeated ones driven into exile, never abdicated. As professional hereditary rulers they knew defeat was an occupational hazard that time might reverse (witness Dost Muhammad, Shah Shuja, or Abdur Rahman). Neither overthrow nor exile could ever extinguish their right to rule as long as they lived (and kept their eyes). Had Amanullah fled to Qandahar without first abdicating, he would have been in a much stronger political position to reclaim the capital by arguing that his authority as amir had never lapsed. From this perspective, no matter how many nights the new brigand amir occupied his palace it could never imbue him with true royal authority. The other and more significant difference in this civil war was the emergence of such an interloper in national politics. Unlike their nineteenth-century predecessors, the Kohistanis had not sought out a Muhammadzai royal to replace Amanullah but had instead placed one of their own on the throne. Naming a Tajik bandit amir sent shock waves through the political establishment. Not only was he an outsider, he was not even a Pashtun.[26]

The reign of Habibullah Kalakani has been excoriated in Afghan history. Invariably referred to by his opponents as Bacha Saqao (son of a water carrier), he represented the most reactionary elements and promptly abolished all of Amanullah's reforms. Though he proved to be a poor ruler, leaving Kabul in chaos during his nine-month reign, he was a crafty fighter. Without any foreign aid or international recognition, he defeated Amanullah's allies in Mazar by bringing the most prominent clergy there to his side, and later he took at least nominal control of Qandahar and Herat. He skillfully divided the Pashtun tribes for a surprisingly long time, keeping them at odds with one another by appealing to their local mullahs (who approved of his reactionary policies) as well as playing on traditional animosities between the Ghilzais and Durranis. And as much as they tried to cover it up later, many in Kabul who had worked for Amanullah also initially proved willing to work for Habibullah, even arranging for his marriage to a Muhammadzai wife. In the end, however, Habibullah Kalakani suffered from two fatal weaknesses. The first was financial. Once the estimated £750,000 he found left in the Kabul treasury ran out, which he was using to buy influence and pay his troops, there was no way to replace it. The second was his status as an outsider. The amirs of Afghanistan had been drawn exclusively from the Durrani elite for so long that even the most powerful regional and tribal leaders could not conceive of it being otherwise. Amanullah had proudly described his politics as revolutionary, but granting recognition as amir to a Kohistani bandit who came from the bottom ranks of Afghan society was such a radical break with the past that it made the thought of unveiled women walking the streets of Kabul seem tame by comparison.

Habibullah Kalakani's elevation to the amirship was only possible because the rebels seeking to topple Amanullah's government had never agreed on who should replace him. During the Anglo-Afghan wars this issue had never arisen because regional faction leaders invariably aligned themselves with some member of the royal line who used their support to establish his own authority. In the First Anglo-Afghan War Dost Muhammad's son Akbar had done this by assuming overall leadership of the resistance, paving the way for his father's return in 1843. In the Second Anglo-Afghan War Abdur Rahman had received recognition of his new government by both the resistance forces and the withdrawing British in 1880. Although the movement against Amanullah was led by powerful clerics, such religious leaders never saw themselves as possible rulers. The Kohistani factions therefore supported Habibullah, one of their own, while the Shinwari Pashtuns proclaimed Ali Ahmad, the general that Amanullah had originally sent against them, as their new amir. Ali Ahmad was also an outsider in that his descent was from the Qandahari Loinab sardars, but he was an established member of the old elite. Ali Ahmad's hopes were dashed, though, when his army disintegrated after a failed Shinwari attack on Habibullah's forces. He fled to Qandahar, but was later captured and returned to Kabul, where he was brutally executed by being blown out of a cannon.

After the collapse of Ali Ahmad's army, the eastern Pashtun tribes and clergy reconsidered their original opposition to Amanullah. He had already promised to drop his reforms and strike a new bargain with the tribes and clergy. The Durrani Pashtuns in Qandahar had rallied to him, and he had the support of the Hazaras as well. Fearing that Habibullah might well consolidate his power, many eastern Pashtuns now joined with their southern brothers to oppose him. They pledged to restore to the throne the very amir that they had only a few months earlier declared an infidel and driven from office. Since Afghan politics has always been renowned for its side switching, both parties overlooked the recent unpleasantness so that they could deal with an enemy they now feared more. Amanullah had encouraged this alliance by playing on the Pashtun chauvinism, insisting that such a proud people could never accept a Tajik bandit as their amir. He also fell back on the timeworn accusation that the British were to blame for all of Afghanistan's problems. He accused them of driving him from power so that Habibullah could rule the country as their agent. Yet as much as the British disliked Amanullah, the uprising against him was of his own making and none of their doing. On the other hand, they did nothing to help him regain power either. Declaring a policy of neutrality, the British refused to grant Habibullah's regime diplomatic recognition, but also blocked Amanullah's attempts to gain access to the Afghan arm shipments that were being held up in India. In spite of this problem, Amanullah's position in the east appeared to improve with the arrival in Afghanistan of Nadir Khan and his brothers from France in February 1929. Nadir had strong ties with the eastern tribes, and he and his brothers took the lead in organizing them against Habibullah (who had by then put a price on Nadir's head). There are those who later accused Nadir of coming to Afghanistan with the intent of making himself amir, but if so he played a subtle hand. By March, Amanullah was riding such a wave of support among the eastern tribes that Nadir was careful to position himself as an enemy of Habibullah allied with Amanullah without ever making it clear whether or not he supported Amanullah's restoration.

Amanullah's prospects took a sudden turn for the worse in late May, when his army marched north out of Qandahar toward Kabul and was ambushed by the Ghilzai near Ghazni. Fazl Omar, the Mujaddedi Hazrat of Shor Bazaar and a long-standing enemy of Amanullah, had induced his followers there to support Habibullah and attack their traditional Durrani rivals. According to British reports, Fazl Omar had brought the Ghilzais into the fray with the understanding that Nadir, with whom he was in close communication, would become amir. Faced with continued attacks by both Habibullah's troops and the Ghilzais, and having received word that Herat had fallen to Habibullah's forces too, Amanullah soon took

Nadir's advice that he should leave Afghanistan for exile in Europe. Nadir now took the lead in fighting Habibullah as the Pashtun champion. Fazl Omar issued a fatwa declaring Habibullah a tyrant who deserved condemnation. Nadir challenged Habibullah to put his claims of rulership to the test in a loya jirga of tribal leaders—a contest that the Tajik would surely lose. But Habibullah's hold on power remained tenacious. Nadir and his brothers attacked Kabul four times in summer 1929, only to be repulsed on each occasion. Even in the absence of Amanullah (or perhaps because of it), the Pashtun tribes remained fragmented and unwilling to unify against Habibullah. Nadir lacked the money needed to buy their support, and many tribal groups appeared to be content with the absence of any government. In the end it was a tribal *lashgar* of twelve thousand Wazir tribesmen from the British side of the frontier assembled by his youngest brother, Shah Wali Khan, who took Kabul on October 13. In the absence of pay, the Wazirs looted the city before returning home. Nadir was proclaimed king two days later. Two weeks later Habibullah was hanged, along with around a dozen of his followers.[27]

Act II: The Musahiban Dynasty, 1929–78

Habibullah's defeat opened the question of who should rule Afghanistan. Nadir recommended that an assembly of notables act as a jirga and decide the issue. Nadir's brother explained that his "position was that once the civil war had ended, the Afghans should choose their monarch in the time honored way," although he disclaimed any interest in the job himself. The assembly immediately rejected Amanullah's restoration and enthusiastically chose Nadir to replace him—a decision particularly welcomed by the armed tribesmen still on the streets of Kabul who refused to leave until he took the kingship. Nadir did so, saying, "Since the people so designate me so, I accept. I will not be the king but the servant of the tribes and the country."[28]

Let there be no doubt that this was a dynastic change. The descendants of Dost Muhammad were being replaced by a collateral line of Muhammadzais, the Musahibans, Peshawar sardars who had never before been considered candidates for the amirship. Perhaps for this reason Nadir renamed himself Nadir Shah. Just as Dost Muhammad had dropped the title

of shah in favor of amir in 1826 because it was so associated with the Sadozais that he was replacing, a century later Nadir did the opposite but for
the same reason. He needed to symbolically distance himself from Amanullah's line because they had a stronger claim to the throne than his people
did. A change in titles made that a bit less obvious. Abdur Rahman's earlier
grant of elite status to the Muhammadzais as a class had also helped by
blurring the distinctions among the lineages within it (which was one reason why he exiled those families that he judged as having any political
ambition). A more creative justification used to defend Nadir's legitimacy
was the assertion that his election by a jirga representing the people was
Afghanistan's "time honored way" of choosing its rulers. In reality it was an
invented tradition that had little historical basis. The last jirga to play such
a role was the one in 1747 that chose Ahmad Shah Durrani. After him, the
choice of the ruler remained the exclusive monopoly of a dynastic elite
composed first of Sadozais and then of Muhammadzais. Though contend-
ing dynastic factions often sought the support of different tribes, regions,
or clerics to put themselves in power, they were never elected by them. In
any event, previous Afghan rulers had always seen their people as subjects
to be ruled, not constituents to be courted. It was probably Amanullah's
own frequent calling of loya jirgas to ratify his laws and approve his policies that, ironically, set the stage for then using one to select a ruler to replace him. Lacking any hereditary claim to the throne, Nadir needed such
a justification to preserve himself from the charge of usurpation and legitimate what would become a new dynasty. Another way of doing this
was by repositioning the legal foundation of the Afghan monarchy away
from the near divine right basis championed by Abdur Rahman to a more
consent of the governed model embodied in Nadir's claim that he was now
"the servant of the tribes and the country." Afghanistan remained a monarchy, but its rulers were changing with the times. Still, like Abdur Rahman, the Musahibans acted much more autocratically after they entrenched
themselves in power than when they were competing for it.

Amanullah and his followers did look on Nadir's succession as an usurpation. On Habibullah Kalikani's death he had expected to be invited back
as the rightful amir, believing that he had not abandoned his claim to the
throne, but had only left the country to avoid needless bloodshed. In addition, Amanullah continued to claim that Nadir had fought the war in his

name, not as an announced pretender. So too if a loya jirga was to settle the issue by determining the will of the people, then the rump group that assembled in Kabul on Nadir's arrival in the city was illegitimate because it was too small, did not adequately represent Amanullah's followers, and had not heard the strong arguments in favor of his restoration. Nadir's faction used his newspaper, *Islah*, to rebut these charges, rejecting the claim that Nadir had been fighting in the ex-amir's name and presenting Amanullah in the worst possible light. They asserted that only Nadir had the capacity to restore stability to Afghanistan, and that far from scheming to take power, it was thrust on him.

> If Amanullah Khan was so much loved by his nation, how could the Great Revolution of Afghanistan take place? Nadir Shah and his family did not arrive in Afghanistan to reign but rather to save the country. He did not want to become King. Kingship was thrust upon him "in the presence of the delegates of the nation and the diplomatic corp." It was under the repeated pressures of the *jirga* that he accepted the burden of his reign.[29]

For all practical purposes this succession contest ended when the British formally recognized Nadir's regime in mid-November 1929, and began providing him with money and arms to stabilize his government. Six months later he reciprocated by confirming the existing treaties between Afghanistan and Britain.[30] He still faced opposition in Afghanistan, however, and during summer 1930 needed to call again on the Pashtun border tribes to put down revolts by the Shinwaris and Kohistanis—the very peoples who had first risen against Amanullah. He also imprisoned and executed many of Amanullah's liberal supporters, who had remained in the country. After finally putting down the last remnants of opposition against his regime in the north and west, Nadir assembled a loya jirga in September 1931 of 510 members, who approved an official declaration of deposition (*khal*) that formally abrogated the rights of Amanullah and his heirs on the grounds that he had violated sharia law.[31]

This proved a timely decision because in November 1933 Nadir was assassinated in a revenge attack and was immediately succeeded by his young son, Zahir Shah, who was to remain king of Afghanistan for the next forty years.

Musahiban Policies: Stability über Alles

For the Musahibans nothing was more important than preserving the internal stability of Afghanistan, which they defined as maintaining their own rule over the country. Such a goal may not seem ambitious but it was far from easy to achieve. Power remained highly concentrated within Nadir's extended family over the course of almost fifty years. In a country of weak institutions, their success in remaining united (or at least keeping the fights within the immediate family) provided the ballast to keep the ship of state on an even keel. They also had a long-term vision about how to structure the relationship between state and society to avoid conservative rebellions while still modernizing the country. It was a strategy of limited and gradual social change accompanied by economic development. Changes would begin in Kabul and move outward in a manner that would facilitate change without imposing it. To this end, the Musahibans realized that most Afghan rural rebellions that were later justified in Islamic terms had initially been provoked by the state's economic demands for money and conscript troops. They still needed cheap manpower for the military, but they did seek to reduce the state's economic pressure on the countryside in return for greater political subservience. Over the decades, taxes on rural production and people gradually declined in real terms until they were no longer a significant revenue source. In their place the Musahibans put the revenue burden on trade tariffs, government monopoly enterprises, and (particularly in its last twenty years) foreign aid and loans.

These strategies had developed in reaction to the Amanullah's difficulties, and were designed to both prevent the turmoil that brought his regime down and reestablish an unchallengeable central government. The Musahibans perceived the greatest threat to their rule as arising from any alliance between Afghanistan's disaffected rural population and the conservative Islamic establishment, but over time its own policies made these groups ever more marginal and less politically significant. As the state gradually eliminated rural taxation (and thus the need for corrupt tax officials who scoured the land to collect it), the tension between Kabul and the countryside subsided. Similarly, the Musahibans gradually marginalized the clergy and Sufi order leaders who played a powerful role in the 1930s, until by the 1960s they were no longer able to set state policy and had been pushed into the background. The success of both these strategies appeared sealed by the mid-1970s, when the government easily suppressed a new nonclerical Islamist movement that had attempted to foment a rebellion in the countryside. Not only was there no positive response to the call for insurrection; the imprisonment of many established clerics during the ensuing government's crackdown produced little protest. But the very strategies used to sideline the conservatives had also empowered the modernist ideological descendants of Amanullah who believed that the Musahiban rule was too reactionary. Underestimating these people would prove the dynasty's undoing.

MUSAHIBAN LEADERSHIP ROLES

This solidity of the Musahiban brothers was apparent from the beginning. When Nadir chose to split with Amanullah in the mid-1920s his brothers all joined him in France. They returned together to Afghanistan, and it was only their close cooperation in the war against Habibullah that brought Nadir to the throne. Nadir immediately reinforced these ties by giving his brothers the most powerful government posts when he became king. He named Hashim Khan as premier, Shah Wali Khan as the minister of war and commander in chief, and Shah Mahmud as the minister of the interior. Although Zahir Shah assumed the kingship at age nineteen on Nadir's death, he remained largely a figurehead until the last decade of his reign—his aging and more balding head marking the passage of time on Afghanistan's banknotes. From 1933 to 1946 the real strongman was Hashim Khan, who turned the premiership over to his brother Shah Mahmud when he became ill. Mahmud was the dominant figure from 1946 to 1953, when he retired as prime minister in favor of his nephew Daud Khan.

The appointment of Daud marked not just a change in generation but also the beginning of a twenty-year tarburwali rivalry between him and his cousin Zahir Shah. Daud, whose own father had died in an assassination in Berlin weeks before Nadir was also shot, had long been groomed for

power by his uncle Hashim Khan. Hashim had never married (highly unusual in Afghanistan) and so treated his nephews as surrogate sons. Since
Zahir Shah's uncles had been the real powers ruling the country since
1933, this strongman succession to Daud in 1953 merely continued this
pattern. He resembled his stern uncles in his personality and ruling style.
Nadir's brothers and Daud were all more feared than loved by ordinary
Afghans. Daud's rule as prime minister ended in 1963, when Zahir Shah
finally took the reins of power himself. To maintain his supremacy, Zahir
Shah approved of a new constitution in 1964 that prohibited members of
the royal family from holding any ministerial posts. The limits of such
paper prohibitions became apparent when Daud returned to power in a
largely bloodless coup mounted while his cousin was in Italy in 1973.
Daud's declaration of a republic may have formally ended the monarchy,
but it did not end Musahiban rule or its monarchical style, as the appearance of Daud's own bald head on the country's currency soon attested.

SOCIAL CHANGES

Under Amanullah, Afghanistan had been at the forefront of change in
the Islamic world, but his regime had been unable to sustain it. Under
Musahiban rule Afghanistan was stable yet stagnated. By whatever indexes
of modernization one chose to examine, Afghanistan would persistently
lag behind practically every other Muslim country. Amanullah had wanted
his country to be seen as innovative; by contrast, his immediate successors
attempted no reforms that had not already been introduced in other countries of the Middle East or south Asia at least a generation earlier. One
reason for this was the bargains that they had struck with the clergy and
tribes on coming to power. The most powerful tribes were exempted from
conscription, and the Ministry of Tribal Affairs tended to their needs. The
constitution of 1932 was effusive in its praise for all things Islamic and
gave supremacy to the Sunni Hanifi school in legal disputes. Nadir made
his ally Fazal Omar Mujadedi the minister of justice, putting the state legal
system in the hands of religious conservatives—where it remained for more
than a generation. As in Amanullah's time, these conservatives were keener
to block social changes than restrict government power, and so made no objection when the Musahibans reinstituted Amanullah's state-centralizing bu-

reaucratic reforms such as registration cards and conscription, and created a powerful gendarmerie under the control of the Ministry of the Interior.

After the precipitous decline in education as a result of the civil war, Hashim Khan made the delivery of modern education a key government goal, but the task was so overwhelming that even twenty years later the results were meager. As Vartan Gregorian concluded, "The needs and short-comings of education in Afghanistan were staggering."

According to both Soviet and Western estimates, by 1948 only 8 per-cent of the population was literate. At the time there were only 2,758 teachers and 98,660 pupils. According to a UNESCO mission in 1949 less than 10 per cent of school age girls were in educational institu-tions. As late as 1954, the total school enrollment in Afghanistan, ex-cluding Kabul University [which was founded only in 1946], was 114,266, or about 4.5 per cent of the approximately 2.4 million school age children.[32]

Of the small number of students who were able to enroll in secondary education at the end of the 1950s, it was estimated that only about 26 percent completed their studies. Even more troublesome for the country's future was the ever-widening gap between Kabul and the rest of the coun-try. In 1959, 73.8 percent of the country's secondary school students re-sided in Kabul, a city whose population constituted only 1.8 percent of the total Afghanistan population.[33]

Given the high concentration of modernizing institutions in the capital and the more liberal attitudes of its population, the Musahiban strategy for making social changes was to introduce them first in Kabul quietly rather than as parts of noisy national programs. Most of these changes, however, came only after the Musahibans had been in power for more than thirty years. The best example of this was the end to the mandatory veiling for women that had been reintroduced with the fall of Amanullah. Rather than issue a proclamation or engage in any consciousness-raising debates, Prime Minister Daud simply had the wives of the royal family and high government ministers sit unveiled in the reviewing stands at the National Day parade in 1959 where everyone could see them. Word went out that the government no longer considered the veil mandatory and would de-fend women who chose to appear without it. When conservative clerics denounced Daud's government for this action and called for its downfall, Daud had fifty of them arrested on charges of treason.[34] There was no popular uprising in support of the conservatives, and the issue soon faded from the public stage. The lack of a response was predictable; the reform was seen as overdue in Kabul, and few unveiled women appeared outside the capital. Choosing to frame the issue as a choice versus compulsion also weakened the critics because women continued to observe strict purdah in more conservative areas.* But perhaps a greater reason for the muted response was that when Amanullah proposed abolishing the veil, he had made it part of a larger project designed to transform Afghan life through the emancipation of women more broadly. This included restrictions on the age of marriage and proof of consent—limiting bride price payments and wedding expenses—and prohibitions on polygamy for government officials. By contrast, the list of social changes introduced under the Musahiban monarchy was small and mostly visible in Kabul. They feared making any broad-based reforms lest it put their regime at risk. By making it clear that they were restricting such reforms to an urban elite that already wanted them, they reduced the veil issue to the status of a fashion statement divorced from the larger and more contentious question of women's rights in general.

ECONOMIC CHANGES

Implicit in the Musahiban strategy of gradual social reforms was the belief that modernizing the economy should take precedence. Amanullah had been keen on development too, but his enthusiasm proved greater than his achievement. Initially the Musahibans had limited resources at their disposal. Still fearful of outside influence, they were unwilling to allow foreign investment in the country or to engage in large-scale international borrowings. Instead they sought government control over domestic merchants, whose profits from trade could be used to finance small-scale industrialization and agricultural development. The government helped to

---

* As the use of the full veil fell out of fashion in Kabul over the next twenty years, it would become more widespread in the countryside as a status marker because it had previously been a practice followed only by the urban upper class, whose women did not need to work.

create the first modern corporation in the country by chartering the Bank Melli Afghan in 1932 as a joint stock company with thirty-four million afghanis (US$3.5 million) in capital. In return, it demanded an ownership share and later created its own Da Afghanistan Bank in 1939 as a rival institution. Granted monopolies over many types of exports and with the political influence to see its projects to completion, Bank Melli Afghan saw its assets rise to 454 million afghanis ($40 million) by 1948. By 1950, these two banks had combined assets of 660 million afghanis ($60 million)—a substantial amount of money in such a cash-poor country.[35] The government benefited not only from its ownership shares but by imposing export tariffs and currency exchange controls as well.

On the ground, the greatest economic impact of this new policy was the establishment of a new export cotton industry centered on Kunduz in the north. Former malarial swamps were reclaimed, and the cheap land attracted settlers from many parts of the country, including previously rebellious Pashtuns deported there from the south following the Safi Rebellion of 1946. In the mid-1930s, the region produced only four hundred tons of cotton but within ten years this number climbed to ten thousand tons. Factories for processing the cotton were imported from the Soviet Union, Britain, and Germany, and cotton was exported north through Uzbekistan. The Spinzar (White Gold) Cotton Company became the dominant economic institution in the northeast—one of the only important economic enterprises not centered in Kabul. The karakul lambskin business, from a special breed of sheep also found in the north, became an even larger export industry. A traditional export of central Asia, this lambskin was highly profitable due to the demand in the West as well as India. It accounted for 40 to 50 percent of all Afghan exports between 1935 and 1945, when exports doubled from 1.5 to 3.3 million skins annually.* Another 40 percent of export trade during this period was in agricultural products (fruits, grain, cotton, and opium). These exports financed the imports of manufactured goods, petroleum products, all types of equipment, metals, and machinery. One reason that the economy did not diversify more was because Afghanistan's infrastructure was so poor. Electricity

---

*For this reason, the Afghan consulate in New York City was located in the downscale fur district on Thirtieth Street, rather far from other diplomatic missions, to attend to this major export business.

was rare outside Kabul, as were telephone and telegraph lines. The country's road system remained rudimentary despite Nadir's success at pushing a route north through the Hindu Kush using corvée labor. This helped internal trade, but since Afghanistan continued to lack railroads there was no way to develop the country's considerable mineral wealth, which would have required massive investments of foreign capital in any event. Instead, the government proudly pointed to the construction of light factories for processing sugar, packing fruit, or weaving cloth. Many of these used equipment that had first been purchased by Amanullah, so getting them into operation marked significant progress. Still, they had little impact on the overall economy. The Soviet scholar R. T. Akhramovich estimated that such internal production met only 10 to 15 percent of its domestic demand for textiles, sugar, shoes, and other simple consumer goods at midcentury.[36] Thirty years later the percentage of domestic production was not much greater, even though at that time Afghan Communists would insist that the existence of such factories proved that Afghanistan had passed through its capitalist phase and was now ready for socialism—a position that even their Soviet comrades less than politely dismissed as wishful thinking.

In fact, throughout the Musahiban period the national economy remained subsistence based. Even in the 1970s, the export of sheep products raised mostly by nomads made up 30 percent of the county's exports. Only 20 percent of the country's annual wheat production entered the market for sale. Until a paved road system was constructed in the 1960s, each region remained economically isolated, with no way for areas of grain surplus to meet the demands of deficit regions. Gas deposits developed in the northwest were piped directly to the Soviet Union as part of a barter trade system in the 1960s that had little impact internally. If the basic economy had not shifted much, though, the government's relation to it had. Taxing export trade generated revenues that were much easier to collect than the land and animal taxes traditionally levied against farmers and pastoralists. As Maxwell Fry has shown, the importance of such direct taxes declined sharply as the government turned to other revenue sources. Indeed because the tax rates were never raised to reflect inflation, eventually it hardly mattered whether or not they were paid. Land and animal taxes that made up the bulk of the government's revenue in the 1920s had declined to only

30 percent in the early 1950s, and accounted for less than 1 percent of government revenue in the 1970s. Taxation in other areas did not rise much either, so that Afghanistan's "tax effort" (the percentage of potential revenue versus that collected) was next to last in a comparison of fifty developing countries.[37]

The declining percentage of revenue gained by domestic taxation and trade tariffs needed to be made up from elsewhere, particularly as the size of the government began to rise sharply as did its expenditures for new development projects. The Musahibans therefore turned to a finance strategy first pioneered by Ahmad Shah Durrani himself when he conquered India: meet the dynasty's needs by extracting revenue from foreigners. From the time of Dost Muhammad to Abdur Rahman these external resources had taken the form of British subsidies. While these had disappeared with Afghanistan's independence in the 1920s, the world situation in the 1930s began evolving in ways that again allowed Afghanistan to manipulate great power rivalries to advance its own interests. This started in a small way during the prewar period when Afghanistan sought aid from the Axis powers (Germany, Japan, and Italy) to offset British and Soviet influence, but achieved its greatest success in the postwar period when it manipulated the rivalry between the Soviet Union and the United States. Beginning in the 1950s with the modernization of the Afghan army, the building of a true road infrastructure in the 1960s, and a vast increase in the number of educated young Afghans by the 1970s, Afghanistan's most rapid and far-reaching period of development would be financed by foreigners. The government itself became so dependent on foreign aid and loans that by the 1973, two-thirds of its annual revenue was derived from foreign grants and loans.[38] The old strategic great game was paying rich new dividends, and Afghanistan became a rentier state, clipping its coupons to pay expenses. This strengthened the ruling dynasty in two ways. First, it was able to provide new benefits while lowering the domestic tax burden. Second, it allowed the dynasty to fill a unique role as an intermediary (and circuit breaker) between an insular Afghan society suspicious of outside influences and the international community from which the government drew an ever-larger percentage of its income. The latter role required a degree of sophistication that none of the government's internal rivals had mastered.

FOREIGN AFFAIRS

In a country that often cultivated a reputation for isolation and xeno-
phobia, Afghan leaders had always proved remarkably shrewd in dealing
with the outside world. Historically they negotiated even with their worst
enemies if they thought they could come to a useful accommodation. This
required great skill because for Afghanistan the world situation became
much more complex in the twentieth century than it was in the nineteenth. The Soviet Union replaced Russia after the First World War. The
British would withdraw from India following the Second World War, leaving Afghanistan to deal with new successor states. As the United States
came to replace Britain as the major power concerned with possible Russian expansion in the region, Afghanistan lost none of its potential strategic importance. The Musahiban plan was to warm Afghanistan with the
heat generated by the great power conflicts without getting drawn into
them directly.

During the nineteenth century, Afghanistan's main goal was to avoid
incorporation by the czarist empire to its north and the British raj to its
south. In the twentieth century its existence as a nation was less at threat,
but Nadir returned to the old Afghan policy of not provoking his powerful
neighbors unnecessarily, even if that meant taking actions that were unpopular domestically. He concluded a nonaggression pact with the Soviets
in 1931 and repressed the remnants of the basmachi movement, which
had considerable support within Afghanistan. Similarly, he stopped Afghan aid to the Pashtuns in the NWFP who were engaged in armed resistance against the British. To this policy of accommodation the Musahibans
added a new strategy of seeking out powerful patrons from outside the
region to develop the country. They believed it was safer to accept aid from
such powers because they had no common borders with Afghanistan and
therefore no interest (or ability) to take Afghan territory. They could also
be employed as a "third force" to offset the political pressure exerted by
their immediate neighbors. Germany, Japan, and the United States were
the most natural candidates for this position in the 1930s. Germany had
always been the most popular European power among the Afghans because it had fought against both Russia and Britain as an ally with Muslim
Turkey in the First World War. Japan was a self-made Asian economic and

military power that had become the equal of the European powers. The United States had the world's largest economy and took an anticolonial view of European empires.

But in seeking out new allies the Afghans faced a problem. What could they offer such distant lands to induce them to take an interest in playing such a role? The Japanese signed a treaty of friendship with the Afghans in 1930 and increased their level of trade, but Afghanistan was well beyond that country's east Asian sphere of interest. Despite Afghan overtures, the United States showed little interest in the country. It had waited until 1934 to recognize the new Musahiban government and did not establish a diplomatic mission in Kabul for another decade. In spite of this coolness, the Afghans granted an unprecedented seventy-five-year oil and mineral monopoly concession to a U.S. company in 1937. Much to the chagrin of the Afghans, the company quickly surrendered the concession on the grounds that Afghanistan's potential oil wealth was too inaccessible, and would thus require hundreds of millions of dollars to develop and export. It was risky to begin such an investment with the world on the brink of war again. Yet the same move to war had renewed German interest in Afghanistan. By 1939 the Nazi regime had sent hundreds of experts to Afghanistan, where they served throughout the government. Unlike Japan and the United States, the German government was willing to provide long-term credits for trade and investment. It would exchange machinery for Afghan cotton and agreed to provide financing for 80 percent of the Afghan government's purchases made through the state bank. The Afghan modernists looked on this increased German cooperation as wholly positive because it would better offset the influence of Russia and Britain.[39]

If the Second World War had not broken out, the use of German capital and expertise might have spurred Afghanistan's modernization in the 1940s. Instead, before the promised machinery and money could arrive in Afghanistan, Germany was at war with Britain in 1939. In a seeming replay of the First World War strategy, the Germans tried to get the Afghans to assist the Axis powers in causing trouble for India. As before, the Afghans made a secret agreement to join the Germans if and when their armies arrived in central Asia, but otherwise maintained formal neutrality. After the Germans attacked the Soviet Union in October 1941, the Afghans received an ultimatum from the British and Russians to expel all

Axis subjects working in the country. Aware that only a month earlier neighboring Iran had been invaded and divided by the British and Soviets for being too pro-German, the Afghans reluctantly acceded to this demand. But to preserve himself from the opprobrium that had rained down on Habibullah when he gave in to similar British demands during World War One, Hashim Khan was canny enough to call a loya jirga to ratify this decision. In the name of securing the country from attack, he also used the same assembly to win approval for a new law that increased the size of the army through more widespread conscription and a tax increase that would have ordinarily aroused widespread opposition.[40]

The war had a devastating impact on the Afghan economy. Its modernization was stopped in its tracks, and capital fled the country for India. Prices rose as the economy declined, impoverishing ordinary people and creating social unrest. As the Axis powers went down to defeat, all that seemed left of the German alliance was the lasting belief inculcated by Nazi ideologues that Afghanistan was the "homeland of the Aryans"—a racist concept that had displaced the old tradition that the Pashtun tribes were descendants of the Jewish lost tribes.

If the First World War had shattered the old Ottoman Empire and transmuted the czarist Russian Empire into the Soviet Union, the Second World War initiated the process of dissolving the West's Asian colonial empires. Since the beginning of the nineteenth century, the British raj had been the dominant power in south Asia with the most significant impact on Afghanistan during times of both war and peace. The British announcement that they would withdraw completely from India in 1947 was therefore a tectonic shift that shook Afghanistan with all the force and suddenness of a catastrophic earthquake, leaving the political landscape transformed in its wake. The Afghans had been dealing with the British for so long that the implications of their leaving were practically beyond comprehension. Since Afghanistan had historically played the role of a buffer state, how would the dissolution of the raj in the south affect its ability to deal with the Soviet empire to their north? And how should Afghanistan respond to the British partition of the subcontinent that would create a new state, Pakistan, along its border? The answer to the first question was to seek a new world power patron, the United States, to counter Soviet influence. The answer to the second was to demand the return of Pashtun land earlier ceded to the British or make it independent as part of a new "Pashtuni-stan." The first would make Afghanistan a target of competition during the cold war between the Soviets and the United States. The second would periodically poison the relationship between Pakistan and Afghanistan through disputes that continue to this day. It would also put Afghanistan's international politics on two tracks: one dealing with the big powers and international agencies, and the other with its neighbors in the region.

The cold war provided Afghanistan the development aid and expertise it had sought earlier from Germany. In the postwar period Afghanistan considered the idea of joining the various U.S.-sponsored alliances aimed at containing the Soviet Union. In the end it remained neutral because the United States was unwilling to formally guarantee its security against a Soviet attack or provide direct military assistance to modernize Afghanistan's army. Both these decisions had their roots in the closer relationships between the United States and neighboring Iran and Pakistan that made Afghanistan seem peripheral in U.S. eyes. Having been refused military aid by the United States, in 1956 the Afghans turned to the Soviets, who were happy to comply with $25 million worth of tanks, jets, and other arms. With this help the Afghan government finally had a military force that appeared capable of overwhelming any internal opposition—a task that had still proved difficult in the 1940s. Going back to Sher Ali, the Afghan government's first priority in its relationships with friendly foreign powers was to build up the military. With that on the way to accomplishment, the Afghan government under Daud Khan's leadership moved to improve the country's primitive infrastructure.

The arrival of Soviet weapons and advisers changed the U.S. calculus about Afghanistan's importance. The U.S. government decided to compete with the Soviets for influence by providing economic aid. The United States had been involved in the development of the Helmand Valley irrigation scheme in the south since 1946, but this experience had been less than satisfactory as each side blamed the other over its many problems. In the wake of the Soviet military aid, the United States increased its investment here and expanded into new infrastructure of many types to compete with the Soviets. The Afghans put their long experience at manipulating international rivalries to good use. For example, they got the Russians to build silos and the Americans to then fill them with wheat. More significantly, the Afghans arranged for the construction of a fifteen-hundred-mile paved ring road to knit the country together and link it to the outside world. About half the sections were constructed by the United States (mostly east-west) and half by the Soviets (mostly north-south). The most spectacular of these projects was the road and tunnel system built by the Soviets that pierced the Hindu Kush at the Salang Pass north of Kabul. At the time it was the highest motorable pass in the world, built over six years and opened in 1964. With Western aid, education also expanded greatly to about 5,700 students attending Kabul University in 1970, and 580,000 students enrolled in about 3,000 primary and secondary schools. Over the next decade the number would almost double, so that in 1979 the number of primary students topped a million, with 136,000 secondary students and 23,000 enrolled in higher education. All in all, Fry estimated that over a billion dollars in the form of grants, loans, and barter deals flowed into Afghanistan, permitting the country's development budget to exceed its regular budget in the 1960s. The economic modernization sought by Amanullah was coming to fruition in many areas, but it had also made Afghanistan heavily dependent on foreign aid. Since the government received this aid, it was able to secure its own power but did little to transform the country as a whole.[41]

The Decline and Fall of the Musahibans, 1963–78

Historically, the modernization process has sloughed off monarchies like a growing snake sheds its skin. The Musahiban plan to develop the Afghan economy, society, and infrastructure, while preserving its own power, was therefore embedded in both a contradiction and wishful thinking. The greater the Musahibans' success in achieving their goals, the more likely they were to be displaced by the very interest groups they helped to create.

Before these development projects began in earnest in the late 1950s, the Musahibans had successfully restricted power to a select few for thirty years. They had been able to do this in part by organizing the state's relatively small bureaucracy and military as "servants of the palace," patrimonial institutions with little political influence and no autonomy. The desire to create a more modern military, however, demanded the training of a larger professional officer corps that would command tank battalions and air forces that could as easily topple a small elite as preserve it. The expansion and professionalization of the military was soon followed by a similar development in a civilian bureaucracy. These changes proved fatal to old patrimonial ties as mid-ranking individuals in both the military and bureaucracy came to see themselves as instrumental in preserving state power no matter who held the reins of command. Their previously close identification with the monarchy and its interests atrophied, and was transferred to the state structure itself.*

A hint of this problem arose as early as 1948, when the "Liberal Parliament" spawned a variety of small new parties (Marxist, nationalist, Islamist, and democratic) that demanded more political openness and shared antimonarchist views. Although such parties were quite small and had few connections beyond Kabul, the government's response was to ban them, close their newspapers, and reinstitute more dictatorial rule under Daud in 1953. His policy combined co-optation with repression—a tactic long successfully employed by his uncles. The growing government apparatus needed trained personnel so it was relatively easy to incorporate the rising but still small numbers of secondary school and university graduates into its service. These institutions included the military, the civilian bureaucracy, the educational system, and industries that the government either owned or dominated. All of these began to grow significantly, particularly in the 1960s. It was during this period that King Zahir Shah ended Daud's rule and experimented with a parliamentary system put in place by the constitution of 1964. While the new parliament became a place of lively debate, no political parties were permitted, and real power remained in the hands of the king and his relatives.

This experiment in democracy ended in 1973, when Daud mounted a coup and declared a republic, which finished the monarchy but not the Musahiban dynasty. Much as he had done twenty years earlier after a similar period of liberalization, Daud took power with an eye toward imposing

---

*I later saw an example when a mujahideen "shadow minister" of agriculture in Peshawar requested current fertilizer production statistics for me from the PDPA ministry in Kabul in the 1980s. He explained that the functionaries were happy to comply with such requests because they wished to demonstrate how necessary they were to the operation of any government.

tighter political control over the country. Unlike previous family disputes that toppled existing rulers, such as those that littered the nineteenth century, Daud had not relied on the mobilization of tribes or the clergy to put himself in power. He instead looked to factions within the military and the leftist political parties that had grown dissatisfied with Zahir Shah and sought a greater role in setting government policy. These new political forces had been a product of Afghanistan's rapid development. Even among those who did not benefit directly, the changing economy and political ferment in Kabul created a revolution of rising expectations in terms of public services, infrastructure, and the standard of living that the government was failing to adequately address. Nowhere was this more obvious than among the graduates of Afghanistan's expanding educational system. They represented a generation of newly educated Afghans who saw the monarchy as an obstacle to the country's progress (and their own).

Education has always been touted as the key to economic development because a modern economy cannot operate without educated people. In many developing countries, however, the capacity of the government and economy to absorb such individuals is limited. Thus, like the sorcerer's apprentice who wished into existence a few helpers who then kept multiplying beyond his control, the Musahibans enlarged the class of educated Afghans only to discover they could not limit its growth. Although the total number of schools and graduates in Afghanistan still remained low by international standards, within a decade widespread unemployment struck the very class of people who had the highest expectations for their own futures. During the 1950s and 1960s, the government absorbed practically all graduates who had secondary and university training. By the 1970s this was no longer possible. Government employment was now growing at a much slower rate, and getting more education no longer guaranteed employment. Even for those who had such jobs, the rate of pay was so meager that it encouraged endemic low-level corruption. The private sector could not support them either. Most of Afghanistan's industry was state owned and starved of resources, especially since the government made foreign investment difficult or impossible. Education in Afghanistan also created a cultural divide because university graduates, and even those with only a secondary education, considered it beneath their dignity to return to villages, where farming and pastoralism still predominated.

Kabul University became a particular hotbed of political radicalism, spreading among the disaffected. Advanced educational opportunities drew talented youths from the countryside; they were introduced to new ideas, new opportunities, and each other at the university. After graduation, they stayed in the capital whether or not they found employment because it was the country's primary city, overshadowing everywhere else. Radical politics flourished in Kabul within secret societies formed to seek the overthrow of Afghanistan's social and political order. At opposite ends of the spectrum, the two most important actors were the Islamists and the Communists, who often clashed violently on campus and in the streets of Kabul.

The Islamists had their base in the Sharia Law Faculty at Kabul University, where a student group called the Muslim Youth Organization formed. Formalized as a party in 1973 and later renamed Jamiat-i-Islami (Islamic Society), its founders included such faculty members as Burhanaddin Rabani and Ghulam Rasul Sayyaf along with Gulbuddin Hekmatyar, a former student at a technical university who had been jailed for murdering a leftist student earlier. Drawing inspiration from the Muslim Brotherhood in Egypt, they sought to establish a state based on sharia law in which politics and religion were intertwined. The Islamists were multiethnic and came out of the state educational system rather than traditional madrasas (religious schools), as did the ulema. They were provincials, not Kabulis, and what little experience they had with the outside world was exclusively with Islamic countries.[42]

The Communists formed the PDPA in 1965 under the leadership of Nur Muhammad Taraki and Babrak Karmal. By 1967 it had split into two factions. The largely Pashtun Khalq (Masses), under the leadership of Taraki and Hafizullah Amin, recruited heavily among the disaffected Ghilzai Pashtuns in the Soviet-trained military, while the mainly Persian-speaking Parcham (Banner), under the leadership of Karmal, had its center of power in the bureaucracy and educational institutions. Though both were Marxist and pro-Soviet, the Khalq faction was in favor of an uprising that would bring down the old order and open the way for a quick progression to socialism. Parcham was more willing to cooperate with progressive forces within the existing elite and envisioned a slower economic transition. It was multiethnic, but most members were Kabul born, and many were tied by clientage or marriage to the Musahiban elite. They attended prestigious secondary schools, but their higher education remained within Afghanistan. By contrast, the Khalqis were not only Pashtuns but also eastern Pashtuns who came to Kabul via tribal boarding schools or the military academy. They had no marriage ties with the old elite.[43]

The membership of such radical groups was tiny for a country the size of Afghanistan. The PDPA later claimed it had eighteen thousand members in 1978, but activist membership was probably only a third of that. The Islamist parties had even fewer members, although they overlapped with the much larger number of traditional ulema and Sufi orders. They were able to play an outsized political role because in Afghanistan national politics was restricted to Kabul and focused on the state. Neither the Islamists nor Communists created countrywide links or built up a rural political base. Both had as their objective the seizure of the state apparatus so that they could use it and its resources to implement their respective ideologies. It was not surprising, then, that the Communists' first effective appearance on the political stage was as the junior allies in Daud's coup in 1973 that established an Afghan republic.

Recognizing the changing nature of Afghan politics and society (at least in Kabul), Daud had ignored the ulema and tribes that had been the backbone of his uncle Nadir's rise to power in 1929. Instead, he allied himself with the leftist educated urbanites who already held positions within the existing Afghan government, uniting the heirs to Amanullah's dreams with the toughest living member of the dynasty that had ended them. That the Parchamis would follow Daud's lead was evidence of just how tenaciously the aura of dynastic prestige lingered in Afghan political culture: even those envisioning an eventual socialist revolution found it hard to shake off the presumption that they could not succeed without the assistance of a member of the royal family. The coup itself was practically bloodless and generated no immediate opposition. The pictures of Zahir Shah that adorned every government office and many shops in the bazaar immediately disappeared, miraculously replaced in days by framed portraits of a scowling Daud. Daud promised to end corruption by punishing those who engaged in it. Fearful officials stopped taking bribes for a few weeks, but soon decided that the president's eyes and ears could not be everywhere, and so simply demanded even larger bribes to compensate for the additional risk they were now taking.

At the time many in the countryside wondered whether Daud had become a Communist himself, but it quickly became clear that he was not sharing power with anyone. His leftist military allies were soon squeezed out of important posts for men that Daud trusted more. Civilian Parchami activists were posted to the countryside as government officials to get them out of Kabul. When confronted with the true complexities of governing, they either quit and came home or took to accepting bribes, making themselves indistinguishable from the officials that they had replaced. Within two years, Daud felt secure enough to drive the Parchamis from the government entirely and ban the party. While sidelining his leftist allies, Daud also attempted to wipe out the Islamists, forcing most into exile after uncovering a plot in the military against him. A series of small-scale insurrections by Islamists in 1975, including one by Ahmad Shah Masud in the Panjshir Valley, failed to generate any local support and were easily crushed. Daud used these uprisings as an excuse to arrest more mainstream Islamists as well. This included many members of the Mujaddidi family, the Hazrats of the Shor Bazaar, who had played such a powerful role in government under Nadir and his brothers.

Daud's seizure of power demonstrated that Afghan national politics was still the domain of a small elite based in Kabul that had little connection with the rest of the country. There was no popular resistance to his new government in the name of the ousted king or the "New Democracy" parliament. Why should ordinary people become involved in a family dispute, especially since Daud was not implementing any radical new policies and was a known quantity from the decade he ruled the country as prime minister? Nor did the legitimacy of the regime come under much greater scrutiny. The Afghans had already experienced the autocratic rule of Zahir Shah's uncles and his cousin Daud from 1933 to 1963, so having the puppet masters return to retire the puppet hardly shocked the audience. Other than the label, the differences between the monarchy and republic were few. The country remained under the control of the same family-centered elite, and the Musahibans had always put such ties well ahead of monarchy as an institution. What it did demonstrate was how easily a government might be replaced by a military coup. Both the Marxist and Islamists stepped up their recruiting efforts there, seeking to duplicate Daud's own success. In the absence of a mass political base, such a strike from within was seen as a shortcut to power. The Khalqis in particular made this a priority: "Previously the army was considered a tool of the dictatorship and despotism of the ruling class and it was not imaginable to use it before toppling its employer. However, Comrade Taraki suggested that this too should be wrested in order to topple the ruling class."[44]

Of all the Musahibans, Daud knew these weaknesses of the Afghan government best and had a strategy to overcome them. In foreign affairs he continued to play off the United States and the Soviet Union as before, but also reached out to other countries as well. Daud added Iran as an important ally when the shah, newly emboldened by the post-1973 rush of oil revenue, promised his regime over two billion dollars in aid over ten years, most of which would be devoted to the construction of a rail system through Afghanistan. Improved relations with Saudi Arabia ended the support that Daud's Islamist opponents received from that quarter. They then became completely dependent on Pakistan, a country that Daud had long been at odds with over the Pashtunistan issue. Internally Daud also followed the Iranian shah's model of building a one-party state and a pervasive secret police. As mentioned above, he moved to purge both Islamists and Marxists from the government and military, staffing its upper levels with men of proven loyalty to himself. Army officers were sent for training in Egypt and India to lessen the country's military dependence on the Soviet bloc. In regard to Afghanistan's economic problems, Daud planned to use the increasing levels of development aid to address more of the country's many unmet needs and its redistribution to buy a broader base of political support. Whether or not such a strategy would have worked in the long run became moot in April 1978, when Daud, Afghanistan's last Muhammadzai ruler, was murdered in a coup that brought the PDPA to power in the new Democratic Republic of Afghanistan.

Government and Rural Society in the Mid-twentieth Century

Afghanistan did not appear to be in a prerevolutionary state in 1978. Daud's coup had declared a republic, but his membership in the Muhammadzai royal family meant that his government's legitimacy was still rooted in traditional dynastic descent. Unlike neighboring Iran where a rising tide of street demonstrations against the shah turned violent and finally led to the overthrow of the Pahlavi monarchy, observers in Afghanistan expected nothing of the sort there. The Musahiban government had maintained almost fifty years of peaceful stability in the wake of the 1929 civil war, the longest in the country's history. During this time, Afghanistan had avoided involvement in any foreign wars and experienced no major internal unrest. The last significant regional rebellion by the Safis in Kunar Province had been brutally suppressed in 1946. One reason for this stability was the bifurcation of the country's politics so that events in the capital held little significance for the vast majority of the country's population. For rural folks, a change in government policies or even regimes was the exclusive business of the *kalan nafar* (big guys) in Kabul that had nothing to do with them. While they listened carefully to radio broadcasts, their measure of importance was not what was said but rather what happened on the ground. Little ever did, which was mostly fine with them, but new infrastructure projects did have at least an indirect impact on every region of the country and the lives of their people.

CHANGE BENEATH THE SURFACE

Foreigners who visited Afghanistan during its twenty-year burst of economic development beginning in the late 1950s were often shocked by how little impact it had on the country outside of Kabul. Part of this was cultural. Unlike in Iran or Turkey where Reza Shah and Atatürk had demanded that their people adopt "Western dress" as part of their march to modernization in the 1920s, rural Afghans never abandoned their own clothing. Men continued to wear turbans, long shirts that hung to the knees, and big-waisted baggy pants. Wearing a suit jacket or vest over these clothes was common, but Western-style pants never caught on.* The country's built rural environment also remained strongly rooted in indigenous architectural traditions. Concrete had not replaced pressed mud and mud brick as the basic building materials. People still constructed their own houses using well-tried techniques and designs that were specific to each

---

*Rural Afghan men squat to urinate, asserting that "only donkeys piss standing up." Because pant zippers ride up when squatting, they are viewed as ill designed.

region and ethnic group. Rural Afghanistan was therefore presumed to be stuck in an unchanging past that was described as "timeless," "primitive," "biblical," or "medieval," depending on the writer's imagination.

It is of course true that the level of investment in Afghanistan's infrastructure was low compared to its needs. Electricity was nonexistent outside of major cities, and a single bare telephone line might link a provincial governor to Kabul. Levels of literacy were low, and levels of infant mortality and maternal deaths in childbirth high. But this does not mean that there were no changes that affected rural life. For unlike Abdur Rahman, who made no investment in the country's infrastructure, the Musahibans sponsored a number of projects that had a wide-ranging impact. The first of these were regional investments in agriculture in the northeast and southwest. The former malarial swamps around Kunduz became a cotton-producing center beginning in the 1930s. Taking advantage of Soviet transport systems immediately to the north, cotton became a major export of the northeast. Immigrant farmers were given land on easy terms, and the region's population increased dramatically. An attempt to achieve the same feat in the 1940s in the Helmand Valley was less successful in terms of the money invested, but by the 1960s new dams, a modern irrigation system, and a resettlement policy had brought much new land into production. Yet it was the ring road system that had the biggest impact on rural life, even in regions that it never reached.

Although never fully completed, the paved ring road linked all of Afghanistan's major cities for the first time. Its key element was the Salang Pass through the Hindu Kush Mountains north of Kabul, completed by the Soviets in 1964. The world's highest motorable pass at that time, it linked the capital and the southern regions with the northern provinces, creating a national market for the food surpluses produced there. An example of just how big a difference this made was immediately apparent when the price paid for sheep in Kunduz doubled after the road opened. There were also more subtle changes. Nomads who had been the backbone of the old caravan trade began exchanging their camels for trucks. While this enabled them to increase the volume and variety of goods traded, it meant that they could no longer service their old rural networks in mountainous parts of the country.[45] This change was a contributing factor to the severity of the famines that occurred in mountainous central and northeastern Afghanistan during the severe droughts of the early 1970s. In previous eras, caravan traders would have brought grain into such regions to meet the demand. Now grain surpluses tended to flow along the main road but not beyond it. Planners had been aware of such problems, yet assumed that the Afghan government would finance the secondary farm-to-market roads that would link the main road to the hinterland; it never did.

The road system changed some longue durée aspects of Afghan life. The most significant was shrinking travel time and transport costs. In the early twentieth century, the time it took to get from Kabul to Mazar was only a little less than Marco Polo would have experienced in the thirteenth century. With the ring road, even distant Herat in the west was now no more than a long day's drive to Kabul. Wealthy herd owners found they could inspect their flocks high in the mountains by taking a cheap internal air flight to within a day's walk of their pastures. (One chided me for wishing to go on the ten-day trek with the shepherds by proclaiming, "Only poor people walk!") Exotic goods began permeating even distant bazaars. The bright blue drums of Soviet kerosene bought in major cities were small enough so that pack animals could carry them to distant trading outlets for resale. They supplied the fuel for the lanterns that were used by the remotest villages and nomad camps. Unbreakable drinking glasses from France started replacing porcelain teacups for everyday use. In regions where tea had been considered a luxury it now became more common than water as a drink. Sugar added to tea moved from extravagance to basic foodstuff. Illiterate buyers examined the logos of matchboxes carefully to make sure they were getting the strong wooden matches made in Russia and not the similarly colored boxes of Indian matches that employed inferior materials. In addition to motorized vehicles that were restricted to the roads (an Afghan definition of a road including any track where a vehicle could go without breaking its axle), machines also slowly entered the agricultural economy. Tractors were too expensive to fully replace oxen for plowing, but their numbers began to grow. Small diesel-powered engines started replacing animal power for grinding grain into flour on the plains. The whistle attached to the engine's exhaust produced a thump-thump rhythm that advertised the mill's location and hours of operation. Entrepreneurs used such engines to power pumps to irrigate lands that had previously been unable to produce high-value crops.

There was also an opening in the mental outlook of rural people's lives through radio (television being unavailable even in Kabul until the late 1970s). Owning a battery-powered radio, often combined with a cassette tape player, was a sign of prosperity, but listening to one was open to all within earshot. An Afghan listener could hear Pakistan's government excoriated by an Afghan government channel and get the reverse picture by listening to a Pakistani station. BBC Persian service was popular for international news, yet one could also get Chinese, Soviet, and U.S. shortwave broadcasts. Comedy shows and soap operas that played off social conventions attracted a national audience to Kabul Radio. Music, from whatever source, was particularly popular, and pirated tapes circulated around the country, giving artists a national reputation and making songs from Indian movies famous among people who had never seen a motion picture. People who were illiterate and remained geographically isolated were not therefore cut off from news about what was happening in the rest of the world, although trying to make sense of it was a challenge. When I was informed about the end of the Vietnam War by some nomads who had heard about it on the radio, they insisted that Vietnam bordered the United States. When I objected that the immense Pacific Ocean separated the two by many thousands of kilometers, they said I must be wrong because you could not fight a war with a country unless you were next to it. They were wrong on the facts but perhaps right on the principle.

LOCAL GOVERNANCE

Political stability in rural Afghanistan under the Musahibans rested on the tacit recognition of two distinct power structures: the provincial and subprovincial administrations, which were arms of the central government, and tribal or village structures indigenous to each region. While the central government had been effective in expanding its power into the countryside, its goals were limited to encapsulating local political structures in order to prevent them from causing trouble. It never attempted to displace or transform the deep-rooted social organizations in which most people lived out their lives. Therefore, qawm groups still provided their members with important networks of support outside the official government channels. The strength of such ties varied considerably throughout the country—strongest in the remote mountainous parts of Afghanistan, and weakest in the cities and irrigated agricultural areas, where the government was better established. But even where the government administration was entrenched, qawms remained crucial to daily life. The existence of such a dual organization was not visible from Kabul because officials at the national level resolutely denied its existence, giving it no formal recognition and insisting that only its officials had any legal authority. Anyone who spent any time in rural regions, though, quickly discovered that when people referred to the *hukomet* (government), they often quite literally meant the local government compound—a place rather than a concept. On passing out of its front gate, and particularly after leaving the road that led to it, "government" ceased.

In some ways, the governing institutions imposed by Kabul varied considerably by region and ethnicity. Pashtuns along the Durand Line received special treatment and benefits via the Ministry of Tribal Affairs. Nuristanis had links to the Interior Ministry and military through their coethnics. Hazaras suffered both from neglect of their region and ethnic prejudices that kept them from obtaining government posts and other opportunities for advancement. The Pashtun domination of the Kabul government that appeared natural to the Pashtuns (even those who opposed the regime in power) was strongly resented in regions where non-Pashtuns formed majorities. In other ways, however, there were strong structural similarities across the country. The most important of these was the weakness of the ties between official institutions at the subprovincial administrative level (the lowest unit in a national hierarchy) and the populations they governed. They were the weakest links in what was an admittedly rusty chain.[46]

A good example of just how remote the state was from the lives of ordinary people could be seen in Imam Sahib, a large multiethnic town in the northern province of Kunduz where I did two years of ethnographic fieldwork in the mid-1970s. Located on Afghanistan's northern border with the Soviet Union, the Kabul government's presence was larger than elsewhere because in addition to the interior ministry gendarmerie police there was a unit of border police. Still, despite its pervasive presence in the town and easy proximity to the valley's villages, the Afghan government seemed remote to the local residents. There was no organic connection between them and the government-appointed officials. The enforcement of decisions below this point depended ultimately on the threat of force because the tribesmen and peasants rarely volunteered their cooperation. Government officials could of course seek someone out, but unless in quest of bribes they could extort from wealthy farmers, higher-level bureaucrats generally assigned such tasks to the ill-clothed police conscripts who made up the bulk of their staff. These unwelcome visitors were showered with as many plausible lies as people could invent, the best of which would be passed on to their superiors. If sent on a really serious mission (such as demanding the surrender of a criminal suspect), however, they had the power to move into the offender's home and stay there, eating the family's food, until his relatives delivered him up.

But such direct encounters were rare because the far more common practice was for government officials to deal with villagers by means of local intermediaries. Each village had an *arbab* (also known as *malik*s in Pashtun areas), who was the official link between the village and the local administration. Arbabs were usually literate men with business interests outside the village; often they held urban property. Links to a larger world were important because dealing with government officials required a greater sophistication and experience than most villagers had. The position was not inherently powerful. An arbab could command authority only when he acted on behalf of the government as its agent. He could be safely ignored when he tried to command action on his own. By custom, the arbab was chosen by the people and confirmed by the government, but in many cases the arbab was simply appointed by the government without consultation. The position had a poor reputation because it was associated with trouble, and because many arbabs were known to be corrupt. Indeed, there was a saying that "the pig lives in the jungle, the arbab in the village"— hardly a flattering comparison in an Islamic context.

The real backbone of local leadership was therefore vested in prominent landowners and merchants, who protected the interests of their groups against the government and other communities or ethnic groups. They owed their authority to a combination of wealth, social rank, and political networks. They played a significant role in resolving disputes because people sought them out as mediators. Effective mediators were generally older men with an established reputation for good judgment and honesty to whom the community was willing to defer. Although their authority was informal, it was buttressed by the fear most Afghans had of any dealings with the government. The court system was notorious for its inability to resolve cases in a timely fashion, the need to pay bribes, and the public attention that such cases brought to problems that individuals wished to keep private. In addition, the customary law system was viewed as being more just because mediators using it were guided by concepts of equity, fairness, and the need to maintain social harmony. Unlike government officials, local mediators were well informed about the background on the cases brought before them, and used that information to craft decisions designed to meet with the community's approval. Resolution of minor yet frequently acrimonious disputes at the village level helped to insulate people from the government, keeping village affairs concealed from outside observation. Thus, little of what went on in the community ever came to the attention of local government officials. Government officials at the local level were well aware of this, and the most effective ones delegated sensitive case to such informal mediation as a way to maintain local harmony, even though such actions had no legal basis.

RURAL PERSPECTIVES ON THE KABUL GOVERNMENT

The rural population's alienation from the administration was increased by its lack of participation in it. Persian- and Turkish-speaking regions particularly resented being governed almost exclusively by Pashtuns. Whether Pashtun or not, officials were invariably outsiders with little knowledge of the areas under their jurisdiction. They were part of a highly centralized administrative system in which decisions on appointments for provincial posts were made by ministries in Kabul. Because each ministry maintained its own chain of command, it demanded that any critical issues be referred back to Kabul. Such parallel lines of administrations tended to make each part of government a separate fiefdom, making cooperation at the local level difficult. Officials were therefore more concerned with keeping on the good side of their superiors in Kabul than in forging good relations with the local population. Governors often took a predatory approach in their dealings with local populations, extorting as much money as they could before they were transferred or dismissed. Earlier in the century governors may have been no less corrupt, but because of their longer tenure in office they eventually became part of the local elite, and would begin to represent their interests to the national government. By the 1970s, this form of patronage had all but disappeared as the size of provinces shrank and their numbers expanded.

There was also a growing psychological gap between government officials and the rural population based on differences in social class, education, and the degree of urbanization. Officials were city people who disliked service in the provinces, and who constantly schemed to be transferred to Kabul or at least a bigger town. They dressed in Western suits (at least in public), which set them off from the turban-wearing residents of rural Afghanistan. With few exceptions, government officials expressed their embarrassment at rural Afghanistan, stating that it was a backward place full of backward people. Such contempt was fully reciprocated by the rural population, which found the officials overweight, overbearing, and congenitally corrupt. Moreover, villagers expressed doubts about the religiosity of government officials, particularly over such matters as drinking alcohol and praying regularly. Each group viewed the other as a tricky adversary. Like oil and water, the two never mixed unless shaken together by some conflict or dispute.

In sum, the Musahiban government was effective in rural areas only when it had a specific target for punitive action. The ease with which it expelled, captured, or killed Islamic radicals who had attempted to raise rebellions in the countryside in 1975 was a perfect example of this. Villagers were keen to expel the ringleaders because they were seen as bringing trouble to people who wanted no part of their ideological conflict with the government. But at a more general level, the government did not have the capacity to implement policies that challenged entrenched local interests. These defects were not critical under the Musahiban rule because its administration steered clear of conflicts when it could. Provincial officials had a limited agenda: to keep the peace, suppress banditry, see that conscription went smoothly, and collect what small amounts of taxes the government still demanded. They were not expected to engage in social action projects that might require greater local cooperation than the government was able to muster. As described earlier, at the time of Daud's republic the strategy of the national government was to free itself from the need to maintain political, financial, or ideological support from the provincial population in order to carry out its policies. National politics and programs were thus largely divorced from rural areas. This would now change with the fall of the Musahibans.

ACT III: THE WORST OF TIMES, 1978–2001

The Rise of the Radical Khalqis and the Revenge of the Ghilzais

The PDPA was correct in seeing the Afghan government's greatest vulnerability as an attack from within. Nevertheless, its coming to power was a close-run thing. It was Daud's own strike against the PDPA leadership in April 1978 that pushed its military allies into action prematurely. This has led some to declare the coup accidental, while others have insisted it was inevitable given Afghanistan's problems.[47] Inevitable or not, the PDPA took its prize by stealth with the help of junior military officers and without having to mobilize a popular following, as calling the coup the Saur Revolution (for the Afghan month in which it occurred) implied. The more radical Khalqis quickly became the dominant faction in the PDPA government. They were not just interested in ruling Afghanistan but also in transforming the country through revolutionary policies of land reform, education, and changes in family law. They moved to destroy all who opposed them, including their Parchami rivals, the traditional rural landowners, the old military establishment, and Islamic clergy. They abandoned Afghanistan's historic policy of power-balancing neutrality for a direct alliance with the Soviet Union. The regime also rejected the country's traditional Islamic symbols of legitimacy by striking religious salutations from their speeches and decrees, and changing the color of the flag to red. As revolutionaries, they justified themselves and the legitimacy of their government in Marxist terms. This rhetoric was alien to most of the population, except in the north, where it was all too familiar to the descendants of refugees who had originally fled from Soviet central Asia in Stalin's time.

The structure of the new government and its personnel also marked a sharp break with Afghanistan's long history of Durrani rule—even sharper than Habibullah Kalakani's displacement of Amanullah in 1929. While the government remained as Pashtun dominated as it had ever been, the old Persian-speaking Muhammadzai elite was displaced by eastern, mostly Ghilzai, Pashtuns. They had stronger tribal backgrounds than did the old elite and were native Pashto speakers. These eastern Pashtuns were members of the tribes that had provided the backbone of the resistance against the British that kept Afghanistan independent in the nineteenth century. They began the revolts against Amanullah that put Nadir Shah on the throne in the early twentieth century. During these previous periods they had always willingly ceded power to a Durrani ruler when the fighting ceased. Such Durrani leaders had repaid the eastern Pashtuns by using state power to suppress them, most particularly during Abdur Rahman's campaigns against the Ghilzais in the 1880s, but extending to the Safi rebellion in Kunar as late as 1946. As a result, they were rarely welcomed into the highest levels of government, yet did come to staff important positions within the interior police and military. It was such junior Ghilzai military officers who ousted Daud in 1978, to then claim the top positions in the new regime and finally displace their old Durrani rivals from power after 230 years. Of course as Marxists they did not portray their victory in this old-fashioned way, but it is striking that during the next twenty-three years of intense fighting it would be the eastern Pashtuns, Ghilzais mostly, who would supply most of the leading Pashtun political and military figures on all sides in the conflicts to come, whether as PDPA rulers (Taraki, Amin, and Najibullah), Islamic resistance leaders (Hekmatyar, Abdul Haq, and Jalaludin Haqqani), or Taliban holy warriors (Mullah Omar). By contrast, top-level Durrani leadership on any side was quite rare.

PDPA PROBLEMS

The Saur Revolution brought in its wake three interconnected problems for the victors. The first was how to establish the legitimacy of their government. Abolishing the Musahiban dynasty opened up this question with a voice not seen since Amanullah was replaced by Habibullah in 1929. The second was how the PDPA would relate to Afghanistan's existing political establishment and who within the party would set policy. In defiance of Leninist principles, the Afghans had two Communist parties

(Khalq and Parcham), which were unified in name only and whose leaders hated one another. They held opposing positions on whether the government needed to broaden its political base. The third was how best to implement their new social and economic policies. Such policies were bound to pit the Kabul modernists, who beginning with Amanullah, had envisioned a secular nationalist state, against their rural and provincial opponents, who wished to preserve or reinforce Afghanistan's Islamic traditions and maintain the country's long-established social structure. The Musahibans had carefully worked around this divide but never fully overcame it. These issues were closely connected because the greater the degree of opposition to the changes that the new government wished to impose, the more its legitimacy would be challenged and its authority undermined.

In Afghanistan before 1900, there were few barriers between the de facto seizure of power and the de jure recognition of that fact by the population. Traditional Islamic legal thought forbade popular rebellions against an established Muslim ruler by his subjects on the grounds that it created too much social disorder. This helped preserve the power of existing rulers, but also laid the groundwork for their replacement. The popular rebellions that characterized the two Anglo-Afghan wars were justified on the grounds that Muslims should not be ruled by infidels or the Muslim rulers, who were seen to be their clients. Rulers such as Dost Muhammad and Abdur Rahman were insistent that once the British were gone, however, so was any political justification for rebellion. The civil war that drove Amanullah from power had been a product of internal rebellions. His opponents claimed that even a previously legitimate amir could be replaced if he lost his status as a Muslim ruler by implementing "un-Islamic" policies. But since Sunni Islam lacked a hierarchical clergy, such declarations often failed to stick because they were the personal opinions of the clerics issuing them. Indeed if a rebellion failed, such clerics frequently lost their heads—a doubly useful punishment for the ruler, since the binding power of a fatwa on any issue was deemed ended on the death of the cleric who issued it. Thus, when the PDPA came to power it was within a political milieu prone to accept even a usurper's rights if he held power firmly. Despite his bandit origins and Tajik ethnicity, Habibullah had received widespread internal recognition of his regime before it was toppled by the Musahibans. Flush with victory and believing in its own ideology, though, the Khalq faction of the PDPA declared itself a revolutionary government led by a vanguard party that represented the interests of the working class. It was not only a secular government but also an anticlerical one that praised the atheistic Soviet Union. The Khalqis dismissed fears that such moves would open the government to the charge of being un-Islamic and hence illegitimate as the last cries of an old feudal establishment that the PDPA expected to wipe from politics, just as the Soviets had succeeded in doing in their central Asian republics. Those who rejected its right to rule were counter-revolutionaries, who would be crushed in the name of the people.

Questions about the new government's legitimacy were exacerbated by its internal disunity and penchant for violence. The Saur Revolution inaugurated a frenzy of bloodshed at a level not seen in Afghan politics since the nineteenth century, beginning with the murder of Daud, his family, and many other key figures of the old regime. These included Islamists previously jailed by Daud as well as members of the established ulema such as the influential Mujaddidi family, seventy of whom were murdered in February 1979. Members of minority groups such as the Nuristanis (who had influential positions in the old government) and the Hazaras (who demonstrated against it) became targets of the regime, alienating their home regions. This violence was not restricted to "reactionary elements" but also applied to the Khalq and Parcham factions themselves. Although they initially agreed to share power evenly with Karmal as deputy premier and the "Great Leader" Taraki as president and premier, by July 1978 the Khalqis had purged the Parchamis from government. Its most prominent leaders, including Karmal, went into exile abroad, but those remaining within the country found themselves targets for arrest and execution, often in greater numbers than outright opponents of the regime. Khalq members soon turned on one another as Hafizullah Amin chipped away at Taraki's power. Amin was made the prime minister in April 1979, and replaced Taraki as president in September. He murdered the Great Leader a month later after discovering his involvement in a Soviet-backed coup attempt, leaving the Khalqis divided between pro-Amin and pro-Taraki factions. This internal conflict was so extreme that, using their own figures, of the PDPA's eighteen thousand original members and the twenty-eight thousand who joined in the aftermath of the coup, half would be killed, purged, or leave the party in the twenty months before it was toppled.[48]

Far from solidifying its base of power, the PDPA seemed intent on destroying it, even before its enemies could make common cause against it.

While still busy purging its own membership, the PDPA launched a sweeping series of radical economic and social programs in the countryside. Promulgated in a series of edicts, the declarations required land reform, equality for women, the abolition of marriage payments, and the cancellation of many types of rural debts, among many other goals.[49] Some of the declarations, like those on women's rights and limiting marriage payments, were first initiated by Amanullah, but the economic ones centering on land redistribution and rural debt were new. The Parchamis and the regime's Soviet advisers were opposed to making such far-reaching changes so rapidly in a country as socially conservative and economically underdeveloped as Afghanistan. They warned of doing too much too soon, particularly before the new government (already divided internally) had put down strong roots. But the Khalqis saw transforming Afghanistan as their revolutionary duty, and one that should not be delayed. If they met any resistance they could always employ military force to intimidate opponents. Their confidence was based on the belief that a modern military was invincibly stronger than any rural or tribal militia, so their opponents would have no real power to resist them—evidence for which could be seen in the Musahiban dynasty's success in reducing the influence of tribal groups and religious leaders in national politics. There had been no significant rebellions against the government since the military was modernized during the 1950s. Yet impressive as Kabul's jets, rockets, and tanks appeared on the parade ground, the real secret behind that success had been political rather than military. The Musahibans had so reduced their own political and economic footprint in the countryside that there was little to rebel against. The PDPA's program for revolutionary change would alter that equation without weighing the consequences.

THE REVOLUTION GOES SOUR

When the Khalqis went beyond pronouncements and attempted to implement their policies in the countryside they met with armed resistance. These uprisings were uncoordinated and tended to focus on local rather than national issues, but they soon became widespread. Even by the

PDPA's own account, by the beginning of 1980 they controlled only 5,500 of the country's estimated 35,500 villages. Attempts to use military force against this opposition proved ineffectual because the army itself started to dissolve under pressure. In the twenty months of Khalqi rule the troops loyal to the regime declined to less than 60,000, or half of the troop strength under Daud. Similarly, the interior police numbers fell to 8,000, or 60 percent fewer than before the coup. The higher ranks had been purged, and the lower ranks consisted predominantly of conscripts, who deserted in large numbers, including the mutiny of whole units.[50]

Many of these rebellions were the products of resistance to the PDPA's programs demanding the radical transformation of the rural economy. Although this period of radical reform was short-lived, it alienated people in the provinces. The economic program was poorly conceived, structurally flawed, and badly implemented. The land reform decree, for example, failed to recognize that land was often less significant than water for agricultural production. Likewise, abolishing traditional forms of rural debt without providing reliable substitute credit meant that even if poor farmers received land, they would still not have the money to buy the seed or rent the traction animals necessary to get a crop planted and harvested. The existing systems of land rentals, sharecropping, and hired labor that the PDPA wished to abolish were at least adapted to these conditions. At a cultural level, the uncompensated seizure of land from its legal owners to redistribute free to others was seen as a form of theft not sanctioned by Islamic tradition. Since most rural landowners in Afghanistan lived in the same communities as those who worked for them, they were bound together by a web of social relations that transcended mere economics. Qawm affiliations too were important: even those who might benefit by receiving land would stand against its redistribution to "outsiders." Many in the north associated the PDPA's rhetoric about land redistribution with the Soviet collectivization schemes that their grandfathers had fled to Afghanistan to escape. This belief was reinforced by the government's plan to create rural cooperatives, whose officials would link individual farmers to government institutions, replacing traditional qawm or village leaders. In reality, the land reform program had little permanent impact on rural villagers since most of the land that was redistributed was already state owned. While the Khalqis announced that 340,000 families had received farmland when they declared a successful end to the program in July 1979, the PDPA later admitted that the program had never really been completed, and that the true figure for land under production by new owners was 85 to 90 percent less than originally claimed.[51]

From its inception, the land reform program was less about economics than politics. The PDPA's goal was to break down the qawm-based political structure by which rural communities had insulated themselves from the central government and its officials for generations. For this reason, one of the most common flash points that incited violent opposition was the PDPA's compulsory literacy campaign requiring the attendance of young unmarried women and men in mixed classes. It pitted rural notions of propriety and social honor against the goals of the revolutionary vanguard. While seizing land and breaking down such cultural barriers was one of the main strategies that the Soviets employed to transform their provinces in central Asia, they had relied on a large number of trained party cadres to implement their programs. In Afghanistan there were few such people to be found in the rural areas, so the government relied instead on the existing Musahiban administrative structure to achieve its goals. This strategy was fatally flawed, not only because local officials there were not very committed to the party's goals, but also because government in rural areas under the Musahibans had always been passive and employed a "live and let live" policy that avoided confrontations whenever possible. The government was certainly not equipped to implement radical policies that struck at the core of the rural economy and society. The PDPA also failed to consider the ramifications of many of its actions. Issues it considered purely economic had social components, and many of its social reforms affected such basic values as family honor. For example, when the PDPA declared that its government was established on a secular base, it undercut its legitimacy in the eyes of the rural population. In Afghanistan nothing was ever completely secular: slaughtering a sheep, praying to finalize a contract, or giving money in thanks for good fortune—all had some religious overtone. There was a strong belief that a non-Islamic government had no legal authority, and that a Muslim had the right, even the duty, to rebel against it.

The PDPA's confidence that it could impose its will rested on the illusion that its opponents had no power to resist them because the Musahiban dynasty had already broken the power of tribal and religious groups in national politics. Yet the PDPA failed to recognize that the Musahiban governments achieved this success by ignoring rather than confronting Afghanistan's rural areas. Social and economic reforms had only marginally involved the rural population, and the government had not challenged traditional beliefs or economic patterns. In contrast, changes in provincial Afghanistan were the centerpiece of the PDPA program because rural Afghanistan was the source of what the new government most objected to. Lacking its own rural organization, the PDPA planned to use the old provincial administration inherited from the Musahibans to carry out its reforms after staffing the upper levels with party members.[52]

When the PDPA implemented its policies, the brittle links between the local government and the villages that it administered broke down under pressure. The Khalqis soon discovered that their writ ran only to the edge of town. By confronting the rural population in its own backyard where community leaders were at their strongest and the central government was at its weakest, the balance of forces was more even than the Khalqis anticipated. In Kabul the national government might seem all-powerful, but the deeper it reached into the countryside, the less it was able to project that power. By contrast, traditional local-level leaders had the ability to bring their neighbors together using kinship ties and personal contacts. They used the old political language of Afghanistan, calling on their followers to defend their property, the faith of Islam, and the honor of their families against outsiders. Their objections to the PDPA's economic policies were combined with objections to its social policies, especially those relating to marriage customs and women. (Villages that did cooperate tended to have kinship links with PDPA officials that outweighed these ideological concerns.) The parochial nature of this type of opposition was pervasive but noncentralized, resulting in the seeming paradox of the PDPA government becoming weakened to the point of near collapse without having an easily identifiable enemy at the national or international level.

Wittingly or not, the PDPA raised the same issues that brought about the downfall of Amanullah. The combination of rural rebellions against government reforms and the failure of state institutions under pressure was reminiscent of the crisis that ended Amanullah's reign. But there were a number of significant differences. Amanullah's most controversial reforms were those mandating the equality of women, a more secular legal system, and interference with customary practices related to the family. The PDPA program was much broader and more radical. It included not only social reforms but also attacked the economic foundations of rural life: landownership. If successful, it would have brought direct government control down to the village level—the goal of all modernizing states, whether socialist or not. In 1929, the opposition to Amanullah and his reforms had been confined to the usual suspects: the Pashtun east and Tajik Kohistan. By contrast, opposition to the PDPA programs and resistance against them was nationwide. In this respect the mutiny of the army garrison in Herat in March 1979 and periodic street demonstrations in Kabul were particularly telling because they proved that opposition to the PDPA was not limited to rural areas.[53] Yet the biggest difference was the international context. Amanullah was dependent entirely on domestic resources and had no foreign alliances to protect him from internal rebellion. The PDPA had bound itself closely to the Soviet Union, a superpower that was unwilling to accept the collapse of a socialist government. Having declared Afghanistan a member of the Soviet bloc, its government could not be allowed to fall.

The Soviet Invasion

The Soviet Union watched the disintegration of the new socialist regime with alarm. A month before the first anniversary of the Saur Revolution, Taraki had traveled to Moscow to demand Soviet troops to bolster his government and prevent its collapse. The Russians refused, fearing they would be viewed as aggressors and put in conflict with the Afghan people. But as the months progressed, the regime continued to lose strength and internal cohesion. Its very survival came into question, even in the absence of a unified opposition. The Soviets put the blame for this situation on Hafizullah Amin and the Khalqis. Strangely enough for a leader guilty (in Soviet jargon) of "left deviation" by his pursuit of policies deemed too radical and destabilizing, Moscow was most suspicious of Amin's meetings with the U.S. embassy in Kabul. In justifying the need for intervention after rejecting such an action nine months earlier, a report signed by the Soviet politburo explained that after Amin's murder of Taraki,

> the situation in Afghanistan has been sharply exacerbated and taken on crisis proportions. H. Amin has established a regime of personal dictatorship in the country, effectively reducing the CC [Central Committee], PDPA and Revolutionary Council to entirely nominal organs. . . . H. Amin deceived the party and the people with announcements that the Soviet Union had supposedly approved of Taraki's expulsion from the party and government. By direct order of H. Amin, fabricated rumors were deliberately spread throughout the DRA [Democratic Republic of Afghanistan], smearing the Soviet Union and casting a shadow on the activities of Soviet personnel in Afghanistan, who had been restricted in their efforts to maintain contact with Afghan representatives. At the same time, efforts were made to mend relations with America as part of the "more balanced foreign policy strategy" adopted by H. Amin. H. Amin held a series of confidential meetings with the American charge d'affaires in Kabul.[54]

So ingrained was the tradition of Afghan leaders seeking to play one world power against another that the Soviets were convinced that Amin was about to desert the socialist bloc and ally with the West. In reality, the United States never saw him as a possible ally and still held the regime responsible for the death of the U.S. ambassador in Kabul in February 1979. All Amin shared at those meetings with the charge d'affaires was tea.[55]

To prevent Amin's defection and restore order to Afghanistan the Soviets invaded on December 27, 1979, using provisions of the Soviet-Afghan Treaty of 1978 as their justification. They killed Amin and installed Karmal as the country's new ruler. Using the analogy of their invasion of Czechoslovakia in 1968, the Soviets assumed that they could begin withdrawing their troops after a few months when order was restored. Instead, the intervention marked the beginning of a decade-long occupation that would result in the death of one million Afghans, the flight of four million refugees to Pakistan and Iran, and the displacement of millions of others internally. The upending of the old social order that Amin had sought would now proceed apace, but in a very different way than he imagined, through the crucible of war and the violence it spawned.

The Russian intervention in Afghanistan mobilized a mass opposition against it. Before the invasion, rural resistance was pervasive but decentralized. Olivier Roy describes the standard way that local insurgencies developed:

> The revolt usually took the form of a mass uprising preceded by preaching and followed by an attack on the government post of the principal town of the district, using small arms (including flintlock guns). The post was usually captured with heavy casualties on both sides. The communist activists were executed, non-communist soldiers and officials allowed to go. The revolt would spread to the whole area in which there was tribal solidarity. The people who had taken part in the attack then spread out throughout any neighboring villages of their own ethnic affiliation. When the frontier of the territory of the ethnic or tribal group was reached, the dynamic phase was over. Members of the resistance did not attempt to go beyond their own territory.[56]

In the aftermath of the Soviet intervention and the reorganization of the PDPA government, the resistance became more national in scope and its goals broadened. Whatever local grievances they had against the PDPA previously, those in the resistance all agreed that expelling the Soviets from Afghanistan was the movement's primary objective. As with earlier resistance movements, this one took the form of a jihad against the infidel invaders because that was the classic way to overcome the qawm barriers that normally prevented unity among Afghan factions. It was also a legacy of Abdur Rahman, who had so permanently fused the defense of the nation with the defense of Islam that the two seemed inseparable after that. Thus, regardless of their different backgrounds and goals, the resistance fighters all styled themselves mujahideen.

But while organizing the resistance to foreign invasion as a jihad followed a well-worn cultural track, the seizure of its leadership by the exiled Afghan Islamist parties based in Pakistan did not. Although a wide coalition of Afghan parties were opposed to the Soviet invasion—including royalists, nationalists, regional groups, and even non-PDPA leftists—the

Islamist parties in Pakistan quickly became paramount since only they had access to foreign money and arms. Control of these resources was critical because the cost of opposing the Soviets would be exponentially higher than opposing the PDPA alone and impossible to sustain on domestic resources. Foreign help was readily available because by breaking the cold war status quo the Soviets had provoked both the United States (by moving beyond its postwar boundaries) and Saudi Arabia (by invading a Muslim country). Together the United States and Saudi Arabia were willing to bankroll the resistance in Afghanistan in amounts that eventually reached a billion dollars a year in the mid-1980s. Pakistan agreed to channel the money and arms to the Afghans through its own intelligence service, but insisted on limiting the distribution to the Sunni Islamist parties, which were already its clients. (The much smaller Hazara Shia parties received aid from Iran's Islamic revolutionary government, which acted in a similarly divisive way.) The Islamist parties thus became the public face of the resistance in the same way that the PDPA was the face of the Kabul government. Neither was representative of the aspirations of ordinary Afghans.[57]

The Islamist parties played an insignificant role inside Afghanistan before 1980, and their leaders never established a base of national support there. Those who escaped imprisonment in Kabul had been living in Pakistan since the mid-1970s after their opposition to Daud failed. They came to prominence only after Pakistan made them the monopoly suppliers of arms and other aid in the wake of the Soviet invasion. This soon included the distribution of humanitarian assistance within the massive Afghan refugee camps, where they established powerful patronage networks and recruited soldiers. Resistance groups based within Afghanistan were required to affiliate with one of these Islamist parties if they wanted to get weapons and money. Because the groups fighting in Afghanistan had little or no interest in the political ideologies of these parties or their leaders, affiliation was most frequently based on personal relationships, regional and ethnic ties, or simple opportunism, inducing many commanders to hold membership in two or three parties simultaneously. The non-Pashtun Sunnis in the north and west tended to align themselves with Burhanadin Rabbani's Jamiat-i-Islami, while Pashtuns in the south and east joined more often with Gulbadin Hekmatyar's Hizb-i-Islami, although he competed with two smaller Islamist Pashtun-based parties led by Abdul Rasul

Sayyaf and Yunis Khalis. These two smaller parties were rooted more in animosity to Hekmatyar than differences in ideology. Three much-weaker traditionalist parties were led by scions of established Sufi families (Gailani and Mujaddadi) or ulema (Muhammad Nabi Muhammadai). They incorporated the secular nationalists and royalists, who were not allowed to establish independent parties in Pakistan. Given the complex nature of Afghan politics, local rival groups would join different mujahideen parties regardless of ethnic ties and would defect from one party to another if they could get a better deal. (Jamiat-i-Islami, for example, was about 25 percent Pashtun.) The various parties were also at odds with one another: Hekmatyar in particular was as likely to authorize attacks against rival mujahideen and their caravans as he was on the Soviets.[58]

Immediately after putting Karmal in power, the Soviets had him repudiate Hafizullah Amin's policies. In 1980 the regime freed political prisoners, rescinded the signature Khalqi decrees on land reform, rural debt, and women's rights, and abandoned the revolutionary red flag for a version of Afghanistan's old tricolor one. They made overtures to the ulema by restoring religious blessings in government decrees and adding mullahs to the government payroll. But having intervened to preserve a socialist revolution in Afghanistan, the Soviets under Leonid Brezhnev were still unwilling to compromise with the opposition if that meant relinquishing the PDPA's power monopoly. This presented a dilemma because if they could not broaden the government's political base they would never be able to leave and expect the regime to survive. Karmal especially was so closely tied to the Soviets that he won the unpleasant distinction of being labeled a new Shah Shuja, another feckless ruler entirely dependent on the presence of foreign troops to maintain his power.[59] As we shall see, Karmal would not be the last Afghan ruler to face this problem.

The initial Soviet strategy was to employ a heavy military force against the resistance with the expectation that they could pacify Afghanistan as they had done in the central Asian republics during the 1920s and 1930s. They did not expect to win friends in this process, just make their occupation and the PDPA appear so permanent that their opponents would eventually tire and come to an accommodation with it. To this end, they took direct control of Afghanistan's urban population centers and key strategic transportation links while attacking districts in the countryside that supported the resistance. They also rebuilt the PDPA military with the expectation that they would eventually do most of the fighting. This policy gained little traction. Despite air bombardments, the widespread use of land mines, search-and-destroy sweeps, and the depopulation of much of the countryside, the Soviets were unable to dislodge the resistance. Nor was the resistance willing to come to an accommodation with the PDPA as long as Soviet troops appeared set to remain in the country indefinitely. The Soviets also discovered that even after building up the Afghan army's strength to 90,000, Kabul regime commanders were still not willing to take the offensive. Instead, they and the mujahideen usually established zones of truce and agreed not to fight one another. At the same time the mujahideen grew more sophisticated in their use of weapons and tactics, particularly after they were provided with Stinger antiaircraft missiles in 1986, thereby greatly reducing Soviet air superiority on the battlefield.[60]

The military situation became stalemated. While the 111,000 Soviet troops in Afghanistan were not enough to pacify the country (most were assigned to garrison duty), they were powerful enough to keep the resistance from overthrowing the government. But as Soviet casualties grew (the Soviets eventually acknowledged the loss of least 15,000 troops killed) perceptions of the war in Moscow changed, especially after the death of Brezhnev, who had ordered the invasion. The estimated financial cost of the occupation was running at five billion dollars annually, and the Soviets had little to show in return. The diplomatic cost was also high (as annual UN condemnations of the invasion demonstrated), and the war became increasingly unpopular within Russia itself. It was these considerations rather than defeats on the battlefield that caused the Soviets to reexamine their rationale for continuing to occupy Afghanistan. The politburo had ordered the invasion of Afghanistan on the belief that this would be both a short-term measure and one that would reinforce their international power by proving that the Soviets would never desert a client. As the years progressed neither of these assumptions proved correct, and Moscow began to look for a way out. When Mikhail Gorbachev took power in 1985, he shifted Soviet strategy to give primacy to negotiations and to reorganizing the PDPA government to give it more internal stability. Najibullah, the head of the country's feared secret police, replaced Karmal as leader of the PDPA. Gorbachev then gave the Soviet military a last opportunity to win militarily in 1986, and when that failed accepted the offices of the United Nations to begin negotiations for a peace that would allow the Soviets to withdraw their troops. The Kabul regime strategy of seeking local accommodations with resistance groups in return for their neutrality became Soviet policy as well.[61]

Although born in Kabul, Najibullah was from an Ahmadzai Pashtun family and was particularly well-known for his skills in Pashto oratory. Preparing for the time when the Soviets withdrew, he sought to broaden his government by reaching out to the resistance and attempting to wash the PDPA of its Marxist past, beginning with his own name. Before 1986 he was known as Dr. Najib, but on taking power he restored the traditional *ullah* ("of God") to give his name a more Islamic flavor. Similarly, he reorganized the PDPA and renamed it the Hizb-i-watan (Homeland Party), abandoning socialism for nationalism. Additional clerics were put on the payroll, and the government began restoring damaged mosques. The Democratic Republic of Afghanistan reverted to Daud's Republic of Afghanistan. More significantly, Najibullah proposed forming a coalition government that would reserve key posts to the resistance. (Ahmad Shah Masud was offered the Defense Ministry.) The mujahideen leaders in Pakistan (and Pakistan itself) were vehemently opposed to such a compromise because they anticipated toppling Najibullah once the Soviets left. It was equally opposed by Khalqi and other PDPA hard-liners for whom the Najibullah's abandonment of socialist policies was a betrayal of the revolution. In fact, no power-sharing proposal coming directly from the Kabul regime was credible while the Soviets still occupied the country, but Najibullah realized that the political dynamic would alter dramatically once they left. He understood that opposition to the Soviet occupation was the force that held the disparate parts of the resistance together.

The mujahideen were already seriously hamstrung by the distance between the political party leaders, who had access to funding, and the mujahideen commanders, who actually did the fighting. Based in Peshawar, Pakistan, the political party leaders earned a reputation for venality and self-centeredness that alienated them from their commanders inside Afghanistan. In a culture that glorified military achievement and bravery in battle, their failure to fight the Soviets personally or even venture into Afghanistan undercut their authority as potential national leaders. They were also seen as too willing to sacrifice Afghan interests to maintain their ties with Pakistan's Inter-Service Intelligence (ISI). But the leaders within Afghanistan who had earned reputations as commanders found it difficult to move beyond the regional level of organization.[62]

In the absence of a national organization inside Afghanistan, its regions and their leaders became more important. Masud created a protogovernment in the resistance-controlled areas of the northeast, as had Ishmail Khan in the west. Although both men were members of Jamiat, neither of them looked for guidance from Rabbani, the party's head in Pakistan. Hizb-i-Islami was much more centralized under Hekmatyar, whose party organization resembled the PDPA in structure, if not in ideology. Hekmatyar, however, had many rivals in the Pashtun east and found it hard to control the charismatic commanders actually doing the fighting there, such as Abul Haq and Jalaludin Haqqani. The tribes there were also historically fragmented in opposition to one another and inclined to reject any leader seeking to centralize power. The Durrani south was divided among a number of resistance parties, some of which joined with the PDPA, as had many Uzbeks in the north.

What all these parties and leaders had in common was the inordinate amount of time they spent just keeping their coalitions together. At the local level units were loyal only to their own commanders, and such commanders saw themselves as independent agents. Using ibn Khaldun's dichotomy, regional mujahideen leaders (and the party leaders in Peshawar) were more like chieftains who had to cajole their followers into taking action rather than rulers who could command them. Subordinate commanders could and did defect to another resistance party or even the PDPA if they felt abused or were attracted by a better deal. Because local resistance groups were tied to the population of the districts in which they fought, they were often willing to agree to formal cease-fires or follow a policy of neutrality to avoid the PDPA or Soviet retaliation that came in the wake of active fighting.

The moment of crisis for both Najibullah and the mujahideen arrived as the last Soviet troops left the country between May 1988 and February 1989. Under the terms of a UN-sponsored withdrawal agreement, the United States and the Soviet Union promised to halt further military aid to their respective clients. Both continued to do so covertly, however, providing many years worth of arms and ammunition to each side. Few observers considered this breech very serious because it was universally believed that once the Soviets left, the mujahideen would overrun government outposts, take the regional cities, and then march on Kabul in triumph in a matter of months, if not weeks. Foreshadowing this possibility was the fact that during 1988, the Kabul regime had experienced a rising level of attacks from the mujahideen as well as a big decline in its ability either to attract defectors or strike agreements of neutrality with local commanders because their survival prospects appeared so poor. The ISI, wishing to act as soon as possible after the Soviet troops were gone, pushed the seven Peshawar-based resistance parties into forming a provisional government to prepare for victory. The plan was to install this government inside Afghanistan after seizing the eastern city of Jalalabad and expand its reach from there. The project collapsed when the PDPA beat off the mujahideen and prevented them from taking the city in March 1989.[63]

In retrospect, it was clear that the resistance had been given a task they were incapable of accomplishing. The mujahideen had no previous experience in assaulting heavily defended cities, and their forces had never been integrated into a common command structure. They withdrew when the battle went poorly—an excellent guerrilla tactic yet one that exposed their inability to fight as a conventional army. The high level of distrust among the factions after the defeat made a quick second attack all but impossible. In a political culture where the perception of being a winner (or loser) often plays a decisive role in turning that perception into reality, Najibullah now looked like a leader who could hold his own without Soviet troops. By contrast, the conviction that the mujahideen would soon take Kabul was replaced with uncertainty, causing leaders everywhere to reconsider their positions. Although the resistance overran many isolated PDPA outposts and districts elsewhere (most notably Khost in the east) in the months that followed, they did not succeed in driving regime troops from their core areas. After Jalalabad the number of commanders willing to cut deals with Najibullah rose sharply, as did the number of autonomous militia groups that allied with his government now that it appeared to have more life left in it. More important, with the Russians gone Najibullah was able to frame the ongoing conflict as an internal Afghan affair, a dispute among fellow Muslims that could not be justified as a jihad. As the situation evolved, the Peshawar Islamists had to fight the perception that they were Pakistan's clients, intent on imposing their own radical regime on the country if Najibullah fell.

THE SOVIET WAR'S CONSEQUENCES

Even more than in the nineteenth-century Anglo-Afghan wars, the Soviet invasion generated an unprecedented level of national opposition. The collapse of central authority in rural areas and the rise of locally based resistance groups transferred real power into the hands of communities previously administered by distant officials assigned there by the central government. By framing the conflict as a jihad, it was possible to unite a large number of people and deprive the Kabul government of legitimacy. As during the British occupation, the Afghan resistance was rarely able to win set-piece battles against its Soviet enemy because of its better organization and firepower. The Russians found it impossible to permanently suppress the opposition in spite of inflicting heavy casualties, though. Of course since the Afghan definition of victory consisted of a Soviet withdrawal, all the resistance needed to do was to make the country ungovernable and a drain on Soviet resources. By the mid-1980s, the Soviets came to the same conclusion that the British had reached a century earlier: the direct occupation of Afghanistan had a high cost for few benefits. Gorbachev also concluded that the best policy was to take a more indirect approach and let the Afghans handle their own affairs.

In other respects, however, the defeat of the Soviets in the twentieth century was quite different from the Anglo-Afghan wars of the nineteenth. In the Anglo-Afghan wars, the occupations had been relatively short, and the damage to Afghanistan's economy and people was limited. The Soviet occupation, by contrast, lasted a decade, and did immense damage to the country and its people. The agricultural economy was so disrupted that the Afghan people became dependent on imported food aid, particularly in the cities. The cities themselves grew in size as villagers sought safety there. This war-induced urbanization tripled the population of Kabul, and the regional cities grew by as much or more. The regional cities also became more important as the Soviets invested in new infrastructure for them. Previously, for example, Kabul University had been Afghanistan's only university, but now each major city had its own institutions of higher learning. The educational system at lower levels also grew, raising rates of literacy and expanding the number of teachers, especially women. Those refugees who fled the country may have been even more transformed by the war. Coming from subsistence village economies, they found themselves in large refugee camps that were bureaucratically run and tied to political parties. People who had never been outside their own province were now living in foreign countries surrounded by strangers. The assistance they received, though modest by international standards, raised expectations about what services a government owed its people. More negatively the war offered an opportunity for young men to earn a living as soldiers, whether for the resistance or the PDPA. Within rural Afghanistan, the old elite of landowning khans and elders were replaced by young military commanders, who could offer their communities protection or simply demand more respect because they had guns.

The Afghans also found themselves embroiled in deadly conflicts on behalf of those who provided them aid. Both sides adapted themselves to appeal to their sponsors in ways that pandered to their prejudices at the expense of their indigenous followers. The PDPA received its military and economic support from the Soviet Union, but the mujahideen would not have been competitive without access to similarly large sums of money and arms, which were supplied by the United States and Saudi Arabia. This meant that the Afghan resistance was as dependent on international aid as its Soviet-supported rival was. As a result, the Afghan mujahideen found themselves sucked into two larger conflicts: the ongoing cold war struggle between the United States and the Soviet Union, and a new struggle by Saudi Salafis to make the war in Afghanistan the vanguard of a transnational jihad that they hoped would bring about Islamic revolutions in the Sunni Arab world and beyond.

The international funders justified their support of the Afghan conflict in ways that had little relevance within Afghanistan. They portrayed the struggle in Afghanistan as a Manichaean conflict of competing ideologies (e.g., Islam versus atheism, socialism versus capitalism, freedom versus oppression, feudal reactionaries versus progressive patriots, modernists versus traditionalists). Afghans never saw the war they were fighting in such black-and-white terms because politics in Afghanistan was less ideological and more personal. It was a world where yesterday's enemy might become today's ally, meaning you should take no one for granted. The mujahideen parties, for instance, had good connections with Kabul government bureaucrats throughout the war and could generally get any information they needed from them. Such bureaucrats sent the message that no matter who held the top positions and set policy, they were the functionaries who kept a government running. Defections from one side to another were based more on personal disputes and private interests than on any ideology. If a village son rose high in the PDPA's ranks, one could be sure that the district would throw its lot in with Kabul. If he defected or was purged, that district was sure to discover the merits of the resistance. Even more common was spreading risk by placing different community members in rival camps to protect the group as a whole. At the national level, the philosophical differences between the resistance and the Kabul regime, which seemed so sharp when the war began, blurred with time. The PDPA government denounced its earlier radical policies as mistakes after the Soviet invasion and later renounced socialism itself. While party leaders in Peshawar may have remained hard-line Islamists, internal mujahideen commanders who originally shared their ideology, such as Masud, adopted more practical policies to hold their regional coalitions together. But changing government policy and flexible ideologies had their limits. They failed to blunt the continuing opposition to the PDPA government as long as Soviet troops remained in the country.

The Soviet Union's withdrawal in 1989 removed this bedrock objection to Najibullah's legitimacy. Once he survived the initial period of military uncertainty, his political flexibility greatly expanded. Najibullah portrayed himself as a good Muslim and Afghan nationalist who could protect Afghanistan's interests better than the Peshawar-based party leaders. He offered mujahideen commanders cease-fires and leadership positions to run their own autonomous militias. This policy had a substantial impact since it was estimated that only around 12 percent of the active mujahideen fell into the irreconcilable camp. Thus, the number of active mujahideen engaged in fighting peaked at an estimated 85,000 in 1988–89 as the Soviets were pulling out and then declined to 55,000 by 1990. Attracted by offers of arms and money, 20 percent of former mujahideen groups defected and joined Najibullah's militia system, while another 40 percent agreed to cease-fires. They saw little reason to fight against Najibullah's regime if their own needs were met and the Soviets were gone. In Herat, long a stronghold of resistance, government militia strength grew from around 14,000 in 1986 to 70,000 in 1991. This radically altered the military and political structure of Najibullah's regime. Militia forces of all types reached 170,000 in 1991 and accounted for more than half his forces. By contrast, troops under direct government control (in the army, paramilitary police, and secret police [KhAD, State Information Agency]) declined precipitously from a perhaps-inflated high of 400,000 in 1989 to 160,000 in 1991.[64] These government troops became more fragmented and politicized as well. The radical Khalqi minister of defense, Shah Nawaz Tanai, attempted a coup against Najibullah in April 1990. It failed when the Khalqis proved too divided to act as a group and Tanai defected to Hekmatyar in Pakistan.[65]

For those who saw the war in ideological terms, Najibullah's success at winning support from his old enemies was inexplicable, but he followed a well-known strategy that had proved successful in the past. Like the British-funded amirs before him, he planned to use continuing aid from the Soviet Union to consolidate his power through networks of patronage and by maintaining a powerful military. In 1988, seven hundred thousand people were already receiving salaries or in-kind payments from the government in a salaried workforce of three million.[66] The expansion of the militia system increased that number significantly and gave more people a vested interest in seeing his rule continue. Of course, such a strategy required a large and continuing flow of resources. This appeared guaranteed by the Soviet Union's ongoing willingness to provide Najibullah with food, fuel, cash, and (covertly) weapons. Neither Najibullah nor his enemies ever imagined that his superpower patron might suddenly disappear from the world stage, as it did at the end of 1991.

THE FALL OF NAJIBULLAH

After 1989, Najibullah's administration of Afghanistan was characterized by the de facto devolution of power to the country's regions and its leaders. This marked an enormous structural change. For one hundred years the Kabul government's power had been so dominant that it was assumed that Afghanistan's regions would never again play a significant role in national politics. But as the Soviet occupation progressed, Kabul's hold over the country weakened, and both the PDPA and the mujahideen fell back on using these regions as their basic building blocks of Afghanistan. The mujahideen had done this from necessity, since their resistance had welled up from the grass roots and depended on alliances of local-level commanders that never transcended the regional level. Masud founded the Supervisory Council of the North, and Ismail Khan was known as the amir of Herat whose power encompassed the west. The mujahideen in the Pashtun areas of eastern and southern Afghanistan were more confined to their localities, because tribal rivalries and infighting among the Peshawar-based political parties thwarted attempts at regional integration there. Initially the PDPA continued the tradition of a Kabul-centered government, not surprisingly since that is where the bulk of its members were. Yet as the war progressed they divided the country into seven military zones, which had more internal cohesion than the unwieldy provincial structure. These received considerable autonomy, particularly in the north, where a new Uzbek dominated province (Sar-i-pul) was created and Balkh Province signed its own electricity agreement with Uzbekistan.[67] The emphasis on the north was deliberate: it bordered the Soviet Union, and the government hoped to build this region up as a counterweight to the Pashtun south and east, reversing the policies of earlier Afghan amirs. The devolution of power quickened when the Soviets began withdrawing. Najibullah needed to ensure that his vital transit routes to the Soviet border were not cut off after they left. For a leader who planned to preserve his regime through patronage and the redistribution of Soviet aid, nothing could be more dangerous than the interruption of such aid. For this he did not rely on the army (still dominated by Khalqis) but rather on the northern militias, whose leaders thereby became power brokers in their own right.[68]

While militias were recruited from a variety of sources and regions, the strongest and most effective were drawn from the northern minority communities that had suffered discrimination in the past. The Ismailis in Baghlan had long been viewed as heretical by their Sunni neighbors and were ignored by previous Kabul governments. Their leader, Sayyid Mansur Nadiri Kayani, therefore chose to ally himself with the PDPA in opposition to local Pashtuns and Tajiks, who had joined the resistance. By 1989, he commanded a militia of thirteen thousand that protected the northern approach to the Salang Pass, a key link in the route from the Soviet border to Kabul. His control of the transit trade and access to Soviet aid put him at the center of a powerful patronage network, including the mujahideen he paid off to keep the truck traffic flowing. Abdul Rashid Dostam rose from an impoverished social background to become the feared commander of the Jauzjani militia, composed mainly (but not exclusively) of his fellow Uzbeks. Eventually numbering forty thousand men, it was one of the few militia units that fought effectively outside its home territory in northern Afghanistan. Dostam became one of the most powerful military commanders in Najibullah's government and gave the Uzbeks a national political importance they had not had in 150 years. Such militias were far less important in Pashtun regions, although the regime did organize some border guards in the tribal areas and Najibullah's own Ahmadzai Ghilzais backed him with militia troops.

Najibullah's continued survival put the resistance leaders in Peshawar in a difficult position. After the Soviet Union departed, their international patrons had less incentive to fund them. The United States had financed a war to bloody the Soviets, and achieved that result. The Saudis had paid for a war to expel an infidel occupier, who was now gone. Only Pakistan saw benefits from further fighting because it desperately wanted to dominate Afghanistan's postwar government. Pakistan's goal was the installation of a Pashtun Islamist regime in Kabul led by Hekmatyar, a man whose animosity toward the United States was well-known. That Pakistan persuaded the United States to support its policy of continued resistance to Najibullah's regime to achieve this end was remarkable. Had the dead spirits of the British raj arisen to give their advice on the matter they would surely have advised their American cousins to cut a deal with Najibullah now that he had become an Afghan nationalist and proved his staying power. After all, Abdur Rahman had been on the Russian payroll for many years and had proved quite a successful choice in bringing stability to the country in the 1880s. Given the alternative of Najibullah or the mujahideen leaders in Peshawar backed by Pakistan, the British would have said the choice was clear. There were certainly also charismatic resistance leaders within Afghanistan who had previously been excluded from consideration by their rivals in Peshawar. They had begun to display their own independence by forming the National Commanders Shura (NCS) in opposition to the external party leaders in October 1990. They still favored toppling Najibullah, but planned to accomplish this without a direct attack on Kabul in a slower province-by-province approach. If they had succeeded, the NCS would have likely displaced the Peshawar parties in determining Afghanistan's postwar future.[69]

Najibullah's ability to balance the disparate factions that now made up his power base collapsed when the Soviet Union was formally dissolved in December 1991 and aid to his regime stopped. Deliveries of such assistance had already begun declining substantially in the aftermath of the failed coup against Gorbachev in August by hard-liners, leaving Afghanistan without enough fuel and food for the winter. The Soviets had promised 230,000 tons of food that year, but by October had delivered only half that amount and only 10 percent of the promised amount of fuel. The only thing still arriving in quantity were new Afghan banknotes printed in Russia, the distribution of which by the container load generated a high rate of inflation. Desertions from the armed forces started rising at an alarming rate, and the regime lacked funds to pay its affiliated militia forces, some of which turned to crime. Corruption was so rampant that the government bureaucracy absorbed 85 to 90 percent of the Soviet aid intended for the population as a whole. Since Najibullah's strategy had depended on his redistribution of Soviet aid, the sudden end of such outside assistance was a fatal blow to his regime. He agreed to accept a transition process that would create a new government through a UN-brokered conference. This caused a realignment scramble by all factions, mujahideen and Kabul regime forces alike. These new alliances were based largely on region and ethnicity, so that the radically socialist Khalqis joined Hekmatyar's radical Islamist party to unite the Pashtuns. Dostam's Uzbeks and Kayani's Ismaili militias revolted against Najibullah's regular troops in the north, and then allied with Masud's Tajiks, who had been overrunning the northeast. The Shia Hazara Hizb-i-Wahdat party joined them. When word reached Masud that Hekmatyar and the Khalqis intended to take Kabul for themselves in April 1992, he occupied the capital a day before they arrived. Unable to escape the country, Najibullah sought asylum from the United Nations and disappeared from view. The Communist regime was not so much defeated militarily as it was reorganized when its components defected to various mujahideen factions.[70]

The Mujahideen Civil War

Once he was in Kabul, Masud's allies urged him to take charge as leader of a provisional government. The fate of Afghanistan might have taken a different turn had he done so. He was well-known as a conciliator who regularly crossed political and ethnic lines to create coalitions, and thus was best placed to broker a new peace. Although a Tajik, even Pashtuns admitted that he was one of the most outstanding military commanders who had fought against the Soviets. His NCS was broad based and supported by the leaders who had done most of the actual fighting. As Neamatollah Nojumi observed, the NCS was also best placed to integrate the still well-organized ex-government forces with the victorious mujahideen factions to create a national army capable of preserving order. This would have been the best guarantee for preserving security in Kabul[71] and facilitated cooperation with the now-powerful regions. Most important, it would have had the best chance of preventing the country's descent into civil war. Masud unfortunately proved to be a far more skilled commander than politician. Fearful of provoking ethnic conflict, he left the formation of the new government to the Peshawar party leaders with the expectation that they would do what was best for the country and arrange for future elections. But they had no intention of seeking a consensus or presenting themselves for any electoral approval. This was their chance to seize power, and they snapped at the opportunity like hungry dogs.

The last remaining thread that had bound the mujahideen into a marriage of convenience broke when they no longer had a common enemy. Their new Islamic State of Afghanistan was a mere shell. Its leaders had no clear goals because their unity had been based on resistance against the Soviet Union and its client Afghan government, not on any popular political platform. None of the seven Peshawar party leaders who agreed to the new government had done any fighting inside Afghanistan themselves or created a national political base. They were naturally opposed to any open system of government that might expose their unpopularity or narrow base of support. They were particularly vehement in their insistence that Zahir Shah, the former king, should play no role in government, not even a symbolic one. Royal legitimacy through recognized tribal lineage still held enough sway among ordinary Afghans to undermine the Pakistani-backed mujahideen party leaders. The most powerful of them, Rabbani and Hekmatyar—the leaders of Jamiat-i-Islami and Hizb-i-Islam, respectively—lacked prestigious social origins or a strong tribal following of their own, and so they feared being swept aside by those who had such advantages.

A mujahideen power struggle was therefore inevitable once the PDPA dissolved. It was not the result of some Afghan penchant for blood feud or tribal rivalries (although these did play a part) but rather the predictable consequence of having armed and funded political-military factions in Pakistan that had long waited for such an opportunity to arise. Each faction leader realized that if he did not obtain power now, he never would. And since the parties were based more on personality than ideology there was little basis for compromise, particularly since the rise of one predominate leader would mean an end to all the smaller factions. The agreed-on distribution of power failed immediately after the Peshawar party leaders arrived in Kabul. Despite attempts at mediation by Saudi Arabia, the "prime minister," Hekmatyar, refused to enter the capital and remained encamped in the hills south of Kabul, from where he began shelling the city and the troops of his "president," Rabbani (1992–95). Kabul, which had been spared any fighting during the war because of its many lines of defenses, was devastated over the next three years, and large parts of the city were reduced to rubble. Many of its residents fled the city, seeking safety elsewhere, and twenty-five thousand people were believed to have died as a result of the fighting. A stalemate ensued, in which neither side was able to dislodge the other. In an attempt to break the deadlock, Hekmatyar cut a deal in January 1994 with the Uzbek leader Dostam, who once again betrayed his former allies to join what he hoped would be the winning side. This was an odd couple: the most fundamentalist mujahideen commander embracing the hard-drinking former Communist general. The venture failed to bring down Rabbani's government. The fighting in and around Kabul intensified as the Tajiks led by Masud in one part of

the city continued to fight bitter battles with the Hazaras led by Ali Mazari
in the other. All sides committed atrocities, and what prestige the mujahideen factions had gained by expelling the Soviets was lost as they fought
each other in the ruins of Kabul.[72]

In previous periods of such turmoil, Afghan leaders had arisen to reestablish political order in the country by combining some recognized claim
of political legitimacy with substantial aid from the outside world. The
more a leader had of one, the less he needed the other. But both of these
conditions were now lacking. Because the Soviet war had thrown contenders on to the Afghan political stage from previously marginalized social
groups, they were all in the awkward position of needing to take power
before they could legitimize their right to it. This was proving impossible
to achieve since no leader had the strength to eliminate his rivals permanently. Unlike earlier Afghan civil wars that were restricted to small sets of
Durrani competitors, this struggle was a free-for-all potentially open to
anyone. While this made access to outside resources even more critical for
political success, such resources had now become scarce. The great game
finally appeared over. Russia had closed the book on the Soviet Union's
misadventures there and was content to let the Afghans live as they pleased.
And with the Soviet Union dissolved, the United States wished no further
involvement in a resourceless country on the verge of collapse that had
become strategically irrelevant. Not bothering even to reopen its embassy
in Kabul, which had been closed since the Russians invaded, the United
States withdrew its aid and personnel from the whole region, including
Pakistan. (Pakistan was denied assistance on the grounds that its barely
secret nuclear program violated U.S. laws previously overlooked in the
context of the cold war.) Even die-hard Saudi Islamists found it hard to
generate funds to assist one group of Sunni Muslims to better kill another.
The United Nations continued to provide emergency humanitarian aid,
but it had no mandate to impose a political solution, and no means to
accomplish such a task if it did. Of the neighboring states only Pakistan
retained a keen interest in Afghan affairs. It had always expected to install
a friendly regime in Kabul, and that task remained undone.

The inability of the factions to find any common agreement about what
a future government should look like, let alone who should run it, made it
impossible to unify the country politically. Nor was there the prospect of

unifying the country militarily either, since each faction was strong enough to defend its own home region but too weak to extend its power beyond it. This placed Kabul in a uniquely vulnerable position. Timur Shah had chosen to make it his capital in the late eighteenth century because it lay on an ethnic fault line—a Tajik city just outside the Pashtun tribal belt to the south and east. For centuries Kabul's location aided successive amirs in projecting national authority: a Pashtun-dominated government wielding power over Tajiks to the north and Hazaras to the west from a capital that shared no common territory with any of the Pashtun tribes. But during the mujahideen civil war Kabul's location proved a recipe for disaster. Hekmatyar's Hizb-i-Islam faction was ensconced in the city's Pashtun southern flank, Masud's Jamiat troops had control of Tajik Kohistan, and Mazari's Hizb-i-Wahdat troops were able to support Kabul's Hazara neighborhoods with aid from central and northern Afghanistan. It was thus hard for any faction to drive the others far enough away to secure the city from further attack. As the nation's capital, Kabul also held an iconic status that made it an irresistible target for every leader who wished to claim national power.

By 1993, the country was divided into regions that closely matched the provinces of nineteenth-century Afghanistan. Ismail Khan secured Herat and the west (including Badghis, Farah, and Ghor). Dostam ruled the north from Mazar in alliance with the Hazara Hizb-i-Wahdat and the Ismailis in the Baghlan. Masud controlled Kabul and the northeast. The Nangarhar shura in Jalalabad led by Haji Qadir oversaw the east, while the southeast was divided between Jalaludin Haqqani in Paktia and Mulla Naqibullah Akhund in Qandahar. Unlike the failing state of Yugoslavia that was collapsing into ever-smaller ethnic states at the same time, however, even in this weak condition Kabul was never challenged by regional or ethnic separatist movements. No Afghan leader saw the collapse of central power in Kabul as an opportunity to seek independence. Instead, the regions backed one of the two major contenders for national power: Rabbani and Masud's Shura Nazar (Supervisory Council), or Hekmatyar's Shura-i-Hamabangi (Coordination Council). While this division is often described as strictly regional and ethnic, it was not. Although seeking Pashtun hegemony, Hekmatyar recruited Dostam's Uzbeks and Mazari's Hazaras as allies to buy time against Masud and Rabbani. Similarly, the divisions among the Pashtuns were strong enough to undermine any attempt to unite them under a single leader. The Nangarhar shura declared its neutrality in the struggle for national leadership, while Mulla Naqibullah Akhund in Qandahar remained loyal to Rabbani's Jamiat faction.[73] In Afghanistan, opportunism could always be counted on to undermine any other "ism" (Islamism, nationalism, socialism, etc) in this fight. In terms of outside support, Pakistan backed Hekmatyar, while Iran and Russia provided aid to Rabbani and Masud. As the world changed, Masud found himself drinking tea with the very Russians that he had expelled from Afghanistan but who now supplied him with weapons and ammunition.

Viewed from Kabul, Afghanistan was now a failed state that had dissolved into complete anarchy, with its national institutions bankrupt and powerless.[74] But the picture was not uniform because the country's regions differed so markedly in their levels of security and ability to sustain ordinary life. Unlike Kabul, not all regional cities experienced ongoing fighting and the disruption that this produced. The largest sat at the center of their respective regional territories (Mazar in the north, Herat in the west, Qandahar in the south, and Jalalabad in the east), where one faction was more likely to become dominant. In terms of daily life, the non-Pashtun regions had higher levels of security and economic prosperity than did the Pashtun regions, because their local economies were stronger and their administrative structures were more coherent. The government in Qandahar, for example, never established regular order over its surrounding region, and it fell prey to armed militias whose major source of income were roadblocks that extorted money from the international transit trade between Pakistan and Iran. They also abused the local population, engaging in rape and pillage without fear of punishment.

As the mujahideen civil war intensified around Kabul, these regions grew ever more autonomous, and Afghanistan reverted to nineteenth-century patterns of rule that had been well adapted to such conditions. The local elites declared nominal fealty to Kabul yet otherwise went their own way. Kabul returned the favor by extending them patronage. In the absence of any national military force, "the most important element that sustained the connection between Kabul and the local and regional forces was the financial support sent by Rabbani and Masud to these local groups. This financial support came in the form of cash printed in Russia and transported to Kabul."[75]

Also similar to the nineteenth century was how contenders competing for national power around Kabul lived in a world apart from those who held regional power. They headed shifting alliances among the different factions but had no independent regional power base of their own. Rabbani may have been president of the Islamic State of Afghanistan, but his writ did not run beyond the palace. His rival Hekmatyar commanded a powerful army attempting to displace him, but it was an army that did not control a region itself. Hekmatyar was so fixated on seizing national power that he placed his troops on the outskirts of the capital and never left, leaving civil administration to his local commanders, wherever they happened to be. Not only were the most important towns and cities of the east, Jalalabad, Khost, Ghazni, and Gardez, not under Hekmatyar's direct control, they were held by men whose loyalties were first to themselves.

Rabbani and Hekmatyar were in this situation for the same reasons. Both lacked a strong base inside Afghanistan similar to those that regional military leaders had developed during the course of the war. By contrast, Hekmatyar and Rabbani were party political leaders who had sat out the war in Pakistan. Their power rested on the redistribution of resources and their international connections rather than fighting. More significantly, the social origins of both men made it all but impossible for them to become powerful figures regionally on their return to Afghanistan. Rabbani was a Tajik from Badakhshan, a poor mountainous region that was already part of Masud's territory. Masud commanded his army, and the troops were loyal to him, not Rabbani. Hekmatyar was a Ghilzai Pashtun, but he had no home community in the east because his people had been resettled in the north before he was born. This cut two ways: negatively, he had no immediate ties to the Ghilzais of the east that would have guaranteed him their support in a bid for regional power, but in seeking national power he could proclaim himself leader of a Pashtun movement clear of the internecine rivalry that dogged local commanders when they moved upward. Such a competition also satisfied the regional power holders, who played the role of kingmakers. From their perspective, supporting the rise of a structurally weak national leader was superior to a seeing the reemergence of a powerful central government that would have the capacity to displace them.

The Rise and Demise of the Taliban

Historically, Afghanistan got rid of foreign occupiers by making the country so ungovernable that they wanted to leave. This strategy, perfected during the decade-long struggle to expel the Soviets, now came to haunt the Afghans themselves. Having achieved the sobriquet "graveyard of empires" for their nineteenth- and twentieth-century successes against the superpowers of the age, the Afghans now began digging a grave for themselves. No faction was able to establish either political legitimacy or military hegemony, but none was willing to compromise with its rivals either. It was as if the country had developed an autoimmune disorder: powerful antibodies fatal to foreigners were now directed at the Afghan body politic itself. This made the country vulnerable to opportunistic attacks by groups and ideologies that under other circumstances, would never have gained a following or been easily suppressed. The Taliban arose and spread in such a context.

THE TALIBAN MOVEMENT

The Taliban was a cross-border movement led by Afghan Pashtuns trained in Deobandi madrasas in Pakistan. Its ideological roots lay there, and its Afghan leaders had close ties with religious parties in Pakistan. The madrasas had grown at a tremendous rate in Pakistan under Zia al Haq, attracting a large number of Afghan refugee boys by offering free room and board along with education. During the Soviet war, the schools' graduates joined the mujahideen to fight in Afghanistan in defense of Islam through the existing Peshawar party structure. But because the civil war now pitted Muslim against Muslim, the Taliban movement's goal shifted to ending the disorder while also reforming Afghanistan's religious and cultural practices by creating a pure Islamic state along Salafist lines. This ambition was shared by the religious parties within Pakistan, but the disorder in Afghanistan gave the Taliban a better chance of achieving it.[76]

The Taliban was unlike other Afghan political movements not only in the exclusively clerical origin of its leaders but in the refugee origins of its followers too. The Soviet war lasted for so long and the refugee flow into neighboring countries was so great that over time they created a new class of people: refugee Afghans born in Pakistan who had never seen the country or experienced life there. Refugee camps are notorious hotbeds for radical movements of all types because they are generally poor, provide few opportunities for young people, and are under the control of political factions that manipulate their populations. The hope of recovering a lost homeland is a particularly powerful ideal, but as time passes the view of this homeland becomes more and more mythical because refugee children know of it only by hearsay. The past is idealized because the present is so miserable and the future is so uncertain. Groups with extreme messages, whether their ideologies are political, ethnic, or religious, galvanize their followers not only with the visions of reclaiming a lost homeland but also of then transforming it. Refugees in Afghanistan did better than most. They experienced a tactical victory when the Soviets withdrew and in theory could return to their homeland.

But the fighting among the mujahideen foreclosed that option for most. Even when the refugees did return, their homeland was not what they had known when they left it. Although poor before the war, the Afghan economy at least functioned, and there was general security for life and property. Now there was none. The mujahideen, who had been heroes in the anti-Soviet jihad, lost respect when they became mere factions engaged in self-interested and violent struggles for power with other similar groups. The Taliban drew on this discontent in two ways. First, they recruited men who had been too young to participate in the anti-Soviet war and gave them a chance to participate in a new type of jihad—one that would bring a "truer version" of Islam to Afghanistan. Jihad had been the focal experience for young men throughout the Soviet war, and a new generation of refugee youths was looking for a goal that was equally as idealistic. That the Taliban's view of Islam was far more radically reactionary than any existing in Afghanistan previously meant little to people who had nothing to compare it with. For them it was far easier to imagine an ideal Afghan way of life, and to enforce it on others, because they drew their lessons from religious schools rather than the give-and-take of everyday life. Their hostility toward women may well have stemmed from being removed from their families and female relations at an early age to grow up in all-male religious schools. Second, the Taliban drew on the discontent of the population living in areas where chaos prevailed. For them, any ideology or regime that could bring about stability was preferable to the status quo.

The early development of the Taliban movement and how much it owed to Pakistan are subject to dispute. By their own account, they organized themselves in Qandahar in mid-1994 in response to the failure of mujahideen leaders there to provide security. Their leader was Mullah Omar, a minor cleric who had not previously been involved in politics. His religious students, or *taliban* (hence the name), had complained about how badly local commanders were abusing the population, so he instructed them to disarm these bands. They then proceeded to unblock the region's roads and took control of Qandahar. Other observers trace their origin to Pakistan's frustration with Hekmatyar's lack of success in the civil war against Rabbani and the need to create a more effective alternative movement to replace him. They note that the first massing of Taliban fighters was within Pakistan, and how easily they came to seize a large arms depot from Hekmatyar's forces at the main border crossing of Spin Boldak just inside Afghanistan before moving on Qandahar. With Pakistani help and large cash payments to its mujahideen commanders, they induced the city to surrender without a battle in early November. The Taliban quickly added the opium-rich Helmand Province to their base, giving them control of the southwest and a substantial source of income from the drug trade. Regardless of their origins, the Taliban introduced a new political force into Afghanistan. The movement was widely popular in the south because it promised security of life and property to a region that lacked both. Its "law-and-order" platform initially overshadowed the movement's radical Islamist ideology, which the Taliban did not implement in full until they were better established.[77]

Afghanistan and Pakistan's NWFP were familiar with ephemeral rural uprisings led by religious visionaries who claimed to be acting on God's command to bring about some divinely inspired change. Their leaders were almost always charismatic clerics who exploded on the political scene by rousing the tribes to resistance, asserting that their success was preordained. Paradoxically, their leaders' low social origins reinforced this perception, because how else could such men have risen so high except by God's direct assistance? Conversely, the failure of their movements ended their careers and often their lives. The British dismissed such religious leaders as "mad mullahs," who were troublesome rabble-rousers but otherwise ineffective, because their tribal military forces were poorly organized and went home when they ran out of supplies. Their movements rarely proved long lasting when the central government was strong and could suppress their uprisings with a regular army. But the Taliban movement was not opposed by a central government or indeed any coherent military force. It seeped into the lawless vacuum of southern Afghanistan, which had no powerful regional leader of its own to maintain order, as the Nangarhar shura had done in the Pashtun east.[78]

Although the Taliban may have resembled similar mad mullah movements in its socially marginal clerical leadership, recruitment of religious students as fighters, and unorthodox religious ideology, they also had a professional military arm that previous such movements lacked. From the beginning, the first targets of Taliban attacks were always the weapons depots of their rivals. These not only provided their foot soldiers with small arms but also heavy weapons, armored vehicles, and aircraft. Since tank maintenance and piloting jets or helicopters were not subjects taught in madrasas, the men who supplied these skills were professional soldiers, mostly ex-Khalqis trained by the Soviets. These professionals had first joined various mujahideen factions when Najibullah fell, and now agreed to grow untrimmed beards and serve the Taliban, who were at least fellow Pashtuns. (How becoming the military backbone of a Salafist movement seeking to reestablish a seventh-century Islamic caliphate appeared to these champions of the Saur Revolution can only be imagined.) Pakistan also provided direct military aid and advisers to the movement, including the delivery of supplies and transport, without which the Taliban could not have survived.

TALIBAN EXPANSION

After taking control of Qandahar in 1994 the Taliban expanded quickly, but not without setbacks. They moved north to attack Kabul, taking Ghazni in late January 1995. Along another line of attack they took control of the eastern Pashtun provinces of Paktia and Paktika. This advance so undermined Hekmatyar that he was forced to flee east, abandoning his own siege of Kabul and his heavy weapons. Strikingly, Hekmatyar's party (and those of the other Peshawar leaders) proved so weakly rooted within Afghanistan's Pashtun regions that their military units dissolved in the face of the Taliban advance. The Taliban simply swept them aside until they stood at the gates of Kabul. Taking advantage of the long-running conflict between Masud's Tajiks and Mazari's Hazaras in Kabul, they gained the support of Shia Hizb-i-Wahdat for an attack on the capital in March. But here Masud's experience triumphed over Taliban enthusiasm. The Taliban's string of earlier successes had been achieved indirectly by exploiting internal rivalries among their enemies, encouraging defections with promises of reappointments within their own administration, or simply bribing militia leaders with large amounts of cash. These strategies were so successful that the Taliban had not yet engaged in a battle against a serious foe determined to fight. Yet as they entered Kabul they encountered Masud, a commander far more familiar than they with the bloody tools of war. His artillery rained destruction down on the Taliban troops as they fled Kabul and retreated south. Along the way the Taliban murdered their erstwhile-ally Mazari, earning the undying enmity of the Hazaras who had trusted them.

This defeat encouraged Ismail Khan to attack the Taliban from the west. Although still engaged in fighting with Dostam in the northwest, he forced the Taliban to retreat back toward Qandahar in March. If Rabbani had joined in this attack strongly from the north, the Taliban might have been expelled from the country, but the success of one region's leader invariably generated more jealousy than support from rivals elsewhere. Rabbani worked to undermine Ismail Khan in Herat by encouraging his enemies there to displace him, and Dostam dispatched technicians through Pakistan to repair the Taliban's jets. Meanwhile, the Taliban raised a large number of recruits in Pakistan for a counterattack in August that broke through the defenses of the overstretched Herati forces. When their retreat became a rout, the Taliban were able to secure Herat in early September with little fighting. With southwestern and western Afghanistan now firmly under their control, the Taliban made a new bid to take Kabul. This time, though, they attacked from the east, first destabilizing the Nangarhar shura by dividing its members after an attack through Paktia. In September 1996 they captured Hekmatyar's last-remaining arms depots and took Jalalabad, which also had a large supply of arms. The Taliban then moved on Kabul from the east and outflanked Masud, who had not anticipated the collapse of the Nangarhar shura. Masud retreated from the city to his base in the Panjshir Mountains without giving battle. He was the only commander in Afghanistan skilled enough to carry out such an operation and still keep his forces intact. So even though he lost Kabul, Masud inflicted a severe beating on the Taliban troops that pursued him and established a line of defense against them on the Shomali Plain north of Kabul. Dostam now joined Masud as part of an anti-Taliban Northern Alliance, but he had his own internal troubles and was driven into exile for a time.[79]

The Taliban used their bases northwest of Herat to mount an attack on northern Afghanistan in May 1997. After subverting these Uzbek commanders charged with defending the region, their troops dove into Mazar unopposed and began to take charge. While their leaders addressed a crowd of uncomprehending Persian and Uzbek speakers in Pashto at the main mosque, another group of Taliban decided to shoot up the Shia Hazara districts of the city. They forgot that these people were still well armed and thus were forced to retreat when they came under fire themselves. On hearing of this setback, the Taliban's new Uzbek allies decided they had acted too hastily and started shooting at them as well. Hundreds of Taliban were killed as they retreated west, and around three thousand were taken prisoner. Few of these survived the wrath of the northerners. Since all Afghan factions were quite small (the Taliban were estimated to have twenty-five thousand troops in total), such a loss was catastrophic. It punctured their aura of invincibility and made the recruitment of new Afghan troops more difficult. From this point on the Taliban forces relied even more heavily on raw Pakistani recruits from religious schools and international jihadists (Arabs, Uzbeks, Chechens, etc.), who were viewed as invading foreigners by other Afghans. Yet the depth of this non-Afghan recruitment pool allowed the Taliban to regroup, and they retook Mazar in August 1998 with the help of the local Pashtun population there. The Taliban then engaged in a wholesale massacre of Mazar's Hazaras, who had driven them from the city the year previous. The next month they occupied Bamiyan, the Hazara center, leaving the Taliban in control of the entire country except for the northeast, where Masud still stood alone against them for the next three years.[80]

TALIBAN GOVERNMENT

Mullah Omar took the title of Amir-ul Momineen ("Commander of the Faithful") of the Islamic amirate of Afghanistan. His authority was absolute because obeying his commands was religiously obligatory—a demand by God (*fardh*), resistance to which merited execution. The Taliban saw themselves as returning to the early days of Islam, in which the community was ruled by a small council of religious leaders. This produced a two-track government. The real power lay in a six-member Inner Shura led by Mullah Omar, while the regular administration and foreign relations were in the hands of a nine-member Central Shura that reported to Mullah Omar. This structure was poorly adapted to ruling a country or running a bureaucracy. In 1999, the Taliban therefore overhauled their administrative structure. The Qandahar Inner Shura was still dominant, but the government in Kabul now adopted the old offices previously employed by Zahir Shah and filled various ministries with Taliban appointees. Even this change was largely cosmetic, however, because the Taliban proved unwilling to make the transition from a social movement to a government. Taliban governors continued to serve as military commanders reporting directly to Mullah Omar and not to the ministries in Kabul. More debilitating, Mullah Omar refused to leave Qandahar, so his ministers in Kabul found themselves outside the decision-making process. The ministers would make agreements or announce policies in the name of the government, only to rescind them after being overruled from Qandahar with little explanation.[81]

The Taliban were initially lauded for bringing peace and security to the regions they captured, but their social and religious policies became widely unpopular thereafter, particularly in the cities. Taliban religious ideology was a crude mixture of Salafi Islam and Pashtunwali, the cultural code of the Pashtuns. Their religious interpretations were often idiosyncratic and tended to dress local custom in the guise of religion. On the other hand, many aspects of Taliban policy were not local custom at all. The movement was hostile to Sufism as well as the veneration of saints and shrines—elements that were deeply embedded in the popular Islam of Afghanistan. The Taliban banned all forms of entertainment, especially music, and attempted to eliminate all images of living things (going so far as to black out pictures of cows on imported cans of dried milk). They drove women from all public arenas, banned their education, and enforced a strict code of veiling and seclusion. Lawbreakers could expect harsh Islamic punishments not seen in Afghanistan for many generations, including the amputation of hands for thieves, collapsing mud walls on top of homosexuals, and stadium-style public executions for murderers and women caught in adultery. The newly created religious police took it on themselves to arrest men who trimmed their required beards or violated some other Taliban regulation. The opposition between the Taliban and the local populations was most intense in cities such as Kabul and Mazar, which were the strongholds of the modernists, who chafed under the rule of men they considered ill-educated rural bumpkins. Taliban policies inspired less complaint elsewhere because their vision on social policies was less rooted in Islam than in rural Afghan values.

In many ways the Taliban proved themselves a mirror image of the PDPA, intent on imposing radical doctrines of foreign origin (this time religious) on a population that was strongly opposed to them. This opposition had two distinct strands—one intellectual and one ethnocentric. At an intellectual level, it was argued that the Taliban had no business enforcing sharia law because their knowledge of it was rudimentary and flawed. This view was supported by the al Azar–trained Egyptian clerics, who met with Taliban leaders in a failed attempt to forestall the destruction of the Bamiyan Buddhas in 2001. They were appalled to find that "because of [the Taliban's] circumstances and their incomplete knowledge of jurisprudence they were not able to formulate rulings backed by theological evidence. The issue is a cultural issue. We detected that their knowledge of religion and jurisprudence is lacking because they have no knowledge of the Arabic language, linguistics, and literature and hence they did not learn the true Islam."[82]

Of course, the Soviets had voiced similar complaints about the PDPA leadership's deficiencies in Marxist dialectics, so the Taliban were not the first Afghan political movement to ignore such carping criticism. The ethnocentric resistance to the Taliban policies was more diffuse but cut much deeper because it touched on Afghan pride and honor. Ordinary Afghans believed their existing practice of Islam was already so inherently superior to that of other Muslims that it needed no change. Calling for its improvement was oxymoronic because Afghans were the victors of a successful jihad and the inhabitants of the only country in the region that had never come under colonial rule. Advice for improvement from foreign Muslims who could claim neither distinction had little to recommend it.

As the first government run by clerics, the Taliban marked a sharp break with Afghan political tradition. Religion had always played a significant role in Afghan politics, but previously Muslim clerics had always been servants of the state, and not its masters. The failures of the mujahideen leaders, particularly in the Pashtun regions of the country, provided them with a unique opportunity to sideline the existing factions by appealing to a broader commonality that rose above ordinary tribal divisions. Indeed, one of the reasons for their particular success among Pashtuns was their ability to sidestep existing tribal leaders hamstrung by local rivalries. As was noted in chapter 2, ibn Khaldun argued that religion was uniquely suited to bringing tribes together because it is "then easy for them to subordinate themselves and unite (as a social organization)."[83] By this logic the Taliban could argue that they were now best suited to rule Afghanistan because their religious movement had the potential to transcend all ethnic, political, and regional barriers. They squandered this advantage, however, by failing to expand their core leadership beyond a parochial Pashtun base. For non-Pashtuns, the Taliban were just turbaned chauvinists seeking to regain a Pashtun political hegemony that they had lost during the Soviet war. Overt favoritism to minority Pashtun groups in the north, pogroms against the Shia Hazaras by Taliban troops, and the forced removal of Tajiks from Taliban-held parts of the Shomali Plain reinforced this view. More debilitating was the Taliban's increasing reliance on foreigners in what was a civil war from the Afghan point of view. In the absence of an external enemy, the Taliban found it difficult to gain legitimacy internally when so many Afghans saw its regime as too dominated by Pakistan and al Qaeda Arabs.[84]

TALIBAN AND EXTERNAL RELATIONS

As a movement of poorly educated clerics, the Taliban's leadership had far less experience in foreign relations than previous Afghan regimes. Even if they had been skilled diplomats, they would found it difficult to cope with the loss of Afghanistan's strategic position in world politics after the collapse of the Soviet Union and the end of the cold war. But the Taliban could not garner even minimal international recognition of their government. Only three nations—Pakistan, Saudi Arabia, and the United Arab Emirates—ever established diplomatic relations with the Taliban, and the latter two soon downgraded them. This put the Taliban in a difficult position because their stability as a state remained dependent on a continual flow of foreign resources from international donors, by now reduced largely to neighboring Pakistan and the United Nations.[85]

Pakistan had helped to create the Taliban, and continued to supply the movement with vital military aid and access to its religious schools to recruit new soldiers. But Pakistan was a poor country that lacked the resources to substitute itself for the richer powers that had historically met Afghan government shortfalls to feed the population, finance economic development, and subsidize the government services. Nor could Afghan domestic revenues, even including such illegal sources as the highly lucrative export of opium and smuggling untaxed consumer goods into Pakistan, begin to meet such needs. The Taliban thus turned to the United Nations for assistance. In the absence of bilateral relationships, only the United Nations had both the funds and the regional infrastructure to deliver humanitarian assistance, especially food aid. This set up an immediate conflict because the United Nations stood for international human rights, which included the freedom of religion, gender equality, and the protection of minorities, all of which the Taliban violated continually. Yet despite the movement's hostile rhetoric and regular threats to throw the international agencies out of the country, Taliban and UN officials in Kabul generally managed to come to some accommodation that kept the aid flowing, even over the objections from hard-liners in both Qandahar and New York. Unlike North Korea, a place to which Afghanistan was sometimes compared in its extreme isolation, the Taliban understood that no Afghan government could expect to retain power if the population began to starve. The Taliban also realized that as long as they did not actually expel the United Nations and other donor organizations from Afghanistan, the international community would continue to ship food and other aid to the country. Although the Taliban had murdered and castrated Najibullah in the UN compound when they captured Kabul, did not hold Afghanistan's UN seat in New York, violated every UN norm, and was hit by a series of UN sanctions for protecting al Qaeda's bin Laden, the humanitarian imperative was so strong that the United Nations could never bring itself to cut funds to Afghanistan below a minimal level. Since such supplies forestalled civil unrest in the cities where they were most hated, the Taliban carefully weighed their economic necessity against their desire for Islamic purity that working with non-Muslim institutions sullied. This codependency made divorce impossible and had the unintended consequence of providing the Taliban with the economic foundation they needed to continue the civil war on an uncompromising basis.[86]

In their five-year rule of Afghanistan the Taliban not only failed to win wider diplomatic recognition, they demonstrated a talent for alienating possible allies while creating ever more new enemies. They had no friends in the region, with the exception of Pakistan. The Taliban's anti-Shia rhetoric and the murder of the Iranian consular staff in Mazar when they took the city in 1998 almost provoked a war with Iran. They frightened Uzbekistan and Tajikistan with loose talk of spreading Islamic revolution north and providing sanctuary for groups seeking to overthrow their secular governments. In both cases the Taliban denied any intention of doing their neighbors harm. They insisted that they had no interest in the internal politics of the central Asian states and excused the killing of Iranians by Taliban troops as the products of regrettable errors by local commanders. Such explanations eased regional tensions but never reduced their neighbors' enmity. Iran provided aid to groups opposed to the Taliban, and Tajikistan allowed weapons to pass through its territory to arm the Northern Alliance resistance.

Beyond their immediate neighborhood the Taliban took many actions that made dealing with them politically poisonous. The U.S. government, which published some positive statements about the Taliban in 1996 with an eye to developing a natural gas pipeline from Turkmenistan, quickly backtracked when outrage over their treatment of women became a domestic political issue. Neutrality turned to hostility in the wake of the al Qaeda attacks in 1998 on two U.S. embassies in East Africa that resulted in a cruise missile strike against a training camp in Afghanistan. That same year, the Saudis recalled their diplomatic staff from Kabul after Mullah

Omar refused their request to expel bin Laden from the country and insulted the Saudi government for good measure. India felt itself a victim of the Taliban in 1999 when hijackers seized an Air India flight and flew it to Qandahar, using the Taliban as intermediaries to negotiate the release of jailed Islamist radicals, who were flown to Afghanistan in exchange for the passengers. Russia, always fearful of fundamentalist Islam creeping northward to its borders, reinforced its hostility to the Taliban when they granted separatist Chechens full diplomatic recognition in 2000. If the Russians had ever considered ending their aid to Masud's last-ditch resistance against the Taliban, they now had every reason to keep that aid flowing. The Taliban blew up the Bamiyan Buddhas in 2001 to demonstrate their hatred of idol worshippers, unmoved by the world's anger and seemingly ignorant of the fact that Buddhist Japan had been providing Afghanistan with hundreds of millions of dollars in humanitarian aid. The *Economist* magazine wrote in an editorial on May 26, 2001, that "soon there will be no more religions for the Taliban to insult." The next week, however, the Taliban demanded that Sikhs and Hindus in Kabul wear badges to distinguish them from Muslims, and later arrested some humanitarian aid workers on suspicion of being Christian missionaries.

Mullah Omar's limited grasp of world affairs and how they affected Afghanistan exacerbated the situation. His only experience outside Afghanistan was in neighboring Pakistan, and even that was confined to dusty Baluchistan, far from the sophisticated cities of Lahore or Karachi. Nor did Mullah Omar have any trusted aides within his inner circle who could fill the role of sophisticated intermediary with the outside world, since they were all men remarkably like himself. The progressive alienation of the Taliban regime from the world community, including other Muslim states, did not faze Mullah Omar, however. As leader of an aggressive monotheistic movement, he took a view similar to that espoused by the seventeenth-century English religious Puritan Oliver Cromwell, who declared, "If God be for us, who can be against us?" and acted accordingly.[87] Mullah Omar particularly welcomed international jihadi groups to Afghanistan, most notably bin Laden's al Qaeda Arabs, but also including Chechens, Uzbeks, Indonesians, Uighurs, and Kashmiri separatists, among others. Some of these people had been in Afghanistan during the Soviet war, but most represented a new generation of Islamic movements that sought to replicate the Taliban's success in their own countries. Such foreign groups brought money with them, but they also served as the regime's shock troops in the still-ongoing civil war in Afghanistan. Basing themselves in Afghanistan had many advantages in addition to the Taliban's sympathy for their goals. As a failed state, Afghanistan lacked the ability to control their actions, yet could still protect their members from extradition to their home countries. Afghanistan also had a symbolic importance as the place where a superpower had been defeated. In the wake of the Soviet Union's collapse, radical Islamic leaders reinterpreted the Afghan war from one in which a resistance movement successfully forced foreign troops to withdraw to a broader claim that Islamic warriors had destroyed the Soviet Union itself. They now wished to internationalize the Afghan war, and begin a new jihad that would topple existing Muslim governments, destroy the West, and create a caliphate that would rule the world. It was from Afghanistan in 1996 that bin Laden issued his "A Declaration of Jihad," although it was widely ignored at the time.[88]

The Taliban provided foreign Islamists with bases and rhetorical support, but they did not share their expansive view of jihad and had always been quite careful to restrict their jihad to one country: Afghanistan. Ethnocentric to the core, they believed that while Afghans had a duty to risk their lives in a jihad to expel infidels from their own country, they had no obligation to die in other Muslim lands. If foreign groups wished to conduct a jihad against their own governments that was their affair, and they wished them well, but it had nothing to do with the Afghans. In an old Soviet revolutionary terminology, Mullah Omar was a Stalinist who believed in Islamic revolution in one country, while bin Laden was a Trotskyite who believed in fighting a world Islamic revolution. This divide was demonstrated most clearly by how few Afghans ever sought to join international movements such as al Qaeda, and their lack of participation in activities outside Afghanistan or the Pakistan border region. One reason for this was that few Afghans (even clerics) spoke Arabic, the lingua franca of the international jihadists, while another was the belief that they had already contributed a full measure to the cause during the Soviet war. But at a deeper level Afghans were repelled by their nihilism, which glorified death seeking at the expense of life. The blood spilled in two decades of warfare in Afghanistan had long since extinguished any romantic notions about warfare. Martyrdom in battle might be a noble sacrifice that gained entry to paradise, but becoming a ghazi, the living victor of a jihad, was better. Afghans therefore rejected the tactic of suicide bombings so popular among Arab jihadists, and did not employ them even during the Soviet war. They also disapproved of terrorist attacks that deliberately targeted noncombatants because they were dishonorable and not justified by Islamic law. In Afghanistan, where today's enemy might be tomorrow's ally and where blood feuds created rifts that were hard to mend, indiscriminate slaughter was ultimately counterproductive. Of course, groups like al Qaeda had their own reasons for not seeking Afghan recruits: they were too independent minded and failed to follow orders when they disagreed with them.

THE FALL OF THE TALIBAN

Beginning in 1998, the presence of bin Laden in Afghanistan was the main source of conflict between the Taliban and the international community. Saudi Arabia and the United States both wanted to extradite bin Laden for the various terrorist attacks that al Qaeda had mounted. Failing that, they demanded that he be expelled from the country. Mullah Omar was unwilling to do this, citing the Pashtunwali obligation of hospitality (*melmastia*), which required a host to protect his guest even at the risk of his own life. But since by the same code a guest must accept the authority of his host, Mullah Omar assured the world that he had forbidden bin Laden from engaging in any improper activities on Afghan soil, and so that was the end of the matter. The Taliban had not weighed the real cost of giving protection to all these foreign jihadists, though. While the world might condemn Taliban policies within Afghanistan, no country was willing to pay the cost of intervening in its affairs. By contrast, giving protection to foreign jihadists who had decided to mount a campaign of terrorism against the world's remaining military superpower could easily change that equation by returning Afghanistan to the center of the world stage in a battle not of its own making. This was a situation that more experienced Afghan rulers had always been keen to avoid, even if it meant betraying old allies. Afghan rulers who so often encouraged resistance movements against the British raj and the Soviet Union, including tribal jihads in the NWFP, the khalifat movement in India, or the basmachi resistance in central Asia, dropped that support (and even brutally suppressed their former allies) when events reached the point of endangering Afghanistan itself.

On September 11, 2001, that line was crossed when al Qaeda operatives struck New York and Washington, DC, in a series of airline suicide attacks. Two days earlier, their agents had finally succeeded in assassinating Masud in a suicide attack designed to throw the Northern Alliance into disarray and derail an expected U.S. counterattack. When the United States threatened the Taliban leadership with destruction if bin Laden and al Qaeda were not expelled immediately, Mullah Omar refused that demand as well as pleas from his Pakistani patrons to cut his losses now before Afghanistan was attacked and his was movement destroyed. The Pakistanis then deserted him and cooperated with the United States, as did all of Afghanistan's other neighbors, leaving the Taliban isolated. Seeking domestic support for his intransigence Mullah Omar called for an assembly of clerics to meet and affirm his claim that because bin Laden was a guest of the country, he could not be given up. With a nuanced approach that would have done credit to any Pashtun tribal jirga, the three hundred assembled clerics told Mullah Omar that he must indeed protect his guest, but that because a guest should not cause his host problems bin Laden should be asked to leave Afghanistan voluntarily as soon as possible. (It is notable that the question that Mullah Omar tabled was not one of sharia jurisprudence but rather an issue of Pashtunwali.)[89]

In October, U.S. jets struck Taliban positions from the sky while their Northern Alliance allies moved against them on the ground. Mullah Omar had already played his graveyard of empires' card, threatening the United States with the same fate as the Russians and British if it entered Afghanistan. As if to back him up, the Western press ran many stories of "unconquerable Afghanistan" and the invincibility of Afghan guerrillas. Within ten weeks of the war's beginning, however, Taliban positions unraveled completely. They first collapsed in the north and west, where Pashtun control had always been most resented. Kabul fell in early November after the Taliban abandoned the city, hoping to regroup in the Pashtun heartland. But this proved no sanctuary when the traditional Pashtun tribal leaders used the opportunity to regain power and expel the Taliban from Qandahar.[90]

The war did not have any decisive battles. Just as the Taliban had come to power by persuading people that they were winners without fighting and buying the defection of wavering commanders with suitcases full of hundred dollar bills, they lost the war in a reverse process. After the fall of Mazar they were seen as losers, and their nominal allies deserted them. It was an easy choice. The United States, the homeland of hundred dollar bills, was paying for defections by handing them out by the trunkload while threatening the recalcitrant with precision-guided bomb strikes. More compelling was the fear that their local rivals might cut a deal. Only the foreign jihadists appeared willing to seek martyrdom in a fight with the infidels. But they were betrayed by their own Afghan allies, who had always maintained lines of communications with the resistance and now used them. Keen to have a place at the table in a postwar Afghanistan, they abandoned the fight, leaving Mullah Omar and bin Laden without the resistance force they anticipated using to wage a guerrilla war in Afghanistan. Both fled the country for Pakistan, with bin Laden barely escaping with his life. Far from rising up against the infidels and demanding that the foreign troops leave, the Afghan population saw them as a bulwark against the return of civil war and the abusive warlords who waged it. Back in the world's spotlight they now clamored for basic security for the country's reconstruction.

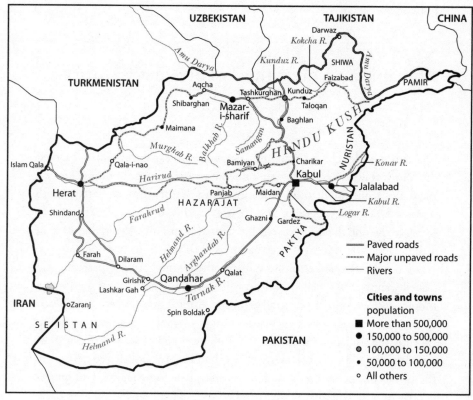

Map 7. Contemporary Afghanistan

CHAPTER FIVE

Afghanistan Enters the Twenty-first Century

The arrival of the United States in Afghanistan to expel the Taliban marked the fourth time in 160 years that a foreign power put troops on the ground there. But while the British in the nineteenth century invaded with plans to replace the existing regimes, and the Soviets invaded in the twentieth to preserve the one they supported, the United States invaded Afghanistan at a time when the state structure had ceased to function. It would need to create a new state to restore stability in the country. In the past this was done by supporting a client political elite in Kabul that would use foreign money and weapons to centralize power. After a quarter century of warfare, however, such a strategy was no longer as viable. There was no political elite in Kabul able to take the reins of power and get others to accept its authority. In addition, too many people had become politicized, at least to the extent of demanding a share of power in the new regime and greater control over local affairs. Yet perhaps because Afghanistan appeared so backward to outside observers, no thought was given to devising a new type of government for this changed situation. Instead, the international community hurried to restore the highly centralized government first imposed on Afghanistan by Abdur Rahman, albeit one in which the government's legitimacy was to be based on elections rather than dynastic right. The weaknesses of this model in terms of leadership, functionality, and legitimacy became apparent soon after Hamid Karzai took power.

To be successful, the leader of a centralized state needed to remove the existing power holders who were determined to undermine state power or make them subservient. Karzai, for all his admirable characteristics, was seen as passive, weak willed, and prone to compromise. Far from acting as a state builder, Karzai adopted a patrimonial model of the state in which its offices and resources were redistributed on a personal basis to buy the support of existing power holders or play them off against one another. Such tactics encouraged maladministration and corruption, failings that debilitated earlier Afghan governments, and these became worse as time passed. Holding loya jirgas and elections meant little if they could not ensure popular participation in government or make government respond to popular complaints. When the Afghan government proved unable to provide the level of security and economic development that the population expected, it was forced to rely ever more heavily on its international backers to maintain itself. This only highlighted Karzai's weakness and undermined his legitimacy in Afghan eyes, particularly when these foreign efforts on his government's behalf proved, as an American idiom has it, "a day late and a dollar short." Still, it was not until the Taliban insurgency flared up in 2006 that the dangers of complacency began finally to be recognized, although little was done until the Obama administration reversed U.S. foreign policy to focus on Afghanistan in 2009. That the situation was not worse owed much to the desire of the Afghan people to see normality restored to their country—a goal that the Taliban had little hope of delivering by reintroducing war into a country that had seen too much of it. Whether new policies could bring peace and stability to Afghanistan was the question that now hung in the balance.

Although nothing is more problematic than sorting through recent events, the consequences of which are unknown (or worse, misapprehended), it is revealing to set the establishment of the Karzai government and its development in the context of earlier similar efforts in Afghanistan. The focus in this chapter is therefore less on events per se than on how they illuminate the process of Afghan state rebuilding (in theory and practice), its leadership, and the role that the international community has played in Afghanistan. For the United States, all was new; for the Afghans, much was recycled. How this period would turn out depended on both of them. Keeping in mind the famous response reputedly made by Chinese prime minister Chou En-lai that it was "too soon to tell" when asked about the impact of the French Revolution of 1789, the consequences of this interaction may become finally apparent only long after all the current actors have left the stage.

THE UNITED STATES IN AFGHANISTAN, 2001–

In 2001, the world community sought to restore peace and stability to Afghanistan after the fall of the Taliban. This goal was well short of being achieved as the country approached the end of its first decade in the new century. Depending on how you looked at it, Afghanistan was either once again on the verge of chaos as a failed state or was surprisingly stable given the problems it faced. There were many positives. The presence of international forces and outside aid had ended the civil war. Millions of refugees had rapidly returned from exile in Iran and Pakistan. A political process for creating and ratifying a constitution had run smoothly, allowing the popular election of a national leader, Hamid Karzai, for the first time in Afghan history. On the other hand, the military and financial resources allocated to the country were grossly inadequate to provide security and improve one of the world's lowest standards of living. The large sums of money pledged for reconstruction at first raised the expectations of ordinary Afghans to unreasonable levels, but as the years passed people had a right to be disappointed by how little was being accomplished at such great expense. Worse, project priorities were set by the funders, not the Afghans, so they rightly questioned the wisdom of building schools and hospitals without teachers and doctors to staff them, or repairing roads with foreign labor while local people remained unemployed. The Taliban tapped into this frustration, but the return of what had been a discredited force was less a measure of their popularity than a response to the failures of the Karzai government, particularly in Pashtun areas. The Taliban could not hope to overthrow the government, yet could reduce its effectiveness through threats of violence, and raise questions about both its legitimacy and staying power. Nevertheless, given Afghan history, what was more surprising was the patience that the Afghans displayed in dealing with outsiders who had little or no understanding of Afghan culture or values. Now the concern was that these outsiders would leave before stability was restored.

Land of Contradictions and Surprises

Afghanistan is one of those places in the world in which people who know the least make the most definitive statements about it. It was common knowledge that the Afghans had risen up against all previous invaders, and so any army would find itself immediately bogged down in a guerrilla war such as the Soviets had experienced. The people there also hated foreigners so much that they would never cooperate with them in the country's postwar reconstruction. It was an artificial country riven by ethnic division and doomed to collapse into pieces like the former Yugoslavia. All of these maledictions proved well off the mark. Despite Mullah Omar's confident predictions, the invasion failed to inspire a national insurrection against the Americans and their allies. Far from decrying the arrival of international forces, the vast majority of Afghans took a wait-and-see attitude, viewing them as a way out of the civil war disorder that had torn up the country since 1992. Their major criticism was the failure to provide enough of them and restricting their deployment to Kabul. Afghans were also eager to cooperate in the rebuilding of their country, and as many as three million refugees would return home from exile by mid-2003. No faction moved to divide the country, despite the weakness of the center. How can such unexpected outcomes be explained? The most basic reason was that Afghanistan had always been more complex than the simple picture painted by the press. Nor was Afghanistan in 2001 the same place with the same attitudes that it had been two hundred, one hundred, or even twenty-five years before.

WELCOME INVADERS!?

There was a surprising level of popular support within Afghanistan for the U.S. intervention, especially among non-Pashtuns. But then again, a drowning person is not too picky about who throws him a line. Since the fall of the PDPA regime in 1992, Afghanistan had either been ignored or abused by the outside world as it descended into chaos. While the Taliban regime had come close to gaining total control of the country by 2001, it had done so only by increasing the numbers of Pakistanis, Arabs, and other foreign fighters in its ranks. Afghans resented such outside interference in their affairs, particularly the common Pakistani boast that Afghanistan had become its "fifth province." During interviews in 2002, when I expressed surprise that there had not been more opposition to the United States, a United Front commander explained that it was a case of using one set of foreigners to drive out another; not a desirable situation perhaps, but a resolution to a problem beyond Afghans' capacity to solve. And although they may not have been aware of it, the Americans held an advantage in

Afghan eyes because they came from a distant land that did not border their country. Afghans always perceived the most dangerous threats to their sovereignty as coming from contiguous powers (czarist Russia/Soviet Union in the north and the British raj/Pakistan in the southeast) because these states had viewed Afghanistan as a territory that could be annexed to those they already ruled. More distant powers such as Germany and the United States were assumed to have no territorial ambitions in the country, and thus made safer allies.

From the Afghan perspective, there was also a striking difference between the U.S. invasion and that of the Soviets and British: there were practically no Americans to be seen during the war against the Taliban. The U.S. military had so ignored Afghanistan that it had not even drawn up any contingency plans for attacking it. It declared that it would take six months or more to position troops for a conventional attack. Unwilling to wait, the Bush administration turned to an unconventional approach. It tasked the Central Intelligence Agency with coordinating existing anti-Taliban forces, mostly in the north and northeast, and provided them with money, weapons, and supplies. It also embedded a small number of Special Operations Force troops with Afghan fighters, some on horseback, who could call in precision air strikes using laser- or GPS-guided bombs and missiles. Because the United States saturated Afghan airspace with jets that simply circled above, waiting for coordinates to attack, the aircraft could be called in at a moment's notice to devastating effect. For example, the well-prepared Taliban defense lines around Mazar-i-sharif were taken out from the air simultaneously with an Uzbek cavalry attack on them. In the south, mobile Taliban troops that had previously used swarms of light trucks to overwhelm their opponents now found these so vulnerable to air attack that they could not even reach the front line.

This high-tech–low-tech combination proved deadly to Taliban forces, and led to their rapid disintegration. So many Afghan factions deserted them to join the winning side that by the war's end, the only identifiable losers were those who fled to Pakistan. Most everyone else could make some claim to being part of the winning coalition, making political accommodations much easier to achieve in the months that followed. And as the war wrapped up, each side congratulated itself on having used the other to achieve its own ends. The anti-Taliban Afghans did the deals and fought the fights using U.S. money and firepower without having to surrender the country's sovereignty. The United States expelled al Qaeda from Afghanistan and toppled the Taliban regime without deploying any of its regular ground troops. Of course where their interests did not coincide, the results were less favorable: bin Laden and many of his al Qaeda fighters escaped from the mountains of Tora Bora into Pakistan precisely because the United States' new Afghan allies refused to stand in their way. It was not their fight.

Even though the expulsion of the Taliban had gone smoothly, the history of Afghanistan led to firm predictions that the country would revolt against any foreigners who remained there, as it had against the British in the nineteenth century and the Soviets in the twentieth—if not immediately, then within a year. Bin Laden himself was sure that if the United States invaded Afghanistan, it would provoke a guerrilla war that would be a repeat of the one against the Soviets. This did not occur because what ordinary Afghans wanted most was protection against the indigenous factions that had destroyed the country in their struggles for power. The decade of civil war that followed the end of the PDPA had so undermined the legitimacy of all internal factions, whatever their origin, that at best their leaders retained support only in their home areas. Thus, for ordinary people the defeat of the Taliban was less significant than the belief that the U.S. intervention would put an end to the civil war that had brought such ruin to the country. They saw the international forces as a bulwark against anarchy they feared would reemerge if they withdrew. The expected role for such troops was modest too: simply to police those warlords who might think of disrupting the peace. Unfortunately this unexpected measure of goodwill from the Afghan people in 2002 was heedlessly squandered in the coming years by inept policies that failed to bring security to many regions and did little to improve people's dire economic condition. The popularity of the U.S. intervention and the Kabul government therefore began declining, most sharply in the Pashtun south and east, where these problems remained the most acute.

A UNITED PEOPLE IN A FAILED STATE

The belief that Afghanistan was an artificial creation doomed to collapse was rooted in confusion between the effectiveness of its state institutions and the cohesion of its people. In 2001, Afghanistan was a failed state but not a failed nation. Its lack of an effective central government was counterbalanced by a strong sense of national unity forged during the Soviet war as well as the refugee experiences in neighboring Pakistan and Iran. In living as refugees abroad and fighting the Soviets at home, the Afghans came to realize that what united them far outweighed the differences that divided them. This sense of national unity was not rooted in an ideology of nationalism but rather in the will of its people to persist together, united by a common experience that transcended ethnic or regional differences. Despite the collapse of central authority and the rise of ethnically based militias during the civil war, Afghans never feared that their country might disintegrate.* Understanding that all Afghan factions wished to hold the country together, and not divide it along ethnic lines into ever-tinier parts (à la the former Yugoslavia), was an underappreciated Afghan strength that would allow its leaders to rebuild a central government through a process of consensus.

That a notoriously fractious people would not want to break the country up, as so many people had confidently predicted, might seem puzzling. Everyone else seemed to be doing it, as the ever-expanding number of UN General Assembly seats suggested. The Afghans had four good explanations.

1. The persistence of the old central Asian view of political order that never linked ethnicity with nationalism.

The belief that nation-states and ethnic groups were naturally coterminous may have inspired Western ethnonationalists, but this idea never had the same force in central or south Asia. There, multiethnic states and empires were the norm, and not a historic injustice that demanded redress. The issues subject to contestation was who would be politically dominant in such a multiethnic system and how power would be shared. Nor did Afghans often use broad ethnic labels like Pashtun or Tajik inside the country because they did not capture the myriad divisions within each group. Such gross ethnic labels, moreover, lacked the potential to mobilize people who saw themselves as sharing a common history, not parallel universes. The Afghans had also seen some of the difficulties inherent in the ethni-

---

* The situation was the reverse in neighboring Pakistan, which despite strong state institutions, never developed a secure national identity and has been preoccupied by fears of internal disintegration throughout its sixty-year existence.

cally based states that emerged in central Asia when the Soviet Union collapsed. Their common ethnic ties could not overcome the regional rivalries that divided them internally. Drawing boundaries on the basis of ethnicity also tore apart regions that were formerly economically integrated, frequently leaving one state with the equivalent of four extra hands but no feet while its neighbor had plenty of feet but no hands.

2. Each ethnic group in Afghanistan felt secure enough in its own region to cooperate with others as partners at the national level.

During the Soviet occupation, the emergence of regional militias with local leadership created more parity among different ethnic groups and guaranteed them a seat at the table. In 2001, they entered into negotiations to create the new Afghan state so firmly entrenched at the local level that they no longer feared being displaced by a restored central government. Such a government would in fact need their cooperation to function. The pre-1978 ethnic hierarchy that gave Pashtuns a monopolistic control of the Afghan state had been destroyed. The Pashtuns themselves grudgingly accepted the reality that they were unlikely to restore their dominance of government institutions that was the hallmark of the status quo ante. The choice of working together was infinitely more practical than starting a new conflict to break up the country. In this respect, Afghan leaders were like poker players who wanted to continue gambling whether or not they won or lost a particular hand. They had no interest in ending the game by dividing the table on which it was played.

3. The negative consequences of disunion outweighed internal frictions.

Afghan regional leaders recognized that if they broke the country apart, its smaller pieces could be more easily dominated or even attacked by their neighbors. As a unified country the size of France, Afghanistan could better hold its own. This would allow regions such as Herat to maintain close ties to Iran, knowing that they could rely on a central government to keep external meddling within tolerable bounds. The same logic applied to relations with Uzbekistan and, most important, Pakistan—the country that Afghans most suspected of wishing them ill. That no region proposed an amalgamation with a neighboring state was equally practical. The last thing that neighboring countries wanted was a piece of unruly Afghanistan and its troublesome people. The last thing that any Afghan wanted was to be a subordinate part of someone else's state, particularly those they had no liking for. Thus, in spite of non-Pashtun groups regaining much of the autonomy that they had lost at the end of the nineteenth century, they never sought independence from the Afghan state, or an amalgamation with coethnics in Iran or central Asia. Nor did Pashtuns in Afghanistan, despite their continued rhetorical support for an independent Pashtunistan to be carved out of Pakistan, ever envision themselves as being a minority part of this state. Besides, you cannot smuggle if there is no border, and Afghans made large profits moving untaxed goods across boundaries where a single ethnic group straddled both sides, especially across the Durand Line, which separated Afghanistan from Pakistan. Being part of a single state would have destroyed that business.

4. Afghans had few illusions about the nature of state politics, and the compromises necessary to engage in them.

The Afghans who negotiated the composition of a new central government treated it as an arranged marriage, not a love match. They had none of the romantic illusions fostered by ethnic nationalists, who asserted that "their people" were so entitled to a state of their own that compromise was out of the question. Afghans had little time for such idealized and uncompromising views of ethnicity: there was no immutable history or commonality that could not be jettisoned if self-interest required it. Afghan ethnic groups often cooperated with other groups that they did not like and had even fought with, just as they divided within a single ethnic group when their interests diverged. They were well aware that in the long history of Afghanistan, no enemies (or friends) were ever permanent. And Afghan factions well understood that the resources of the international community could only be effectively tapped if there was a single national government to deal with the outside world, even if only to cash the checks and redistribute the money. This could not be done effectively at the local level, and ethnic ministates could expect to receive only minigrants or perhaps nothing at all.

A FORCED TRANSFORMATION

Looking at the mud-brick architecture and traditionally dressed people in rural Afghanistan today, it would be easy to assume that little had changed in the country for centuries. In fact, Afghan society had been profoundly altered in almost all aspects as a result of the Soviet invasion and Afghan civil war. Before 1978 it was common to talk to men in rural Afghanistan who had never left their province or region, except for the time they might have served as conscript soldiers in the national army. Women were even less likely to have left their villages. But as the Soviet war progressed it drove huge numbers of people from their homes. Three to five million people fled Afghanistan to become refugees in Iran and Pakistan, while an almost equal number sought safety in Afghanistan's cities and towns. Kabul's population rose from a half million in the 1970s to two million in the 1980s. For a people so closely attached to their localities, the massive displacement of Afghans either as refugees or internally displaced people was traumatic, affecting at least a third of the country's population. Nor were the estimated three million people who returned to Afghanistan in the years immediately after 2001 the same people who had fled. They had experienced a wider world and returned with different expectations. Many who had left as small children or who were born abroad had never even experienced life in Afghanistan. Because so few young people had acquired the skills needed to farm, many chose to resettle in Afghanistan's cities rather than return to the rural areas that were home to their parents. By 2009, it was estimated that Kabul was home to three to four million people.

Most of the refugees in Pakistan had relied on international agencies for food and shelter. The camps also provided medical care and some educational facilities. Poor as these were by international standards, for Afghans who had come from villages with few schools, and no electricity, running water, or health care facilities of any type, the realization that government agencies or nongovernmental organizations (NGOs) could provide needed services on a large scale was a revelation. Those who sought refuge in Iran were less dependent on refugee camps and tended to find work within the larger Iranian society, providing cheap labor for road-building projects, agriculture, and construction. They too availed themselves of educational and health care facilities that were well beyond what they had known at home. For in Afghanistan, the government had supplied little or nothing to rural areas, where it was associated primarily with predatory police, the conscription of young men, and greedy government officials who demanded bribes. Returning refugees now had a new model of government against which to test the actions of their own. They knew that it was possible to provide much more than the Afghan state had done before. A new government would therefore be held to a much higher standard by the returnees.

There was a much smaller set of Afghan refugees who resettled in Europe and North America. Many were members of the old Kabul elite but they also included most of Afghanistan's professional class. The fall of the Taliban would induce at least some of them to return to reclaim lost property, start businesses, or enter government. While the international community saw them and their skills as a vitally needed addition to the country, resident Afghans and returning refugees from Pakistan and Iran often accused them of being opportunistic carpetbaggers, using their familiarity with the West and foreign-language skills to benefit themselves. ("Dog washers" was the insult of choice because it implied that these upper- and middle-class returnees had been reduced to taking demeaning jobs abroad.) While this was the newest split in the Afghan body politic, it merely resurrected the old division between Kabul-based modernists and the more conservative rural majority that was now a least a century old.

MILITIAS AND WARLORDS

In prewar Afghanistan, landowning khans had been the backbone of the rural political order. They were generally allies of the state (or at least respectful of it), even when they opposed particular policies. During the war, this old elite was replaced by a new generation of younger, self-made military commanders fighting for the mujahideen against the Kabul government. To this group was added the militia leaders created by Najibullah as the Soviets withdrew. They became the dominant figures during the Afghan civil war after 1992, and although the Taliban killed or exiled many prominent regional commanders, they could not as easily displace the structure of local commanders. It was the defection of these local commanders that sealed their defeat during the U.S. invasion. These local commanders had no strong links with the national state, which had ceased to exist after 1992 in any event, but did have connections to higher-order commanders who returned to their regional power base following the collapse of the Taliban. From Kabul's (and the international community's) perspective, these commanders were oppressive warlords who needed to be removed from power as soon as possible. Indeed many were accused of committing war crimes. But from a local perspective, particularly in the non-Pashtun regions of the country, commanders had their own political bases among their coethnics, who were willing to overlook their excesses because they promised to bring security and prosperity to their home regions. As usual the Pashtun regions were more fragmented, but they too usually saw their own militia leaders in a similarly favorable light. The existence of these armed militias led by men who expected to have a future in a new government would complicate any process of state building, particularly one that saw a highly centralized government as its goal.

The Historical and Cultural Template for the Bonn Accord

Toppling one Afghan regime required replacing it with another. Beginning with the British installation of Shah Shuja in the First Anglo-Afghan War, Western powers that intervened in Afghan affairs simultaneously anointed one Afghan leader while removing his predecessor. This was a tricky maneuver that usually proved short-lived because such imposed rulers found it difficult to establish their political legitimacy. Prior to 2001, however, all foreign invaders had at least selected a candidate for the job—some better than others perhaps—before they commenced their wars. The United States was unique in launching a war in Afghanistan without having anyone in mind for the job. It turned to the United Nations for this task, which in turn convened a conference in Bonn, Germany, to hammer out the structure of a provisional government and apportion leadership roles in November 2001. This group included representatives of the United Front fighting in Afghanistan, the Rome faction composed of exiled Zahir Shah royalists, and the Peshawar mujahideen faction based in Pakistan. The Taliban were excluded from the talks, and because of their previous ties to the Taliban, the Pashtuns had poorer representation than they would have normally expected. Despite this disadvantage, the conference selected a

Popalzai Pashtun from Qandahar, Hamid Karzai, to head the provisional Afghan administration, while the United Front took over most of the key ministries. The ex-king was given an honorary position. The whole regime was to be subject to a vote of approval by a national loya jirga, to be held in Kabul within a year.

That the Afghans could come together so quickly to create a provisional government was astounding given what the world had been told of their fractiousness. (The United States would never get such agreements from the Iraqis under similar circumstances.) Less commented on was how closely their agreement hewed to past political patterns. A victorious non-Pashtun United Front had defeated the Pashtun-backed Taliban and yet still agreed to accept a Pashtun as head of state. Even more remarkable it marked the return of the royal Durranis to national power, since Karzai's Popalzai clan was descended from Ahmad Shah, the founder of the Durrani Empire. The Durranis had almost completely disappeared from national politics after the last Muhammadzai, Daud Khan, was overthrown in 1978. From that time forward it was the Ghilzai Pashtuns who had constituted the Pashtun power elite, whether in the PDPA (Taraki, Amin, and Najibullah), the mujahideen parties (Hekmatyar, Khalis, and Sayyaf), or even the Taliban (Mulla Omar and his inner circle).

How was it possible that the more militarily dominant eastern Pashtuns had been so outmaneuvered by their Durrani rivals with the support of the non-Pashtuns and the international community? One explanation was that the Afghans had rebuilt failed states in the past and had a template for how this was done. In this template, the Durranis held substantial advantages over their Ghilzai rivals because they were more skilled in the arts of peace than they were in those of war. The template also continued a historic bargain by which non-Pashtuns ceded executive power to Pashtuns because they believed that they could not hold it themselves. But in choosing among Pashtuns, they sided with the Durranis over the Ghilzais, if a choice was available, precisely because they were perceived as more accommodating. Whether Karzai could actually make a stable state using this template would depend on his skill at extracting resources from the international community and his ability to prove himself a strong ruler. In Afghanistan's long experience, weak rulers rarely lasted while strong ones laid the foundation for long periods of peace.

Durranis versus Ghilzais Redux

The Ghilzais thrived politically in times of war and chaos, and regularly produced major military figures who were self-made men. Most of the important Pashtun military leaders—whether for the PDPA, the mujahideen, or the Taliban—had been of Ghilzai origin. The Ghilzais had also played an equally dominant role in the Anglo-Afghan wars of the nineteenth century. By contrast the Durrani base of power was the Afghan state itself. The Durranis jealously guarded their dominance within it during times of peace and set themselves up as the only possible candidates for its restoration in the aftermath of state collapse. They had come out on top politically following the two Anglo-Afghan wars, the civil war of 1929, and the U.S. invasion. "Tribal competition" was less a factor than the political niche that each group held and how well it was adapted to changing conditions within Afghanistan.

DIFFERENCES IN SOCIAL AND ECONOMIC STRUCTURES

The eastern Pashtuns had long proved themselves superior to the Durranis in times of war and disorder, because their social and political structure was better adapted to cope with it. Intensely egalitarian, a characteristic shared with the Karlanri Pashtuns of Pakistan's Federally Administered Tribal Area (FATA), their leaders lacked royal authority. They needed to engage in constant consensus building to implement any major decision. Any individual could compete for leadership, and did so by displaying special skills in mediating problems within the tribe or successfully organizing the tribe militarily against its enemies. It was a structure that put a premium on aggressive risk taking as the quickest way to build a reputation. Even when a man achieved a position of leadership he could never rest on his laurels. There were always new rivals from lower-ranking lineages seeking to push their way up, and times of war provided them with more opportunities than times of peace. Nor was a leader free from challenges by his own relatives (particularly patrilineal cousins, or *tarbur*), who were ready to replace him if the right opportunity presented itself. For these reasons, leadership rarely remained for long within a single lineage.

The maintenance and persistence of this egalitarian ethos was rooted in the poor economic conditions of eastern Afghanistan and the NWFP's FATA. These regions were resource poor and marginal to the urban centers. The scarce arable land there produced little in the way of surplus food or cash crops. In such a subsistence economy, it was difficult to accumulate substantial wealth when what existed was consumed in meeting the obligations of hospitality and other expressions of generosity that maintained social status. It was rarely enough to sustain a family's superior position across many generations. Seeking outside revenue was a possible way out of this low-resource trap, but that was a double-edged sword. Subsidies from governments or political movements allowed resident leaders to attract more followers but could also provoke jealousy—generosity's evil twin.[1] Leaders in eastern Afghanistan or FATA were therefore not able to soar high enough above their rivals to subordinate them permanently. And public acceptance of such subordination would in any event violate the basic principle of political autonomy that undergirded the Pashtunwali mind-set. Yet if the eastern Pashtuns refused to accept the cultural legitimacy of hierarchy and were unwilling to subordinate themselves to others, they paid a high price for it: poverty, isolation, lack of economic development, poor education, and minimal services. Those groups that moved to richer areas to seek a higher living standard found that they could not maintain the same degree of autonomy as those in the hills, but as compensation their internal leadership became more stable. For this reason, the eastern Pashtun groups that inhabited the interface regions between areas of tight state regulation and the uncontrolled hinterlands, such as the Ahmadzais of the Suleimankhel, tended to provide more powerful leaders than other Ghilzai groups.

The Durrani Pashtuns of southern Afghanistan lived under very different conditions. Their territories generally lay within the zone of state control, and they had access to dependable sources of wealth based on irrigated agriculture, with access to trade and cities. This helps explain why they developed a much more hierarchical social and political structure. Benefiting from the large tax-free land grants first given to them by Ahmad Shah Durrani in the eighteenth century, they had developed a ruling class whose inherited power lasted centuries. As a result, their leaders were generally better educated and more culturally sophisticated than their rural Ghilzai counterparts. Durrani leaders also had the ability to command their tribal followers because they had long ago reduced so many of them to the status of clients whose support they could count on.

Unlike among the Ghilzais, where any lineage might see its status rise rapidly if it produced a talented leader or fall if it failed to do so, the inherited authority of Durrani lineages in Qandahar was well entrenched and difficult for outsiders to challenge. The Durranis did, however, face competition from other equally well-established clans. The most famous of these long-running Durrani rivalries was between the Popalzais (Karzai's clan) and the Barakzais (Zahir Shah's clan) over which would control the Afghan state. The former had produced the Sadozai lineage of Afghan shahs who ruled from the founding of the Durrani Empire in 1747 until 1818, while the latter produced the Muhammadzai royal lineage that ruled Afghanistan from 1826 to 1978. Below them were other rivals: the Alikozai and the Achakzai clans, which had not achieved the same national prominence but did constitute powerful regional elites in southern Afghanistan. All of these groups benefited from their links with kinsmen who ran the national governments in Kabul. These ranged from eighteenth-century land grants to twentieth-century irrigation projects. The limits of the Helmand Valley and Argandab River development schemes neatly coincided with Durrani tribal distribution—something quite apparent to the eastern Pashtuns, whose regions received no such extraordinary investment.

There were weaknesses in such a system of concentrated power, though, because it made the Durranis more vulnerable to coercion than the eastern Pashtuns. The river valleys and flat surrounding deserts in the south were more susceptible to military attack than were the more isolated mountain villages of the east. Landed estates were subject to confiscation, and the irrigation network itself was exquisitely vulnerable to disruption. As a result, Durrani leaders were more risk averse than their Ghilzai counterparts because they had more to lose. They played only a small role in the Anglo-Afghan wars of the nineteenth century (even the famous Battle of Maiwand was fought by troops from Herat). The war with the Soviets was also more intense in the east and north of Kabul than it was in the south. Even the Taliban, who had their headquarters in Qandahar, were dominated by Mullah Omar's Hotaki Ghilzai lineage. They followed the eastern pattern to power by which a new and more aggressive leadership shoved aside the older southern Durrani elite. One stark example of this was the Taliban-inspired assassination of Hamid Karzai's father, Abdul Ahad Karzai, in 1999. Even though he had moved to Quetta, Abdul Ahad's authority as the leader of the Popalzai in Qandahar remained so entrenched that the Taliban considered him a significant threat to their stability.[2] With the collapse of the Taliban under American pressure, however, conditions changed markedly. The road to political power and influence would now move through the channels of diplomacy, patronage and deal making, arenas where the Durranis historically excelled.

A TALE OF TWO LEADERS: ABDUL HAQ AND HAMID KARZAI

A dramatic example of these different leadership styles and the rapidly changing political ecology in Afghanistan in 2001 could be seen in the tragically different fates of two Pashtun leaders, Abdul Haq and Hamid Karzai, who both entered Afghanistan to raise revolts against the Taliban just before the United States invaded.

Haq was a member of the Jabarkhel clan of the Ahmadzai tribe from Nangarhar Province who became one of the most charismatic mujahideen commanders in the war against the Soviets. Even though he had largely withdrawn from Afghan politics during the civil war, he ran afoul of the Taliban, and left for Dubai after they murdered his wife and daughter in Pakistan in 1999. Haq returned to Peshawar after 9/11, hoping to raise the tribes in eastern Afghanistan against the Taliban under his leadership. He believed that if he could unite them and bring about the defection of wavering Taliban factions, then he would be able to forestall the faction fighting among the Pashtuns that would otherwise surely occur when the Taliban regime collapsed. But because he was unable to secure the sponsorship of the United States (and knowing that the Pakistani ISI would do anything to stop him), he was strongly advised by friends to abandon his plans. Haq refused and entered Afghanistan in October. His whereabouts were quickly betrayed to the Taliban, who then captured and executed him.[3]

Haq's impetuous decision to go into eastern Afghanistan despite the high risk was characteristic of an eastern Pashtun leadership style. He had already been wounded sixteen times and lost a foot to a land mine during the Soviet war. Such leaders believed that grand enterprises demanded bold leadership if they were to succeed. The greater the danger overcome, the greater the reward. Yet part of the danger was the lack of cohesion among the factions in eastern Afghanistan. Haq was returning not to lead a group ready to support him but instead to create such a group. It was the first stages that were always the most hazardous in such a venture, and Haq was captured before he could raise an army. If he had been able to establish himself in Afghanistan then perhaps he, and other eastern Pashtuns, would have played a more significant postwar role. As Haq had feared, however, the collapse of the Taliban did produce a power vacuum in the east and new faction fighting there. As the question of who should rule the nation was being settled in Bonn, the eastern Pashtuns fought over which of them should rule Jalalabad.

Karzai, by contrast, was neither a warrior commander nor a particularly charismatic political figure, although his Sadozai Durrani descent gave him an impeccable Afghan lineage. Educated in India, he had remained in the shadow of his father until the Taliban assassinated him. Following Durrani custom he then inherited the leadership of the Popalzai, since most of his other brothers had earlier moved to the United States. In the wake of 9/11, it was the Popalzai themselves who had approached Karzai to ask him to return to southern Afghanistan and lead them against the Taliban. Thus, even though he entered the county almost alone on a motorcycle, he found an organized group of supporters awaiting him and sworn to his protection. While both the ISI and the Taliban were keen to capture and kill him, as they had Haq, they were unable to do so, given the security provided by his own people. As the war progressed Karzai also gained the assistance of American Special Operations advisers, who brought air support to his aid, allowing his outnumbered forces at Tarin Kot to beat back Taliban attacks. While many southern Pashtun groups had turned against the Taliban when their grip on power weakened, Karzai was one of the few Pashtun leaders who had actually organized resistance against them. As the hostilities were wrapping up (and after almost being killed by friendly fire), Karzai received a satellite phone call from Bonn informing him of his selection as head of the new provisional administration. No eastern Pashtun leaders had even been considered for the job.

In a continuing conflict situation, Karzai would have never emerged at the top. Yet in choosing a national leader the Afghans in Bonn were not looking for an überwarlord but rather someone who could successfully deal with the outside world—resources from which would be critical in bringing stability to Afghanistan. None of Afghanistan's existing faction leaders had the required characteristics: education, linguistic skills, cultural sophistication, and experience in dealing with the outside world. Of course, these characteristics had not been as highly valued in times of war. The deceased Ahmad Shah Masud aside, it would be hard to imagine any of the existing faction leaders winning the support of the American or European public, let alone capturing their imagination, as Karzai was to do. He also had an advantage internally because the Durrani elite stood to support him regionally as a way back to national prominence for the Pashtuns as a whole and the Qandaharis specifically. By contrast, the eastern Afghan leaders were not secure enough to make a play for national power, and even if they had been better organized, they were unlikely to agree on a single candidate.

The Grand Bargain Redux

Explaining how the Durranis outcompeted their Ghilzai rivals at the Bonn talks leaves open the question of why newly empowered non-Pashtun United Front leaders proved willing to cede the top job to them. The United Front's resistance movement owed nothing to the southern Pashtuns, who had previously backed the Taliban and had turned against them only when it became clear they had no future. Since the United Front's troops controlled Kabul (a situation that Pakistan had vainly tried to prevent), its leaders were in a position simply to dig in their heels and declare "to the victor go the spoils." Their Panjshiri Tajik military commander, Marshal Muhammad Qasim Fahim could have declared himself ruler of Afghanistan in the same way that Habibullah Kalakani had done in 1929 and dared the Pashtuns to remove him. There would have been little that the United States could have done about this since it had so few troops on the ground. So why did the United Front representatives cooperate in the Bonn Accord to anoint a Durrani Pashtun as national leader? The answer was that after a quarter century of war in Afghanistan, no faction was keen to engage in more fighting if a political compromise was possible. Nor did any faction wish to dismember the country—another alternative. They also had to consider the small number of candidates available who would be acceptable both domestically and internationally. At a deeper level the belief that only the Pashtuns, particularly the Durrani Pashtuns, could be considered for the top job was still deeply ingrained, even among non-Pashtuns.

The situation might have been different if Masud had not been assassinated just before the U.S. invasion. He was a true national hero both in his successful resistance against the Soviets and his long fight against the Taliban. Indeed, Afghanistan had probably never produced such a skilled military mind. But unlike most other commanders, Masud had a reputation as a cultured man who thought deeply about the problems before him and his country. When the PDPA collapsed in 1992 and his troops occupied Kabul, Masud refused entreaties to rule the country himself and ceded power to the mujahideen leaders formerly based in Pakistan. The mujahideen leaders' misrule and the civil war it sparked had led to the rise of the Taliban. Had Masud been alive and running the United Front, it is unlikely that he would have made that mistake again.

If the non-Pashtuns were to renew their old bargain and choose a Durrani leader, however, the more natural choice to head the government was not Karzai but Zahir Shah, the old deposed king who was living in exile in Italy. He still had many supporters, some of whom were keen on the restoration of the monarchy as an institution. But Zahir Shah had always been known as a weak ruler, and this combined with his advanced age made him a poor choice for any executive position. Still, restoring him as head of state and leaving the running of the country to someone else did have considerable merit because Zahir Shah had an unquestioned political legitimacy in the eyes of most Afghans, particularly in the rural south.

Two obstacles stood in the way of this canny compromise. First, the Afghan factions could not agree on who would fill the executive role. Second, the Americans were opposed to the idea. George W. Bush had loftier goals for the United States in Afghanistan than restoring a monarchy, as his father had done in Kuwait. Perhaps a deeper reason for agreeing to set him aside was the question of who would succeed him. Afghans gave unspoken credence to the ibn Khaldunian notion that dynastic lineages were prone to burn themselves out after three or four generations—a notion given some credibility by the lack of enthusiasm generated by any of Zahir Shah's long absent sons and other collateral heirs. Other contenders included Rabbani, who because he had been president of the mujahideen government before the Taliban took Kabul in 1996, asserted that his authority had never lapsed and moved back into the palace. Even members of the United Front felt that the country needed to move on and refused to back his bid to return to power.

Faced with this situation, the negotiators in Bonn looked for a compromise that would achieve immediate consensus within Afghanistan. This ruled out the most powerful commanders of the United Front (Fahim, Ishmail Khan, or Dostam), who the Pashtuns and factions within the United Front would have rejected. But if they were to select a Pashtun, they needed one who would not immediately be challenged by other Pashtuns. Here, reaching back to the Durrani lineages that had supplied Afghanistan's rulers in the past, was a trump card. The Durranis, long out of power, appeared willing to support anyone of their number who might emerge from the process, preferably the king but Karzai as well. The Ghilzais would have to get behind the agreement because it at least put a Pashtun at the top, even if it were not one of their own. Besides, they had few representatives at the Bonn conference.

The path of least resistance was to follow the model used in 1842, 1880, and 1929, in which those most responsible for toppling an existing Afghan government justified themselves by returning power to the Durrani Pashtuns who had founded the state. The more recent transfers of power that took a different path (the PDPA in 1978, the Soviets in 1979, the mujahideen in 1992, and the Taliban in 1996) had all failed to unify the state and bring stability to Afghanistan. Reviving the aura of Durrani royal authority (while sidelining its last living representative) had enough drawing power to serve as the basis for compromise once all factions concluded that they could not come to power by force of arms. An additional factor was the requirement that a leader have the ability to strike a deal with the foreign powers to provide Afghanistan with resources for rebuilding the country and protecting its territorial integrity. Dost Muhammad and Abdur Rahman had both dealt effectively with the British raj in the nineteenth century, and in the twentieth century Nadir Shah had also stabilized his own power with British support. Karzai appeared ready-made for this role in the twenty-first century because he had the tools to deal with the outside world that none of his rivals could match. Karzai's elegant dress and mild manner made him a brilliant and unthreatening representative for the country as a whole, and his skill at languages allowed him to move easily on the diplomatic stage. He would receive a rapturous reception on state visits and at international conferences, achieving a level of international prominence that no other Afghan ruler (save perhaps Amanullah) had ever experienced.

REBUILDING THE AFGHAN STATE

While the details differed, the post-2001 political deals that the Afghans struck among themselves were remarkably similar to those in earlier periods. It was not that Afghan politicians were keen students of history but instead that the problems they faced were comparable. Yet attempts to restore stability in Afghanistan based entirely on old institutions and old ideas had their limits. In the wake of so much war and political upheaval, Afghanistan was now a profoundly different place than it had been before 1978. It was not clear that the solution to its current problems was the restoration of a Kabul-centered government run by a Kabul-based governing elite, especially because demands for regional autonomy and wider political participation were now much stronger than in the past.

During the nineteenth and twentieth centuries, rulers had always been able to restrict participation in the national government to a small elite based in Kabul. But implementing such a strategy was now problematic. The mass mobilization of the population during the Soviet war and succeeding civil war had raised the level of popular political participation in the country to new heights.[4] If in the past ordinary people had been all too willing to see government as none of their business, they now demanded a greater role in it. This set up a conflict between those who saw restoring stability in Afghanistan as the reimplementation of a centralized, top-down, kinglike authority, and those who insisted that the country needed a new model of political organization derived from the cooperation and consent of the governed. If looked at from a longer time perspective, this demand for a more consultative government was not new at all but rather a reversion to the country's most stable political and economic equilibrium, in which Afghanistan's historic regions and social groups (qawm, religious sect, or locality) regained the political influence that they had held earlier. Over the longue durée, these regions and solidarity groups had never been displaced as the established building blocks of whatever kingdoms, empires, or national states they became a part of. While leaders in Kabul often presented this situation as a challenge to the national state, it could also be seen as a healthy counterweight to Kabul's previous excesses.

State Building in Theory

For the international community, the process of restoring the Afghan state began by seeking the approval of the population for the establishment of an interim government and the creation of a constitution, to be followed by elections for president and parliament. Reaching these consecutive milestones, each with a higher level of political inclusion, would then result in a government that was legitimate in both the eyes of its international backers and (it was assumed) the Afghan population. Whether such a process had any real meaning for the majority of Afghans, though, was never asked. It was simply assumed that the "age-old" loya jirga process would do the trick, and that its approval of a constitution would give the government legitimacy. But while the international community focused on process, Afghans wrestled with a more basic question about whether the new Kabul government could provide the necessary level of law and order to be considered a state. For them, endorsing the results of the expensively produced series of loya jirgas and elections was a bit premature. Only time would tell whether they truly marked the creation of a new and viable political order, or were just the latest *tamasha*—a public performance or spectacle that tends toward farce.

THE LOYA JIRGA AS AN INSTITUTION

Karzai and the international community assembled an "Emergency Loya Jirga" in Kabul in 2002 to ratify the decisions made at Bonn because they said this was the way Afghans had always selected their leaders. This assertion was an excellent example of an "invented tradition," however—

one that was believed to be deeply rooted in time but in fact was of recent origin or altered in a way that changed its original pupose.[5] A jirga had selected Ahmad Shah as ruler of the new Durrani Empire in 1747, but its membership was confined largely to the Abdali Pashtuns and it failed to set a precedent. There were no loya jirgas of any type held in the nineteenth century either to select a ruler or set policy. Far from seeking approval from the people, Abdur Rahman had demanded that they renounce any role in Afghan politics by signing his "Covenants of Unity" of 1896. This proved to be the high watermark of traditional autocracy in which subjects were viewed as having no legitimate role in national politics. Habibullah felt it necessary to convene a loya jirga in 1915 to support his policy of neutrality during the First World War. This was in response to a new wave of nationalism and enthusiasm for a more participatory government that put Afghan rulers under pressure to ground their regimes in constitutions and later through the establishment of parliaments. While this did little to curb the autocratic tendencies of Afghan rulers, it did reduce their tendency to treat the country as their personal patrimony.

Amanullah was the first Afghan ruler to revive the loya jirga institution for domestic policy during the 1920s. But he sought approval for his constitution and other reforms, not ratification of his right to rule. Nor were these loya jirgas popular assemblies (Amanullah determined their composition and the issues to be addressed). Nadir turned the institution against Amanullah in 1929, when he first ratified his usurpation of the throne by having it approved in a loya jirga, albeit one hastily assembled and composed only of his followers. He was insecure enough to call another in 1931 to formally disinherit Amanullah. Nevertheless, while Nadir's Musahiban successors continued Amanullah's practice of assembling loya jirgas to approve weighty issues (such as Afghanistan's policy of neutrality in 1941, support for the Pashtunistan movement in 1955, and the constitutions of 1964 and 1977), they never again felt the necessity of seeking public approval for their leadership. Zahir Shah ascended to the throne without a loya jirga in 1933, and Daud consulted with no one when he declared himself president in 1973. Although their reasons for doing so differed sharply, no successor regime (PDPA, mujahideen, or Taliban) ever assembled a loya jirga to legitimize its leaders either, although the PDPA used one to ratify its constitution in 1987.

An invented tradition is most effective when people believe it is a long-existing practice. What made the loya jirga appear to be such a tradition was its similarity to the smaller-scale jirgas used by Pashtun communities to resolve problems and approve collective actions. Raising the jirga to a national level could be made to appear as part of that tradition, even though historically it was not. The jirga process also fit the dynamics of Afghan politics well in three respects. First, its legitimacy depended on meeting an accepted level of participation. If enough people, particularly influential ones, refused to attend or walked out during the process, then the jirga itself would be viewed as illegitimate. This made calling a jirga risky since you had to be sure the major political actors would participate. It also gave the jirgas themselves a theatrical air as opponents of some position would storm out, promising never to return, only to be cajoled back after some backroom dealing and private compromises patched up the problem. Second, votes on individual issues were never taken during a jirga; only when a consensus on a total package was agreed on would the results then be approved by acclamation. In this way all parties could proclaim themselves winners. Third, the people who participated in a jirga agreed to be bound by its results and stand behind its decisions. It was therefore a particularly good process for creating a new regime by proving that it had popular support, even if it had rarely been employed in this way before.

The National Commanders Shura had unsuccessfully urged Masud to convene a loya jirga to create such a fresh start in 1992. They wanted to outflank Pakistan-based mujahideen party leaders, whose political base within Afghanistan was too weak to risk a loya jirga process to ratify its leadership. To their credit, the organizers of the Bonn process believed that they could do so. All who attended would be bound by it, and the failure to attend risked political isolation. The use of the loya jirga in this way was innovative, though, because it was an explicit acknowledgment that the Afghan people had a legitimate role in choosing their national leaders—a principle rejected by all previous Afghan rulers. While resistance by the Afghan population to foreign occupation had been critical in preserving the country's independence during both the nineteenth and twentieth centuries, they had always been excluded from government (and often abused) once a new regime took power. The balance had now shifted. No future

Kabul government could expect to survive if it attempted to act as unilaterally as had its predecessors, particularly because its international backers (the United States, its coalition allies, and the United Nations) were committed to creating democratic government institutions there.

THE EMERGENCY LOYA JIRGA OF 2002

The emergency loya jirga was held in Kabul in June 2002. It was asked to accept the provisional government for two years until a constitution could be produced and elections held. The loya jirga was composed of one thousand elected representatives and five hundred delegates chosen by the organizers, with a last-minute addition of forty-five unelected militia commanders (pejoratively labeled warlords by their critics). Despite seating these commanders, the assembly was more broadly representative of Afghanistan's regions and ethnic groups than any held previously. It also included more women representatives, thanks to international pressure. While in retrospect the outcome seemed foreordained (Karzai was eventually confirmed as the head of the government along with his cabinet), the assembly took on all the raucous uncertainty of a real jirga with harsh words and walkouts before reaching a consensus. In particular, the southern Pashtun supporters of Zahir Shah moved to make him the head of state and they were supported by many non-Pashtuns. Only when the U.S. special presidential envoy for Afghanistan, Zalmay Khalilzad, strong-armed the king into throwing his support behind Karzai did the leadership contest end. The obviously forced nature of the king's withdrawal and its embarrassing televised presentation undermined Karzai legitimacy because to many Afghans it appeared that it was the United States that was calling the shots.

THE CONSTITUTIONAL LOYA JIRGA OF 2003

The constitutional loya jirga was held in December 2003. Its five hundred members, a quarter of whom were women, were representative of the various Afghan political factions and ethnic groups, except for the Taliban. The key issue was whether the Afghan government should be highly centralized or federal. Institutionally, the debate was between those who wanted a powerful presidential system and those who favored a parliamentary system with a prime minister. The diversity of Afghanistan argued for a federal system, especially because a century of highly centralized rule from Kabul had been so detrimental to the regions. Two decades of war had also made the regions much more autonomous and less likely to take orders from Kabul that they disagreed with. Yet supporters of a centralized political system countered that any devolution of power away from Kabul would pave the way for the country's future dissolution. They were joined by Afghan modernists who had always looked on a powerful national government as their tool to bring about change. Many Pashtuns also saw a strong presidency under Karzai as the means to restore their dominance in government after the setbacks they received with the fall of the Taliban. (Their infallible belief that Pashtuns would always lead Afghanistan blinded them to the risk that such an arrangement might prove a liability if this powerful presidency fell into the hands of another ethnic group.)

Those favoring a more federal system found themselves at a disadvantage in this argument. They were tarred with the brush of ethnic chauvinism for supporting more regional autonomy, and accused of being reactionaries by those who equated a Kabul-centered government with modernization and decentralization with rural conservatism. The international community was also more strongly supportive of a presidential system than a parliamentary one, and adamantly opposed devolving power to the regional or provincial level. Indeed, for all their talk of consultation and inclusivity, representatives of the international community in Afghanistan were happier working with a powerful president and centralized bureaucracy than they were with a messy legislature or regional power structures. This included the United States, which despite having the world's oldest federal constitution, preferred all-powerful strongmen abroad (a structure that the Bush administration of course would have preferred to have at home too).

The original draft of the constitution attempted to please both sides by proposing both a president and a prime minister—a structure similar to Zahir Shah's 1964 constitution, on which it was largely based. The prime minister position was dropped in favor of a single strong president on the grounds that Afghanistan needed a unitary power center. The appointment of governors, the right to taxation, and the provision of government services all remained monopolies of the central government. The new constitution therefore had a strong monarchal flavor. In fact, it was later discovered that the original Persian version had failed to delete the many references to the king in constitutional articles that were lifted wholesale from the 1964 document.

Since the jirga process required achieving consensus, there was flexibility on other issues, however. The new parliament was given the right to approve cabinet officers and dismiss them for cause. The provinces and districts could elect local assemblies, although it was unclear just what authority they would have. Ethnic minorities and their languages were given official recognition for the first time. Shiites were granted legal parity with Sunnis in matters of family law. The mujahideen faction was allowed to stiffen the requirement that all laws created by the government be compatible with Islamic principles, although (as in previous constitutions) just how such determinations would be made remained vague. The constitution steered clear of the historic minefield of women's rights, indirectly recognizing them (because women were full citizens like men) but attaching no specific protection to them as a class through an equal rights provision.

Setting the qualifications for important offices reopened the rift between the mujahideen faction and the educated technocrats who had returned to Afghanistan after long periods in the West. Each saw the other as unfit to hold office—the former because they were generally ill educated, and the latter because so many of them held dual citizenship. The dispute was settled with a compromise that required all cabinet-rank officials to have an advanced degree of some type (including religious ones) and renounce any dual nationality. The legitimacy of the degrees presented by the mujahideen side was questionable, but then again the renunciation of the dual nationality was mostly symbolic.

In classic jirga fashion, drafts of the constitution's articles were continually revised to bring about consensus, yet its sections were never voted on individually by the assembly. Instead, the entire final version was approved unanimously by voice vote, although it took a number of weeks before a definitive text was finally issued.[6] Some critics objected that this printed copy differed from that which had been approved by acclamation, but by then the assembly had been dissolved.

THE PRESIDENTIAL ELECTION OF 2004

The high point of the constitutional process came with the successful presidential election in October 2004. While there had been parliamentary elections in the past, this was the first time in Afghan history that a national leader had ever sought electoral approval. Karzai was therefore keen to see elections held quickly once the constitution had been approved despite the concerns of international critics, who doubted the ability of the Afghans to organize the balloting and feared that the election would be marred by violence. The Afghan people instead seemed genuinely motivated by the election process and turned out in large numbers, including a relatively high participation by women. Opponents of the Karzai regime, including the Taliban, failed to disrupt the process, in part because it had such popular support. Despite many irregularities the election was deemed relatively fair. While a total of eighteen candidates qualified for the ballot, only four were serious contenders. In addition to Karzai, these included Qanuni (a Panjshiri Tajik leader running as the head of a reconstituted United Front party, Hizb-i-Nuhzhat-i-Milli Afghanistan), Dostam (the Uzbek militia leader and founder of the Junbesh-i-Milli Islami party), and Mohaqiq (a Hazara leader closely associated with the Shia-backed Hizb-i-Wahdat party). The balloting produced a majority for Karzai, who garnered 56 percent of the approximately eight million votes cast. While both the eastern and southern Pashtuns were strikingly united in their support of Karzai, he also garnered enough support in other areas of the country, particularly among Tajiks, to avoid a second round of balloting. The vote totals for the Hazara and Uzbek candidates were confined to their own ethnic groups or the regions they dominated.[7]

While the election strengthened the legitimacy of the Karzai government in the eyes of its international backers, it did not have as strong an impact within Afghanistan. For the international community, a free and fair election in itself established a democratic leader's political legitimacy. The relationship between elections and political legitimacy was less clearcut for Afghans. The presidential election was an innovation that while allowing the expression of popular opinion, could not by itself create political legitimacy. It merely gave the victor an opportunity to legitimate themselves by their future actions. An Afghan friend explained the difference in cultural perceptions to me this way: "You Americans pray before the meal; we Afghans pray only after we have eaten it." Karzai needed to prove that he could live up to the role he now filled and provide the people with what they expected: security, economic improvement, and a functioning government. An electoral victory would mean nothing if he failed to do so.

THE PARLIAMENTARY ELECTION OF 2005

The constitutional process flagged during the organization of the parliamentary elections in 2005, which had already been postponed for a year. While Karzai had been eager to improve his own standing through the presidential election, he was far less enthusiastic about seeing a new branch of government equally empowered. Like Zahir Shah before him, Karzai expressed a visceral disdain for political parties as institutions and refused to give them legal recognition. (For this reason, he even refused requests by his own followers to form a "King's Party" that would back him in the new parliament.) Claiming that Afghans associated political parties with the Communists, and that reviving them would be confusing to voters, he forced parliamentary candidates to run as individuals. To further weaken the emergence of an organized opposition, candidates could not even identify themselves as members of a political party on the ballot. This put a premium on nonpolitical factors (such as name recognition, ethnicity, region, and social standing), which in turn promoted division. Since in some cases over a hundred candidates ran for a single seat with no provisions for a runoff, the choice of a "first past the post" system of balloting meant that most winning candidates got less than 10 or even 5 percent of the total votes cast in their provinces. This reduced the legitimacy of the parliament, since the chances of winning a seat better resembled a lottery than a political contest.[8]

Despite Karzai's attempts to weaken it as an institution, the parliament quickly became the locus of political opposition to his administration. In 2006 the parliament rejected his leadership slate for the body, and in 2007 it forced him to reorganize the judiciary when they rejected his reappointment of a conservative Islamic cleric with no higher education as the Supreme Court chief in favor of a Western-trained technocrat.

State Building in Practice

The practical aspects of successful state building depended on getting the structure right and having skilled people run it. Neither condition needed to be met perfectly. A badly flawed structure might succeed if run by a talented leader while a more expertly designed structure could survive the mistakes of a poor one. What a fragile state could not easily survive was a badly designed government in the hands of a poor leader. With the best of intentions, the international community helped Afghanistan get both because it misconceived the political realities there and promoted a leader whose flaws were magnified rather than mitigated by the centralized government it had created. Since Afghans judged the legitimacy of a state by its actions rather than the process that created it, these errors had significant consequences.

THE PUSH FOR A CENTRALIZED GOVERNMENT

Although Afghanistan's regions had become autonomous during the Afghan civil war, the UN Assistance Mission in Afghanistan (UNAMA) and the United States both pushed to reestablish a highly centralized government of the type that had failed repeatedly in the past. Abdur Rahman created the first centralized Afghan state in the late nineteenth century only after many bloody military campaigns, but his political goals had been limited to destroying internal rivals, preserving his supremacy, and maintaining order. Later rulers who thought they could use his state model to impose change on the country soon found that it was not up to the task. The reforming King Amanullah was overthrown, and his state collapsed in 1929, requiring two generations to fully restore. Only the Soviet invasion in 1979 preserved the unpopular PDPA regime from a similar collapse after it too found the Afghan state institutions weaker than expected. During the civil war that followed the dissolution of the PDPA in 1992, Afghanistan reverted to its older pattern of regional autonomy that even the Taliban could do little to change. Arriving UNAMA officials saw the lack of a strong centralized state as a symptom of Afghanistan's problems and moved to restore it. Though written to serve monarchs, the constitutions of 1923 and 1964 were used as templates for the constitution of 2004. This new constitution made the Karzai government responsible for everything from appointing provincial governors to paying local schoolteachers.

The enthusiasm for restoring a highly centralized government was confined to the international community and the Kabul elite that ran it. Many other Afghans saw such governments as the source of Afghanistan's past problems. Critics contended that decentralization better suited Afghanistan because such governments had so badly neglected the rest of the country. The nondemocratic regimes that had ruled Afghanistan previously saw this as an acceptable price for the greater political control it gave them, particularly by preventing the reemergence of powerful regional elites, which had characterized Afghan politics before 1880. But the impact of twenty-five years of warfare changed this situation. Regions wanted a direct choice in how they were to be governed at the local level. The international community saw assertions of such regional autonomy as signs of disorder that needed to be curbed. They dismissed decentralization proponents as supporters of warlords who would bring the country to ruin. In fact, establishing governmental order and services by region, rather than centrally from Kabul, had considerable merit. It would have proven more effective and given people more of a stake in local administration. In addition there was always the risk that if a highly centralized government faltered, the consequences would be nationwide.

Any prospect of central state failure was dismissed by those who touted Karzai as a sure bet for success after he steered the country through the constitutional process and his own election as president in 2004. Afghans were less sanguine because they saw Karzai in a different light, as a vacillating leader who was unwilling to confront his enemies or discipline his allies. Rather than dismiss incompetent or crooked governors, Karzai transferred them from one province to another when complaints against them mounted. Powerful regional militia commanders were left in place (such as Dostam and Muhammad Ata in the north) or brought to Kabul as cabinet ministers (such as Ishmail Khan from the west and Gul Aga Sherzai from the south). Taliban sympathizers continued to dominate the judiciary, making the task of bringing the rule of state law to the country all that much more difficult. This strategy of appeasing the discredited leadership from the civil war period wedded Afghanistan to its failed past rather than charting a new future. It was no wonder Afghans increasingly complained of the Karzai administration's corruption, incompetence, and inability to meet the basic requirements of governance. In a system designed to operate effectively only with firm direction from a strongman at the top, this was a recipe for disaster.

One reason for the failures of the government was that Karzai was not really interested in building an institutionalized state structure. Despite the large sums that the international community was investing in "institution building," Karzai's model of government was patrimonial, in which the government administration and its assets were an extension of the ruler. In such a system, personal relationships determined everything from who would amass personal wealth to who would be thrown in jail. Karzai did not use the assets of the state to centralize power so much as he used them to create a patronage network of personal clients bound to him.[9] One key area that he did not really control, however, was the military. Funded and trained by the United States for the purposes of taking on the insurgency, the military was receiving the majority of U.S. assistance after 2006 (even leaving aside the cost of U.S. troops deployed there). While this strong U.S. presence prevented Karzai from making the military part of his patrimonial system, U.S. deference to his government also kept the military out of politics. Whether this would continue as the institutional capacity of the military grew while the civilian administration stagnated was little discussed but had long-term implications.

ALTERNATIVES IGNORED

The constitutional push to shore up central government eliminated promising options for devolving some power to the regional and local levels. In this respect, it harked back to earlier times when Durrani rulers praised the mobilization of the population to win Afghanistan's wars and then excluded their leaders from power in the aftermath. As noted earlier, this was relatively easy to do in the nineteenth century because there was a cultural predisposition to return national power to members of the old elite with the belief that only they were entitled to hold such offices. Nadir's success in removing Habibullah Kalakani from power in 1929 demonstrated that this tendency was still strong, as did the choice of Karzai in Bonn in 2001. But the concept of dynastic exclusivity had lost much of its strength despite Karzai's elevation to power. The Pashtuns maintained their monopoly over the appointment of the Afghan head of state, but this did nothing to reconcile the rivalry between the southern and eastern Pashtuns over the share of power each was entitled to. As the presidential election of 2009 approached, it was no surprise that the main Pashtun contenders seeking to displace Karzai had eastern roots.

The non-Pashtuns still appeared to be willing to cede the palace to a Pashtun ruler, yet only in exchange for much more local autonomy. They were unwilling to accept a return to a government in which Pashtun appointees had the power to run their lives. One way to achieve this would have been to have local governors chosen by election or at least confirmed by parliament. This would not only have made them more responsible to their constituents than to Kabul but also have served as a way to integrate local power elites into the national system. Instead, governors and other officials remained Karzai's personal appointees. When their misdeeds became the focus of local outrage, the Karzai government got the blame for appointing them in the first place. In the past people had seen themselves playing no role in government at any level, but now they pushed back at the local level. Karzai's response was to transfer the offending officials when the pressure mounted yet do nothing to change the structure, which would continue to produce the same negative outcomes. Complaints were similar in other areas: Kabul was responsible for all the nation's schools, but regularly failed to provide supplies or pay the teachers. In such a situation there was no means to redress these complaints against a distant and unresponsive ministry in Kabul.

Afghan Leadership Styles and State Building

In the absence of a strong institutional base, the characteristics of a leader still played a more critical role in state development and maintenance in Afghanistan than in other countries. Therefore, although the international community gave primacy to process (such as through the constitution and elections) and institution building (such as via ministries, courts, and police), the Afghans focused their attention on the quality of Karzai's leadership and his actions. They had their own templates by which they categorized his performance that ranged from a strong autocratic leader to a powerless figurehead. Rulers of the former type, although they were not always successful, dominated Afghan politics for the periods they governed, while the latter were dominated by others. Even though having Karzai as the head of the provisional government and then president at first appeared to be a perfect choice to start a new regime, the question remained as to what type of leader he would be. For those taking bets, the odds for success would be long in either case. Since the peaceful death of Abdur Rahman in 1901, no Afghan head of state of whatever political stripe had avoided assassination or being driven from office by force.

STRONGMEN

The strong autocratic leader was the most archetypical figure in Afghan politics. From the founding of the Afghan state in the eighteenth century by Ahmad, such men seized power, destroyed their enemies, and built or maintained centralized governments. The most notable were Dost Muhammad, Abdur Rahman, and Nadir Shah. All restored order after periods of war and created stable states, then inherited by their successors. They used their military talent and social prestige to first gain acceptance to their rule, and then employed the office of amir or king to build autonomous governmental institutions and create a strong state.

More problematic were those strongmen who ruled effectively while in office, but found themselves overtaken by events that destroyed them and their governments. They had powerful personalities and a clear sense of what they wanted to accomplish, yet miscalculated the stability of their regimes. Amanullah underestimated the strength of the conservative opposition to his reforms and overestimated the capacity of his military. Daud was the strongest Muhammadzai ruler of his generation both as prime minister and president, but lost his life in a military coup mounted by the leftists who had once been his allies. Najibullah built a state structure strong enough to survive the Soviet withdrawal from Afghanistan in 1989, although not strong enough to survive the dissolution of the Soviet Union itself.

As discussed earlier, an even larger group of strong personalities competed for national power during civil wars or internal power struggles, but could not consolidate their hold on it. In the twentieth century these included Habibullah Kalakani, Hafizullah Amin, Ahmad Shah Masud, Gulbadin Hekmatyar, and Mullah Omar. Habibullah's nine-month rule in 1929 shook Afghan politics to its core, though in the end he lacked the revenue needed to fend off his enemies and was killed by Nadir. A half century later, Amin purged his Parchami rivals to dominate the PDPA, but was murdered by the Russians when they invaded Afghanistan in late 1979. Masud was the most successful war leader against the Soviets and occupied Kabul in 1992, but refused to compete for the top job. He was driven back into the Panjshir Valley by the Taliban in 1995 and assassinated in 2001. Hekmatyar, the leader of the Hizb-i-Islami, desperately wanted to displace Masud, yet failed and was forced into exile by the Taliban of Mullah Omar. But Mullah Omar's refusal to leave Qandahar or establish a functioning government revealed him to be a leader with no talent for state building.

FIGUREHEADS

Figurehead rulers were most characteristic of foreign intervention and had an impressively dismal record of failure, as also described earlier. Shah Shuja was restored to power by the British, but lost his life months after they were expelled from Kabul during the First Anglo-Afghan War. Yaqub Khan ruled less than a year, in 1879, after being put on the throne by the British during the Second Anglo-Afghan War. He was widely reviled for signing the Treaty of Gandamak, which relinquished Afghan sovereignty over much of what became the NWFP. Although not associated with foreign intervention, Zahir Shah spent all but the last ten years of his rule taking orders from his uncles and his cousin Daud before Daud finally ousted him in a coup.

The PDPA had its share of figureheads as well. Taraki was the formal head of state but remained under the thumb of Hafizullah Amin, who murdered him in October 1979. Karmal, the Soviet-backed replacement for Hafizullah Amin, was so ineffectual that they exiled him in 1986 in favor of the more dynamic Najibullah. Rabbani was the head of the Jamiat Islami and the president of the mujahideen government, but everyone knew his power rested on Masud's military skills. Figurehead leaders were never successful in ending civil wars in Afghanistan for the simple reason that somebody else had to do the real work of fighting them. More often than not assertive military strongman who fought in the name of an established leader revealed their true colors as soon as victory was in sight (for instance, Nadir edged out Amanullah when he tried to stage a comeback after his abdication).

At first glance, it might appear that it was association with foreign occupiers that doomed figurehead rulers since the two generally went in tandem. A closer inspection, however, reveals something more complex. While true puppet leaders (Shaha Shuja and Babrak Karmal, most notably) did have a fatal dependency on the foreign backers who put them in power and alienated the Afghan people, they all also had reputations for poor judgment and had weak personalities as well. These character flaws were only magnified when they came to power in Kabul, and not just in Afghan eyes. The British had a much higher personal opinion of Dost Muhammad, even after he surrendered to them, than they did of Shuja. The Soviets displayed a similarly dismissive attitude toward Karmal. By contrast, leaders picked by foreign powers in anticipation of their withdrawal from Afghanistan did better. They included Dost Muhammad after the end of the First Anglo-Afghan War, Abdur Rahman at the end of the second one, and Najibullah during the Soviet withdrawal. In such cases, the foreign power was looking for a leader who was independent minded enough to rule Afghanistan, yet calculating enough to keep the flow of foreign aid coming. The trick was to be seen by the Afghans as protecting the integrity of the country while also doing so.

It perhaps goes without saying that had there been a classically strong leader available to rule Afghanistan in 2001, he would not have waited for a telephone call from Bonn to determine his fate. He would have already been in Kabul making calls to Germany, demanding that the Bonn participants recognize his legitimacy and swear their allegiance—or expect to live in exile, if they did not. In the absence of such pressure the Bonn participants chose Karzai, for the reasons outlined earlier. But what style of leadership did Karzai bring to the table? He had the advantage of being a plausible Afghan choice even though he did not have a reputation for being a strong leader. Indeed, beginning with his initial appointment, Karzai displayed a worrying inability to make hard decisions and stick to them in the face of opposition. For example, immediately after becoming the head of the provisional government, he appointed Mullah Naqibullah, a powerful Alikozai leader, as governor of Qandahar, only to be ignored by Gul Aga Sherzai, a Barakzai supported by Pakistan's ISI and the few U.S. forces on the ground. Sherzai had already moved into the governor's palace and refused to leave. This proved to be an early test of Karzai's character—a test that most observers believed he failed. As Ahmad Rashid observed,

> Karzai's indecisiveness was to now emerge for the first time for all to see. He had waited too long for the Taliban to surrender Kandahar, the seizure of which proved worthless because all the Taliban had escaped to Pakistan. Then he waited two more days, until December 9, before entering the city and was forced to appoint Sherzai governor. It was the first of many showdowns with the warlords that all too often ended in a humiliating compromise or climb down for Karzai.[10]

While even the Iron Amir would have found the task of rebuilding a failed Afghan state daunting in 2002, Karzai's inability to act decisively made the task all the more difficult. Over the course of the next seven years, he would shuffle powerful warlords from one position to another but never eliminate any of them. Corrupt government officials were never punished, and this generated ill will for Karzai's administration. Expensive and ostentatious new mansions built by prominent public officials popped up in Kabul's best neighborhoods—a sign to all of their new wealth and their lack of fear in displaying it.[11]

Karzai's weak internal position was exacerbated by his obvious dependency on American support. That U.S. guns and money undergirded his regime was less corrosive to Karzai's standing among Afghans than the belief that he was as ineffectual in dealing with them as he was with the warlords. This was manifest publicly in his relationship with Zalmay Khalilzad, who served as Bush's special presidential envoy for Afghanistan in 2001 and was named ambassador there in 2003. An Afghan American with strong White

House connections, Khalilzad often better resembled a proconsul than a diplomat. He had made his first appearance on the Afghan political stage pressuring Zahir Shah to step aside in favor of Karzai at the emergency loya jirga in 2002. On his return as ambassador, he spent more of his nineteenth-month tenure in Kabul at the palace than at the embassy. He then became so engaged in the country's domestic political deal making that some Afghans referred to him as "America's warlord."

A vivid demonstration of Khalilzad's influence occurred in 2004, after a paroxysm of factional fighting in western Afghanistan involving Ismail Khan, a warlord who was the governor of Herat province. It was clear to Khalilzad that Khan needed to go, but Karzai was hesitant. So Khalilzad flew to Herat for discussions with Khan and announced that Khan would be moving to Kabul to become a cabinet minister. A few days later, Karzai issued an edict to that effect. "Karzai was being his usual indecisive self, so Zal drove the steel rod up his spine," said a U.S. official. That tactic, applied repeatedly, earned Khalilzad some detractors. "Khalilzad's approach fundamentally weakened Karzai," said a veteran Western diplomat. "Karzai was seen by many Afghans as a puppet of the Americans. It delegitimized him."[12]

U.S. attempts to encourage Karzai to govern more autonomously after Khalilzad's departure failed to improve the situation, though, because Karzai acted even less decisively in the years that followed.

Although these defects were widely known, Karzai retained enough esteem to win the presidential election of 2004 easily. After 2005, however, his popularity declined significantly because of his inability to create an effective administration, a deteriorating security situation, and a lack of economic progress. The personality flaws that had been excused previously now came under ever sharper attack from domestic critics. Karzai's impotent public demands for policy changes in response to U.S. air strikes that killed civilians only reinforced an Afghan perception of his weakness each time he made one. Karzai also began to find himself at odds with the international community. The international community's earlier praise of him as the "indispensable man" for Afghanistan shifted to disparagement of his weak leadership as well as his inability to curb corruption and drug production, particularly after his staunchest U.S. supporter, Bush, left office in 2008. When detractors began to make barbed comparisons of him to the British-backed Shuja of 1841 or the Soviet-backed Karmal of 1981, Karzai must have started to worry that both the Afghan people and foreign powers were in the market for a new Dost Muhammad, Daud, or Najibullah. As the Afghans themselves often opined, their resentment of tough leaders was leavened by a belief that Afghanistan required them. Karzai's only consolation was that his opponents would never agree on who should replace him.

INTERNATIONAL RELATIONS

Despite Afghanistan's well-deserved reputation for independence, no government there was ever stable without access to foreign sources of revenue. While such income took many different forms, obtaining it remained a high priority for every Afghan regime. Ahmad Shah Durrani mounted raids on India and took tribute from there in the eighteenth century. Nineteenth-century rulers made peace deals with the British raj in exchange for substantial subsidies and access to modern weapons. The Musahiban rulers of Afghanistan exploited the cold war rivalry between the Soviet Union and the United States to modernize Afghanistan's military and develop its economy. The PDPA was entirely dependent on resources from the Soviet Union to keep it afloat. The Karzai government was equally dependent on the United States and other Western countries.

The problem for Afghan rulers was that under ordinary circumstances, there was little incentive for foreign governments to provide the assistance that was vital for their regimes' survival. The only way to overcome this obstacle was to make Afghanistan seem important (or dangerous) enough to justify these payments. But here Afghan rulers were faced with a difficult task. They were acutely aware that they lived in a world where their country's primary interests were always at the bottom of someone else's agenda. Even taking the country seriously earned the rebuke of critics in nineteenth-century Britain; they coined the term "Afghanistanism" for those who exaggerated the significance of events in distant and obscure places. Yet time and time again, Afghanistan returned to the world stage with an importance that always belied this gloss and generated the revenue it was seeking. In the nineteenth century, Afghanistan's successful resistance against the British gave it a central place as the frontier of the raj—negatively as a potential threat to India's NWFP, and positively as a barrier to Russian expansion. In the latter part of the twentieth century, the Soviet Union and the United States each feared "losing Afghanistan" to the other. This gave a country with no developed resources or vital strategic location a remarkably crucial significance until the cold war ended with the dissolution of the Soviet Union. It recovered that position when Islamic terrorism became a new world security issue and keeping Afghanistan free of it an international priority.

The U.S. invasion that expelled the Taliban and al Qaeda from Afghanistan created an odd circumstance in its wake. The usual priority among the Afghans of expelling foreign invaders was replaced by a tacit strategy of keeping them there to guarantee security and finance the development of the country. This was because the Afghan population was looking for stability after decades of war and protection against predation by factions within Afghanistan as well as from neighbors seeking to exploit its weaknesses. But accepting such assistance needed to be carefully balanced: a Kabul government that was dependent on it could be labeled a puppet regime unless it proved itself independent enough to protect Afghan interests and values. It was also dangerous to assume that the initial willingness of the Afghan people to accept foreign intervention had no expiration date. To be successful, foreign military assistance to the Afghan state needed to be self-liquidating, and foreign economic assistance needed to improve ordinary lives.

Opportunities Squandered

Afghanistan required three specific types of international assistance to restore stability after the expulsion of the Taliban. The first was the deployment of international troops to all the country's major regions in order to improve security. This would end (or at least restrict) the power of the local warlords. It would also send a message to Afghanistan's neighbors that change there was permanent. The second was a large-scale investment in agriculture for rural Afghans, the bulk of the population, which would include irrigation schemes, crop improvement, and farm-to-market roads. The third was the rapid restoration and expansion of the country's infrastructure (trunk roads and electric lines particularly), which would create employment opportunities and improve urban life. Together these would create a momentum that would harness the new optimism of the Afghan people and reduce the appeal of factions that wished to drag the country back into war. Unfortunately for Afghanistan this assistance was not provided at the levels needed. International forces were small in number and restricted to Kabul, the rural economy got no attention, and progress on infrastructure repairs and improvements moved at a glacial pace despite large outlays of money.

The underlying reason for this failure was the short-term political calculation driving U.S. foreign policy in 2002. The Bush administration was gearing up for its war on Saddam Hussein's Iraq, which would begin a year later, and so wished to keep U.S. assets deployed in Afghanistan to a minimum. The United States therefore had no interest in becoming involved in Afghanistan's reconstruction. It hoped to leave that task to UNAMA, which was supposed to coordinate the international community's projects throughout the country. As a result, international efforts in Afghanistan really amounted to nothing more than stopgap measures—just enough to keep immediate problems at bay with the hope that the situation would improve on its own in the future. It did not.

MILITARY SHELL GAMES

The United States maintained only a "light footprint" in Afghanistan after its victory over the Taliban. Initially it was so light as to be invisible. During 2002–3, Washington committed only seven thousand troops to a country the size of France with a population of thirty million people. Most of the U.S. troops were tasked with tracking down the remnants of al Qaeda and the Taliban in the south and east of Afghanistan as part of "Operation Enduring Freedom." The responsibility for securing Kabul, the capital, fell to a separate military command, the UN-mandated International Security Assistance Force (ISAF), initially comprised of five thousand troops drawn from forty nations.*

---

* By comparison, NATO had deployed fifty-four thousand troops to Bosnia in 1996 (a place one-twelfth the size and about one-sixth the population of Afghanistan), and New York City alone had a civilian police force of thirty-five thousand at the time.

Because the United States initially opposed the expansion of ISAF's mandate beyond Kabul, most regions outside the capital had no international military presence. By the time that Washington came around to supporting the ISAF expansion in 2003, allied support for sending additional troops to Afghanistan had waned. Countries that might have been willing to make substantial additional commitments in 2002 refused requests to do so a year later, in part because the unity of the international coalition in Afghanistan was damaged by a split among the North Atlantic Treaty Organization (NATO) allies over the Iraq War. Afghanistan got the worst of both worlds: the United States and Britain argued that they could not send any more troops because of their commitments in Iraq, while France, Germany, and Turkey expressed their displeasure with the United States' Iraq policy by being less helpful in Afghanistan. International troop presence did not substantially increase until the run-up to the Afghan presidential election in October 2004. The ISAF numbers then doubled to ten thousand, and U.S. forces increased to twenty thousand. Some of this increase was absorbed by the deployment of new "Provincial Reconstruction Teams" designed to provide security for civilian groups and government officials delivering local aid. Because most of these teams were dispatched to parts of the country that were generally progovernment and staffed by only sixty to ninety soldiers and civilians, however, their significance was more political than military.

The failure to extend the ISAF beyond Kabul in 2002 and the focus by U.S. troops on confronting an al Qaeda enemy that had largely decamped to Pakistan created a power vacuum. Because a national Afghan army and police force had not yet been trained (even by 2004, the national army of nine thousand could deploy only forty-five hundred troops), the new Afghan government lacked the capacity to extend its power into the provinces. As a result, the former regional military leaders of the old United Front retained their political importance in the non-Pashtun regions of the north and west even after their militias were officially demobilized. In the Pashtun east, U.S. forces coped with their limited troop strength (and lack of familiarity with complex tribal divisions) by recruiting local militia allies to assist them. This was an easy short-term solution but highly divisive politically. (In a land where factionalism was rife, an alliance with one group guaranteed making an enemy of another, regardless of ideology.) The south, except around Qandahar, was left to fend for itself.

EPHEMERAL AID

Since the mid-nineteenth century, Afghan central governments had relied on foreign subsidies to help them finance their governments, equip their armies, and build infrastructure without taxing their own people. It was control of this revenue stream that gave Kabul its ability to centralize power through an elaborate system of patronage that rewarded allies and punished opponents. But the situation after 2001 put the Afghan government in a paradoxical position. Although more economic aid poured into the country than ever before, the vast majority of it was distributed directly by foreign donors for projects that they planned and implemented. This practice ended the central government's monopoly over such resources and crippled its ability to rule through patronage. More significantly, the amount of money pledged to Afghanistan, while seemingly large, could not begin to meet either the country's needs or the population's expectations.

Given the Bush administration's reluctance to engage in "nation building," the role of the United States in Afghanistan was initially presented as one of facilitating reconstruction. Never was a term a greater misnomer, since even before its wars began in 1978, Afghanistan had been one of the least educated and poorest populations in the world, with an infrastructure to match. Bringing the country back to prewar conditions would still leave it at the bottom of any development index. What the Afghans needed was construction and capacity building, not reconstruction to pitiful prewar levels. Yet the major projects planned for Afghanistan hardly began to meet the country's needs. For example, the critical fifteen-hundred-mile ring road that first linked the country's regions together in the 1960s was not an impressive divided highway but instead a dangerously narrow two-lane road. Restoring it barely met the engineering standards required of a rural farm-to-market road in the United States or Europe. Similarly, only slightly more than 10 percent of Afghanistan had been electrified before 1978—at a time when the population was half that of today.

While other nations recognized the need for nation building in Afghanistan, the amount of money available, even had it been well spent, was insufficient to do the job. Pledges to Afghanistan amounted to $10 billion in the first three years after 2001, and an additional $14 billion was pledged to cover the period from 2005 to 2011. While the total figures appeared impressive, many pledges never materialized, and the amounts delivered were low on a per capita basis. In 2003, international aid amounted to only $50 per person and rose to only $66 two years later.* Worse, a substantial portion of the aid to Afghanistan was swallowed up by the expenses of providing it. The Agency Coordinating Body for Afghan Relief estimated that in 2008, of the $15 billion in reconstruction assistance given to Afghanistan since 2001, "a staggering 40 percent has returned to donor countries in corporate profits and consultant salaries."[13]

The Afghan government, meanwhile, was treated less as a partner than as a nuisance. Because most projects were handled by foreign contractors or international NGOs, 75 percent of aid funds were disbursed and delivered outside official Afghan government channels. This reduced the capacity of Afghans to manage such contracts themselves and increased the costs devoted to security.[14] It also divorced the reconstruction process from the political one, reducing its utility as a source of positive patronage to build support for the new regime, since NGOs plastered their own logos on projects rather than the government's insignia. While the decision to work around the Afghans as opposed to through them allowed some large construction projects to be completed more easily (albeit at a much higher cost), it reduced the projects' economic benefits to local communities because it failed to provide local job opportunities, which were particularly important to support returning refugees. One response to this was the spectacular rise of the opium economy, which soon provided 90 percent of the world's illegal production. By 2007, the export value of the drug trade was estimated at $4 billion and internally constituted more than 12 percent of Afghanistan's licit gross domestic product.[15]

Spending large amounts of money that generated disappointing results at the local level exacted a political price when rural Afghans came to be-

---

*This fell well short of postconflict aid packages elsewhere at the same time, such as Mozambique ($111 per capita) or Serbia and Montenegro ($237 per capita).

lieve that their needs were being ignored. Rural Afghans were also suspicious of attempts by a modernizing Kabul elite supported by international aid givers to engage in social engineering. To those in Kabul planning projects, there was s self-evident need to provide gender equality, better representation of the poor and minority groups in decision making, and access to secular education. This was not so self-evident to rural Afghans, since the question of how and in what ways Afghanistan needed to change had generated political problems since the 1920s. It was easy for conservative opponents of the Karzai regime to claim that such projects undermined traditional Afghan cultural values and that their non-Muslim backers were seeking to undermine Islam itself. The number of examples did not have to be large (or even real) to have a political impact. An international NGO that saw itself as doing good by helping women get divorces was seen by Afghans as encouraging home wrecking in a country where divorce (by a man or a woman) was socially unacceptable.

This problem was exacerbated because international decision makers had little familiarity with Afghanistan's culture or history. This situation was in fact typical of international responses to rebuilding failed states generally, of which Afghanistan was only one of many. Since the inhabitants of failed states had obviously proved their inability to govern themselves, they had little to offer the professional international experts brought in to rehabilitate their governments and societies. As Rory Stewart acidly observed, such

> post-conflict experts have gotten the prestige without the effort or stigma of imperialism. Their implicit denial of the difference between cultures is the new mass brand of international intervention. Their policy fails but no one notices. There are no credible monitoring bodies, and there is no one to take formal responsibility. Individual officers are never in any one place and seldom in any one organization long enough to be adequately assessed. The colonial enterprise could be judged by the security or revenue it delivered, but neo-colonialists have no such performance criteria. In fact their very uselessness benefits them. By avoiding any serious action or judgement they, unlike their colonial predecessors, are able to escape accusations of racism, exploitation, or oppression.

Perhaps it is because no one requires more than a charming illusion of action in the developing world. If policy makers know little about Afghanistan, the public knows even less, and few care about policy failure when the effects are felt only in Afghanistan.[16]

Of course the Afghans noticed, and neocolonialists got no more respect from them than their forbearers gave to true colonialists. But policy failures in Afghanistan, unlike in some other similar places, would eventually have international repercussions.

The Price of Neglect

In 2005, Afghanistan was being presented as a "mission accomplished" despite the problems outlined above. The levels of conflict remained relatively low, the presidential election had gone off without violence, and no big problems appeared to be on the horizon. Washington was so sure of this that it reduced its budgeted aid request for Afghanistan by 38 percent (from $4.3 billion in fiscal 2005 to $3.1 billion in fiscal 2006).[17] In December 2005, the U.S. Department of Defense announced plans to reduce the number of U.S. troops there by three thousand in the coming year, although a larger NATO force would replace them. This new NATO command would take responsibility for all of Afghanistan except for the east, where the United States would retain direct control.

From inside Afghanistan the view was less upbeat. The positive goodwill and enthusiasm that the Afghan people displayed on the expulsion of the Taliban in 2001 through the presidential elections of 2004 began to decline. Universal complaints of insecurity, governmental malfeasance, corruption, and abuses of power steadily reduced domestic confidence in the Karzai administration in the absence of any serious steps to curb them. This coincided with a growing dissatisfaction at the slow pace of the country's economic development, in which few improvements ever reached the rural areas where most Afghans lived. Even the more favored residents of Kabul complained that the government appeared to be incapable of meeting such basic needs as electricity, drinking water, and transportation. More ominously, security started to deteriorate, particularly on the borders with Pakistan, where suicide bombers appeared for the first time.

Unmistakable signs of trouble appeared by mid-2006. On May 29, a riot sparked by a fatal traffic accident involving U.S. troops and local Afghans engulfed Kabul. Although it ended by evening, the rapid spread of the unrest, the ineffective response by the police (some of whom joined the rioters), and its antigovernment character demonstrated both the danger of complacency and the declining popularity of Karzai even in normally progovernment Kabul. Later in the summer, British and Canadian troops deployed to Helmand and Qandahar confronted a well-armed and full-blown insurgency led by a reinvigorated Taliban. While they expected to meet some opposition, their plans and training had focused on providing a peacekeeping shield that would facilitate the introduction of new economic development projects, not combat. Instead they experienced the fiercest fighting ever. Although NATO forces inflicted severe casualties on the Taliban and many of them thus retreated back into Pakistan, troop levels were too low to expel them permanently from the region. There was also trouble in eastern Afghanistan, which experienced a sharp rise in cross-border attacks from Pakistan's autonomous tribal territories, where al Qaeda and Taliban forces were becoming dominant.

Evidence for this new level of violence was clear statistically. Between 2005 and 2006, suicide bombings increased by more than 400 percent (from 27 to 139), the use of improvised explosive devises more than doubled (from 783 to 1,677), and armed attacks nearly tripled (from 1,558 to 4,542).[18] America's "good war" was now badly off track, and the seemingly discredited Taliban were back in the south and attempting to spread outward. The Taliban southern offensive in 2006 was premised on the assumption that NATO troops were simply covering for a U.S. departure from Afghanistan, as indicated by the troop-cut announcement in 2005. Believing NATO to be a less-committed foe than the United States, the Taliban risked fighting conventional battles with the expectation that they could take Qandahar when they withdrew. In fact the reverse happened, at least militarily. Despite disputes among the allies over their willingness to deploy troops into combat zones, NATO fought effectively. The United States increased its troop commitment, and allied governments did not withdraw from Afghanistan.

The explanation for this deterioration lay in the defective policies that were never corrected to adjust to a changing situation. No one of them was so flawed that it alone caused the crisis, but together they produced a situation that was difficult to correct.

The Insurgency

> We are not going to ever defeat the insurgency. Afghanistan has probably had—my reading of Afghanistan history—it's probably had an insurgency forever, of some kind.
> —Stephen Harper, Canadian prime minister, March 2, 2009

The assumption that Afghanistan has always been an unstable state perpetually beleaguered by armed rebels is now taken as fact. Yet as I have shown in earlier chapters, Afghanistan actually experienced relatively few insurgencies, and most of these lasted less than eighteen months. Those that were generated by the invasions of the British ended as soon as they were gone. The many violent civil wars in the late eighteenth and nineteenth centuries were not insurgencies but rather succession struggles in which rival members of the ruling elite mobilized their followers to take or hold the throne. The violence ceased whenever one of them came out on top. No ruler was ever seriously challenged by nonrelatives. This pattern of endemic succession struggles ended in the late nineteenth century, when Abdur Rahman ruthlessly centralized power and violently eliminated all potential challengers to his rule. There would be no civil war succession struggles within the dynasty for the rest of its history.

It was Abdur Rahman's increasing the power of the central government at the expense of his subjects that created the country's first domestic insurgencies. Whereas earlier wars of succession were fought over who should wield state authority, these new insurgencies were uprisings against state authority itself, provoked by the Kabul government's attempts to change or abolish customary relationships. An insurgency of this type was mounted by the Ghilzais (1886–88) against their political subordination by Abdur Rahman and his taxes. It was the first serious mass resistance to a Kabul government based on its domestic policies and provided a model for later uprisings. Still, considering how many wars Abdur Rahman conducted during his reign, it was easy to overlook the qualitative differences between his suppression of the Ghilzai Rebellion and his conquests of lands that Kabul had never controlled (Hazarajat and Nuristan) or wars against his own relatives (Ayyub in Herat and Ishaq in Turkistan).

Abdur Rahman was so successful in suppressing opposition to the Kabul government that his successors remained unchallenged for more than a generation. It was not until Amanullah attempted to implement his reform policies that another insurrection, the Khost Rebellion of 1924, again challenged state authority. Limited to parts of eastern Afghanistan, this rebellion was suppressed only with the aid of tribal levies. The civil war that erupted five years later was much more serious because both the Kohistanis north of Kabul and the Pashtuns in the east rose up simultaneously against Amanullah and his policies. The insurgency, however, quickly reverted to a succession struggle when the Kohistani rebel leader, Habibullah Kalakani, declared himself amir in Kabul. The Pashtun tribes then dropped their opposition to Amanullah and shifted their goal to ensuring that Afghanistan's rulers remain Pashtun. Nadir used this opportunity to displace Amanullah and establish a new dynasty. He granted the formerly rebellious frontier tribes special political status and turned them into allies. This bargain proved so successful that over the next half century, Nadir's Musahiban successors faced no serious revolts. They easily repressed the few nascent insurgencies that did arise: the Safi Rebellion in 1945–46 by Pashtuns in Kunar Province, a rebellion in 1959 by the Pashtun tribes in Qandahar resisting a new provincial tax (and schools for girls), and the Islamist uprising in 1975 in the Panjshir Valley. Nor was Daud's republic toppled by an insurgency of any type; it fell victim to a classic military coup.

It was only during the period of resistance against the Soviet occupation (1979–89) that Afghanistan experienced its first national insurgency. Previous rebellions, even against foreign invasion, had been confined to the regions immediately north and east of Kabul. The other parts of the country remained aloof from these struggles or acted opportunistically. By contrast, the Soviet occupation was met with resistance throughout the country and by all ethnic groups. The Soviets also had a more profound impact on

Afghanistan than did the British. They were there longer (ten years versus three), deployed troops more widely (every city versus the British focus on Kabul, Qandahar, and Jalalabad), and created an unprecedented flow of refugees. The Soviet departure from Afghanistan did not bring an end to the insurgency. One reason for this was that the mujahideen rebels maintained access to their foreign funding and bases in Pakistan, whereas earlier rebels had subsisted entirely on domestic resources. But the Russian withdrawal of their troops (while continuing their aid) so reduced the level of opposition to the PDPA regime that Najibullah remained in power until the Soviet Union itself collapsed.

It was the post-1992 mujahideen civil war and rise of the Taliban that created the impression of never-ending insurgencies in Afghanistan. But since no faction had obtained complete control of the country, this was not a situation of insurgency but rather civil war or, worse, chaos. The Taliban had come closest to taking control of the country. They had ousted the indigenous regional commanders in the west, north, and center, while co-opting those in the east. By September 2001, they were on the verge of expelling the last of their enemies in northeastern Afghanistan following the assassination of Masud. The U.S. invasion reversed that process dramatically, and within months the Taliban were gone and the new Karzai government was installed. If Afghanistan were truly a land of unending insurrections, one should have arisen somewhere against the United States in 2002. Despite the weaknesses in the Karzai government and its obvious foreign backing, though, even in the Taliban heartland of the south it took many years for a significant insurgency to develop. Yet that insurgency was far from nationwide, and Afghanistan's receptivity to a returned Taliban was decidedly local.

Two Afghanistans

Within Afghanistan, political and economic conditions varied so much by region that it often appeared there were two different countries: the north, west, and center, which were relatively stable; and the south and east, which were not. Since the south and east were predominantly Pashtun, this division had an ethnic component as well.

Stability in the non-Pashtun north and west rested on more adequate security and a rising standard of living. Herat received close to a half-billion dollars in investments and infrastructure from Iran, linking the economy of western Afghanistan much more closely to its richer neighbor. Northern Afghanistan had reached out internationally to tie itself into central Asia's electricity grid and was poised to take advantage of new bridges across the Amu Darya. Iran and the central Asian states were also friendly with the Kabul government and hostile to the Taliban, so there was little threat of cross-border trouble. Their domestic economies were stronger as well because the north and west had been blessed with Afghanistan's most productive irrigated agricultural land. Although much poorer, Hazarajat was also a zone of stability, in part because so many of its local officials were now Hazara themselves and able to bring small-scale development projects to the region. These places thought they had closed the door on Afghanistan's recent troubled past and had no desire to return to it.

By contrast the Pashtun south lacked security, had a stagnant or declining standard of living, and had become dependent on opium as a cash crop. It bordered Pakistan, a state where the Taliban leadership had reconstituted itself in neighboring Baluchistan and from where it could stir up trouble. As a result, the foreign-funded development projects planned for the region moved slowly or were abandoned because of the poor security situation. The south also had difficulty adjusting to its reduced political significance at the national level. Although the Karzai government was increasingly dominated by Durranis, it was unable to deliver the generous subsidies and political favoritism that had flowed to the region in earlier times. The best it could do on that score was to shield the region's opium production from outside interference, but this came both at the cost of alienating the regime's international backers and subsidizing enemies such as the Taliban. The east was a paler reflection of the south, with the opium economy there waxing and waning depending on the benefits available from Kabul. Its Durand Line border with Pakistan was outside state control, although the deployment of U.S. troops there gave the Kabul government more influence than in the south. Indeed, the strongest base for Islamists inside eastern Afghanistan was not among the Pashtuns but instead among the more remote Nuristanis in the high mountains northwest of Jalalabad.

Kabul sat on the fault line of these two Afghanistans. In terms of security and prosperity it topped the list of successful Afghan cities. ISAF maintained order, and the bulk of the international funding for the country as a whole seemed to gravitate as if by magic to the Kabul Basin. Kabul was the center of government power and by far Afghanistan's largest city. The people there had the strongest commitment to putting the past behind them. But because Kabul bordered the more discontented south and east, it was unsettled by the trouble originating there. At first this was quite distant, but attacks once confined to isolated rural areas began to spread to the capital. The Kabul-Qandahar Highway, repaved at great expense during the run-up to Karzai's election in 2004, was considered dangerous to travel only two years later and was pockmarked with craters made by improvised explosive devices.

That the trouble was coming out of the Pashtun regions was a particular problem for Karzai as a leader. It was his own coethnics that were the most discontented with his government, in spite of the fact that they played a dominant role in it. More significantly, it was Karzai's home region (the Durrani south) where the unrest was most pervasive. Attempts at appeasement through promises of more money and appeals to "moderate Taliban" had little impact there. They only alienated the non-Pashtuns living in the more secure parts of the country. These non-Pashtuns questioned the wisdom of devoting resources to places and people that caused the most trouble at the expense of those that were at peace. In particular, Karzai's inability to bring order to the south undermined the implicit bargain by which the non-Pashtuns agreed to back a Pashtun ruler as a way to bring stability to the country. Such a concession was for naught if Karzai could not command the loyalty and obedience of his own people in return. If Afghanistan were ever to break apart, it would not be out of ethnic hatred or nationalist ideology but rather out of pragmatism. Those who wished to continue on that trajectory of progress already achieved in their own regions would be quite willing to leave the Pashtuns in the south and east to their own devices. If that happened Kabul, Mazar, and Herat would constitute the foundation of a new state of Khorasan (the old Persian name for the entire region, which had the great advantage of having no ethnic connotations), and the Pashtuns would get their wish to have a Pashtunistan.

Two Insurgencies

The ease with which the United States expelled the Taliban in 2001 induced complacency. There was no military follow-up designed to ensure that they could not return to mobilize their followers, who had simply returned home after their defeat. Nor was Pakistan pressed hard enough to end its covert aid to the movement and its support of other jihadist groups. These failures did not seem important because the Taliban were judged to be a spent force as late as the elections of 2004. But that did not mean they lacked the potential to reorganize. It was as if a patient stopped taking an antibiotic when the immediate symptoms had ended, disregarding his physician's warning that a full course was required to eliminate the infection. Goals that might have been relatively easy to achieve in 2002 were much more daunting in 2006.

The Pashtun areas along Pakistan's border with Afghanistan became the seedbed of an insurgency against the United States, its coalition allies, and the Kabul government. This was not a new insurgency, however, but a continuation of the older one that had begun against the Soviets and had fragmented during the Afghan civil war. While joined by al Qaeda elements and new Pakistani allies, the insurgency's leaders were the same as during the Soviet period, albeit changed by time from angry young men into aging graybeards. All the insurgent groups maintained a radical Islamist line with demands that foreign forces leave the country and that the government follow strict sharia law, but they had no unified command or common plan of action. They did maintain close ties with Pakistan's ISI, and received direct support and sanctuary under their auspices. Unlike the Soviet period, the non-Pashtun regions of the country did not join in this fight despite their own dissatisfaction with the Karzai government.

THE BLOWBACK INSURGENCIES

Blowback is the unforeseen negative consequence of an earlier covert action—in this case, facing armed opposition from some of the mujahideen parties and leaders in eastern Afghanistan that the United States had lavishly funded in the 1980s to fight the Russians. When the United States drove the Taliban from power, these groups reemerged under their old leadership, some of which allied with the United States while others opposed it. Whether allied or opposed, the U.S. invasion resuscitated the political careers of these older mujahideen leaders, since the Taliban had earlier forced them into subordination or driven them into exile by the late 1990s. Those who took the path of insurgency simply revived their old networks, shifting their opposition from the Soviets to the United States. Because they had an already-existing command structure and willing support from Pakistan, it did not take them long to breathe new life into an old conflict.

Hekmatyar's Hizb-i-Islami was the best known of those factions opposing a foreign presence in Afghanistan. It was most influential in the provinces of Kunar, Nangarhar, and Nuristan. The lack of early U.S. resistance to Hekmatyar allowed Hizb-i-Islami forces to take control of many villages in mountainous Nuristan, where they linked up with al Qaeda forces on the Pakistan side of the border. Despite Hekmatyar's radical rhetoric, some members of his party joined the Kabul government, and Hekmatyar hinted at a willngness to cooperate if Karzai ceded enough power to him. A more radical insurgency based on Pashtun tribal networks arose further to the south in the provinces of Paktia, Paktika, and Khost that straddled the frontier with Pakistan's FATA. Commanded by Jalaluddin Haqqani, a prominent resistance commander against the Soviets, its greatest influence was among the resident Pashtun tribes, particularly Haqqanni's own Zadran people in Afghanistan and FATA's north Waziristan, where he had his headquarters. Haqqani's influence extended well beyond the frontier. His network orchestrated the majority of terrorist attacks in Kabul itself (at the behest of Pakistan's ISI, according to the Afghans). His faction also included many foreign fighters and was closer to al Qaeda than Hekmatyar's Hizb-i-Islami.

THE SOUTHERN INSURGENCY AND THE RETURN OF THE TALIBAN

The largest and most intense insurgency was centered in Qandahar and Helmand provinces, and led by Mullah Omar's Taliban. The Taliban regained the capacity to mount an insurgency in the south among a people who had failed to raise a hand to defend them in 2001 by taking advantage of discontent with the Kabul government and the late arrival of international troops as well as by modifying their own ideology. The absence of any earlier economic development left the region dependent on an illicit opium economy. This provided the Taliban with a revenue source to tax and gave them allies among those benefiting from the illicit trade. In the absence of any significant international military presence, the Taliban were able to regroup unimpeded in an area they knew well for at least two years before NATO troops were deployed to confront them. The Taliban also took advantage of the discontent with the Kabul government's inability to maintain local security, offer services, or establish the rule of law. These defects also reinvigorated local militia leaders, who exploited the public discontent with the officials dispatched from Kabul to position themselves as protectors of the local population. As significant, the Taliban changed their ideological stance. They now portrayed themselves less as Muslim zealots and more as God-fearing nationalists seeking to expel infidel foreigners from the country. They played on the suspicions of the rural population that the Kabul government and its international backers were attempting to impose alien values on them, harking back to old hot button issues. They downplayed their earlier demands for strict adherence to Salafist Islam and implied that if given power again they would not be as intolerant of other sects.[19]

While the Taliban benefited from the defects of the Kabul government and lack of an international counterforce, their surprisingly well-equipped forces could not have been supplied without Pakistan's help. Similar complaints against the Kabul government existed in other parts of Afghanistan, but it was only along the Pakistan frontier—where they had access to cross-border support and bases—that it erupted into open warfare in 2006. Although Pakistan had officially abandoned its support of the Taliban when it acquiesced to the U.S. invasion of Afghanistan in 2001, it did so under duress. In reality, it never abandoned its covert support for the movement and provided its leadership with refuge in Baluchistan. Pakistan turned a blind eye to the existence of their training camps and the Taliban's recruitment of new troops through Islamist madrasas. Although the Pakistanis claimed to be unaware of their presence, Taliban leaders had homes in Quetta and showed no fear of arrest. While the Musharif government proved willing to hunt down foreign al Qaeda members, Pakistan still saw the Taliban as allies, and had not abandoned its goal of controlling Afghanistan through a Taliban regime or faction in government when the United States withdrew.[20]

TALIBAN DILEMMAS

The weaknesses of the Karzai government were well-known, but the Taliban had their own legitimacy problems that undermined their ability to conduct a successful insurgency. It was a divided movement whose leaders had different interests and bases of support. Despite Pakistan's assertion that the Taliban had solid Afghan roots, these had atrophied over time and would be hard to rebuild. Taliban ideology was more Pakistani than Afghan, and while its popularity surged in Pakistan's NWFP, fewer Afghans saw it as a model for the future. Its Pakistani-based leadership could not wage an insurgency without the recruits, bases, and safe refuge it had access to there. If Pakistan ever reversed its policy of support, as it did to Mullah Omar in 2001, the insurgency in Afghanistan would be dealt a fatal blow.

The Taliban's dependence on Pakistan also had some additional negative consequences within Afghanistan. Their condemnation of the Karzai regime as subservient to the United States looked hypocritical in light of their own subservience to Pakistani interests. More crucially, it forced the Taliban to accede to a Pakistani strategy on how the insurgency should be run. For a movement that stressed its willingness to outwait its opponents for decades ("You have the watches, but we have the time!"), moving the southern insurgency into the open around Qandahar in 2006 by using conventional warfare was risky. It was similar to the ISI attempt in 1989 to organize the mujahideen for a conventional military assault on Jalalabad after the Soviets withdrew. In both cases the aim was to establish a rival provisional government within Afghanistan to challenge the regime in Kabul, leading some to wonder whether it was the ISI rather then Mullah Omar that drew up the battle plan. Also in both cases the assaults failed because neither the mujahideen nor the Taliban were equipped to take on a well-organized conventional force. After their 2006 defeat, the Taliban reverted to the more classic insurgent strategy of basing themselves where coalition forces were weakest, and returning to their older tactics of ambush and roadside bombings.

The greatest vulnerability for the Taliban, however, was that southern Afghanistan had never served as a successful base for insurgenices in the past. Successful resistance efforts against Kabul or foreign occupation had always had their epicenters in the Pashtun regions of eastern Afghanistan and the Tajik regions north of Kabul. Throughout Afghan history, Qandahar and the south had either come to an accommodation with the occupying power or been a secondary area of resistance. Indeed, the south had rarely served as a center for successful rebellions of any type because in geographic terms it offered little to sustain an insurgency. The terrain was flat with little ground cover for troop movement, its supply routes were vulnerable to attack, and there were no mountains to take refuge in. The region's population was also historically inclined to sit on the fence rather than take the lead in warfare. These people were unwilling to put their valuable farms at risk, fearing that any sustained warfare would destroy their vulnerable irrigation systems, without which the land would return to desert. Their leadership therefore saw politics rather than military prowess as the best long-term strategy.

Although the Taliban were able to replace the traditional leadership structure in southern Afghanistan during their rise to power in the late 1990s, it had returned when the Taliban were driven from power in 2001. Having lost out once to Mullah Omar and company, the traditional leadership had good reason not to accommodate the Taliban again if it thought the insurgents would be defeated. Southern areas therefore came under Taliban domination only in the absence of significant Kabul government or international forces to oppose it. And it was the failure of the Kabul government to provide economic benefits, security, and justice that made the Taliban look like an attractive alternative, rather than any sympathy for their ideology. This was a dangerous situation for an insurgent political movement because it meant that the groups they depended on could be convinced to defect based on self-interest. To the extent that this forced the Taliban to depend more on non-Afghan fighters, it undermined their status as an indigenous insurgency for which Afghans were willing to sacrifice.

Obama's War

As the new decade came to an end, Afghanistan was at a tipping point. After years of stasis under Bush, the new Obama administration swiftly moved Afghanistan to the top of the U.S. foreign policy agenda. It revised the strategy for dealing with the insurgency and became more openly critical of the Afghan government's performance. It also recognized that Pakistan was as much a part of the problem as a part of the solution. If the United States was keen to break new policy ground, however, Karzai was not. Determined to win reelection as Afghanistan's president, Karzai looked to the political past to maintain his power even at the cost of weakening the state structure. In this Karzai followed the path blazed by earlier Afghan rulers who had ridden to power on the backs of others and then excluded them from government in favor of a personal patrimonial clique. But this weak system of government was now threatened by the possibility that outsiders, the most serious of whom had served as Karzai's former cabinet ministers, might depose him through an electoral process that was under international scrutiny. Just as an astrologer might marvel at portents derived from a particularly unusual conjunction of the planets when plotting a horoscope, political analysts of Afghanistan began prognosticating on the special consequences of the unusually close proximity of the American and Afghan election cycles.

Elections and Illegitimacy

Despite new policies and a new commitment of troops that broke from the Bush era, the Obama administration inherited the dysfunctional Karzai as the head of the Afghan government. Karzai's erratic behavior made coordination with his government difficult, but he had no intention of leaving voluntarily. Unlike the British or Soviets who had ruthlessly replaced unpopular client leaders with more viable ones, the United States hesitated to take advantage of the opportune electoral timing to oust Karzai, lest it be accused of interfering in the country's internal affairs. This puzzled the Afghans. By having an army in the country the United States was already up to its eyeballs in Afghanistan's domestic affairs. But because bringing democracy to Afghanistan was one of the benchmarks of success that the U.S. government had set for itself, it would be up to the Afghan electorate to show Karzai the door. The Afghans, however, convinced that it was the United States that would choose their next president, saw no reason to risk opposing the existing regime until the United States made its own intentions clear by implicitly anointing another candidate or making it apparent that it would welcome alternative leadership.

In this gap of mutual incomprehensibility, Karzai saw an open path to reelection in spite of the high levels of domestic and international opposition to his government, which in most other countries would have doomed his prospects. In the absence of American opposition, the Afghans would presume Karzai remained the U.S. choice and blame it for the failings of his regime. The United States would resign itself to defending the principle of "people's choice" and blame the Afghans for failing to appreciate the responsibilities that came with a democracy.

The presidential election structure favored Karzai. He had prevented the formation of political parties, so that those who wished to oppose him had to run as individuals. Forty-one candidates qualified to appear on the ballot because the threshold was set so low, hopelessly dividing the opposition. In seeking allies to create an electoral majority, Karzai's reelection campaign recruited so many of Afghanistan's old warlords to his banner that one might have thought the election was being held in 2002 rather than 2009. To the particular outrage of UNAMA officials, who many believed had him on their list of possible war criminals, Karzai selected Marshal Fahim, the former Tajik United Front commander, to be his vice presidential candidate. The leaders of ethnic minorities were lured by promises of new provinces and control of government ministries. The Hazara leader Mohaqiq proudly announced that Karzai had promised him five ministries. Others were content with simple cash payments. Karzai also played on Pashtun fears that they could lose their primacy if he were turned out of office, pressuring other powerful Pashtun candidates to withdraw. His campaign leader in the south was Sher Muhammad Akhundzada, one of Afghanistan's most notorious drug lords. When a *New York Times* reporter questioned his appropriateness for such a position, Akhundzada responded, "They don't take Fahim out of elections? Dostum is not criminal? Mohaqiq is not criminal? Just me?"[21] Karzai appeared to revel at the dismay that this warlord reunion tour produced among his international backers, proving he was not their puppet. But for a regime that would not survive a week if left to the mercies of such allies without international support, it demonstrated a disturbing disconnect with the reality of his situation.

In the months preceding the election, Karazi was prejudged the inevitable first-round victor. Even U.S. officials who had strongly criticized Karzai in the first months of the Obama administration quieted their objections on the assumption that they would have to work with him in the coming years. Only as the election came closer did this aura of inevitability fade as his former foreign minister, Abdullah, unexpectedly surged in the polls. Although there was no doubt that Karzai would win a plurality of the votes in the first round, if it went to a second round his opponents would have a single figure to rally around. The challenge was all-the-more serious because if Karzai lost the election, despite all the advantages of incumbency, his U.S. backers would insist that he leave office.

Karzai was therefore determined to win a first-round majority victory at whatever cost. He committed massive (and obvious) electoral fraud to achieve that end. His fear of a second round of elections was rooted in the historic dynamics of Afghan power politics: since he was expected to win outright, the failure to do so would allow his rivals to paint him as a loser. In particular, it would send the message that the United States was not opposed to his replacement because otherwise it would have ensured his first-round victory. If that were the case, Karzai faced a possible stampede of his wavering self-interested allies to a new coalition led by Abdullah. Leaders and regimes in Afghanistan never declined gradually but fell almost instantaneously when their ability to maintain themselves in power became uncertain. What the international community saw as a first-round floor of support that Karzai could easily build on in a second round, Afghans took as a ceiling that could collapse at any moment. Avoiding that risk was worth the cost of delegitimizing the authority of his government because Karzai would still have the power to fend off rivals as long as international troops remained in the country. When enough votes were disqualified to force a runoff election, Karzai made sure that his handpicked Afghan Electoral Commission rejected all the changes proposed by Abdullah and the international community to prevent fraud from reoccurring. Abdullah then quit the race in disgust and Karzai declared himself the victor. While successful, Karzai's victory came at the cost of alienating his international backers while doing nothing to improve his reputation among Afghans. In this he bore an unfortunate resemblance to his Sadozai ancestor, Shah Shuja, whose miscalculations terminated that dynasty and fueled a violent uprising against his British backers.

The U.S. Policy Shift

Afghanistan had always been the "other war" under the Bush administration, starved of resources, attention, and troops in favor of Iraq. By mid-2009 that status was reversed. The number of casualties and war costs in Afghanistan exceeded those in Iraq for the first time. The first surge of seventeen thousand U.S. troops was designed to both provide greater security for the Afghan election in August 2009 and lay the foundation of a new counterinsurgency strategy. That strategy was confirmed in December, when after months of deliberation, President Obama announced the dispatch of another thirty thousand additional troops to Afghanistan, putting U.S. forces over the one hundred thousand mark in 2010.[22] The planned size of the Afghan army and police was also greatly increased. At the diplomatic level, the Obama administration tasked a high-powered diplomat, Richard Holbrook, to deal with what was now inelegantly called "AF-PAK." Critics noted that had this attention been paid to Afghanistan in 2002, when the Taliban were at their low point and the Afghans' enthusiasm was at a high point, there might have been no insurgency to confront. That being said, 2009 marked a serious change in the U.S. determination to deal with the problems of Afghanistan rather than let them fester.

In rethinking its Afghanistan strategy, the United States introduced a string of revised civilian and military policies designed to restore stability to Afghanistan. All were deemed necessary, but each had the potential of producing negative consequences if not handled carefully.

1. The deployment of an increasing number of U.S. and coalition troops to rural areas in the south and east was double-edged. Intended to improve security for the local population and put the insurgents on the defensive,

their very presence in the heart of rural Afghanistan was potentially destabilizing, particularly if they were seen as defenders of an unpopular Kabul
regime rather than the local population. A balance needed to be struck
between demonstrating a determination to invest in the long-term and the
ability to promise a rapid departure once the situation stabilized.

2. Eliminating debilitating corruption that undermined government
institutions and allowed large criminal drug syndicates to flourish was a
long-term necessity, but attacking the problem posed an immediate danger
if the spoils of corruption proved to be the only glue holding the existing
system together. Similarly, improving the efficiency of the Afghan government by appointing officials based on technical competence rather than
personal connections threatened the whole structure of patrimonial government that Karzai had so carefully nurtured.

3. Growing the army and police was deemed vital for fighting the insurgency and replacing foreign troops with Afghan ones. The target of 80,000
army troops was raised to 134,000 at a projected cost of $10 billion over
five years. Raising it to a proposed 240,000, as some favored, would be even
more expensive. Some plans also called for the police force to double from
80,000 to 160,000, although past goals in this area had always come up
short. The unintended consequence of such growth was an enormous gap
between the funding (and professional training) available to the security
forces and those supplied to their civilian counterparts. In the absence of
effective civilian government, it potentially laid the foundation for the
emergence of a military regime in Afghanistan—perhaps the only variety
of government that Afghanistan had not yet experienced.

4. U.S. approaches to fighting the Taliban favored empowering the
local population and dealing with their community leaders directly. This
was against the political interest of a centralized Kabul government that
sought to reduce the autonomy of local communities and marginalize their
leaders. On this score the United States could easily find itself pleasing no
one: local communities could object to U.S. support of Kabul-appointed
officials over whom they had no control; Kabul could complain that the
United States was undermining it by encouraging alternative models of
governance that bypassed the formal state structure.

5. Devoting an increased percentage of development resources to the
Pashtun areas that were at the center of the insurgency might be a political

necessity, but it promised to generate animosity in the other, more stable (and mostly non-Pashtun), parts of Afghanistan that saw themselves neglected. Proposals to create and arm local militias against the Taliban stirred fears elsewhere that the ground was being prepared for a new civil war in which their disarmed regions would be threatened.

6. The United States need to get Pakistan to end its support for the Taliban was stymied by a lack of the necessary leverage to make it happen. That such an agreement was still missing eight years after the United States entered Afghanistan highlighted the contradiction between Pakistan's official status as an ally of the United States and its barely covert assistance to an insurgency that would likely wither without it. Not even the rise of a Pakistani Taliban that directly challenged the national cohesion of the Pakistani state could convince successive governments there of the dangers inherent in supporting violent Islamist movements over which they had little control.

Neither the problems that the Americans confronted nor the policy approaches that they took were new. Both the British and Russians had confronted similar difficulties in Afghanistan, and had designed similar plans, the success of which varied considerably. The lesson that could be learned from their experiences was that all foreigners entered Afghanistan intoxicated by high expectations of easy victories and quick transformations of the country in their own image. All left Afghanistan more sober, far less idealistic, and content to let the Afghans handle their problems in their own way. The one thing they had all needed to ease their way out was the partnership of a strong Afghan leader who could maintain the country's stability with only "over the horizon" assistance and could ensure that their vital interests would not be threatened from Afghanistan. This Afghan leadership element was notably absent from the Obama strategy.

Growing domestic opposition to more troops in Afghanistan led many American politicians to demand a reduced rather than increased effort there. But attractive as that option was to a domestic audience, it hinged on the assurance that Afghanistan would not revert to its pre-9/11 status of a nation that served as a haven for Islamic extremists with international ambitions. In the absence of effective Afghan leadership, abandoning Afghanistan was highly risky. Any attack on the United States that originated from there after a drawdown would end the political life of the administration on whose watch it occurred. And once the United States left Afghanistan, it would have little capacity to intervene there later, no matter how serious the threat—a difficulty that had been manifest in the Clinton administration. Indeed, despite its difficulties, Afghanistan was the only place in the region that the United States had a direct presence that could prevent the reconsolidation of Islamic extremists, and serve as a base for responses to potential state collapse in the surrounding countries of central Asia and Pakistan. And the fear that nuclear-armed Pakistan might either disintegrate in the face of an Islamist insurgency or that its government could be seized by a radicalized military faction that supported the insurgency's cause gave a U.S. presence in Afghanistan even more importance. As had many foreign powers before it, the United States found its Afghan policy as much driven by events in south and central Asia as those within Afghanistan itself. As the second decade of the twenty-first century dawned, Afghanistan could expect to remain the focus of world attention for years to come.

CHAPTER SIX

Some Conclusions

Both Afghans and foreigners remain tied to visions of what they wish the country to be that obscures its present reality and possible futures. The long view of Afghanistan and its history present possibilities for resolving the country's current problems, but it also presents warnings about how even the best planned policies can fail. One aspect missing from most projections for the country's development are the surprising number of new conditions that may set Afghanistan on a different and more positive course.

THE PAST AS A GUIDE TO THE FUTURE IN AFGHANISTAN

Governance

The belief that Afghanistan and its people are inherently ungovernable has become an unfortunate conventional wisdom that drives policy decisions. It is based on Afghanistan's contentious relationship with its most marginal regions (and those least significant to the state), which had a long history of rejecting government control. In reality, the vast majority of the population and economically most productive regions historically accepted the legitimacy of state rule and rarely rebelled against it, if only because they accepted the classic Islamic political premise that disorder, sedition, and civil war was too high a price to pay to substitute one set of power-hungry rulers for another. While it is true that thirty years of war have deeply damaged the traditional structures of Afghan governance, the major problem of restoring stability has been the uncritical support for a centralized model of administration that is ill adapted to the country's need.

The most successful model of Afghan governance employed the Swiss cheese approach, in which regimes expected their writs to run completely only in the most populated and economically prosperous parts of the country. The peoples in the poorer high mountains, steppes, and deserts were left to fend for themselves as long as they did not challenge state authority. If they did, the state resorted to a range of weapons well short of direct rule to get them to cease. These included support of internal rivals, denial of access to vital urban markets, and one-off punitive campaigns designed to emphasize the cost of resistance. The goal was to intimidate a population and its leaders into acquiescence without changing the existing political structure. It was a strategy that required constant maintenance. A change in policy or local mismanagement could quickly turn cooperative groups into enemies, but none of these enemies were so beyond the pale that they might not be co-opted if the right opportunity presented itself. Rulers effectively controlled Afghanistan for many centuries with this model of government, and the fall of one regime and its replacement by another rarely resulted in chaos since the structure remained intact.

Based on Abdur Rahman's late nineteenth-century success in creating the country's first centralized state, successor Afghan governments developed a taste for American cheese models of governance that posited a single rule of law and administration. Those regimes that attempted to make theory a reality (Amanullah, the PDPA, and the Taliban) experienced state collapse because they provoked more opposition than they could handle. By contrast, the long-lived Musahiban rulers of Afghanistan maintained fifty years of peace and stability by proclaiming their right to rule everywhere in theory, but recognizing that enforcing such a vision was neither practicable nor desirable.

The post-2001 model of government in Afghanistan that attempted to restore a direct-rule model remains at odds with the realities of Afghanistan, especially rural Afghanistan, and the Kabul government lacks the military and administrative capacity to implement it. Ironically, it was the United States and Britain that rediscovered the virtues of the indirect approach while seeking to bring order to the Pashtun regions in the south and east. They quickly realized that local order could be more easily had if negotiated directly with local political leaders, enabling them to circumvent the dysfunctional national institutions. In this respect, the foreign forces became more traditionally Afghan in their willingness to strike deals, while the Kabul government became more dogmatically Western in its insistence on state dominance. A democratic government respecting the will of its own people would be more naturally compatible with the Swiss cheese approach, albeit one that replaces premodern forms of coercion with political accommodation. Kabul needs to recognize that the menu has changed by popular demand. Afghanistan is governable, but it requires a government adapted to its needs.

Modernization and Social Change

For almost a century, attempts to bring about social change in Afghanistan have been led by governments in Kabul determined to modernize the country. For an equal period of time, they have been resisted by the inhabitants in rural Afghanistan as well as conservative Islamic clerics who distrusted such changes and saw them as a threat to their traditional way of life. The most contentious policies concerned women's rights, secular education, the primacy of state law (including family law) over customary law, and reducing the autonomy of Islamic clerics. Although Afghanistan's initial attempts at reform in the 1920s under King Amanullah were far less radical than contemporaneous movements under Reza Shah in Iran, Ataturk in Turkey, or the Bolsheviks in central Asia, they provoked a stronger opposition. The Afghan government not only failed to achieve its goals, it incited rebellions that destroyed the state in 1929. For the next half century, government pressure to modernize was restricted to urban areas that were largely sympathetic to the policies. This changed when the PDPA took power in 1978 on a platform of radical social change. Only the intervention of the Soviet Union kept that regime from going the way of Amanullah's. With its fall in 1992, Afghanistan entered a period of reactionary government in which the values of the urban elite were replaced by those of rural religious ideologues, the most radical of whom were the Taliban. The U.S. invasion of 2001 ousted the Taliban, and the new government pressed ahead on the same project of social reforms first begun in the 1920s. Indeed, Afghanistan's international backers insisted that the country had a positive duty to implement them in order to comply with the many international treaties that various Afghan governments had signed over the years.

What the Kabul government's foreign allies did not appreciate was how contentious these policies still remained in Afghanistan. Economic issues aside, the Karzai government policy closely resembled the modernizing efforts of Amanullah and the PDPA. The new Afghan government thus took on a set of tasks that were difficult to achieve, thereby creating political opposition it could ill afford. This was particularly true when its opponents argued that such policies were foreign imports designed to destroy Afghan culture. Although this was certainly an exaggeration (Amanullah had first proposed them), foreign governments and international NGOs rarely attempted to address popular suspicions that these policies engendered. Because they worked almost exclusively with urban elites (who saw international support as the means to achieve a goal they had long sought), foreigners failed to realize just how shallow support for these policies was. Assuming their good intentions were self-evident, they never felt the need to persuade ordinary Afghans of their programs' value, let alone weigh the consequences of how changes designed to help individuals might alienate their communities.

Establishing security, creating a competent government, and facilitating economic development are immense tasks, but at least there was general agreement among Afghans that the country required them. This was not the case concerning the long-running conflicts over issues of social change. They have provoked armed conflict and led to state collapse more than once when not handled carefully. A look at the historical record demonstrates that peace and stability in Afghanistan have best been ensured by governments that pursued policies of social change in urban areas where they were welcome, and then let them spread to the countryside only after prejudices against them had waned. This strategy, though inelegant, strikes a balance between the minimalist approach in which Afghan governments had no concern for how people lived and a maximalist vision that demanded the state transform people's lives regardless of their own wishes. In such a process foreigners may supply the funds, but they cannot take the lead nor can they dictate the outcome.

Political Legitimacy

In premodern Afghanistan questions of rulership were relatively easy to resolve. Whoever gained power and could hold it was deemed legitimate as long as he could provide security and fend off rivals. Disputes rarely impacted the population as a whole nor did fights among rivals within the same ruling family constitute true civil wars. The Anglo-Afghan wars changed this dynamic because the foreign armies that invaded Afghanistan were only driven out after the population as a whole mobilized against them. Despite this popular participation in warfare, national leadership historically reverted to the established Durrani royal lineages after each state collapse. The pattern broke in 1978 when the PDPA took power and proclaimed an end to the dynasty that had ruled Afghanistan for 230 years. From that point onward the question of who had the right to rule and on what basis became more difficult to resolve. The PDPA assertion that it was a vanguard party leading a proletariat revolution was so alien to Afghanistan that its legitimacy was fatally compromised, particularly after the Soviet invasion. As the Soviets withdrew, Najibullah backtracked and grounded his legitimacy in the cloak of nationalism along with the premodern convention that those who held the reins of power were legitimate if they could provide security and governance. The mujahideen parties that replaced him in Kabul in 1992 could do neither. The Taliban grounded their right to rule in religion—proclaiming Mullah Omar the Commander of the Faithful—but their ability to restore order carried more weight. After the U.S. invasion, the Karzai government grounded its legitimacy in the loya jirgas held to approve it and later through elections. Despite this democratic veneer, however, the Karzai regime better resembled the royal Afghan governments that provided the model for the constitution of 2004, although it lacked their grounding in tradition.

Had Karzai been able to establish security and extend his government's control throughout the country, he would have met the basic premodern test of legitimacy. Holding elections did not compensate for his government's failure to meet this bedrock benchmark. But Karzai failed to meet another criterion particular to Afghanistan: that he be perceived as independent of foreign control. Rulers whose power rested on the protection of foreign troops were naturally suspect, and the weaker their governments, the greater the risk of rejection. Initially Karzai had been given considerable leeway in this regard, and his election as president in 2004 was a genuinely popular one. But as dissatisfaction grew in the coming years, that support melted away. His most able cabinet members quit or were fired during his first term, and Karzai himself became increasingly isolated in the palace. Fearing any possibility of rejection at the polls, he committed such blatant fraud to ensure his reelection that his victory proved truly pyrrhic. At the end of the process, he was a ruler who met neither Afghan nor international standards of legitimacy.

Afghan history portents an unhappy end for a such a ruler, whether at the hands of his foreign patrons or his own people. A tree whose roots are rotten may still stand, but it is only a matter of time before it crashes under its own weight or is blown over by a windstorm. Once again a new Afghan ruler will seek to establish his authority and legitimacy. The country's past suggests that to be successful, such a ruler will need to convince the Afghans that he will not be beholden to foreigners, even as he convinces these very same foreigners to fund his state and military. In the absence of such a figure, and the departure of foreign forces, Afghanistan will not survive as a unitary state. The most likely event in that case would be a sundering of the country along regional lines, since these have always been the true political bedrocks of the country.

The Persistence of Regions

The persistence of Afghanistan as a national state may be problematic, but not the regions that make it up. They have survived over the millennia, and have long outlived the states and empires that once claimed them. The same is true today. Herat in the west, Qandahar in the south, Mazar in the north, and Kabul in the east remain the leading cities that dominate their own large regions. For this reason, the U.S. military has used a regional template in preference to a provincial one for their organization (as did the Soviets before them). The civilian side has been less astute in recognizing that the ever-growing numbers of provinces are too small and too varied to facilitate coherent economic planning or practical administration. Nor should they be since they are the products of successive Kabul regimes seeking to increase the power of their centralized governments by diminishing their regional rivals through ever-greater division. Afghans themselves recognize this by their persistent use of older names that encompass these historic regions—Loya Qandahar for the south, Hazarajat for central Afghanistan, Turkistan for the north, or Qataghan for the lowlands of the northeast, to mention just a few.

A more stable Afghanistan therefore requires less reliance on a Kabul government and more emphasis on Afghanistan's key regions. This makes strong economic sense because projects integrated at the regional level have the capacity to reinforce one another. It also makes sense politically because each region has its own interests to defend and better capacity to unite its inhabitants. Ideally this could be done through a federal system of government, but this is not a necessity. Earlier rulers of Afghanistan who claimed supreme power for themselves recognized it was more efficient to allow de facto autonomy than impose centralized rule. Partnering with regional elites proved more successful than displacing them and created regimes that were less prone to collapse. Indeed, in such systems a displaced ruler often retreated to one of these regions to stage a comeback after losing power in the capital. While rewriting the Afghan constitution of 2004 might be the clearest way to proceed, a more moderate use of the existing institutions would suffice if a ruler retained centralized power of appointment but chose not to use it as recklessly as Karzai. The greatest Afghan rulers realized the importance of consultation and accountability in making appointments, giving both the officials and the people they administered a vested interest in each other's success.

Breaking with Precedent: Fundamental Changes to a Timeless Land

Afghanistan's past will remain a reliable guide to its future as long as its economy and social structure stay unchanged. And as one of the most underdeveloped countries in the world it often appears that nothing could alter either. Yet because Afghanistan was left undeveloped as a deliberate policy by earlier rulers, the assumption that it lacks the capacity to change may be incorrect. Afghanistan has rich mineral resources (iron, copper, and gemstones) in a world economy ever more eager to develop them. It could once again become the hub of a new transport network of overland trade that links landlocked Eurasia to the outside world. It could also become the transit route for the export of central Asian energy (oil, gas, and electricity) to the rapidly expanding economies of south Asia. In addition Afghanistan may have its own energy deposits, which could allow the country to become self-sufficient, or even an exporter of oil and gas. It has never fully utilized its rights to the water that flows through its territory in an arid region where such resources are ever more scarce and costly. Afghanistan could harness these for its own use or negotiate payments not to do so from its downstream neighbors, who now exploit them for free.[1]

The development of all these resources comes at a time when Afghanistan's population is changing. The conservative rural population that has always constituted a majority will be challenged by the growth of cities in which an ever-greater percentage of the population resides. This urban population is more open to change, and less bound by the old ties of qawm and region. The relative youth of the population will also challenge old norms and political practices, as younger Afghans attempt to create a world that better meets their needs.

Economic Developments and Their Consequences

A NEW OUTLET TO THE SEA

Afghanistan is landlocked and has always been dependent on Pakistan's port of Karachi for access to the sea. This has given Pakistan considerable leverage over Afghanistan—leverage that it has periodically utilized to pressure governments there. This situation changed in September 2008 when India completed construction of a 135-mile road that connected the Iranian container port of Chahbahar with Afghanistan's Nimroz Province. Part of a larger billion dollar reconstruction scheme within Afghanistan financed by India, it created a new transport corridor that ends Pakistan's monopoly on seaborne transit trade to Afghanistan. This not only allows

India to trade directly with Afghanistan, it makes Iran (via Afghanistan) the most efficient transit route into central Asia. For millennia the old silk route caravan trade made Afghanistan's cities rich, and their decline coincided with the atrophy of these overland routes. New motorized transport by rail and road promises to restore the importance of these old routes as investment in Afghanistan's infrastructure fills the missing gaps. As this happens, Afghanistan's strategic position will change from an isolated buffer state to a transit state—the stability of which will be of vital concern to all its neighbors.

The new link to the Persian Gulf may also change regional power dynamics. India now has the capacity to dispatch troops and supplies directly to Afghanistan via Iran if it chooses to do so. Should the United States decide to withdraw from Afghanistan, India may well be tempted to step in to preempt the possibility of a Taliban takeover. While this prospect appears unlikely now, that could change if Pakistan-based jihadists mount more attacks within India itself. Given its deteriorating relationship with Pakistan, the United States itself may eventually come to see the Indian option as a better long-term solution to its Afghan problem. Both the United States and India have given priority to eliminating the power of radical Islamists, and hence are more in sympathy with each other than either is with Pakistan. Such an alliance, if it were to occur, would mark the end of the cold war legacy that has undergirded U.S. support of Pakistan for more than a half century.

ENERGY CONDUITS

The Soviet Union invested heavily in the hydropower of mountainous central Asia. Its collapse left the successor states of Tajikistan and Kyrgyzstan with a valuable legacy, but one that was of little practical value because the dams produced electricity only in the summer when it was needed least locally. By contrast, the demand for summer electricity is enormous in south Asia, if it could be exported there. To meet this need, the Asian Development Bank has financed a $500 million project to build a thirteen-hundred-megawatt, high-transmission power line through Afghanistan and across the Khyber Pass to Peshawar, in Pakistan, to be completed by

2013. The realization of this "Central Asia/South Asia Regional Electricity Market" could result in the Punjab region receiving as much as 25 percent of its summer electricity supply from lines that transit Afghanistan. The long-mooted plans for a $2 billion Turkmenistan-Afghanistan-Pakistan-India gas pipeline project have an even greater capacity to change regional trade patterns. Its thousand-mile pipeline would supply ninety million cubic meters of natural gas to south Asia daily from the gas fields in Turkmenistan. All of these projects would generate transit fees for Afghanistan as well as access to the energy itself. More important, they would change the economy of Afghanistan itself, improving the prospects for its own people and (for the first time) integrating its economy with that of the region as a whole.

MINERALS

Afghanistan has long been known to have large mineral deposits, but the government never permitted their development. This changed in May 2008 when China signed a $3 billion mining agreement with Afghanistan that authorized a thirty-year lease to the country's largest untapped copper deposit, which has an estimated value of $88 billion. China also agreed to construct a four-hundred-megawatt power plant for the project that would electrify much of Kabul as well. To get the ore out of Afghanistan, China proposed financing and building the country's first railroad, which would run north through the Hindu Kush Mountains to its western province of Xinjiang. Since Afghanistan's total gross domestic product in 2007 was an estimated $7.5 billion, the size of this investment dwarfed any previously proposed. If this project is completed, China would have the largest direct economic stake in Afghanistan along with the infrastructure to develop Afghanistan's other extensive iron, aluminum, and marble deposits. In addition to making the country one of the world's major mineral exporters, it would begin a process of industrialization in Afghanistan on a scale previously unknown, with opportunities and problems to match. China's investment in Afghanistan would also have a strong indirect effect on its long-standing ally, Pakistan, since China would then have its investments put at risk by insurgents based in Pakistan.

A Changing Society

THE YOUNG AND THE RESTLESS

For the majority of Afghanistan's population—which was born after the Soviets left the country—the country's politics appear stuck in a time warp. Afghanistan's current leaders all came of age in the Soviet war period. The issues they fight over are increasingly irrelevant to a young population with expectations of better economic conditions, broader educational opportunities, and a growing desire for political participation. Within the government itself these younger people make up the bulk of the technocrats with skills needed to make the country work, yet they find themselves taking orders from uneducated political appointees who treat their offices as vehicles for plunder. In the private sector, they find few opportunities for employment and entrepreneurship in an economy that is not growing fast enough. Similar conditions in the 1970s in Kabul alone led to the rise of the PDPA and the end of the Musahiban dynasty. Today such conditions can be found in all major cities throughout the country. But whether this younger generation comes to power as the old generation dies off or they shove them aside, the twenty-first century will be theirs. This bodes poorly for both the Karzai government and the Taliban, since the former has no vision for the future and the latter is fixated on a past that never existed.

URBAN POPULATIONS

For many centuries, Afghanistan's cities have been a small tail attached to a big rural dog in terms of population distribution. This has not been the case in most other underdeveloped countries, where for generations people have flocked to the cities in huge numbers. Lacking good statistics it is hard to know what the distribution of population is in Afghanistan today, but Kabul has perhaps three to four million inhabitants. Provincial cities like Mazar, Qandahar, and Herat that hovered around one hundred thousand each in the 1970s all now have populations of over 300,000.[2] As ibn Khaldun noted long ago, cities are money economy crucibles that break down qawm and regional solidarity groups by empowering individuals. They are doing the same thing in Afghanistan today. The political and social movements that they generate will become dominant as the century progresses. But just what values they will espouse is far from clear. They will not be bound by the strictures of rural conservatism, but their numbers are too vast to be contained by the single visions that characterized the tiny modernizing elite of the 1920s and 1970s. The process of urbanization in Afghanistan and its consequences remains unexplored today—a lacuna that future historians may well find strikingly shortsighted in retrospect.

THE FUTURE

I must study politics and war that my sons may have liberty to study mathematics and philosophy. My sons ought to study mathematics and philosophy, geography, natural history, naval architecture, navigation, commerce and agriculture in order to give their children a right to study painting, poetry, music, architecture, statuary, tapestry, and porcelain.

—JOHN ADAMS, 1780

Afghanistan sits in a dangerous neighborhood and its people are justly proud of their historical ability to maintain their autonomy. That most of this book has focused on politics and war reflects that history. Living in a land whose crossroads status has been as much a curse as a blessing, Afghans have cultivated a puffer fish strategy to repel outsiders. Small puffer fish inflate their highly elastic stomachs with huge quantities of water and air when confronted by a predator, which turns them into a virtually inedible ball many times their normal size. Should their display fail to deter, the puffer fish liver contains a foul-tasting paralytic poison that makes eating one a rarely repeated choice. Afghanistan uses the hyperbole of history (unconquerable and a graveyard of empires) to exaggerate its strengths in order to deter invaders. It has relied on its indigestibility to get them to leave. But like the puffer fish, this is a tactic employed by the weak and vulnerable, not the strong and secure. It comes with a high price tag too, since when deterrence failed, the ensuing conflicts, particularly over the past thirty years, devastated both the country and its people.

To change the status quo, there needs to be an end to violence within Afghanistan and threats to the country from its neighbors. Like Adams, Afghans today see the need for security as the basis to build a better economy, a more stable society, and a brighter future for their children. War holds few attractions for people who have experienced so much of it firsthand. During those centuries when Afghanistan was secure from outside threats, it was far better known for its cultural contributions. The prophet Zoroaster came from ancient Bactria and the medieval Persian poet Jalaluddin Rumi was born in Balkh, both in northern Afghanistan. Herat in western Afghanistan was internationally renowned for its poetry, Persian miniature painting, and architecture during the fifteenth-century Timurid period. In eastern Afghanistan, the second-century Kushans sponsored sculptors in Gandhara who created the first Buddhist statues, fusing classical Greek styles with Eastern iconography. The huge Buddhist monastery complex in Bamiyan (and its famous standing Buddhas) in central Afghanistan attracted pilgrims and scholars from all over central and south Asia during the sixth and seventh centuries. In the Islamic period, Afghanistan was (and remains) a stronghold of Sufi orders. The Chisti Order was founded in Herat in the tenth century, and the many adherents of the Naqshbandi Order (founded in neighboring Bukhara a few centuries later) made Afghanistan their home.

Wars and fighting are of course to be found in these periods as well, but they lie more at the margins of history than at its center. The Mongol conquests of Chinggis Khan are condemned, not celebrated, in Afghanistan because this most skilled of warriors left only death and destruction in his wake. By contrast his distant descendant, Babur (the founder of the Mughal dynasty), has found much more favor as a conqueror who combined his skills on the battlefield with a taste for poetry, a love of Kabul, and autobiographical insight. What Afghanistan sorely lacks today are leaders that have the talent to move the country from war to peace and lay the foundation for a stable future.

In 1973, an Afghan friend heard on the radio that the *New York Times* had sarcastically noted in an editorial that Afghanistan "leaped into the sixteenth century" when Daud proclaimed a republic after overthrowing

King Zahir Shah. After telling me this he quipped, "We may have acted hastily—the fifteenth century was pretty good around here!"[3] But pride in the past is no bar to change in the future. Perhaps the best recent example of this was the Pashtun leader, Khan Abdul Ghaffar Khan, in the NWFP. Inspired by Mohandas Gandhi, he founded the nonviolent Khudai Khitmatgar ("Servants of God"). After taking an oath to foreswear violence, retaliation, and revenge, its eighty thousand members divided into trained regiments, and devoted themselves to village improvement, education, and reform. They also led the resistance to British rule in the region in which hundreds of their members lost their lives in nonviolent protests in the 1930s.[4] When the British left India, Ghaffar Khan remained a gadfly. He was jailed by the Pakistani government in the 1960s when he protested against military dictators there. That such a nonviolent movement could emerge and thrive in a culture that had raised revenge to a holy principle should caution anyone against believing that people or cultures are forever prisoners of the past. It also stands as a challenge to the Afghans themselves to take the lead in breaking the cycle of violence that has generated so much suffering for so little benefit for far too long.

NOTES

Chapter 1. People and Places

1. Braudel, 1972.
2. Tambiah 1990, 742.
3. Barth 1969.
4. Keyes 1976; Geertz 1963.
5. Canfield 1973.
6. Dupree 1980, 57–65.
7. Caroe 1958.
8. Despite their importance, there has never been a published ethnography on any of the many Tajik communities in Afghanistan.
9. Monsutti 2005; Mousavi 1997; Poladi 1989.
10. Nabi 1984.
11. Shalinsky 1994.
12. Napier 1876.
13. Janata 1975.
14. Edelberg and Jones 1979.
15. Wutt 1981.
16. Barfield 1981.
17. Shahrani 1979; Olufsen 1904.
18. Birthe 1996; Olesen 1994; Rao 1982.
19. Shahrani 1979.
20. Tylor 1871, 1.
21. Bourdieu 1977, 78.
22. Chayanov 1966.
23. Szabo and Barfield 1991.
24. Ferdinand 2006.
25. Edwards 1996, 237.
26. Barfield 2005.
27. Monsutti 2005.
28. Humlum 1959, 117.

29. Murra 1985.

30. Humlum 1959, 117.

31. Canfield 1991.

32. Caroe 1958, 26.

33. Subtelny 1994, 48.

34. Khaldun 1969.

35. Ibid., 125, 155.

36. Smith [1776] 1843, 6.

37. Khaldun 1969, 122.

38. For an excellent study of such an institution in Afghanistan, see McChesney 1991.

39. Canfield 1973.

40. Khaldun 1969, 107–8.

CHAPTER 2. CONQUERING AND RULING PREMODERN AFGHANISTAN

1. Herodotus 1987, 330–31.

2. Glatzer 2001.

3. Humlum 1959, 166, 203–4.

4. Hume 1752.

5. Lampton 1981.

6. Kepel 2004.

7. Hobbes [1651] 2008.

8. Barthold 1968, 291.

9. Ibid., 377.

10. Babur 2002.

11. Crone 1980.

12. See Glubb 1973.

13. Sa'di [1888] 1964, 88.

14. Barfield 1989.

15. Ahmed 1980, 141–42.

16. Khaldun 1969, 120–21.

17. Barfield 1989.

18. Lindholm 1986.

19. Khaldun 1969.

20. Ibid., 105–6, 136–38.

21. Compare to Lee 1996.

22. Bosworth 1968, 20–21.

23. Barfield 1989.

24. Sa'di [1888] 1964, 18.

25. Canfield 1991.

26. Fletcher 1979.

27. Manz 1999, 14–15.

28. Caroe 1958, 11–24, 42.

29. Bosworth 1977; Caroe 1958, 131–33.

30. Pandey 1956.

31. Caroe 1958, 231–36.

32. Lockhart 1958, 82–95; Floor 1998.

33. Lockhart 1938.

34. Singh 1959.

35. Ibid., 361–63.

36. Ibid., 342.

37. Elphinstone 1815, 339–440.

38. Ibid., 514.

39. Ibid., 514.

40. Ibid., 400–401.

41. Ibid., 173.

42. Ibid., 173.

43. Ibid., 559.

44. Ibid., 558, 560.

45. For an excellent chart of the complex machinations of all the rival claimants to the throne and the territories they occupied at this time, see Dupree 1980, 344–61.

46. Noelle 1997, 7–8.

CHAPTER 3. ANGLO-AFGHAN WARS AND STATE
BUILDING IN AFGHANISTAN

1. Noelle 1997, 12.

2. Ibid., 38.

3. Ibid., 267–75.

4. Ibid., 275; Harlan 1939, 127.

5. Harlan 1842, 117–72.

6. Lee 1996, 181–82. For the surrender of Dost Muhammad, see ibid., 178–84.

7. Kaye 1857, 2:98; Dupree 1980, 382.

8. Yapp 1964, 339.

9. Ibid., 341.

10. Ibid., 342.

11. Ibid., 339.
12. Ibid., 341.
13. Ibid., 333–81; Hanifi 2001, 58.
14. Yapp 1964, 235.
15. Ibid., 347–60.
16. For a good comparison of these views, see Noelle 1997, 53–55.
17. Yapp 1964, 380.
18. Ibid., 355–60.
19. Ibid., 360–62.
20. Kaye 1857, 453–55; Yapp 1964, 361–62.
21. Yapp 1964, 364–65.
22. Ibid., 381.
23. Greaves 1992.
24. Hanifi 2001, 261; Noelle 1997, 250.
25. Kakar 2006, 161.
26. Lee 1996, 259.
27. Greeves 1992.
28. Compare to Matthee 1996, 389–416.
29. Kipling 1890, 212. A *jezail* was a locally produced Afghan musket.
30. Noelle 1997, 252.
31. Ibid.
32. Kakar 2006, 9; see also Noelle 1997, 387–88.
33. Noelle 1997, 11–13.
34. Kakar 2006, 17–18.
35. Kadir 194?, 134.
36. Kakar 2006, 22.
37. Kadir 194?, 129–30.
38. Curzon 1889, 292, 313–82; Becker 1968, 95–98.
39. Kakar 2006, 26–27.
40. For a full text of the 1879 Gandamak treaty, see Kakar 2006, 234–36.
41. Kakar 2006, 33–41; Gillard 1977, 139–42.
42. MacGregor 1985, 111.
43. Wheeler 1895, 79.
44. Kakar 2006, 44.
45. Tanner 2002, 215–16.
46. Kakar 2006, 61.
47. Dupree 1980, xix.
48. The key sources for this period include contempory British accounts such as Wheeler 1895, and the amir's own autobiography, Rahman 1900, only part of

which he wrote himself. Important scholarly studies on his reign include Kakar 1971, 1979.

49. Kakar 2006, 90.

50. Ibid., 95.

51. Kakar 1971, 139–57.

52. Ibid, 159–210.

53. Kakar 1979, 90–91.

54. Hanifi 2001.

55. Kakar 1979, 90.

56. Kakar 1971, 168.

57. Dupree 1980, 419; Tapper 1983; Kakar 1979.

58. Kakar 1979, 228.

59. Olesen 1995, 89–93.

60. *The Words of the Amir of the Land toward the Encouragement of Jihad* (1886), *Ghaza* (1887), and *The Calendar of Religion* (1889); Kakar 1979, 176–77.

61. Ibid., 178–79.

62. Kakar 2006, 227.

63. Odum 1998, 19–22.

CHAPTER 4. AFGHANISTAN IN THE TWENTIETH CENTURY

1. Rubin 1995, 90, 92.

2. Ibid., 81–84.

3. Kakar 2006, 226–27.

4. For full texts of the covenants, see ibid., 238–40.

5. Ibid., 226.

6. Nawid 1999, 44–46.

7. Ibid., 32–37.

8. Gregorian 1969, 222–23.

9. Sykes 1940, 2:265.

10. Nawid 1999, 42.

11. Nawid 1999, 52.

12. Ewans 2005, 89–97.

13. Kipling 1901, 368. The original coinage is often attributed to Arthur Conolly, a British political agent killed by the amir of Bukhara in 1842.

14. Nawid 1999, 81. For a complete list, see Poullada 1973, 70–79.

15. Poullada 1973, 131–36; Nawid 1999, 82–84.

16. Nawid 1999, 85–86; Poullada 1973, 111–18.

17. Poullada 1973, 92–96.
18. Nawid 1999, 113–22 (quote on 114).
19. Ibid., 124–27.
20. Stewart 1973.
21. Nawid 1999, 140.
22. Gregorian 1969, 259.
23. Nawid 1999, 138.
24. Gregorian 1969, 270–71; Fry 1974, 155–56.
25. Wild 1932, 69.
26. For eyewitness accounts, see McChesney 1999; Habibullah II 1938.
27. Nawid 1999, 182–85; Gregorian 1969, 280–87.
28. Gregorian 1969, 287, 290.
29. Ibid., 289.
30. Roberts 2003, 51–60.
31. Nawid 1999, 185.
32. Gregorian 1969, 356.
33. Ibid., 357.
34. Dupree 1980, 532–33.
35. Gregorian 1969, 362–63.
36. Akhramovich 1966, 11; Gregorian 1969, 361–70.
37. Fry 1974, 155, 183–86.
38. Ibid., 158–60.
39. Gregorian 1969, 378–89.
40. Ibid., 388–89.
41. Rubin 1995, 60–72.
42. Ibid., 93–98.
43. Ibid., 82–89.
44. Arnold 1983, 48; Rubin 1995, 102.
45. Pedersen 1994, 138–45.
46. Barfield 1984.
47. Dupree 1980, 70; Rubin 1995, 184.
48. Giustozzi 2000, 3–4.
49. Charpentier 1979.
50. Giustozzi 2000, 17, 67–68.
51. Rubin 1995, 115–20.
52. Barfield 1984.
53. Arnold 1983, 117–18.
54. Adamec 2003, 409–10.
55. Charles Dunbar, U.S. chargé d'affaires, personal communication with author, 2006.

56. Roy 1990, 106; Rubin 1995, 187.

57. Coll 2004, 21–188.

58. Rubin 1995, 196–225.

59. Arnold 1983, 99–107.

60. Isby 1989; Amstutz 1986, 127–54.

61. Rubin 1995, 109.

62. Nojumi 2002, 78–82.

63. Coll 2004, 194–96.

64. Giustozzi 2000, 189–90.

65. Rubin 1995, 151–52.

66. Giustozzi 2000, 190.

67. Ibid., 77, 142, 210.

68. Nojumi 2002, 78–82.

69. Ibid., 101–9.

70. On the PDPA, see Giustozzi 2000. On the mujahideen, see Coll 2004.

71. Nojumi 2002, 108–13.

72. Barfield 1996.

73. Nojumi 2002, 114–15.

74. Rubin 1995, 265–66.

75. Nojumi 2002, 115.

76. Marsden 2002, 57–63.

77. Rashid 2000, 17–40.

78. Nojumi 2002, 117–24.

79. Ibid., 134–36.

80. Rashid 2000, 41–66.

81. Nojumi 2002, 136–42.

82. Barfield 2001.

83. Khaldun 1969, 20.

84. Rashid 2000; Goodson 2001.

85. Marsden 2002, 102–13.

86. Rasanayagam 2003, 191–210.

87. Carlyle 1846, 143.

88. Calvert 2008, 223–25.

89. BBC monitoring central Asia unit, September 19, 2001, Afghan Taleban leader's address to Ulema, Afghan Islamic Press news agency, Peshawar, in Pashto; BBC monitoring south Asia—political, September 20, 2001, Afghan: Taleban Foreign Ministry official on future of bin Ladin, Al-Jazeera TV, Doha, in Arabic.

90. For a good overview of the military actions, see Jones 2008, 2009, 86–108.

CHAPTER 5. AFGHANISTAN ENTERS THE TWENTY-FIRST CENTURY

1. Lindholm 1980.
2. Mills 2007, 109–10.
3. Rashid 2008, 87–88.
4. Nojumi 2002.
5. Hobsbawm and Ranger 1983.
6. Constitution of Afghanistan [1382] 2003–4.
7. Reynolds 2006.
8. Wilder 2005.
9. Giustozzi and Orsini 2009.
10. Rashid 2008, 96.
11. Chayes 2006 for a bottom-up perspective.
12. Chandrasekaran 2009.
13. Gall 2008.
14. Ghani and Lockhart 2008.
15. UN Office on Drugs and Crime 2008.
16. Stewart 2004, 248.
17. Rohde and Sanger 2007; Neumann 2009, 39–50.
18. Jones 2008, 7–8.
19. Crews 2009; Nojumi, Mazurana, and Stites 2009.
20. Rashid 2008, 240–64.
21. Rubin 2009.
22. Obama 2009.

CHAPTER 6. SOME CONCLUSIONS

1. Barfield and Hawthorne 2009.
2. For 2006 population estimates, see http://www.citypopulation.de/Afghanistan
.html (accessed December 24, 2009).
3. Upheaval in Kabul, *New York Times*, 20 July 1970, 30.
4. Banerjee 2000.

REFERENCES

Adamec, Ludwig. 2003. *Historical dictionary of Afghanistan*. 3rd ed. Lanham, MD: Scarecrow Press.

Ahmed, Akbar. 1980. *Pukhtun economy and society*. London: Kegan Paul.

Akhramovich, Roman T. 1966. *Outline history of Afghanistan after the Second World War*. Moscow: Nauka.

Amstutz, J. Bruce. 1986. *Afghanistan*. Washington, DC: National Defense University.

Arnold, Anthony. 1983. *Afghanistan's two-party communism: Parcham and Khalq*. Stanford, CA: Hoover Institution Press.

Babur. 2002. *The Baburnama: Memoirs of Babur, prince and emperor*. Trans. Wheeler M. Thackston. New York: Modern Library.

Banerjee, Mukulika. 2000. *The Pathan unarmed: Opposition and memory in the North West Frontier*. Santa Fe: School of American Research Press.

Barfield, Thomas. 1981. *Central Asian Arabs of Afghanistan*. Austin: University of Texas Press.

——. 1984. Weak links on a rusty chain. In *Revolutions and rebellions in Afghanistan*, ed. Robert Canfield and Nazif Shahrani, 139–69. Berkeley, CA: Institute of International Studies.

——. 1989. *Perilous frontier: Nomadic empires and China, 221 BC to AD 1757*. Oxford: Blackwell.

——. 1996. The Afghan morass. *Current History*, 38–43.

——. 2001. Idol threats. *Religion in the News* 4 (2): 4–7.

——. 2005. An Islamic state is a state run by good Muslims: Religion as a way of life and not an ideology in Afghanistan. In *Remaking Muslim politics: Pluralism, contestation, democratization*, ed. Robert Hefner, 213–39. Princeton, NJ: Princeton University Press.

Barfield, Thomas, and Amy Hawthorne. 2009. *Afghanistan's other neighbors: Iran, Central Asia, and China*. Boston: American Institute for Afghanistan Studies.

Barth, Fredrik. 1969. Introd. to *Ethnic groups and boundaries*, ed. Fredrik Barth. Boston: Little, Brown.

Barthold, Vasili. V. 1968. *Turkistan down to the Mongol invasion*. London: Gibb Memorial Series.

Becker, Seymour. 1968. *Russian protectorates in central Asia*. Cambridge, MA: Harvard University Press.

Birthe, Frederiksen. 1996. *Caravans and trade in Afghanistan: The changing life of the nomadic Hazarbuz*. London: Thames and Hudson.

Bosworth, Clifford E. 1968. *The political and dynastic history of the Iranian world (AD. 1000–1217)*. Vol. 5, *The Cambridge history of Iran: The Saljuq and Mongol period*, ed. John A. Boyle, 1–202. Cambridge: Cambridge University Press.

———. 1977. *The later Ghaznavids: Splendour and decay: The dynasty in Afghanistan and northern India, 1040–1186*. New York: Columbia University Press.

Bourdieu, Pierre. 1977. *Outline of a theory of practice*. Cambridge: Cambridge University Press.

Braudel, Fernand. 1958. Histoire et science sociale: La *longue durée*. Annales. Histoire, Sciences Sociales 13 (4): 725–53. (English translation, On history [Chicago: University of Chicago Press, 1980], 25–54.)

———. 1972. *The Mediterranean and the Mediterranean world in the age of Philip II*. New York: Harper and Row.

Calvert, John. 2008. *Islamism: A documentary and reference guide*. Westport, CT: Greenwood.

Canfield, Robert. 1973. *Faction and conversion in a plural society*. Ann Arbor: University of Michigan Press.

———, ed. 1991. *Turko-Persia in historical perspective*. Cambridge: Cambridge University Press.

Carlyle, Thomas. 1846. *Oliver Cromwell's letters and speeches*. New York: William H. Colyer.

Caroe, Olaf. 1958. *The Pathans, 550 B.C.–A.D. 1957*. New York: St. Martin's Press.

Chandrasekaran, Rajiv. 2009. Administration is keeping ally at arm's length. *Washington Post*, May 6, A1.

Charpentier, Carl-Johan. 1979. One year after the Saur Revolution. *Afghanistan Journal*. 6 (4): 117–20.

Chayanov, Alexander V. 1966. *A. V. Chayanov on the theory of peasant economy*. Ed. Daniel Thorner, Basile Kerblay, and R.E.F. Smith. Homewood, IL: Irwin.

Chayes, Sarah. 2006. *The punishment of virtue: Inside Afghanistan after the Taliban*. New York: Penguin Press.

Coll, Steve. 2004. *Ghost wars: The secret history of the CIA, Afghanistan, and bin Laden, from the Soviet invasion to September 10, 2001*. New York: Penguin Press.

Constitution of Afghanistan. [1382] 2003–4. Available at http://unpan1.un.org/intradoc/groups/public/documents/APCITY/UNPAN015879.pdf (accessed December 20, 2009).

Crews, Robert, ed. 2009. *The Taliban and the crises of Afghanistan*. Cambridge, MA: Harvard University Press.

Crone, Patricia. 1980. *Slaves on horses: The evolution of the Islamic polity*. Cambridge: Cambridge University Press.

Curzon, George. 1889. *Russia in central Asia*. London: Longsman.

Dupree, Louis. 1980. *Afghanistan*. 2nd ed. Princeton, NJ: Princeton University Press.

Edelberg, Lennart, and Schuyler Jones. 1979. *Nuristan*. Graz: Akademische. Druck- und Verlagsanstalt.

Edwards, David B. 1996. *Heroes of the age: Moral fault lines on the Afghan frontier*. Berkeley: University of California Press.

Elphinstone, Mountstuart. 1815. *An account of the kingdom of Caubul*. London: Longman.

Ewans, Martin. 2005. *Conflict in Afghanistan: Studies in asymmetric warfare*. London: Routledge.

Ferdinand, Klaus. 2006. *Afghan nomads: Caravans, conflicts, and trade in Afghanistan and British India, 1800–1980*. Copenhagen: Rhodos.

Fletcher, Joseph. 1979–80. Turco-Mongolian monarchic traditions in the Ottoman Empire. *Harvard Ukrainian Studies* 34:236–51.

Floor, Willem. 1998. *The Afghan occupation of Safavid Persia, 1721–1729*. Paris: Association pour l'avancement des études iraniennes.

Fry, Maxwell J. 1974. *The Afghan economy: Money, finance, and the critical constraints to economic development*. Leiden: Brill.

Gall, Carlotta. 2008. Afghans lack $10 billion in aid, report says. *New York Times*, March 26, A10.

Geertz, Clifford. 1963. The integrative revolution: Primordial sentiments and civil politics in the new states. In *Old societies and new states*, ed. Clifford Geertz, 105–57. New York: Free Press.

Ghani, Ashraf, and Clare Lockhart. 2008. *Fixing failed states*. Oxford: Oxford University Press.

Gillard, David. 1977. *The struggle for Asia, 1828–1914: A study in British and Russian imperialism*. London: Methuen.

Giustozzi, Antonio. 2000. *War, politics, and society in Afghanistan*. Washington, DC: Georgetown University Press.

Giustozzi, Antonio, and Dominique Orsini. 2009. Centre-periphery relations in Afghanistan: Badakhshan between patrimonialism and institution-building. *Central Asian Survey*, 1–16.

Glatzer, Bernt. 2001. War and boundaries in Afghanistan: Significance and relativity of local and social boundaries. *Weld des Islams* 41 (30): 379–99.

Glubb, John. 1973. *Soldiers of fortune: The story of the Mamlukes*. London: Hodder and Stoughton.

Goodson, Larry. 2001. *Afghanistan's endless war: State failure, regional politics, and the rise of the Taliban*. Seattle: University of Washington Press.

Gregorian, Vartan. 1969. *The emergence of modern Afghanistan: Politics of reform and modernization, 1880–1946*. Stanford, CA: Stanford University Press.

Greaves, Rose L. 1992. Themes in British policy towards Afghanistan in its relation to Indian frontier defence, 1798–1947. *Asian Affairs* 24 (1): 30–46.

Habibullah II. 1938. *From brigand to king; autobiography*. London: Low, Marston.

Hanifi, Shah Mahmoud. 2001. Inter-regional Trade and Colonial State Formation in Nineteenth Century Afghanistan. Ann Arbor, MI: University Microfilms.

Harlan, Josiah. 1842. *A memoir of India and Afghanistan*. Philadelphia: Dobson.

———. 1939. *Central Asia; personal narrative of General Josiah Harlan*. Ed. Frank E. Ross. London: Luzac.

Herodotus. 1987. *The history*. Trans. David Grene. Chicago: University of Chicago Press.

Hobbes, Thomas. [1651] 2008. *The leviathan*. Ed. Michael Oakeshott. New York: Touchstone.

Hobsbawm, Eric, and Terence Ranger, eds. 1983. *The invention of tradition*. Cambridge: Cambridge University Press.

Hume, David. [1752] 1825. Of the original contract. In *Essays and treatises on several subjects*, 444–64. Edinburgh: James Walker.

Humlum, Johannes. 1959. *La géographie de l'Afghanistan; étude d'un pays aride*. Copenhagen: Gyldendal.

Isby, David. 1989. *War in a distant country, Afghanistan: Invasion and resistance*. London: Arms and Armour.

Janata, Alfred. 1971. On the origins of the Firuzkuhis of western Afghanistan. *Archiv für Völkerkunde* 25:57–85.

Jones, Seth. 2008. The rise of Afghanistan's insurgency. *International Security* 32 (4): 7–40.

———. 2009. *In the graveyard of empires: America's war in Afghanistan*. New York: W. W. Norton.

Kadir, Muhammad Abdul. 194? *Royals and royal mendicant: A tragedy of the Afghan history, 1791–1949*. Lahore: Lion Press.

Kakar, Hasan. 1971. *Afghanistan: A study in internal political developments, 1880–1896*. Kabul.

———. 1979. *Government and society in Afghanistan*. Austin: University of Texas Press.

———. 2006. *A political and diplomatic history of Afghanistan, 1863–1901*. Leiden: Brill.

Kaye, John William. 1857. *History of the war in Afghanistan*. 3 vols. London: Bentley.

Kepel, Giles. 2004. *Fitna: Guerre au coeur de l'Islam*. Paris: Gallimard.

Keyes, Charles F. 1976. Towards a new formulation of the concept of ethnic group. *Ethnicity* 3:202–13.

Khaldun, Muhammad ibn. 1969. *The Muqaddimah: An introduction to history*. Ed. N. J. Dawood. Trans. Franz Rosenthal. Princeton, NJ: Princeton University Press.

Kipling, Rudyard. 1890. *Departmental ditties, barrack-room ballads, and other verses*. New York: United States Book Company.

———. 1901. *Kim*. New York: Scribner.

Lambton, Anne. 1981. *State and government in medieval Islam: An introduction to the study of Islamic political theory*. Oxford: Oxford University Press.

Lee, Jonathan. 1996. *The "ancient supremacy": Bukhara, Afghanistan, and the battle for Balkh, 1731–1901*. Leiden: Brill.

Lindholm, Charles. 1980. *Generosity and jealousy*. New York: Columbia University Press.

———. 1986. Kinship structure and political authority: The Middle East and central Asia. *Comparative Studies in Society and History* 28:334–55.

Lockhart, Laurence. 1938. *Nadir Shah*. London: Luzac.

———. 1958. *The fall of the Ṣafavī dynasty and the Afghan occupation of Persia*. Cambridge: Cambridge University Press.

MacGregor, Charles. 1985. *War in Afghanistan, 1879–80*. Ed. William Trousdale. Detroit: Wayne State University Press.

Manz, Beatrice Forbes. 1999. *The rise and rule of Tamerlane*. Cambridge: Cambridge University Press.

Marsden, Peter. 2002. *The Taliban: War and religion in Afghanistan*. New York: Zed Books.

Matthee, Rudi. 1996. Unwalled cities and restless nomads: Firearms and artillery in Safavid Iran. In *Safavid Persia: The history and politics of an Islamic society*, ed. Charles Melville, 389–416. London: I. B. Tauris.

McChesney, Robert. 1991. *Waqf in central Asia: Four hundred years in the history of a Muslim shrine, 1480–1889*. Princeton, NJ: Princeton University Press.

———. 1999. *Kabul under siege: Fayz Muhammad's account of the 1929 uprising*. Princeton, NJ: Markus Wiener Publishers.

Mills, Nick. 2007. *Karzai: The failing American intervention and the struggle for Afghanistan*. Hoboken, NJ: John Wiley.

Monsutti, Alessandro. 2005. *War and migration: Social networks and economic strategies of the Hazaras of Afghanistan.* New York: Routledge.

Mousavi, Sayed Askar. 1997. *The Hazaras of Afghanistan: An historical, cultural, economic, and political study.* New York: St. Martin's Press.

Murra, John. 1985. The limits and limitations of the "vertical archipelago" in the Andes. In *Andean ecology and civilization*, ed. Shozo Masuda, Izumi Shimada, and Craig Morris, 15–20. Tokyo: University of Tokyo Press.

Nabi, Eden. 1984. The Uzbeks in Afghanistan. *Central Asian Journal* 3:1–21.

Napier, George C. 1876. Memorandum on the condition and external relations of the Turkomen tribes of Merv. In *Collection of journals and reports from G. C. Napier on special duty in Persia 1874.* London: Eyre and Spottiswoode.

Nawid, Senzil. 1999. *Religious response to social change in Afghanistan, 1919–29.* Costa Mesa, CA: Mazda.

Neumann, Ronald. 2009. *The other war: Winning and losing in Afghanistan.* Washington, DC: Potomac Books.

Noelle, Christine. 1997. *State and tribe in nineteenth-century Afghanistan: The reign of Amir Dost Muhammad Khan (1826–1863).* Richmond, UK: Curzon.

Nojumi, Neamatollah. 2002. *The rise of the Taliban in Afghanistan: Mass mobilization, civil war, and the future of the region.* New York: Palgrave.

Nojumi, Neamatollah, Dyan Mazurana and Elizabeth Stites. 2009. *After the Taliban: Life and security in rural Afghanistan.* Lanham, MD: Rowman and Littlefield.

Obama, Barack. 2009. Presidential address on Afghanistan. West Point, NY, December 1. Available at http://www.nytimes.com/2009/12/02/world/asia/02prexy.text.html (accessed December 26, 2009).

Odum, Eugene. 1998. *Ecological vignettes: Approaches to dealing with human predicaments.* Amsterdam: Taylor and Francis.

Olesen, Asta. 1994. *Afghan craftsmen: The cultures of three itinerant communities.* London: Thames and Hudson.

———. 1995. *Islam and politics in Afghanistan.* Richmond, UK: Curzon Press.

Olufsen, Ole. 1904. *Through the unknown Pamirs: The second Danish Pamir expedition, 1898–99.* London: William Heinemann.

Pandey, Awadh Bihari. 1956. *The first Afghan empire in India, 1451–1526 A. D.* Calcutta: Bookland.

Pedersen, Gorm. 1994. *Afghan nomads in transition: A century of change among the Zala Khan Khel.* London: Thames and Hudson.

Poladi, Hassan. 1989. *The Hazaras.* Stockton, CA: Mughal Publishing Company.

Poullada, Leon B. 1973. *Reform and rebellion in Afghanistan, 1919–1929.* Ithaca, NY: Cornell University Press.

Rahman, Abdur. 1900. *The life of Abdur Rahman, amir of Afghanistan*. Ed. Sultan Mahomed Khan. 2 vols. London: J. Murray.

Rao, Aparna. 1982. *Les Gorbat d'Afghanistan: Aspects économiques d'un groupe itinérant "Jat."* Paris: ADPF.

Rasanayagam, Angelo. 2003. *Afghanistan: A modern history: Monarchy, despotism, or democracy? The problems of governance in the Muslim tradition*. New York: I. B. Tauris.

Rashid, Ahmed. 2000. *Taliban: Militant Islam, oil, and fundamentalism in central Asia*. New Haven, CT: Yale University Press.

————. 2008. *Descent into chaos: The United States and the failure of nation building in Pakistan, Afghanistan, and central Asia*. New York: Viking.

Reynolds, Andrew. 2006. The curious case of Afghanistan. *Journal of Democracy* 17 (2): 104–17.

Rohde, David, and David Sanger. 2007. How the "good war" in Afghanistan went bad. *New York Times*, August 12, 1.

Roberts, Jeffery J. 2003. *The origins of conflict in Afghanistan*. Westport, CT: Praeger.

Roy, Olivier. 1990. *Islam and resistance in Afghanistan*. 2nd ed. Cambridge: Cambridge University Press.

Rubin, Barnett. 1995. *The fragmentation of Afghanistan: State formation and collapse in the international system*. New Haven, CT: Yale University Press.

Rubin, Elizabeth. 2009. Karzai in his labyrinth. *New York Times Magazine*, August 9, MM26.

Sa'di. [1888] 1964. *Gulistan*. Trans. Edward Rehatsek. London: Allen and Unwin.

Shahrani, Nazif. 1979. *The Kirghiz and Wakhi of Afghanistan*. Seattle: University of Washington Press.

Shalinsky, Audrey. 1994. *Long years of exile*. Lanham, MD: University Press of America.

Singh, Ganda. 1959. *Ahmad Shah Durrani*. London: Asia Publishing House.

Smith, Adam. [1776] 1843. *An inquiry into the nature and causes of the wealth of nations*. Edinburgh: Thomas Nelson.

Stewart, Rhea Talley. 1973. *Fire in Afghanistan, 1914–1929*. Garden City, NY: Doubleday.

Stewart, Rory. 2004. *The places in between*. London: Picador.

Subtelny, Maria Eva. 1994. Central Asia as a part of the modern Islamic world. In *Central Asia in historical perspective*, ed. Beatrice F. Manz, 45–61. Boulder, CO: Westview Press.

Sykes, Percy. 1940. *A history of Afghanistan*. 2 vols. London: Macmillan.

Szabo, Albert, and Thomas Barfield. 1991. *Afghanistan: An atlas of indigenous domestic architecture.* Austin: University of Texas Press.

Tambiah, Stanley J. 1990. Presidential address: Reflections on communal violence in south Asia. *Journal of Asian Studies* 49 (4): 741–60.

Tanner, Stephen. 2002. *Afghanistan: A military history from Alexander the Great to the fall of the Taliban.* New York: Da Capo Press.

Tapper, Nancy. 1983. Abd al-Rahman's north-west frontier: The Pashtun colonisation of Afghan Turkistan. In *The Conflict of tribe and state in Iran and Afghanistan,* ed. Richard Tapper. London: Croom Helm.

Tylor, Edward Burnett. 1871. *Primitive culture: Researches into the development of mythology, philosophy, religion, art, and custom (2 vols.).* London: Murray.

UN Office on Drugs and Crime. 2008. Afghanistan 2008 annual opium poppy survey. Available at http://www.unodc.org/documents/publications/Afghanistan_Opium_Survey_2008.pdf (accessed December 24, 2009).

Wheeler, Stephen. 1895. *The Ameer Abdur Rahman.* London: Bliss, Sands, and Foster.

Wild, Roland. 1932. *Amanullah, ex-king of Afghanistan.* London: Hurst and Blackett.

Wilder, Andrew. 2005. *A house divided? Analysing the 2005 Afghan elections.* Kabul: Afghanistan Research and Evaluation Unit.

Wutt, Karl. 1981. *Pashai: Landschaft, Menschen, Architektur.* Graz: Akademische Druck- und Verlagsanstalt.

Yapp, Malcolm. 1962. "Disturbances in western Afghanistan, 1839–42." *Bulletin of the School of Oriental and African Studies* 25.

———. 1964. The revolutions of 1841–42 in Afghanistan. *Bulletin of the School of Oriental and African Studies* 27 (2): 333–81.

INDEX

Afghans do not have distinct family names and many go by only one name. People are therefore indexed in the ways that they are most commonly known (including use of titles and honorifics in some cases).

British *(continued)*
 Anglo-Afghan Wars); and attempt to
 divide Afghanistan, 143–44; defeat of,
 121–26; Dost Muhammad and, 114–
 18; Durand Agreement and, 48, 153–
 54, 221; English Civil War and, 74; Forward Policy of, 129–30, 140; Habibullah
 and, 178–80; Indian Mutiny of 1857
 and, 129; invasion of Afghanistan, 5–6;
 khalifat independence movement and,
 182; Khost Rebellion and, 183–88; legitimacy and, 70–71, 195–225; Musahiban Dynasty and, 205–8; Najibullah
 and, 247–48; postwar policy of, 132–
 34; and prostitution of women, 120–21;
 raj of, 1, 11, 50, 53, 79, 179, 206, 208,
 247, 268, 276, 292, 311; recognition of
 Nadir by, 197; and restructuring Afghan
 state, 118–21; Sepoy Rebellion and, 129,
 133; Treaty of Gandamak and, 141; Treaty
 of Rawalpindi and, 181–82; withdrawal
 of, 121–26; World War I era and, 177–78
Buddhists, 17, 46, 262, 349
Bukhara, 52, 97, 99, 115–16, 129, 136,
 139, 182, 349, 355n13
Burnes, Alexander, 114, 122
Bush administration, x, 276, 291, 310–11,
 333

camels, 38, 51, 45, 56, 63, 131, 161, 218
Canada, 319–20
cannons, 131; as means of execution, 79,
 193
caravans, 39, 46, 61, 95, 98, 104, 218–19,
 237, 245
Caroe, Olaf, 54–56, 91
Cavagnari, Louis, 141
cavalry, 11, 276; First Anglo-Afghan War
 and, 113, 119, 123, 130–31; legitimacy
 of power and, 75, 85–86, 88, 98–101,
 105; Second Anglo-Afghan War and,
 137, 144
cell phones, 9
Central Asia/South Asia Regional
 Electricity Market, 346

Central Intelligence Agency (CIA), 276
centralization, 8; Abdur Rahman and, 149,
 159–60; 165–66; Amanullah and, 302;
 elitism and, 303; future policy and, 338;
 ignored alternatives and, 304–5; insur-
 gencies and, 320; Karzai and, 302–4;
 Musahiban Dynasty and, 200–201; state
 building and, 302–4; United Nations
 and, 302–3
Central Powers, 178
Chahar Aimaq (Four Tribes), 28. *See also*
 Aimaqs
Chayanov, Alexander, 34
Chechens, 266
China, 46, 54, 67, 77, 80, 87; mineral
 mining and, 346
Chinggis Khan, 1, 20, 66, 76n, 80, 88–89,
 92, 349
Chisti Sufi Order, 42, 349
Chitral, 151
Clinton administration, 336
coin minting, 73, 134
cold war, 1, 12, 311–12, 345; Musahiban
 Dynasty and, 205–10; twentieth century
 and, 205–10, 236, 243, 251, 264
communications: radio and, 217, 220, 349;
 telegraph lines and, 204; telephone lines
 and, 204; television and, 22
Communists, ix, 6, 13, 64; cooperation of
 people and, 173; Daud Khan and, 215;
 factories and, 204; Ghilzais and, 170;
 Leninism and, 226; mujahideen and,
 250–51; Pashtuns and, 170; People's
 Democratic Party of Afghanistan and,
 226–27; Stalin and, 27, 48, 225, 267
Conscription and Identity Card Act, 184–
 85
copper mines, 346
cotton, 203, 218
Covenants of Unity (Abdur Rahman),
 174–75, 295
cows, 28, 37, 45, 61, 262

Da Afghanistan Bank, 203
Darulamam, 183

249; Najibullah and, 239–41; Pakistan and, 171, 249–54; People's Democratic Party of Afghanistan and, 171–72, 241; Peshawar and, 230; Soviet occupation and, 239–42; Tajiks and, 249–51; Taliban and, 255; twentieth century and, 211n, 235–58, 263; twenty-first century and, 282–85, 288, 291–92, 295–96, 299, 308, 322, 326–29; United States and, 243

Musahiban dynasty, 12, 72, 169, 175; British and, 205, 207–8; centralization and, 200–201; cold war and, 205–10; cotton exports and, 203; Daud Khan and, 199–200, 211–16, 224–25; decline and fall of, 210–16; democracy experiment and, 211; economic issues and, 202–5; education and, 201, 210–14; exports and, 203–4; foreign affairs and, 206–10; Germany and, 205–8; as golden age, 170; leadership roles and, 199–200; Liberal Parliament and, 211; military and, 198, 207–16, 221; Nadir Shah and, 195–200, 204–6, 214–15, 226; Pakistan and, 209; People's Democratic Party of Afghanistan and, 213–14; religious power and, 198–99; road system and, 204; rural society in, 216–25; Russians and, 204–10; Saur Revolution and, 225–26, 228, 233, 258; shah title and, 195–96; social changes and, 200–202; stability policies of, 198–210; taxes and, 198, 204–5, 208, 224; United States and, 205–10; veils and, 201

Musa Khel, 25
Mushk-i-Alam, Mullah, 148
Muslims: infidels and, 42; *khalifat* independence movement and, 182; self-superiority of, 42; September 11, 2001 and, 1; Shiite, 23, 26, 29, 40, 49–50, 93, 98; Sunni, 22, 26, 40, 49–50, 73, 94, 200, 236, 246–47, 251. *See also* Islam

Nadir Khan (Shah), 5, 12; assassination of, 197; British recognition of, 197;

leadership style and, 306–7; legitimacy and, 96–98, 101–2; Musahiban Dynasty and, 195–200, 204–6, 214–15, 226; Pashtuns and, 197; shah title and, 195–96; twentieth-century perspective and, 169–70, 173, 181, 189, 194–95; twenty-first century perspective and, 292, 304–5, 321

Najibullah, 171; asylum for, 248–49; fall of, 245–49; leadership style and, 306–8, 311; legitimacy and, 244–45; military and, 244–45; Pakistan and, 247–48; twentieth-century perspective and, 226, 238–41; twenty-first century perspective and, 282, 322

Nakhshbanidya (Naqshbandi) sufi order, 42, 175, 349
Nangarhar, 326; shura, 252, 258–60. *See also* Jalalabad
Naqibullah, Mullah, 252–53, 309
Nasiri, 25
Nasrullah, 177, 180–81
National Assembly, 188
National Commanders Shura (NCS), 248–49, 296–97
National Party, 142
natural resources: copper mines and, 346; deserts and, 28; ecological diversity and, 44–45; energy deposits and, 344; highlands and, 44–47; lowlands and, 44–45; mountains and, 43–47; rivers and, 43–47; settlement patterns and, 35–40; steppes and, 11, 27–28, 39, 46–57, 63–64, 68–69, 74, 77–78, 80, 85–87, 215, 338; watersheds and, 42–43
Nauruz, 55
Nawid, Senzil, 176, 182–84
New York Times, 331, 349–50
Nishapur, 86
nizamnama (state regulations), 182–83
Nojumi, Neamatollah, 249
nomads: archery and, 76, 85–86; bazaar day and, 35; Bedouin, 56–64, 78–82, 84, 154, 156; desert civilization and, 56–60; Durand Agreement and, 153–

Pashto language, 25, 59, 157, 226, 239, 260

Pashtunistan, 216, 280, 295, 324

Pashtuns, 4–5, 12, 18, 51, 63, 65, 67; Abdur Rahman and, 155, 157–58; Achaemenids and, 90; Bonn Accord and, 283–84; civil war of 1929 and, 190–91; code of conduct of, 25–26; Communists and, 170; conversion to Islam, 92; creating state for, 155, 157–58; dominance of, 24–26; Durand Agreement and, 48, 153–54, 221; Durranis and, 25, 66, 89, 103–5 (see also Durannis); Ghilzais and, 25, 89–90, 226, 285–93; Gurghusht and, 25; Habibullah and, 193–95; Herat and, 50; ideologies of, 20, 22; incorporation failures and, 78; Indian frontier and, 92–97; insurgencies and, 321; invaders and, 70; Jamiat-i-Islami and, 237; Karlanri and, 25, 285; Khost Rebellion and, 183–88; Kunar Valley, 157; lineages of, 22, 24–25; Nadir and, 197; Najibullah and, 239; new power base of, 167–68; nomadic, 39; number of, 24; obligatory hospitality of, 268–69; Persian frontier and, 92–97; Peshawar and, 53–54; Qais and, 24–25, 91; resistance to Mughal dynasty and, 70; rise of, 90–97; roots of, 90–91; Shinwari, 126; Taliban and, 7, 255, 258–60, 263, 284; withdrawal of politics by, 166

Pashtunwali, 25, 59, 138, 185, 261, 268–69, 286

pastoralists, 25, 34, 38, 204. See also nomads

Pathans, 25, 350

Payinda Khan, 167; named Sarfraz Khan, 108

People's Democratic Party of Afghanistan (PDPA), 338, 341, 347; aid to, 243; Amanullah and, 232–33; collapse of, 291; Communism and, 226–27; Daud's strike against, 225; dissolution of, 302; Durranis and, 225–26; economic issues and, 231; fall of, 277; figurehead leaders of, 307–8; foreign funding and, 311;

formation of, 213–14; Ghilzai/Durrani issues and, 285; illusion of, 231–32; junior military officers and, 225; Karmal and, 238–39; Khalq faction and, 213–14; kinship and, 232; leadership style and, 307; legitimacy and, 341; Leninism, 226; loya jirga and, 295; membership size of, 214; modernization and, 339–40; mujahideen and, 171–72, 241; murder of Daud by, 170–71; Musahiban Dynasty and, 213–14; Najibullah and, 171, 245–49; opposition to, 171–72; Parcham factions and, 225, 227–29; policies of, 226–29; problems of, 226–29; qawm affiliations and, 230–31; resistance to programs of, 230–31; Russians and, 171, 231, 234–46, 321–22; Saur Revolution and, 225–26, 228, 233, 258; souring revolution and, 229–33; Taliban and, 262; twentieth century and, 170–71, 211n, 213–16, 225–50, 262; twenty-first century and, 275, 277, 284–85, 291–92, 295, 302, 307, 311, 322; uncoordinated uprisings and, 229–30; women and, 229

Persian Gulf, 345

Persian language, 7, 22–23, 42, 46, 85, 88

Persians, 48–51, 54, 69. See also Iran

Peshawar, ix, 25, 43, 46, 93; as administrative capital, 53; Bonn Accord and, 283; contrasts of, 53–54; Dost Muhammad and, 114; historical perspective of, 53–54; invaders and, 70; mujahideen and, 230; mujahideen civil war and, 249; Najibullah and, 247–48; Pashtuns and, 53–54, 91; power lines through, 345–46; sardars and, 175; Treaty of, 128

poetry, 49, 58, 77, 95, 348–49

policy, 15; Bonn Accord and, 283–93, 305; breaking precedents and, 343–48; British Forward Policy and, 140; centralization and, 8, 159–60 (see also centralization); Conscription and Identity Card Act and, 184; Covenants of Unity and, 295; Durand Agreement and, 48,

Sara Roy, *Hamas and Civil Society in Gaza: Engaging the Islamist Social Sector*

Michael Laffan, *The Makings of Indonesian Islam: Orientalism and the Narration of a Sufi Past*

Jonathan Laurence, *The Emancipation of Europe's Muslims: The State's Role in Minority Integration*